Touring the Backroads of North Carolina's Lower Coast

Touring the Backroads of North Carolina's Lower Coast

Daniel W. Barefoot

John F. Blair
Publisher
Winston-Salem,
North Carolina

BOOK DESIGN BY DEBRA LONG HAMPTON
MAPS BY LIZA LANGRALL
PRINTED AND BOUND BY R. R. DONNELLEY & SONS

*The paper in this book meets the guidelines
for permanence and durability of the
Committee on Production Guidelines for Book Longevity
of the Council on Library Resources.*

Photographs on front cover, courtesy of North Carolina Division of Travel & Tourism
Clockwise from top left—
Battleship *North Carolina*, from The Cape Fear Riverfront Tour
Cape Lookout Lighthouse, from The Cape Lookout National Seashore Tour
Orton Plantation, from The Cape Fear Riverfront Tour
A lower coast sunset
Tryon Palace, from The New Bern Tour
Bald Head Island Lighthouse, from The Cape Fear Delta Tour

Library of Congress Cataloging-in-Publication Data
Barefoot, Daniel W., 1951—
Touring the backroads of North Carolina's lower coast / Daniel W. Barefoot.
p.   cm. — (Touring the backroads series)
Includes bibliographical references and index.
ISBN 0-89587-126-2
1. Atlantic Coast (N.C.)—Tours.   2. North Carolina—Tours.
3. Automobile travel—North Carolina—Atlantic Coast—Guidebooks.
I. Title.   II. Series.
F262.A84B37   1995
917.56'10443—dc20   94-47828

*To Kay and Kristie for all of the many
happy miles we've traveled*

Table of Contents

Preface

*And beyond this we saw the open Countrey ris-
ing in height above the sandie shore with many
faire fields and plains . . . as pleasant and delectable to behold, as is possible to imagine.*

Report of
Giovanni da Verrazano
to King Francis I of France,
July 8, 1524

In 1961, Governor Terry Sanford made a plea to the citizens of North Carolina to raise money to save the USS *North Carolina*, the world's first modern battleship, from the scrap heap. As a ten-year-old fourth-grader, I took pride in joining thousands of other schoolchildren all over the state in contributing our nickels and dimes to help bring the great battle wagon to its permanent home on the North Carolina coast at Wilmington.

I well recall the sense of pride and awe that overwhelmed me when I first visited the *North Carolina* after she was dedicated as a war memorial in 1962. Little did I know that, some three decades later, I would be appointed by Governor Jim Hunt to the commission which oversees the operation and maintenance of the majestic ship.

It is with the same sense of pride and awe that I regard the North Carolina coast, the land from whence my grandparents, their parents, and their grandparents came. Indeed, North Carolinians from Manteo to Murphy and people the world over have for centuries been awed by and proud of the North Carolina coast—a land of incomparable natural beauty and great historic significance.

Despite the lavish praise conferred upon the area by the great European explorers of the sixteenth century, the North Carolina coast remained the Rip Van Winkle of the Atlantic seaboard in terms of development until the second half of the twentieth century. During the intervening three and a half centuries, the other Atlantic states witnessed the birth and growth of the great American cities, ports, and resorts along their shores, while North Carolina, because of its unique geography, saw its beautiful barrier islands preserved in their natural state. Treacherous offshore shoals, shallow sounds, and hundreds of nooks and crannies along the irregular North Carolina coast won it dubious acclaim as a pirate haven and a graveyard for ships.

But the centuries of isolation and relative obscurity have now proved to be a blessing. Whereas much of the Atlantic coastline displays the telltale signs of rampant, unplanned development, the North Carolina coast has been largely spared the engineering nightmares evident on the coast of the states to the north and south.

Millions of people travel to coastal North Carolina annually to enjoy the land which has enchanted visitors since the early European explorers. Much of the attraction lies with the unspoiled conditions. Tourists from throughout the United States and from distant parts of the globe revel in the miles of majestic, uncrowded strand, the vast public parks and wildlife refuges, the multitude of family-oriented resorts, and the historic cities and towns, all of which seem to exist in harmony with the natural forces at work on the slender barrier islands and along the sounds, creeks, and other estuaries.

North Carolina possesses the sixth-largest coastline in the United States, following only Alaska, Florida, Louisiana, Maine, and California. Its 301-mile-long coast comprises more than a fourth of the total coast of the original thirteen English colonies. Accordingly, the vast size of the North Carolina coast has necessitated the publication of two volumes of tours.

This volume contains thirteen tours of the lower coast—tours of the barrier islands lying south of Ocracoke Inlet and the portion of the mainland south of the Neuse River.

In July 1524, the famed Florentine navigator Giovanni da Verrazano became the first European to explore the coast of North Carolina when he came ashore somewhere between Masonboro Island and Bogue Banks. His narrative on the lower North Carolina coast is the earliest known description of the shores of what is now the United States.

It is not surprising, then, that the lower North Carolina coast is steeped in history and legend. Over the past fifteen years, I have traveled extensively over the backroads of this unique region to collect stories and bring coastal history to life.

Too often, coastal visitors in a hurry to reach the beach resorts speed by fascinating towns, historic sites, and natural areas without understanding their significance, without partaking of their beauty and charm, and without sampling their briny flavor. And even at the beach resorts, there are intriguing backroads with stories that have either been neglected by historians or forgotten as the region has grown more sophisticated.

As you travel the backroads on these tours, please remember that *change* is a watchword along the coast. While I have taken great care to make the information presented herein as accurate as possible, road numbers change, roads and bridges are rerouted, and historic buildings and other landmarks vanish almost overnight.

This book and its companion volume on the upper coast are not meant to be exhaustive histories of the North Carolina coast. Nor have they been written to provide details on lodging, dining, and shopping facilities. Such information changes constantly and is available from the sources listed in the appendix. Rather, the purpose of these volumes is to introduce the coastal visitor—whether armchair or automobile—to the places, the people, and the events that have indeed made the North Carolina coast "as pleasant and delectable to behold, as is possible to imagine."

Acknowledgments

This book is the realization of one of my fondest dreams: a great, abiding desire to tell the fascinating stories of the North Carolina coast. The realization of my dream has not been achieved without the dedication, assistance, and kindness of many people. To name everyone who has helped in this effort would be impossible, but there are some special people to whom I am especially indebted.

In the entire world, there are no more gracious people than those who live on the North Carolina coast. Whether I was in a library researching local history, on a backroad seeking directions, or at a rural church hoping to get inside on a weekday, the people of the coast were always genuinely interested in lending a helping hand.

The staffs at the North Carolina Collection and the Southern Historical Collection at the University of North Carolina at Chapel Hill and at the State Archives in Raleigh were helpful and considerate on each of my many visits.

The folks at John F. Blair, Publisher, have been a real pleasure to work with throughout this project. In the fine tradition begun by Mr. Blair more than forty years ago, they are truly dedicated to publishing quality books on the history, geography, and culture of North Carolina and the Southeast.

Carolyn Sakowski, the president of Blair and the author of the first book in the *Touring the Backroads* series, saw merit in my manuscript from the outset and has given much of her time and attention to the project from day one. Steve Kirk, my editor, has provided his professional advice and expertise with patience and a smile. Debbie Hampton, Judy Breakstone, Anne Schultz, and the rest of the staff at John F. Blair have worked to make this book a success.

In my hometown, I am grateful to my dear friends Judge John R. Friday and Darrell Harkey for their never-ending support and loyalty.

My family—my wife, my daughter, and my parents—have been a constant source of inspiration and encouragement.

Much of the original manuscript, written in my favorite No. 3 pencils, was typed by my daughter, Kristie. Since her birth, Kristie has been a great travel companion for her parents, and the coast will always be a very special place for the three of us.

Above all, no one deserves more credit for this book than my wife, Kay. Over the course of this long project, she has traveled thousands of miles of coastal backroads and helped make the book as accurate as possible. She has endured hurricanes, torrential rainstorms, howling winds, sweltering heat, and pesky insects; she has asked for directions innumerable times; she has made hotel and ferry reservations; she has missed meals to get from one point to another; and she has read every word of the manuscript over and over and acted as my sounding board. In the bleak moments as well as the good, she has always been there with love, compliments, and patience.

Touring the Backroads of North Carolina's Lower Coast

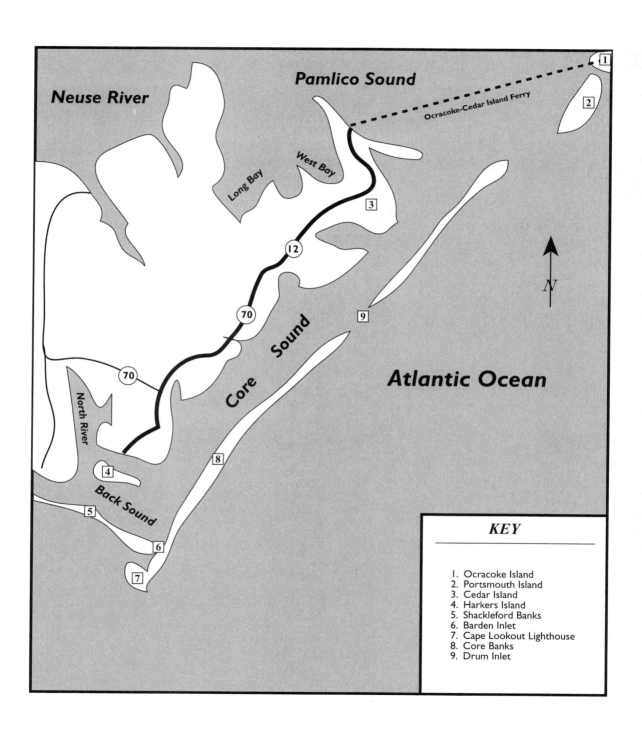

Neuse River

Pamlico Sound

Long Bay

West Bay

Ocracoke-Cedar Island Ferry

① 1

② 2

③ 3

⑫ 12

⑦ 70

⑦ 70

North River

Core Sound

⑨ 9

Atlantic Ocean

N

④ 4

⑤ 5

Back Sound

⑥ 6

⑦ 7

⑧ 8

KEY

1. Ocracoke Island
2. Portsmouth Island
3. Cedar Island
4. Harkers Island
5. Shackleford Banks
6. Barden Inlet
7. Cape Lookout Lighthouse
8. Core Banks
9. Drum Inlet

The Cape Lookout National Seashore Tour

Because the barrier islands that comprise Cape Lookout National Seashore are separated from the mainland by deep inlets and sounds, the park can only be reached by boat. Ferries licensed by the National Park Service depart from Ocracoke, Atlantic, Davis, Harkers Island, and Beaufort to various portions of the park.

There are no improved roads within the national seashore. Thus, only four-wheel-drive vehicles can operate in designated areas.

Visiting all three sections of Cape Lookout National Seashore involves considerable logistical difficulties. Taking this tour from start to finish requires a total of seven ferry rides. And it starts in Ocracoke, which itself is accessible only by ferry. Be sure to call in advance for ferry departure times.

Since you will not be able to complete this tour in a single day, you may want to partake of the lodgings in Ocracoke, Sea Level, Beaufort, Morehead City, or Harkers Island.

Also note that all of your travel within the national seashore will most likely be on foot.

Despite the travel difficulties, most people who make the trip to Portsmouth village or the Cape Lookout Lighthouse judge it well worth the effort. They are rewarded with a unique experience they are not likely to forget.

The tour begins at the ferry dock on Silver Lake in the village of Ocracoke.

This tour is comprised mainly of ferry rides and walking tours of the three sections of Cape Lookout National Seashore, with the only driving coming between ferry landings. It begins with a ferry ride from Ocracoke to Haulover Point on Portsmouth Island. After a walking tour in and around Portsmouth village, the tour returns to Ocracoke, then proceeds by a separate ferry to Cedar Island on the mainland. It then heads southwest by road to Harkers Island, where ferry service is available to Core Banks—the home of the famous Cape Lookout Lighthouse—and to Shackleford Banks.

Among the highlights of the tour are historic Portsmouth village, the story of Shell Castle Island, the Cape Lookout Lighthouse, North Carolina's finest harbor, and the story of Diamond City.

Total driving mileage: approximately 33 miles.

You can park your car nearby. Inquire at the National Park Service visitor center, located near the dock, for information about ferry service to Portsmouth Island.

The ferry ride from Ocracoke will deposit you at Haulover Point, located on the northwestern corner of Portsmouth Island, the northernmost island in Cape Lookout National Seashore.

On most maps and nautical charts, this 18-mile-long barrier island appears to be an expansive body of land. However, visitors find that much of it is nothing more than narrow, sandy barrier beach and marshland just above high water. Portsmouth Island is bounded on the north by Ocracoke Inlet, on the south by Drum Inlet, on the west by Pamlico Sound, and on the east by the Atlantic.

Haulover Point is an ancient landing that served as the gateway to the once-thriving, but now deserted, village of Portsmouth. Here, at its widest point, the island is 2 miles across. Residents of the Outer Banks and other coastal environs know a "haulover" as a shallow spot where it is necessary to actually pull a boat from one area of deep water to another. Much of the maritime history of Portsmouth village was played out at Haulover Point. More than a century ago, great wharves and warehouses stood here.

Clustered in the small village on the southern side of Ocracoke Inlet, twenty-one residents called Portsmouth home in 1946. One of those residents was Captain John Willis, a native of the island. When asked whether he thought that the population of Portsmouth Island was going to increase, Willis responded, "It surely looks that way now, and we people over there certainly hope it would. Wouldn't want our community to become a ghost town."

Captain Willis's prediction proved to be inaccurate. The population of the village dwindled until the early 1970s, when the last two residents of the island moved to the mainland. Today, the village still exists on the northern end of the island, but it has no inhabitants save National Park Service caretakers. It has become a true ghost town.

For most people, the term *ghost town* conjures up pictures of a ramshackle Western town with tumbleweeds blowing down a dusty street. Yet hardy seafaring men established Portsmouth village as one of coastal North Carolina's oldest communities. Only through the cruel fate of human history are its houses now empty and its streets deserted.

To walk the sandy streets of the historic village, proceed south on Haulover Road. To the right of the road, in the direction of Pamlico Sound, you can see the remains of the Old Brick Road—the closest thing to a paved road that ever existed on the island. A number of houses, most of 1900 to 1930 vintage, are located on both sides of Haulover Road.

Near the point where the Old Brick Road merges with Haulover Road stands the Henry Babb House, one of the oldest houses on the island.

As you walk toward the former post-office building, take time to reflect on the three centuries of history to which these sandy lanes have been witness.

The Henry Babb House

In the early part of the eighteenth century, long before a village was officially established at Portsmouth, John Lawson found English-speaking people living on the site. Apparently, the early inhabitants were mariners who settled near this, the site of North Carolina's earliest port activities. Indians also lived on the island at the time of Lawson's visit, and it is certain that they continued to inhabit the island into the nineteenth century.

Portsmouth village was an outgrowth of the desire of the North Carolina colonial government to provide facilities for the growing number of vessels using Ocracoke Inlet as a port of entry. By the middle of the eighteenth century, most of the water traffic from the populous ports of the colony was using Ocracoke Inlet. At that time, the main channel of the inlet was nearer Portsmouth Island than Ocracoke. Big oceangoing ships drew too much water to navigate the relatively shallow inlet. In order to establish a viable port at the inlet, colonial officials recognized the need for wharves, warehouses, and other port facilities where the cargo of the large ships could be unloaded and stored until it was loaded onto vessels capable of navigating the shallow sounds.

It was this process—called "lightering"—which prompted the colonial assembly to enact legislation in 1753 toward "laying out a Town on Core Banks, near Ocracoke Inlet, in Carteret County, and for appointing Commissioners for completing the Fort at or near the same place." Before the town was settled, the legislators named it Portsmouth for the city of the same name in England.

Fort Granville, which never played an important role in coastal history, was completed by late 1757. History does not indicate that a gun was ever

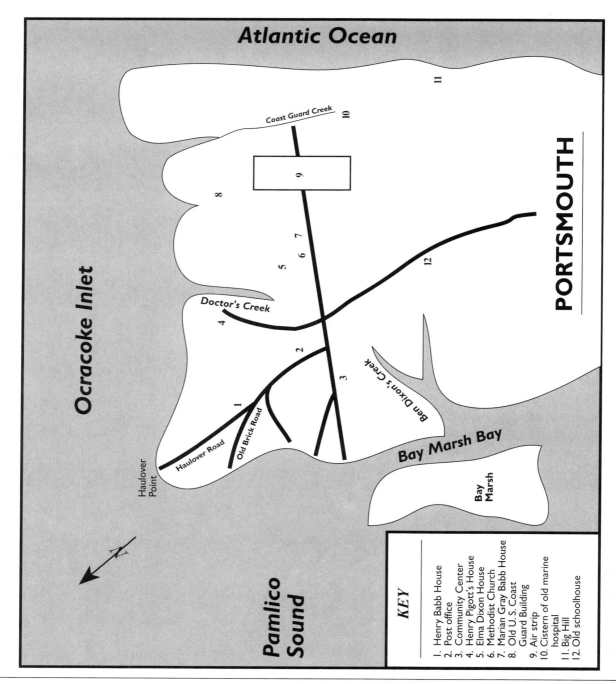

Atlantic Ocean

Ocracoke Inlet

PORTSMOUTH

Coast Guard Creek

Doctor's Creek

Ben Dixon's Creek

Bay Marsh Bay

Bay Marsh

Haulover Road

Old Brick Road

Haulover Point

Pamlico Sound

11

10

9

8

7

6

5

4

3

2

1

12

KEY

1. Henry Babb House
2. Post office
3. Community Center
4. Henry Pigott's House
5. Elma Dixon House
6. Methodist Church
7. Marian Gray Babb House
8. Old U. S. Coast Guard Building
9. Air strip
10. Cistern of old marine hospital
11. Big Hill
12. Old schoolhouse

fired at the fort, but the men stationed there did provide a population base from which the village grew. No remains of the fort exist today.

By the time the first official census of the United States was completed in 1790, Portsmouth had a population of 227, making it the largest town on the Outer Banks. Portsmouth was unique because, unlike the other settlements on the Outer Banks, its future seemed to be filled with nothing but promise.

Subject to severe shoaling and not very deep, Ocracoke Inlet never provided a good natural harbor. However, until a better harbor was available, the settlements near the inlet thrived. Of the three settlements—Portsmouth, Ocracoke, and nearby Shell Castle Island—Portsmouth was the most successful. It quickly grew to be the largest seaport between the Virginia capes and Charleston, South Carolina.

A school, shown as an "academy" on the Coles and Price map, existed in the village as early as 1806.

Due to the heavy port activity at Portsmouth, seamen with various ailments and diseases arrived here. In 1827, the federal government opened a crude hospital facility to quarantine sick sailors on the island. It was replaced in 1846 with a larger, more modern marine hospital that had numerous beds and was staffed by eighteen doctors. A post office, only the second in Carteret County, was opened in the village the same year.

However, another event in 1846 sounded the death knell for the future of Portsmouth as a major coastal port. Although the vicious coastal storm of 1846 did not do great physical damage to the village, it opened two new, deeper inlets on the Outer Banks—Oregon and Hatteras inlets. Suddenly, mariners had alternatives to Ocracoke Inlet.

Despite the threat of competition from the new inlets, Portsmouth was not yet down for the count. In fact, the village enjoyed one of its most prosperous periods from 1843 to 1860. The fact that seventy-seven children were enrolled in the village schools in 1846 attests to the vitality of the community.

In the early days of the Civil War, Confederate forces placed four guns on the beach at Portsmouth at an encampment called Fort Washington. The fort on nearby Beacon Island was burned and abandoned by Southern troops shortly after the fall of the forts at Hatteras Inlet in August 1861. Residents of Portsmouth panicked. A mass evacuation of the island began as Union ships appeared offshore.

Every resident was able to escape the island, save one Miss Rosie Gaskins. Rosie was a rather obese individual who could pass through only one door in her house: the extrawide back door. When the alarm spread that the Yankees were coming, the chubby lady became confused and attempted to leave her house through the front door. Rosie got stuck, and the more she squirmed to extricate herself, the more trapped she became. When Union forces arrived in the village, they found the woman still wedged in her front door. They removed her from her predicament and allowed her to live in her house during their occupation of the island. After the war, Rosie reported to those residents who returned that she had been treated courteously by the enemy.

Census records reveal that, from a postwar high of more than 500, the population of Portsmouth declined to 341 by 1870. Several government projects—among them a weather station in 1876 and a state-of-the-art life-saving station in 1897—helped to breathe temporary life into the village in the last quarter of the nineteenth century. But when the new century dawned, the future for Portsmouth was bleak. Residents continued their exodus after several destructive storms pounded the island.

On August 2, 1927, Marian Gray Babb became the last child born on the island. Ten years later, the Coast Guard station was decommissioned. One by one, age-old institutions on the island fell like dominoes. In 1942, the village school closed, having held the distinction of being the smallest school in North Carolina, and perhaps the nation. Not long afterwards, the last store on the island closed. Thereafter, supplies had to be ordered from the mainland. They were delivered to the village in a skiff poled by an island resident, who made his way to and from a rendezvous with the daily mailboat.

Perhaps the *coup de grâce* for Portsmouth was the weekend storm of 1944, which brought a tide higher than any in the memory of island residents.

A total of thirteen persons lived in the village in 1957, most of them elderly natives of the island.

After 119 years of continuous service, the post office closed on April 11, 1959.

For the next nine years, Hallis M. Bragg delivered the island's mail from the mainland to a skiff in the sound manned by Henry Pigott, a black man who had lived all his life on the island. When Pigott died in January 1971, the last two residents of the island, Elma Dixon and Marian Gray Babb, had no alternative but to move to the mainland. Portsmouth became a ghost town.

Meanwhile, the state was busy purchasing the island for inclusion in Cape Lookout National Seashore. As soon as the village was abandoned, the National Park Service announced that it would not allow any salvageable buildings to deteriorate.

Follow Haulover Road to the small, white post-office building, where it merges with the main village road, which runs the width of the island from the sound to the beach.

For many years, this structure was one of the focal points of the village. Not only did the tiny building serve as the post office, but it was also the last store in the village.

Of the six cemeteries known to still exist at Portsmouth, the most conspicuous is the Community Cemetery. Located about forty yards west of the post office, this serene, shaded spot is the island's largest cemetery, with some forty graves. Near the sound just northeast of this cemetery, a graveyard with thirteen graves is covered with undergrowth.

Just east of the post office lies the village crossroads, where the main village road intersects the north-south road. If you are familiar with old England, you will notice a striking similarity between the layout of Portsmouth village and villages in the English countryside. This Old World atmosphere is enhanced by scattered cottages, wooden footbridges over tidal creeks and marshes, and winding grass paths hedged by yaupon and myrtle.

In recognition of its historic significance, the 250-acre tract encompassing the village has been listed on the National Register of Historic Places. Some twenty-five major structures in various states of repair are located in this historic district. Except for the church and a home restored by the National Park Service as a visitor center, visitors are strictly forbidden to enter the buildings, as many are leased to private individuals. Nevertheless, hours and hours can be spent touring the fascinating village.

Charged with preserving the historic structures in and around the village, the superintendent of Cape Lookout National Seashore has been forced to look for private sources to aid in the effort. Budget constraints and a limited park staff have forced the National Park Service to institute several new programs to prevent the village from falling to ruin. Begun in the early 1990s, a volunteer caretakers' program has attracted individuals who are willing to live in the village for three months at a time to keep an eye on the structures and perform minor maintenance. In a similar vein, another program instituted by park officials allows citizens to lease some of the village dwellings for private use in exchange for restoration of the buildings.

At the crossroads, turn left and walk north to where the road ends at a marshy area called Doctors Creek, on Ocracoke Inlet. Just north of the crossroads, the small cemetery of the Grace family contains four graves.

Near the end of the road stands the home of the last male resident of the village: Henry Pigott. This small story-and-a-half house is painted a distinctive pink color. Three small rooms are located on the first floor, and the rooms upstairs are even smaller. Gutters drained rainwater into a big tank at the rear of the house. This water was then pumped inside for domestic use.

The Henry Pigott House

Behind the house, you will notice a small, roofed, screened box on pilings. Such boxes were the only way of keeping food cool on the island. Fresh sea breezes blew through the box, which protected the food as it was being kept cool. Several of these ingenious contraptions can still be seen in the village.

Henry Pigott, his sister, Lizzie, and their uncle, Joe Abbott, comprised the only black family on the island for most of the twentieth century. Henry claimed his grandmother had been a slave on the island. He spoke with an English brogue. For many years, his sister cut hair for most of the villagers. In Henry's last years, when his health was declining, Junius Austin of Ocracoke provided care for the man who was Portsmouth's last link to the outside world. In 1971, upon Henry's death at the age of seventy-four in Albemarle General Hospital in Elizabeth City, the bell tolled for the village itself.

Even though it was held on a cold, windy, rainy day in January, Henry's funeral at the church in Portsmouth village was attended by throngs of friends and former residents. A bronze plaque was subsequently placed in the church in his honor.

Retrace your route to the crossroads near the post office. Turn left and walk south to the old school building. After this school closed, a young art professor from Huntington, West Virginia, purchased the building in the 1950s for use as a summer retreat and studio. While the artist was in residence, he cut hair for the remaining villagers.

If you are an intrepid hiker, follow the path south from the school for 1.5 miles to the portion of Portsmouth Island known as Sheep Island. Several abandoned houses are located on this extreme southern section of Portsmouth Island, but without question, the most historic spot is the Wallace Cemetery. Now overgrown with vegetation and difficult to locate, the cemetery holds the remains of the legendary John Wallace, governor of Shell Castle.

An integral part of the history of Portsmouth Island is the story of Shell Castle Island.

After the Revolutionary War, Shell Castle Island, made of rock and shells dumped into Pamlico Sound by ships using Ocracoke Inlet, became the site of one of coastal North Carolina's most imaginative enterprises. Located northwest of Portsmouth, the island was never longer than 0.5 mile. It was less than a football field in width. Originally called Old Rock, this diminutive island rivaled Portsmouth for a time in providing lightering facilities for oceangoing ships.

Shell Castle was the brainchild of two of the early entrepreneurs of the North Carolina coast: John Wallace of Portsmouth and John Gray Blount of Washington.

Wallace, a native of England, owned considerable land in the area and was an authority on the navigational problems presented by Ocracoke Inlet.

In 1789, Blount, a member of the Council of State and the North Carolina Colonial Assembly, acquired a state grant of five small islands just inside the inlet, one of which was twenty-five-acre Shell Castle Island. In addition to his shrewd business talents, Blount was the surveyor who accompanied Daniel Boone to Kentucky and made entries of land there. At one point in his life, Blount was among the nation's greatest landholders, his possessions large enough to cover an area about the size of Rhode Island. A fleet of ships owned by Blount and his brother traded with ports in the Northeast, the West Indies, and Europe.

Blount saw the operation at Shell Castle as the answer to his difficulties in moving cargo to and from small vessels plying the sounds and coastal rivers to his fleet of oceangoing vessels at Ocracoke Island. The day-to-day operation of the enterprise fell to John Wallace, who resided on the island and soon became the self-proclaimed "governor of Shell Castle."

Initially, the island facilities consisted of wharves, a warehouse, a gristmill, a windmill, and living quarters for island residents. By 1800, a tavern had been constructed, and the main building on the island stretched some three hundred feet. About the same time, Shell Castle was made an official port of entry, and its future seemed secure.

However, "Governor" Wallace died in 1810 without leaving an heir. Then the War of 1812 disrupted trade, and soon thereafter, the channel serving the island shoaled up. Thus, the island so valuable that a Spanish sea captain once offered to purchase it by covering it with Spanish doubloons was rendered useless and gradually deteriorated.

Shell Castle Island is still shown on nautical charts. No wider than 0.1 mile, it is nothing more than a high spot in the sound today. Although all evidence of the great Blount-Wallace enterprise vanished long ago into the waters of the sound, a picture in the Blount Collection at the State Archives in Raleigh bears a sketch of the facilities at Shell Castle.

Retrace your route to the crossroads, turn right, and walk east on the main village road. Doctors Creek is visible on the northern side of the road. Just east of the creek stands the island's most picturesque landmark. With its tiered steeple dominating the village skyline, the Methodist church is a favorite of photographers.

Inside this large, one-room building, sunlight streams through the arched windows. Old gaslights line the walls. In the chancel area, the old pedal organ remains. It was a gift from a former resident whose husband died at an early age in the employment of the lifesaving service. Visitors are free to tour the church, although the organ is off-limits.

Constructed in 1899, this church was built after its predecessor was destroyed by a storm. Records as early as 1828 make mention of a Methodist church at Portsmouth. Ministers from Ocracoke regularly supplied the pulpit until shortly after World War II. Since that time, the church has been used irregularly.

The Methodist church at Portsmouth village

Among the neatly kept houses surrounding the church are the Marian Gray Babb House and the Elma Dixon House. It was in these homes that the last two permanent residents of the village lived until 1971. Located behind the Babb and Dixon houses, the Dixon Cemetery contains the graves of Henry Pigott and his sister.

In June 1993, Marian Gray Babb, the last survivor among the permanent residents of Portsmouth, died in Beaufort. Now, no one remains alive who experienced life in the last days of the dying village.

Of the thirteen people who lived at Portsmouth when it celebrated its 204th birthday in 1957, most were in poor physical condition. No physician lived on the island, nor were there any health facilities. There was but a single telephone on the island, located in the abandoned Coast Guard station.

There were only two local residents who had any means of income. No stores were open in the village, so all food, clothing, and essentials had to be ordered from the mainland. This was accomplished by providing a list to the skipper of the mailboat, who filled the order and brought the requested items on the next run. No ice was available on the island, and rainwater collected in cisterns provided the only drinking water.

No television was available. Indeed, there was no source of electricity. Several residents had radios powered by batteries. Transportation around the village and down the island was primarily by foot. Not one motor vehicle was to be found on Portsmouth—not that it mattered, because the only roads were nothing more than crude cart paths rutted with potholes.

As you make your way east toward the beach on the main village road, the last structures you will encounter are the former Coast Guard station and its support buildings. After the station was closed, the large structure, with its characteristic watchtower, was used as a hunting lodge. Huge white doors cover the storage space from which surf boats were launched to rescue victims of shipwrecks.

Located nearby is a grass landing strip.

Approximately a hundred yards south of the Coast Guard station is the cistern of the old marine hospital.

Beyond the station, the beach lies about a mile away across a sand flat. The graves of two sea captains who died in the nineteenth century are located along the walk to the beach, but they are often covered by sand and sage grass.

On any given day, when visitors to Portsmouth Island leave the village by foot or by four-wheel-drive vehicle, they can travel down the beach for miles and miles without seeing a human being. No building mars the landscape of the sparsely vegetated, rolling sand flats. Except for the lonely cries of a shorebird and the thunder of the pounding surf and the winds that sometimes whisper and sometimes howl, nothing disturbs the silence.

On the map printed by the North Carolina Division of Transportation for public distribution, Portsmouth Island is shown as approximately 8 miles in length, with Swash Inlet as its southern boundary. This inlet reopened in 1939, but it is now shoaled up and is only awash at high tide. Accordingly, the 8-mile stretch of barrier beach extending south from Swash Inlet to Drum Inlet is considered by many geographers as part of Portsmouth Island.

You will notice a number of interesting geographical features if you take a trip down the island. Most evident is the almost complete lack of dunes on the ocean strand. Coupled with the extremely low elevation of the island, this scarcity of dunes has made Portsmouth highly susceptible to flooding during even moderate storms. Only two relatively tall dunes stand along the entire length. Big Hill, located 0.3 mile south of the village, is a cratered dune that was used by navigators as a landmark for many years. Generations of children from the village played on the dune, and it even provided a high spot of refuge during storms. Near the midsection of the island, George Hills, the tallest dunes, rise almost fourteen feet.

Probably no living person knows or cares more about Portsmouth Island than Don Morris of the village of Atlantic. Don was not born on Portsmouth, but rather on the mainland just across Core Sound from the southern end of the island. Portsmouth has always been a vital part of his life. His father was a commercial fisherman on Core Sound who began taking fishing parties to eighteen cabins he built on Portsmouth just north of the present Drum Inlet. When the state began its acquisition of the island in 1961, the senior Morris sold the 960 acres he owned on the island.

Since that time, the fishing cabins have been leased back to Don Morris. For many years, Don has operated his Kabin Kamp on the island as a concessionaire of the National Park Service. The cabins are clustered midway between Morris's sound-side ferry landing and the ocean. As spartan as these accommodations are, they represent the only lodgings on the island other than several nearby modular units. Camping is allowed on the island, but the lack of water and sheltered areas makes it feasible only for the hardiest and most experienced of campers.

Because the sound-side waters off Portsmouth Island are so shallow, few boaters are able to navigate the treacherous approaches to the island. For many years, Don Morris has operated the only real means of access to the southern end of the island. His knowledge and experience in navigating the waters from Morris Marina at Atlantic to Portsmouth have allowed him to safely ferry thousands of vehicles and passengers to the island. Morris's current ferry is a forty-eight-foot vessel, the *Green Grass*, designed to carry four vehicles and forty-nine passengers.

Passengers on the *Green Grass* can readily understand why only the most experienced of mariners navigate these waters. Small sand sharks swim around and under the boat, which at times scrapes the bottom of the narrow channel.

After providing ferry service to Portsmouth Island for more than forty years, Don Morris wants no other life. In his "Down East" dialect, he once

*The Green Grass Ferry
from Atlantic to Portsmouth Island*

expressed his feelings about his Portsmouth Island ferry operation: "I'm happiest when I'm on the ferry. I'm bringing happiness to people who are going over, and the scenery is beautiful. I might make eight to ten trips a day, but never get tired of it."

If you are interested in riding the *Green Grass*, contact Don Morris in Atlantic, but be aware that it is an extremely difficult 16-mile trek from his ferry landing near the southern end of the island to Portsmouth village. Most visitors to the island find that the ferry from Ocracoke, which lands at the northern end of Portsmouth, better suits their needs.

When you have had your fill of Portsmouth Island, return to the landing at Haulover Point and take the ferry back to Ocracoke. From there, you will need to retrieve your car and take the ferry trip from Ocracoke to Cedar Island. Upon landing at Cedar Island, drive 33 miles south on N.C. 12 to Harkers Island. (For information on the "Down East" country and the small communities lying between Cedar Island and Beaufort, see The Down East Carteret Tour, pages 36–53.)

Cape Lookout National Seashore Visitor Center on Harkers Island

Proceed to Calico Jack's Marina, located on the eastern end of Harkers Island near the Cape Lookout National Seashore Visitor Center. A ferry operated by a National Park Service concessionaire departs from Calico Jack's for the short trip across Back Sound and Barden Inlet to Cape Lookout, located at the southern end of Core Banks. Leave your car at the marina and take the ferry to Cape Lookout.

Three islands make up Cape Lookout National Seashore: Portsmouth, Core Banks, and Shackleford Banks. On the southern side of Drum Inlet, the 26-mile-long Core Banks stands out like a gigantic check mark or a spear with a broken point. Jutting far into the Atlantic at the southern end of the island, Cape Lookout, the central cape of the three famed North Carolina capes, lends its name to the state's second, and younger, national seashore.

As you leave the Cape Lookout ferry, you may well be greeted by National Park Service rangers, who offer a varied schedule of programs and activities, most of which take place at the former lighthouse keeper's quarters. It is here that the park visitor will find the only "amenities" in the national seashore south of Portsmouth. Restrooms, the only ones provided by the National Park Service on Core Banks, are located at the nearby lighthouse complex. Shelter from the storms that often blow up without much warning can also be found at the complex.

Other than the buildings at Portsmouth village, there are few reminders of human habitation on the three islands of Cape Lookout National Seashore. By far the most imposing of the man-made structures is the Cape Lookout Lighthouse.

While visitors were still climbing the steps to the top of the Cape Hatteras Lighthouse for a spectacular view of the Atlantic in 1979, the Cape Lookout Lighthouse had already received a death sentence from the National Park Service. Fortunately, the sea has commuted the premature sentence for this, the prototype for the Cape Hatteras Lighthouse and the other lighthouses built on the Outer Banks.

A lighthouse has stood at Cape Lookout since 1812, when the predecessor to the existing tower was erected. The original ninety-six-foot structure was painted with horizontal red and white stripes. However, mariners complained for many years that the lighthouse was not tall enough. After some unsuccessful efforts to improve the effectiveness of the structure, the federal government decided to erect a replacement.

Construction on the present lighthouse commenced in 1857. Two years later, the imposing red-brick structure stood 156 feet above the Atlantic. It

Cape Lookout Lighthouse

Remnants of original
Cape Lookout Lighthouse

was not only blessed with a majestic appearance, but it was also more functional than its predecessor, no doubt the reason that it was used as the mold for the new lights at Cape Hatteras, Bodie Island, and Currituck Beach.

Constructed close to the first lighthouse, the new tower featured walls that were nine feet thick at their base. Federal architects knew full well that the structure had to be strong enough to withstand the terrible hurricanes and coastal storms that pounded the cape. But the builders did not envision the structural tests to which their architectural masterpiece would be exposed within a few years of its completion.

Shortly after the outbreak of the Civil War, Confederate forces destroyed the lens of the lighthouse in their effort to hamper the Federal blockade off the North Carolina coast. By 1863, the tower was relit, and the Confederacy looked for an opportunity to darken it again. That chance came in the early spring of 1864 through the help of twenty-two-year-old Mary Frances Chadwick of nearby Beaufort, who by that time was already a veteran spy for the Confederate army.

From the intelligence provided by Chadwick, a Confederate raiding party made an undetected landing at Cape Lookout in early April 1864. They immediately proceeded about their task of packing the new lighthouse with explosives. Because the original wooden tower was still standing, it was also rigged to be blown up. When the explosives were detonated, the cape shook. Fire destroyed the older structure, and the new lighthouse sustained extensive damage. Not only was its lamp destroyed, but a large crack ran the length of the brick tower.

It was 1867 before the lighthouse once again sent its beam to mariners in the Atlantic.

Six years later, the United States Lighthouse Board expressed concern that seafarers along the North Carolina coast might be confused by the red-brick lighthouses of similar construction along the Outer Banks. To remedy this dangerous situation, the board issued a directive on April 17, 1873, to make the four lighthouses "more readily distinguishable in the daytime." Cape Lookout would be painted in a checkered design, with black and white diamonds; the Cape Hatteras Lighthouse would be given its now-famous black and white spiral bands; and the Bodie Island Lighthouse would be

distinguished by its black and white horizontal stripes. At the time, the Currituck Beach Lighthouse was still on the drawing board, and the decision was made to leave it unpainted when completed.

Since the initial paint job, the story has been told over and over again that the painting crew put the wrong pattern on the Cape Lookout Lighthouse. According to the legend, the diamond design was meant for the Cape Hatteras Lighthouse, which shines over Diamond Shoals. But research has shown that the painters were not in error, and that the diamond design of the Cape Lookout Lighthouse was meant for it from the beginning.

In 1933, Barden Inlet, which separates Core Banks from Shackleford Banks, reopened. By 1940, the land between the lighthouse and Core Sound had begun to erode. More than 1,000 feet of land were lost by 1979. The waters of the sound were within 279 feet of the first of North Carolina's modern lighthouses when the National Park Service announced that it would do nothing to save the lighthouse. At the time of the announcement, scientists estimated that the lighthouse would tumble into the sound by 1983 if the existing erosion rate continued.

Concerned citizens and state officials were appalled at the National Park

Service's decision. Almost immediately, a citizens' group was formed to save the lighthouse. Thereafter, the danger dissipated when an alternate channel was dredged on the western side of Barden Inlet.

Erosion has been halted for the time being, and the threat to the lighthouse is not as immediate as it was in 1979. Ultimately, steps may have to be taken to salvage the historic landmark. A restoration project completed in the early 1990s repaired many structural and aesthetic defects that had become apparent in the venerable structure.

Since 1950, the lighthouse has been automated. Inside, the spiral staircase has five levels of thirty-six steps each. Near the top, there is a small supply room. Nine more steps lead to the cupola, where the lamp rotates every fifteen seconds.

*Abandoned oil house
at Cape Lookout Lighthouse*

Although visitors to Cape Lookout National Seashore are not allowed inside the lighthouse, they can examine and photograph the exterior of the fascinating structure. Included in the lighthouse complex are the old keeper's quarters, a shed for coal and wood shed, an oil house, and a generator shed.

In the nineteenth century, Cape Lookout village, the only populated place on Core Banks south of Portsmouth village, grew up around the lighthouse. But by 1974, only two residents—a married couple who operated a small store at the site of the old village—lived on the banks.

From the lighthouse, walk 2.5 miles south to Cape Point—Cape Lookout. The hike down the beach to the cape presents an excellent opportunity to reflect on the history of this isolated spot of land.

Few people who walk the lonely shores of the seashore imagine that the Cape Lookout area has figured conspicuously in the history of North Carolina time and time again. During the European exploration of the North American coast, expedition leaders used the bight of Cape Lookout to careen their ships and to obtain fresh water, game, and fish, which were readily available on the banks and in nearby waters. Some historians have speculated that Sir Walter Raleigh's first group of colonists made its initial landing at Cape Lookout. Wherever the first landing was made, it is certain that some members of the party explored the area after a colony was established.

About the time the reign of piracy was ending along the North Carolina coast in the first quarter of the eighteenth century, John Shackleford and

Enoch Ward purchased seven thousand acres of the barrier island from John Porter, who had acquired the land in 1713. Shackleford and Ward's tract extended from Old Drum Inlet to Beaufort Inlet. In 1723, they divided the tract, Shackleford taking Cape Lookout and the western portion.

About the same time, the first permanent settlers reached the Cape Lookout area. Most of these "Banks people" came from the west and north. Few had any formal education, and none had any record of their ancestry, though they claimed and appeared to be of English extraction. Their livelihood came from hunting, fishing, and gardening. Soon, these early settlers were joined by a few whaling families, who arrived from New England around 1725. From the New England whalers, the "Ca'e Bankers," as the early residents were called, learned methods similar to those employed well into this century by whalers in the Azores.

As early as 1755, Royal Governor Arthur Dobbs proposed that a fortification be constructed at the bight at Cape Lookout in order to protect the region from foreign raiders. However, no immediate action was taken on Dobbs's suggestion.

Ironically, Cape Lookout was not fortified until two Frenchmen, Captain Denis De Cottineau and Monsieur Le Chevalier De Cambray, came to America to volunteer for service in General George Washington's army. In 1778, De Cottineau happened to land his frigate at Cape Lookout, and both he and De Cambray, an artillery officer, noted, as had so many mariners before them, that the bight provided an excellent harbor. Because of the cape's value as a safe harbor, the Frenchmen were dismayed to find no fortification here. Anxious to aid the American cause, De Cottineau and De Cambray sought and received permission from North Carolina authorities to erect a fort. When they sailed from Cape Lookout to deliver their letters of introduction to General Washington later in 1778, the Frenchmen left behind a fort with arms, munitions, and barracks.

The gift of the fort was just the first contribution in a distinguished record of service established by De Cottineau in the young country during its battle for independence. Indeed, his greatest moments were yet to come. After he offered his military skills to General Washington, it was De Cottineau's honor to captain one of the four ships in the fleet of America's most famous naval hero, John Paul Jones. Jones's fleet attacked British shipping off the English coast, where his famous ship, the *Bonhomme Richard*, engaged the *Serapis*. From this heated naval battle came one of the most memorable quotes in American history: "I have not yet begun to fight." Many Americans have not heard what happened after the battle was over—the *Bonhomme Richard* sank. John Paul Jones and his crew were rescued from the water by one Denis de Cottineau.

De Cottineau left the naming of the new fort to North Carolina officials, who chose Fort Hancock in honor of Enoch Hancock, the owner of the land upon which the fort was erected. Evidence indicates that the fort was located northwest of the Cape Lookout Lighthouse, close to Barden Inlet. As late as the 1890s, debris from the old fort, including portions of the breastworks, old bricks, pieces of metal, and old coins, could still be found. Twentieth-century attempts to locate artifacts from the fort have failed. Modern aerial reconnaissance has not disclosed any evidence of this French gift to America, which predated the Statue of Liberty by a century. Most likely, the site has been severely eroded and no traces of Fort Hancock will ever be found.

On the trek to Cape Point, there are few visible reminders of the significant American military presence at Cape Lookout during World War II. In addition to the Coast Guard contingent, an army battalion and a small detachment of sailors were stationed here. These military personnel had front-row seats for the warfare conducted by German submarines off the North Carolina coast.

During the war, the bight at Cape Lookout served as a rendezvous point for Allied convoys. However, until the convoy system was perfected, U-boat commanders had some of their greatest successes against shipping in the waters off Cape Lookout in the early months of 1942. Along the beaches of Core and Shackleford banks, shore patrols were greeted almost daily with corpses and debris from U-boat kills.

In the hook of the cape, United States forces constructed a dock, connected to the southern beach by a cement road. At this dock, ammunition and other supplies were unloaded off military boats from Beaufort. Approximately 0.5 mile from the ocean, barracks were erected near a large sand dune on the southern beach. Two large guns with a range of 20 miles were mounted on cement bunkers near the installation to provide protection for

Beaufort Inlet. On the tall sand dunes near the ocean beach were machine-gun nests constructed of stones and sandbags.

A small portion of the old cement road remains intact. Until recent years, the concrete gun mounts could be seen, but the spot where they were located has been reclaimed by the ocean. Now, they are only visible at low tide.

A tour of Cape Lookout National Seashore is not complete without a visit to the cape itself. It is relatively flat, with a cover of sand and grass. Swimming near this hook-shaped cape should be avoided, because of the extremely deep waters of the bight.

Looking out on the Atlantic from this point, you can almost visualize the famous ships that have passed within sight of the cape: the great Spanish galleons laden with newly mined riches destined for the mother country; Sir Walter Raleigh's fleet, carrying the first English settlers in America; the ships of the most infamous pirates of the Atlantic coast, their Jolly Rogers striking terror in innocent seafaring victims; the privateer *Snap Dragon*, commanded by Captain Otway Burns, returning to its home port of Beaufort after another successful raid on British shipping; the massive Federal flotilla heading for the open sea en route to its history-making assault on Fort Fisher; the surf boats from the nearby lifesaving stations on their rescue efforts in the perilous waters of Lookout Shoals; and the Allied convoys desperately attempting to elude German U-boats.

When Royal Governor Arthur Dobbs visited Cape Lookout in 1755, he was impressed by the natural harbor he found here. Describing it as "the best, although small, of any harbor from Boston to Georgia," Dobbs was not the first person to recognize the bight's potential as a protected anchorage. As early as the 1740s, Spanish privateers had used the harbor for shelter and as a hiding place. From that time through World War II, the bight provided anchorage for navies in every war in which America participated.

Despite its long history of use by innumerable ships, no organized attempt was made to realize the commercial potential of the bight until the early part of the twentieth century. In 1912, Congress authorized the construction of a seven-thousand-foot jetty at the hook of the cape to improve the harbor of refuge. At about the same time, the Norfolk and Western Railroad, an industry leader in the coal-transport business, disclosed plans to construct a rail line from the Beaufort–Morehead City area, located across the sound, to the cape, where a coaling station would be located. World War I ended the railroad project before it got off the drawing board.

With the nation's attention turned toward war, the jetty project was halted at forty-eight-hundred feet in 1918. Nevertheless, the bight was serviceable as a rendezvous spot for convoys. To protect these ships, hundreds of shiploads of rock were dumped near the cape to form submarine nets.

Plans were announced for the creation of a commercial port and resort at Cape Lookout almost as soon as World War I concluded. A Beaufort businessman formed the Cape Lookout Development Company in 1921, and lots on the banks were sold in anticipation of the construction of a clubhouse and hotel there.

When the Great Depression enveloped the nation, the North Carolina press clamored for state action to make Cape Lookout a commercial port. At the time, two wooden wharves, one owned by the federal government, stood at the harbor. Plans for the would-be commercial port continued to languish. No state assistance was forthcoming, and, for all intents and purposes, World War II ended the dream for the harbor.

North Carolina has never been able to keep pace with its neighbors to the north and south—Virginia and South Carolina—in seaport revenues and business. The most frequently cited reason for this shortcoming is that Wilmington and Morehead City are not natural deepwater seaports. Ironically, the harbor at Cape Lookout has been termed one of the great natural harbors of the world. Measuring 1.6 miles by 1.75 miles, it is said to be of sufficient size to hold all the navies of the world.

From the cape, return to the lighthouse. North of the National Park Service facilities at the lighthouse, the extremely narrow Core Banks stretches for miles and miles with few landmarks, natural or otherwise, to distinguish one mile from the next. Much of this barrier island is less than 0.4 mile wide, and except for an area of high dunes in the Cape Lookout area, it is exposed to the full brunt of the wind and the ocean waves. With little or no dune protection, the island is frequently overwashed by seawater, thereby preventing any significant vegetation from taking root.

The only development along the northern half of Core Banks is a fishing camp near Shingle Point, located 14 miles north of Cape Lookout, just across Core Sound from the mainland village of Davis. This facility is operated as a National Park Service concession by Alger Willis, who runs a ferry between Davis and the camp.

When you have finished touring Core Banks, take the ferry back to Calico Jack's marina on Harkers Island.

Note that the ferry also runs from Calico Jack's to the eastern end of Shackleford Banks. Make arrangements to take the ferry to Shackleford Banks to complete the final leg of this tour. Another ferry runs between Beaufort and Shackleford Banks, but it deposits visitors on the sound shore near the western end of the island, near Beaufort Inlet.

Shackleford Banks lies closer to the mainland than the other two islands in Cape Lookout National Seashore. It is separated from the mainland and Harkers Island by Back Sound, from Bogue Banks by Bogue Inlet, and from Core Banks by Barden Inlet.

Because of its east-west orientation, Shackleford is geographically different from Core Banks and Portsmouth Island, which both have a north-south orientation. Since Shackleford lies perpendicular to the prevailing winds, it hosts a greater assortment of plants and animals than the other islands. More significantly, it is less susceptible to overwash and inlet formation, because high dunes afford some protection from wind and waves. In addition, these dunes provide shelter from salt spray for the only extensive maritime forest in the national seashore.

Particularly noticeable on Shackleford Banks are the wild horses. When the last permanent residents departed Shackleford, they left behind more than their dwellings. Hundreds of sheep, goats, and cows were left to roam the barrier landscape and to fend for themselves. In addition, approximately a thousand horses, many of them wild, could be found on Shackleford and Core banks at the turn of the century.

These animals were allowed to multiply. Former inhabitants maintained ownership of the horses and cows by branding them from time to time at roundups. Well into the 1980s, these roundups continued to be social events for the former residents and their families.

Suddenly, in 1980, the National Park Service announced its highly controversial decision to remove the animals from Cape Lookout National Seashore. At that time, estimates of the animal population indicated that there

The Capt. Alger *Ferry from Davis to Core Banks*

A herd of wild horses on Shackleford Banks

were 108 horses, 74 cows, 144 sheep, and more than 100 goats. The National Park Service justified the action on the grounds that it was its policy to remove "exotic" or "nonnative" animals from wilderness areas. Specifically, it cited scientific studies that theorized the animals damaged the islands by destroying the vegetation.

By mid-September 1986, the last of the cattle, sheep, and goats had been herded and hauled away from Shackleford Banks under National Park Service supervision. Although the original proposal included the eviction of the horses, a reprieve was granted to a hundred of the animals after the state of North Carolina and concerned citizens argued that the horses had been on the islands before the first permanent human residents.

Of the three islands in the national seashore, only Shackleford Banks now maintains a horse population. Two separate, distinct groups of horses are located at either end of the island. At the current tour stop on the eastern end of the island, the horses are close in size to regular horses. It is believed that these are the offspring of horses from the mainland. On the western end, the horses are smaller. These are the well-known "Banker ponies," the descendants of horses that came ashore centuries ago from European shipwrecks. The development of the Shackleford horses through the years has been influenced by the harsh environment to which they have adapted.

Visitors to Shackleford Banks can watch these remarkable animals as they paw the sand for a drink of brackish water. Only the strongest survive, as the horses are sometimes forced to dig as deep as four feet to find a few sips of water. In the summer, they endure temperatures exceeding a hundred degrees and painful bites from flies and mosquitoes. Winter brings subfreezing temperatures and frigid winds that force the horses to seek shelter behind the dunes. But in spite of the harsh environment, these rugged horses have proved they belong and have earned a rightful place as permanent residents of Cape Lookout National Seashore.

In 1933, at the eastern end of the island, a hurricane reopened the inlet that had separated Core Banks from Shackleford Banks prior to the Civil War. At the time the storm waters broke through, the inlet was nothing more than a stream. But through the intervention of Congressman Hap Barden, local mainland fishermen were provided with a convenient outlet to the sea. Barden gained authorization which allowed the Corps of Engineers to dredge the reopened inlet in 1938. After the initial dredging project, the inlet had a tendency to close, thus necessitating constant dredging to keep it open. Through this process, the Corps of Engineers has maintained a navigable channel which flows directly in front of the Cape Lookout Lighthouse.

This channel—Barden Inlet, known locally as "the Drain"—continues to serve as a passageway for fishermen and other boaters from Core and Back sounds to the bight at Cape Lookout. Scientists have blamed the channel for the increased erosion on the sound side of the lighthouse and the decrease in clams, scallops, and oysters in the waters of Back Sound and portions of Core Sound.

From Barden Inlet, walk west on the island.

Within a few short years, the last persons born on Shackleford and Core banks will be dead. Other than the lighthouse and the horses, little of their heritage remains for park visitors to examine.

North Carolina's development of Cape Hatteras National Seashore, America's first national seashore, provided the impetus for the acquisition of land on Core and Shackleford banks—the nucleus of Cape Lookout National Seashore. By the late 1950s, these barrier islands were sparsely populated and were subject to severe storm damage because of their low elevation and lack of protective dunes. Spurred by the early success of Cape Hatteras National Seashore and by the desire to save Core and Shackleford banks from destruction and commercial development, the state began purchasing land in 1957.

The initial plans for the creation of the state's second national seashore were laid out at a conference between Governor Terry Sanford and Secretary of the Interior Stewart Udall in the summer of 1962. White House approval for Cape Lookout National Seashore came in June 1964 and congressional approval a year later.

Terming the 58-mile string of barrier islands "one of the longest stretches of undeveloped shoreline left along the entire Eastern Seaboard," the Department of the Interior announced comprehensive plans for the development of marinas, campgrounds, picnic areas, ocean access, and interpretive displays in the national-seashore complex.

Somehow, the grandiose plans presented by the National Park Service in the 1960s have never materialized. Primarily because of limited access and the lack of tourist facilities, Cape Lookout National Seashore has never attracted the number of visitors or achieved the visibility of Cape Hatteras National Seashore. Finally, in 1985, the National Park Service proceeded with plans to manage Shackleford Banks as a wilderness area, where "the imprint of man's activities are substantially absent, the environment is affected principally by natural forces and there are opportunities for solitude."

On Shackleford, you will notice some of the highest dunes in the park. Vegetation on the eastern two-thirds of the island is limited to marsh and dune grasses. Located on the remaining third is the only sizable maritime forest in the entire park. Mingled in the forest are live oak, cedar, loblolly pine, American holly, American hornbeam, and Hercules-club. Even "imported" maples can be found in the forest. The long rows of pines growing up and down the dunes were planted by Boy Scouts more than twenty years ago. Evidence of former maritime forests on the island can also be found. Gnarled, lifeless oaks and cedars standing amid shifting dunes are reminders of former groves of trees killed by sand and salt spray.

Remnants of island forest

Sand flats dominate the Shackleford shoreline. Behind the flats, the rolling dunes create valleys which make it impossible to look across the width of the island, even though it is not much more than 0.5 mile wide at its widest point. Of the islands in the park, only Shackleford has permanent freshwater ponds.

Bird watchers are delighted to find that the park is a wintering ground for loons, cormorants, gannets, some geese and swans, and other northern birds. During the summer season, terns, egrets, pelicans, and shorebirds join resident birds such as gulls, herons, hawks, and ospreys. Mammals other than horses are quite rare. Among the reptiles in the park are toads, frogs, lizards, turtles—including the loggerhead—and nonpoisonous snakes.

The 250,000 people who visit Cape Lookout National Seashore annually see what the National Park Service calls "a developing park." Consequently, it ranks ninth out of the ten national seashores in number of visitors. Because of its designation as a wilderness area, Shackleford Banks will have limited visitor facilities in the future. For most of the year, its beaches are virtually deserted.

Camping is permitted without license or permit on both Core and Shackleford banks, except within 0.5 mile of the Cape Lookout Lighthouse. Since no campsites or other facilities have been developed, camping is primitive. Shelter is at a premium in the national seashore. Thus, an adequate tent is essential.

Vehicles are allowed within the park. A free permit must be obtained from the National Park Service prior to bringing a vehicle onto the islands. Four-wheel-drive vehicles are the only ones that can safely and effectively travel the sandy terrain.

In its informational brochures, the National Park Service notes that the park "has been set aside to preserve a fragile natural resource while allowing the public to use and enjoy the area. . . . The visitor will also be provided the opportunity to learn the area's history, both natural and human." However, a hike down Shackleford yields few clues of its past history of human habitation.

As strange as it may seem, the most-populous village on the entire Outer Banks in the latter part of the nineteenth century was located on now-deserted Shackleford Banks. During the latter half of the nineteenth century, five distinct communities were spread along the 9-mile-long island.

Located on the eastern end, Diamond City was the largest community on the island and the Outer Banks in the post–Civil War years. Until 1897, as many as five hundred people called the village home. It stretched from the Drain almost halfway down the island.

Although the village was populated many, many years before 1885, it was in that year that Diamond City got its name, thanks to the design on the nearby lighthouse.

Dominating the Diamond City landscape was an enormous sand dune located near the geographic center of the village. An estimated twelve hundred feet long and four hundred feet wide, the dune was at least forty feet tall. It was so extensive that it afforded some measure of protection for the village from the great Atlantic storms.

Many of the homes at Diamond City were of simple design. These wooden structures were built by their owners, as was most of the furniture inside them. Wood came from the forests which once stood on Shackleford Banks and from the timbers of shipwrecks.

On the extreme western end of Shackleford, the community of Wade's Shore extended for approximately 2 miles. Also known as Mullet Pond, Mullet Shore, Shackleford Banks, and Wade's Hammock, the village covered the most densely wooded portion of the island. Today, a thick growth of cedar scattered among the rolling dunes serves as a mute reminder of the village. At its zenith, Wade's Shore boasted a hundred people. One of the island's two single-room schools was located there.

Between Diamond City and Wade's Shore, three smaller communities—Bell's Island, Sam Windsor's Lump, and Whale Creek—were spread along the middle of Shackleford Banks.

Located just west of Diamond City, Bell's Island was for a time a distinct community known for its big persimmon trees. Eventually, Bell's Island was considered an extension of Diamond City.

Near Bell's Island, in the west-central portion of the island, the tiny settlement of Sam Windsor's Lump bore the name of the only black family on Shackleford.

Farther to the west and adjacent to Wade's Shore, the village of Whale Creek was populated by a number of families who were attracted to this portion of the island because of the dense growth of wild fig trees that once thrived here.

A number of small stores up and down the island met most of the residents' needs.

Visitors to the old port town of Beaufort are often intrigued by the state historical marker on Turner Street that reads, "At Shackleford Banks, six miles southeast by boat, was located a whale fishery of the eighteenth and nineteenth centuries." As incredible as it may seem, a viable whaling industry existed on Shackleford and Core banks from the eighteenth century until the early twentieth century. As late as 1879, four local crews of eighteen men each worked the Cape Lookout area. Fishing was an important way of life for most of the residents of the villages.

A "fish story" of a different sort was told by Charlie Rose, who was born in 1893 in Diamond City. According to Rose, he and two of his cousins from the island were mending their nets one day in 1904 or 1905 when they heard a roar over their heads. Looking up, they saw an airplane, which proceeded to land on the nearby sand flats.

The pilot walked up to the spot where the fishermen were working and offered to give Rose and his cousins a ride. Rose took the pilot up on his offer, and in so doing was most likely the first North Carolinian to ever fly in an airplane. His pilot was supposedly a famous one—none other than Wilbur Wright.

However, experts are agreed that neither of the Wright brothers ever flew a powered airplane on the Outer Banks outside the immediate Kill Devil Hills area.

Although all of them have been washed away by the sea, numerous cemeteries were once located at Diamond City and the other villages. Many were small cemeteries in the yards of homes. However, one sizable cemetery in the heart of Diamond City—called Ben Riles Graveyard—contained as many as five hundred graves.

Throughout the twentieth century, the sea has frequently overwashed the island. By the early 1930s, skulls and other human bones could be found exposed in the sands of Shackleford Banks. Year by year, the relentless sea claimed more and more of the grave sites, and by 1965, virtually no traces of the old cemeteries could be found. Most of the grave markers were made of wood and were vulnerable to the harsh environment. Yet even today, a bone from one of the old graves is occasionally uncovered by the tides.

Vibrant resort towns might exist today at the communities of Diamond City, Wade's Shore, and Cape Lookout had not storms unleashed their full fury in 1896 and 1899. Most of the island residents had weathered many hurricanes, but these two storms were unlike any that had struck before. In August 1899, the worst hurricane to ever hit the Cape Lookout area—at least in the minds of old-timers—produced a storm surge that inundated everything on the islands, save the tops of a few of the tallest sand dunes. When the waters subsided, the giant dune that ran through the center of Diamond City was no more. Countless homes were washed away, fertile gardens were destroyed and replaced with barren sand, wells went dry or were laced with salt water, and sheep, horses, and cattle were killed or driven away. Even more disturbing to many residents was the fact that the graves of loved ones had been uncovered by the relentless sea.

In the wake of the devastating storm of 1899, most residents of Shackleford and Core banks came to the realization that they could not face another

storm of such magnitude. And so during the years that followed, the people of Diamond City, Wade's Shore, and the other tiny communities abandoned the area, and the villages became ghost towns. Not only did the people leave, but they also took their homes with them. Some of the houses were torn down piece by piece and shipped across the sound, where they were reassembled.

The majority of the evacuees moved to nearby Harkers Island. Others moved to Morehead City and other communities on the mainland.

Today, Shackleford Street in Morehead City marks the area to which a number of the families fled. This area became known as "the Promised Land." In fact, some local residents continue to use the name as a point of reference in Morehead City. According to local tradition, that particular part of town acquired its moniker when Bannister Piver, a Morehead City resident, saw a barge loaded with furniture, farm animals, pets, and several families from Diamond City floating by his dock. Piver remarked, "There goes another bunch of Israelites headed for the Promised Land."

By 1902, not a single person lived at Diamond City, and no homes remained. The only remnants of the former town were cemeteries and a few fishing shacks.

When you have fully enjoyed Shackleford Banks, return to the ferry landing near Barden Inlet. Ride the ferry back to Harkers Island to complete the tour.

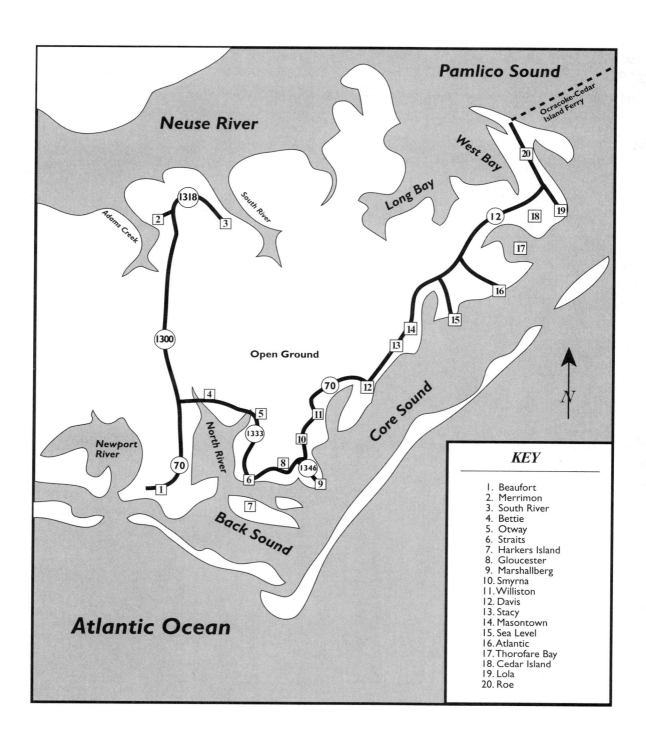

The Down East Carteret Tour

This tour begins with a drive through the area known as the "Open Ground," visiting the villages of Merrimon and South River. Next, it examines the tiny maritime villages along Core Sound, collectively known as "Down East": Bettie, Otway, Straits, Harkers Island, Gloucester, Marshallberg, Smyrna, Williston, Davis, Stacy, Sea Level, and Atlantic. It then visits Cedar Island before ending at the landing for the Cedar Island–Ocracoke Ferry.

Among the highlights of the tour are the largest farm in the eastern United States, the Down East villages, Harkers Island, the story of Shell Point, "the Miracle at Davis," Sailors' Snug Harbor, and Cedar Island National Wildlife Refuge.

Total mileage: approximately 104 miles.

This tour begins northeast of historic Beaufort at the junction of U.S. 70 and S.R. 1300. Proceed north on S.R. 1300.

This route will take you on a 15-mile odyssey to a wilderness region rarely seen by anyone other than locals. Bounded by Adams Creek on the west, the Neuse River on the north, U.S. 70 on the south, and Cedar Island on the east, the Open Ground Prairie Swamp—alternately known as "Open Ground" or "Open Land"—is a desolate 50,000-acre expanse of sand and peat bogs.

In 1926, an attempt to reclaim this vast wilderness was unsuccessful. A wealthy Philadelphian, Georgiana Yeatman, subsequently acquired huge chunks of land just west of Adams Creek, a large waterway at the northwestern corner of Carteret County, in the early 1930s. For several years, she ran an experimental dairy operation with a sizable herd of Guernseys. Later, she spent a fortune transforming a portion of the Open Ground into pastureland. Trainloads of lime were trucked in, and extensive drainage canals were dug. Ultimately, the project was abandoned.

More than forty-five thousand acres of the Open Ground were sold to an Italian conglomerate around 1970. That company invested more than $20 million to begin the largest farming operation in the history of the county. Following several years of difficulties with state and local health agencies, the agricultural enterprise began to prosper. Today, Open Grounds

Farm, which produces corn, soybeans, wheat, cotton, and beef cattle, is the largest farm east of the Mississippi River.

There are only two communities within the confines of the Open Ground.

Merrimon is a small farming hamlet of several hundred persons. To reach it, turn left off S.R. 1300 onto S.R. 1318 approximately 12.3 miles north of the intersection of U.S. 70 and S.R. 1300. Proceed 1.5 miles on S.R. 1318 through Merrimon. The village is located near the banks of Adams Creek, a scenic water course that serves as the route of the Intracoastal Waterway, linking the Neuse River with the Newport River via Core Creek Canal. On clear days, visitors to Merrimon can see the sailing town of Oriental just across the Neuse River.

Retrace your route to the junction with S.R. 1300 and continue 3.3 miles on S.R. 1318 to South River, the second human outpost in the open expanse. Set on the banks of the river of the same name, this small village is a fishing community. A boat ramp provides access to the 9.5-mile-long river.

From South River, retrace your route toward the junction with U.S. 70. For an interesting side trip, turn west off S.R. 1300 onto S.R. 1163 approximately 9.8 miles south of Merrimon. After 2.3 miles, S.R. 1163 intersects N.C. 101. Turn north on N.C. 101 and drive 4.2 miles to Harlowe Creek.

Prior to the completion of the Adams Creek link of the Intracoastal Waterway, the Clubfoot-Harlowe Canal, of which Harlowe Creek is a part, was the main water route from mainland Carteret to the Neuse. Known locally as the Slave Canal because it was deepened to five or six feet by slave labor in the late seventeenth and early eighteenth centuries, it is one of the oldest canals in the United States. It was created untold centuries ago by Indians who dragged their canoes across the lowlands to the Neuse. Though the canal is long and straight, it is extremely narrow and shallow, and lack of maintenance has made it perilous to navigate.

Return to the junction of S.R. 1300 and U.S. 70. Proceed east on U.S. 70.

The only bridge spanning the North River crosses the water 0.8 mile east of the junction. The wide, 10-mile-long North River empties into Back Sound, a body of water separating Harkers Island from Shackleford Banks. An imaginary line runs north from the North River across mainland Carteret County, marking the boundary between the Beaufort–Morehead City–Bogue

Banks resort areas and the northeastern peninsula of the mainland. "Down East Carteret," as this peninsula is known, is one of the last vestiges of the rural fishing and farming economy that once dominated most of coastal North Carolina.

Until World War II, the Carteret communities lying east of Beaufort existed in a state of virtual isolation. Bridges, electricity, and other modern conveniences have come to the area only in the past fifty years. Nevertheless, Down East has not sacrificed its quaint charm. The residents live in peace with the land and sea, as their ancestors did for centuries. Boats, fishing nets, and vegetable gardens are in evidence in the yards of most of the modest white frame homes. In this land of stark natural beauty, man and the coastal environment exist in harmony.

Located 0.8 mile east of the bridge over the North River, Bettie, a small hamlet of three hundred persons, is the first of the Down East communities you will encounter on U.S. 70. Known as the "Gateway to Original Down East," it was named for the daughter of an early settler in the area.

Despite the incursion of the outside world through the automobile and television, Bettie and its sister villages remain among the last places in the nation where visitors can hear "the queen's English"—English spoken as it was when America was first settled. To the uninitiated, this strange brogue may seem uncultured. However, words and expressions still in use by lifelong residents of Down East are found in English literature of the sixteenth and seventeenth centuries. Twice a day, the "toide" (tide) gets "hoigh" (high) for the "Down Easters."

Continue 2.4 miles east on U.S. 70 to the community of Otway, which is separated from Bettie by Ward Creek, a tributary of the North River. Bearing the name of Carteret County hero Otway Burns, this is one of two towns in the state named in honor of the famous privateer. Burnsville, in western North Carolina, is the other. Approximately five hundred people live in Otway.

At Otway, the tour veers away from U.S. 70, making a southern loop around a neck of land separated from Harkers Island by a strip of water known as "The Straits." Turn right, or south, off U.S. 70 onto S.R. 1325. After 0.3 mile on S.R. 1325, turn left onto S.R. 1331 and drive 0.2 mile to S.R. 1333. Turn right on S.R. 1333 and proceed 3 miles to the village of

Straits. Along the route to this small farming and fishing village, you will enjoy a panorama of beautiful farm country and semitropical woodlands. Approximately 0.5 mile north of the community, a bridge affords a spectacular view of the North River at one of the river's widest points.

Because Straits is located just north of the bridge to Harkers Island, it has a high volume of traffic. However, the village was an isolated place until World War II, since the unpaved road from Otway was virtually impassable in bad weather and the ferry landing for the trip to Harkers Island was located 2 miles east, at Gloucester.

Straits is the home of the oldest Methodist church in Down East. This church was built around 1778.

In 1813, the Methodist minister in Straits played an important role in an event that was the basis of one of the most enduring Down East legends. Village residents were starving in the winter of that year. A crop-killing drought the previous summer was followed by deadly winter cold that choked the nearby sounds with ice. Fishing was impossible, and there was no food stored in the village. A wartime blockade by the British fleet prevented trade with the outside world. When almost all hope had faded, the Reverend Starr sought divine intervention. Lifting his voice to heaven, the

Starr Methodist Church

pastor prayed, "If it is predestined that there be a wreck on the Atlantic coast, please let it be here." Whether by coincidence or providence, a ship with a cargo of flour wrecked on nearby Core Banks a few days later, saving the community from disaster.

In the modern village, Starr Methodist Church memorializes the minister who uttered the famous prayer.

In Straits, turn south off S.R. 1333 onto S.R. 1335 for the 1.8-mile drive to Harkers Island. The Straits Fishing Pier, located along this route, is a public facility maintained by the Carteret County Parks and Recreation Department. It affords a beautiful vista of the surrounding waterways.

Many visitors get their first real taste of the salty flavor of Down East Carteret at Harkers Island. Situated almost due east of Beaufort near the mouth of the North River, the 5-mile-long, 1-mile-wide island is bounded on the north by The Straits, on the south by Back Sound, and on the east by Core Sound. Its location on the sounds offers protection from the fury of the wind and sea, which often plagues the nearby barrier islands.

The bridge across The Straits delivers vehicles to the western end of Harkers Island. On the island, S.R. 1335 becomes Harkers Island Road. Proceed east as the road winds its way for 5 miles to the eastern end of the island on Core Sound.

More than three thousand people currently live here, making Harkers Island the most populous of the Down East communities. Over half the population is clustered in the village on the southern shore. Hundreds of other homes and cottages are located along the winding, shady island road.

Its Down East charm and its proximity to the Carteret County beaches have made Harkers Island increasingly attractive to vacationers. At the height of the summer season, the population doubles. Motels and restaurants have been built over the past thirty years to accommodate the growing number of tourists.

On the drive down the island, you will note that the yards of many homes disclose evidence of one of the oldest industries of the island: boat building. Wooden boats of all sizes and in various stages of construction can be seen throughout the year all over the island. This "backyard boat building" has evolved into an important industry that includes a half-dozen boatyards.

Early boatbuilders on the island worked without blueprints. They developed

Fishing fleet at Harkers Island

*Exhibit at Core Sound
Waterfowl Museum*

the distinctive Harkers Island flared bow, now the trademark of island crafts-men. Despite a nationwide decline in sales of wooden boats, boat buyers all along the eastern seaboard are attracted to Harkers Island boats because of their excellent construction and dependability.

Located approximately 3.1 miles from the bridge, the Core Sound Water-fowl Museum is dedicated to the preservation of traditional decoy carving and the history of waterfowl hunting in Down East. Operated by the Core Sound Decoy Carvers Guild, the facility is housed in temporary quarters until a $1.5-million complex containing a museum and gallery can be com-pleted. During the first weekend in December, the guild sponsors the Core Sound Decoy Festival, during which dealers, collectors, and carvers show-case decoys, artwork, and publications.

From the museum, drive east to the end of the island. The recently com-pleted Cape Lookout National Seashore Headquarters/Visitor Center over-looks Core Sound at the end of the road. Park in the parking lot and take a few minutes to enjoy the exhibits and programs at the facility.

Walk across the road to the scenic park overlooking Back Sound. Picnic tables are spread about the grassy area at the water's edge. From the park, you can catch a glimpse of the Cape Lookout Lighthouse on Core Banks, just across Back Sound.

Since the completion of the Cape Lookout National Seashore Headquar-ters/Visitor Center, Harkers Island has served as a gateway to the lighthouse and the southern portion of the park. At a marina near the visitor center, a passenger ferry licensed by the National Park Service provides access to Shackleford Banks and the lower portion of Core Banks during spring, sum-mer, and fall. (For more information on the national seashore, see The Cape Lookout National Seashore Tour, pages 3–32.)

From the waterfront park, walk to the end of the road. Here, at the confluence of Back and Core sounds, is Shell Point. This ancient tip of land holds clues to the history of Harkers Island. Evidence found in this area proves that the island was the site of human habitation for untold centuries. Well into the twentieth century, huge mounds of oyster, clam, scallop, and conch shells left long ago by the Coree Indians were dominant landmarks.

Excavations at the mound in 1928 unearthed three Indian skeletons. On other occasions, teeth, bones, pipes, arrowheads, clubs, tomahawks, and various pieces of Indian pottery have been discovered in the pile of shells.

Shell Point

One piece of Indian pottery is reported to have the word CROATOAN carved upon it, leading some island residents to claim that Harkers Island was the location of the Lost Colony. CROATOAN was the word John White and his men found carved in a tree on Roanoke Island when they returned from England in 1590 and discovered the colony deserted. Although no other tangible evidence has been brought forth to support their claim, numerous historians have concluded that Manteo, the Indian friendly to Sir Walter Raleigh's colonists, was indeed born on Harkers Island.

Conjecture aside, the shell mound covered at least three acres when the first white settlers took up residence on the island. Since that time, it has been significantly reduced in size. So substantial were the shells that Confederate soldiers constructed a horseshoe-shaped fort at Shell Point.

Around 1920, hundreds of tons of the shells were ground up for fertilizer and used on Hyde County farmland. At about the same time, huge quantities of shells were removed and transported to Hyde, Pamlico, and Carteret counties for use in road construction. Apparently, the Indians who were responsible for the mound had discovered many years earlier that shells could be used to build roads. Using shells, they attempted to construct one of the earliest causeways in North Carolina, from Shell Point to Shackleford Banks. Remnants of this early engineering effort can still be traced on the bottom of Back Sound.

In 1926, vast quantities of shells from the mound were used in the construction of the first hard-surfaced road on Harkers Island.

Yet even after all these projects started depleting the mound, it still measured ten to fifteen feet high and extended into the water about seventy-five yards.

From the days of the earliest European explorations along the North Carolina coast, Harkers Island has been known by several names: Crane Island, Craney Island, Davers Island, and Marker Island. Thomas Sparrow acquired the island by grant on March 21, 1714. Ebenezer Harker subsequently purchased the island in 1730 for four hundred pounds. At that time and for the next half-century, the island was known as Craney Island. Ownership of the island eventually fell into the hands of three Harker brothers, who in 1783 gave it their last name.

Until the late nineteenth century, the island was sparsely populated. Dense, junglelike thickets and virgin forests of oak, pine, cedar, and yaupon made travel from one end to the other almost impossible. Several small settlements grew in clearings at the edge of the wilderness.

In August 1899, the island's population more than doubled with the arrival of refugees from the terrific hurricane that lashed Diamond City and the other barrier-island villages just across the sound. Many current residents of Harkers Island trace their ancestry to the "Ca'e Bankers." (For more information on the evacuation of Diamond City, see The Cape Lookout National Seashore Tour, pages 29–32.)

From Shell Point, retrace your route on Harkers Island Road to the bridge.

Before the turn of the century, travel on the island was limited to the shoreline. At high tide, the only way to get from one end of the island to the other was by boat. Around 1900, island residents banded together to cut a narrow path that ran the length of the island. Gradually, this path evolved into the existing east-west road.

When the United States Post Office Department opened a post office at Sea Island—the name arbitrarily assigned to the island—on December 3, 1904, mail was delivered by boat. After the islanders were united by a road, they began to seek improved access to the mainland. An unscrupulous automobile dealer promised a group of Harkers Island men that the government would build a bridge from Beaufort to the island if they would buy at least fifteen automobiles. Not until ten vehicles had been purchased did the naive men realize that the promise was a hoax. They were left with automobiles they could use only on rare occasions.

When the county took over road maintenance in 1926, access to the island began to improve. A north-south road was built to link sea to sound, and a ferry operation between the island and the mainland community of Gloucester was instituted. In the late 1930s, a visitor from inland mistakenly thought he was on U.S. 70 and drove his automobile down the ferry road and into the water. Several occupants of the vehicle drowned, creating a public outcry for a bridge, which was completed in 1941.

Return to Straits on S.R. 1335, then continue 1.9 miles as the road loops south to Gloucester. Named for the coastal town in Massachusetts, this tiny settlement overlooking The Straits has less traffic than it did a half-century ago, when the ferry to Harkers Island departed from the Gloucester waterfront. During the Revolutionary War, a saltworks operated in the village.

To continue the tour, proceed 1.2 miles on S.R. 1335 as it loops north to the intersection with S.R. 1346. Turn right on S.R. 1346 and drive 0.9 mile to Marshallberg.

Of the many great pleasures awaiting visitors to the North Carolina coast, one of the most rewarding is the discovery of an out-of-the-way place where the romance of the sea lives. The mainland shore of Core Sound is one of those places. Marshallberg is the first of many salty Down East communities on the remainder of the tour, which clings to Core Sound for almost 40 miles.

Up and down the North Carolina coast, much of the mainland waterfront has been deemed virtually uninhabitable since the arrival of the first white settlers in the sixteenth century. However, Down East Carteret has been an exception. Here, the interior coastline, punctuated by numerous rivers, bays, and creeks, has been the site of prosperous farms and fishing settlements for more that 250 years.

Marshallberg, one of the most eye-appealing Down East communities, rests on a spit of land bounded by Sleepy Creek and Core Sound. When the first white settlers arrived here around 1800, they found evidence of the existence of a large Indian village at the site. Since that time, many Indian graves have been uncovered. Among the relics are pottery, stone weapons, and large shell mounds similar to, but smaller than, the ones at Harkers Island.

In the first half of the nineteenth century, Marshallberg was known as Deep Hole Creek, a reference to the deep hole left by workmen who excavated swampy soil for use in the construction of Fort Macon on Bogue Banks. A post office opened in the village on February 17, 1889, under the name Marshall. It was so named by the less-than-modest first postmaster, Matt Marshall.

On the picturesque waterfront at Marshallberg, a spectacular panorama of Core Sound awaits visitors. Named for the Coree Indians who once inhabited the area, the sound is one of the most beautiful bodies of water on the North Carolina coast. Though it is relatively narrow—generally no more than 3 nautical miles in width—it is approximately 28 miles long, stretching from Pamlico Sound in northern Carteret County to the bight at Cape Lookout. Probably the most interesting geographic feature of the sound is its lack of depth. Boaters cruising these waters pass by local fishermen standing in the middle of the sound in search of clams.

Some ancient maps lend credence to the local belief that a long, slender island once existed in the middle of the sound. Such an island would explain the shallow depths.

Although Harkers Island is now said to be the center of Down East boat building, the shallow-draft boats that brought fame to the area were first constructed at Marshallberg. George Milney, a New England native, brought the first "sharpie" to the community in the 1880s. Local fishermen discovered that this sailboat, with its high bow and rounded stern, was perfect for the shallow waters of Core Sound. Island craftsmen improved the buoyancy of the sharpie by flaring its bow and exaggerating its fantail. The resulting craft became known as the "Core-Sounder." Boatyards at Marshallberg, Harkers Island, Hatteras, and other places on the North Carolina coast still produce this type of boat.

Numerous well-preserved, whitewashed, turn-of-the-century homes grace the streets of Marshallberg. More than six hundred people live in the community, making it one of the largest Down East villages.

In Marshallberg, S.R. 1346 merges into S.R. 1347. Drive north on S.R. 1347, which tightly hugs the sound for 2.4 miles until it rejoins U.S. 70 at Smyrna.

Situated at the head of Middens Creek, the fishing village of Smyrna boasts 650 residents and is believed to be the oldest settlement in the area. It was named for Smunar Creek in 1785, but the spelling changed over the years.

For more than 140 years, Smyrna has been the center of education in this part of Down East. A one-room school opened in the village in 1850. County funds were used to build a large school building with an auditorium in 1914, and a consolidated high school was completed around 1922. At present, Smyrna Elementary School draws students from Smyrna, Marshallberg, Gloucester, Straits, Otway, Bettie, Davis, and Williston.

At Smyrna, turn north off S.R. 1347 onto U.S. 70. It is 2.6 miles to

Williston. This old fishing community rests peacefully on the shores of Jarrett Bay and Williston Creek. For many years, the only bridge in the village was a four-foot-wide drawbridge spanning the creek. It was subsequently widened to accommodate vehicular traffic.

From Williston, continue 3.5 miles on U.S. 70 to Davis. En route, you will cross still another bridge, one of a dozen or more between the North River and Cedar Island. These water crossings are visual reminders of the difficulties encountered earlier in the century by the builders of the highway through Down East and the settlers who preceded them. Each of these bridges yields a magnificent vista of green marshland and placid bays and creeks.

Of all the Core Sound communities, Davis is the least changed by the passage of time. It is one of the oldest of the settlements, tracing its roots and name to William Davis, who received a grant of 360 acres from King George II in 1763.

Davis lies directly on the shore of Core Sound at the midpoint of a dogleg peninsula formed by Jarrett Bay and Oyster Creek. Prior to the construction of the highway from Beaufort, this village and those to the north were completely isolated from the outside world except by water travel.

Geographic isolation played an important role in a dramatic true story

Davis waterfront

that symbolizes the courageous spirit of the residents of the North Carolina coast. Local people refer to the event as "the Miracle at Davis."

The hardy villagers were accustomed to harsh winters, but no one was prepared for the winter of 1898. Cold weather came early that year, and as it grew harsher, Davis residents found themselves caught in the grip of the coldest winter ever recorded in the area. Food supplies were depleted; fowl that were hunted in happier times sought refuge in warmer climates; and boats could not get out of the harbor because ice choked the sound.

During the bleakest, coldest part of the winter, Core Sound froze solid from the mainland to Core Banks. Many residents became ill. Passage over land for help was impossible. A sense of futility spread through the settlement. In an act of desperation, Uncle Mose Davis, a black leader in the community, recommended that the villagers hold a prayer meeting. All able-bodied people assembled north of the village on the banks of Oyster Creek, where Mose Davis led them in a simple, beautiful prayer: "O Lord, we're gathered here to ask you to help us out of our troubles. We've done everything we can for ourselves, and unless you do something to help us, we are all gonna starve to death. Amen."

Almost as soon as Uncle Mose raised his bowed head, he saw a column of smoke stretching into the eastern sky. Everyone in attendance immediately recognized the smoke as a signal for help from Core Banks. An intense debate followed. Some villagers argued that it would be tantamount to suicide to attempt a rescue. No boat could get through the ice, and, if walked upon, the ice would likely crack, sending a would-be rescuer to certain death. Finally, Uncle Mose chided the reluctant members of the group by asking them how they could ask God for help if they were unwilling to help others in need.

Goaded into action, the rugged seamen of the village tied three lines to the bow of a twenty-foot skiff. Then three brave individuals attached the lines to their waists and began pulling the boat on the ice behind them. They slipped and struggled on the 3-mile sheet of ice, but it proved thick enough to support their weight.

When the rescuers reached Core Banks, they hurried to the top of the dunes, from where they could see a group of stranded sailors huddled around a fire on the beach. Their ship, the *Pontiac*, had wrecked on the nearby shoals. After caring for the victims of the wreck, the Davis residents went about salvaging the ship's cargo. They were delighted to find vast stores of molasses and grain. Because of their efforts to rescue seafarers in trouble even in the face of personal danger, the people were saved from starvation.

Furnishings salvaged from the captain's cabin of the *Pontiac* now decorate a Williston home.

Because of Davis's expansive waterfront on Core Sound, pleasure boaters have made the village one of the favorite ports of Down East. Several marinas and boat landings are in evidence on the waterfront.

The present population of the village is approximately five hundred.

Davis counts among its favorite sons William Luther Paul, born in the village on October 8, 1869. It is believed that Paul was experimenting with a flying machine similar to a helicopter at the time the Wright brothers achieved their success at Kill Devil Hill in 1903. Due to the isolation of Davis, Paul was never able to obtain an engine with enough power to lift his invention into the air. Local historians claim that Igor Sikorsky used Paul's model in the development of the helicopter.

Continue north from Davis. U.S. 70 crosses Oyster Creek during the pleasant 3.6-mile drive to Stacy. This picturesque community of three hundred inhabitants rests on a low, marshy area called Piney Point. No spot in the village rises more than five feet above sea level.

At the waterfront, you will see evidence that Stacy, like most Down East villages, owes its heritage to, and hinges its future on, fishing. Generations of Stacy residents have gone to the sea in boats.

Long before remote coastal villages received advance warning of hurricanes, fishermen had to depend on savvy and raw nerve to survive the horrible storms that often blew up out of nowhere. Lessons learned from a tragic storm in August 1899 have been handed down to successive generations of local fishermen.

Old cemetery at Stacy

On the morning of August 15, a group of fishermen from Stacy and nearby Sea Level set sail for Swan Island, located near the mouth of the Neuse River in Pamlico Sound. They were completely unaware of the massive hurricane, later named San Ceriaco, that was fast approaching from the Caribbean. When the storm struck the Core Sound area two days later, some of the fishermen decided to make the 10-mile run home. But when they were 3 miles into the voyage, the storm swamped their vessels with a twelve-foot wall of water.

All men on board lost their lives. Months passed before the bodies of the victims, save one, were found. Ten wives became widows, and twenty children were rendered fatherless. Now, almost a century after the calamity, the people of Down East maintain a healthy respect for approaching storms.

Beyond Stacy, the highway closely follows the waters of the sound and Nelson Bay as it heads to the three remaining Down East villages. It is approximately 1.5 miles to Masontown, the smallest of the three. This tiny fishing hamlet has a few stores and churches.

Three miles from Masontown, the highway forks. U.S. 70 veers sharply southeast onto a beautiful peninsula bounded by sound and bay, and N.C. 12 makes its way north to Cedar Island. At the fork, continue on U.S. 70 for 1.4 miles. Turn right on S.R. 1373. After 0.2 mile, turn right on S.R. 1385 and proceed 1.5 miles as the road loops around the shore of scenic Nelson Bay. Nestled on the southern tip of the peninsula is the village of Sea Level (or Sealevel), unequaled in charm and beauty in Down East.

Although no one knows why the village was originally called Whit, the name was still in use when a post office was established here on March 11, 1891. Whit became Sea Level twenty-four years later.

Around the turn of the century, four sons were born into the Taylor family, an old family in the village. Daniel, William, Alfred, and Leslie Taylor grew up learning the ways of the sea and acquiring a genuine love for the people of Down East. As adults, the brothers became extremely successful businessmen. Their lucrative commodity brokerage maintained offices in Norfolk and the North Carolina towns of Wilmington, New Bern, and Washington. Despite the wealth they accumulated, the Taylors never forgot their roots in Sea Level. To facilitate access to Ocracoke from their old hometown, they purchased a ferry and operated it between the nearby village of Atlantic and Ocracoke until the state assumed control of the route.

Their concern for the medical needs of the residents of the small coastal communities led the brothers to build a seventy-six-bed hospital at Sea Level. In 1951, this long, one-story facility on the shore of Nelson Bay was dedicated by the Taylors as a memorial to their friends in the area. Homes for

Old Sea Level Hospital

staff, a pier, and a motor inn to accommodate hospital visitors were constructed to complete the medical complex. Over the years, the inn has become a popular overnight stop for people taking the early-morning ferry to Portsmouth and Ocracoke islands.

In 1969, the Taylor Foundation donated Sea Level Hospital to Duke University for operation by Duke Medical Center. During the 1970s and 1980s, the university gradually converted sixty of the seventy-six acute-care beds to extended-care and nursing-home use. In February 1991, the long-feared decision to close Sea Level Hospital was announced by Duke University. Although many Down East residents realized that the hospital did not draw enough patients to make it profitable, a desk clerk at the Sea Level Inn expressed their lingering sentiment: "If the Taylor brothers were still here, it wouldn't have closed."

Following the termination of hospital operations, the old facility was turned over to Carteret County for use as a nursing home.

Despite its small size and isolated location, Sea Level is the home of a nationally known institution. Sailors' Snug Harbor, a retirement home for merchant sailors, relocated to Sea Level from Staten Island in 1976 after an extensive legal battle in New York.

Opened in 1833 on Staten Island's Kill Van Kull, Sailors' Snug Harbor has a fascinating history. It was the brainchild of Captain Robert R. Randall, who earned a fortune from privateering during the Revolutionary War. Upon his death in 1801, his will, penned by his famous friend Alexander Hamilton, established a trust to provide a home for "aged, decrepit, and worn-out seamen." His trust was funded with twenty-one acres in the middle of what became Greenwich Village. Much of the property is still owned by the trust, and rent from it provides income for the operation of the home.

Statue of Captain Robert R. Randall at Sailors' Snug Harbor

The Sailors' Snug Harbor facility was built on an eighty-acre site on Staten Island. It grew substantially during its 143 years of operation in New York. At one time, there were seventy major buildings with a capacity for nine hundred retired and disabled seamen.

In the late 1960s, mounting difficulties with the Staten Island location caused trustees to begin a search for a new site for the home. Negotiations with the Taylor family for a tract at Sea Level began in 1971. Once New York authorities learned of the decision to move the facility, the state attorney general filed suit to block the relocation on the grounds that the charter for the home stipulated that it "overlook the East River or vicinity." The legal dispute was settled in late 1972 with an agreement whereby fifteen acres of the original Staten Island site were transferred to the city of New York for use as a park.

At Sea Level, new facilities were constructed on a 105-acre site. Built to house 122 retirees, the complex features a 100,000-square-foot brick building containing a private room for each resident, a forty-bed infirmary, a physical-therapy center, and a cafeteria. All the artwork and artifacts from the former New York facility are housed at the current home.

Without any advertisements, the home received more than six hundred applications from prospective residents in its first seven years of operation at Sea Level. Admission requirements are few: applicants should have at least ten years of merchant service at sea and a need for a retirement home. In 1981, for the first time, the facility began charging newly admitted residents 40 percent of their income to help defray ever-increasing costs.

At the Sea Level waterfront, turn left, or north, off S.R. 1385 onto S.R. 1373 and drive 1 mile to the intersection with U.S. 70. Turn northeast and proceed 2.5 miles to where U.S. 70 ends at the town of Atlantic.

Oddly enough, the town at the end of the long, serpentine highway is among the most populous of the Down East settlements. Close to a thousand people live in this village, where generations of residents have made their living from the sea.

Throughout Atlantic's long history, other forms of employment have come and gone, but fishing has remained constant. Many residents worked as guides and lodge keepers when duck hunting was popular in the area in the late nineteenth century and the early part of the twentieth century. The popularity hunting once enjoyed in the Atlantic area is evident from the town's earlier name: Hunting Quarters.

Historians believe that the first white settlers arrived in the Atlantic area as early as 1740. Over the years, the villagers developed a keen interest in education. In 1896, the Atlantic Academy opened as the first high school in Carteret County. The town was incorporated in 1905.

In the aftermath of World War II, Atlantic gained a well-deserved reputation for the commercial seafood it produced. By 1954, the town had become one of the largest seafood producers in the state. Today, its waterfront seafood dealers boast of selling the freshest seafood anywhere.

Motorists who venture to the northern reaches of Down East are delighted to find this comfortable, picturesque village near the end of their trail. It is perched on a bluff overlooking Core Sound, Thorofare Bay, and Styron Bay. Myrtle, yaupon, and wind-stunted oak trees grow in the yards of the tidy homes set at odd angles along the winding village streets.

In Atlantic, turn northwest off U.S. 70 onto S.R. 1387. It is 2.9 miles to the junction with N.C. 12. Along this route, the remnants of a World War II landing field used by the United States Marines are visible.

Turn right, or north, onto N.C. 12, which will carry you to the far corner of Down East Carteret. One mile into the journey, you will cross the Thorofare, a channel that connects Pamlico and Core sounds and separates Cedar Island from the mainland.

Cedar Island is bounded on the west by Long Bay, West Bay, and North Bay—arms of the western section of Pamlico Sound. A cluster of islands in Pamlico Sound forms the northwestern boundary. Core Sound lies to the east.

Covering more than 17,000 acres, the island is a vast untamed wilderness, inhabited only on its northern fringes. Almost 80 percent of Cedar Island has been saved from development by its inclusion in the Cedar Island National Wildlife Refuge. Established in 1964 as a nesting and feeding area for migrant and wintering birds, the refuge encompasses some 13,700 acres of irregularly flooded salt marsh and woodlands. The island's hummocks and ridges are covered by red cedar, pine, and gum trees. More than 270 species of birds can be observed throughout the refuge, which is a major breeding area for black rails.

Although the refuge is undeveloped, N.C. 12 runs through it, and other roads provide access to its interior. Approximately four thousand acres of the refuge have been set aside for hunting. Boat landings are located at the bridge over Thorofare Bay and Lewis Creek. Group tours can be arranged at the refuge headquarters, which is located on S.R. 1388 on the northern end of the island.

For nearly 5 miles north of Thorofare Bay, N.C. 12 passes through a desolate grass savanna that stretches as far as the eye can see on both sides of the highway. Because of the rugged, forbidding appearance of the landscape, it is difficult to imagine how humans have survived for centuries at this isolated outpost. Nevertheless, artifacts found on the island and in the surrounding waters disclose that Indians lived in the area many centuries ago. Well into the twentieth century, large mounds of shells similar to, but not as large as, the ones at Shell Point on Harkers Island were found on Cedar Island and nearby Hog Island. When they were excavated for use in road construction, the mounds yielded human and animal skeletons. At low tide, fragments of Indian pottery are often found on the island beach.

Between 1650 and 1700, the first literate white settlers began to make their home on Cedar Island. Strangely enough, these settlers discovered white people already living there. A large Indian population also inhabited the place. Harmony existed between the two groups, some of their number living together as neighbors.

Though the existing white inhabitants spoke English, none of them could read or write. Their lifestyle was that of the Indians, rather than that of Anglo-Saxon Europe. Upon being questioned about their roots, the mysterious people answered that they had always lived there. For many, many years, historians and the residents of Down East have struggled to solve the mystery surrounding the early white residents of the island.

Throughout the recorded history of Cedar Island, families bearing last names identical to those of members of the Lost Colony have lived here. Accordingly, some amateur historians have speculated that Cedar Island may have been home to the Lost Colonists. An ancient oak tree which formerly stood in Croatan National Forest may have been a tangible piece of evidence to support the theory. Early in this century, Ellis Fondrie, a Carteret County native, discovered the giant tree, which bore the letters C-R-O-A-T-A-N. The letters had either been burned or carved into the bark. Unfortunately, the tree was destroyed by lightning prior to World War II.

At the northern end of Cedar Island, N.C. 12 veers sharply to the northwest. After approximately 6.2 miles on N.C. 12, turn east onto S.R. 1388 for a 2.4-mile drive to the eastern shore of the island.

Despite its size, the island has never supported a large population. In the nineteenth century, two separate communities 4 miles apart developed on the northern shore. The remnants of the village of Lola are located along S.R. 1388.

Retrace your route to N.C. 12 and continue in your original direction. Roe, Lola's sister village, is located in this section.

It is 3.5 miles to the landing of the state-operated Cedar Island–Ocracoke Ferry. Virtually all of the five hundred or so residents of Cedar Island live along the highway near the landing. The Cedar Island docks were constructed in 1964. Since that time, the route has ranked as one of the most popular in the state ferry system.

Several small islands with interesting histories of human habitation are visible from the northern shore.

Old cemetery at Lola

Hog Island—actually a cluster of sound islands grouped between Back Bay and Pamlico Sound—is the site of Lupton, now a ghost town. A post office operated in the now-deserted village until May 15, 1920.

Located northeast of Lupton, Harbor Island has been greatly reduced by erosion over the past century. In 1867, a screw-pile lighthouse was built on the island to facilitate navigation of Core Sound. A hurricane subsequently destroyed the lighthouse, and no trace of it remains today. In the 1930s, a hunting and fishing club was constructed on the western tip of the island. The ruins of the old clubhouse are still visible.

Cedar Island Welcome Center

Horse Island, located in the northern portion of Core Sound, also contains the ruins of a clubhouse. For many years, the island has been the source of eerie stories. Two persons are said to have been murdered there. Fishermen have reported seeing ghosts roaming the island.

The tour ends here, at the northern tip of Cedar Island.

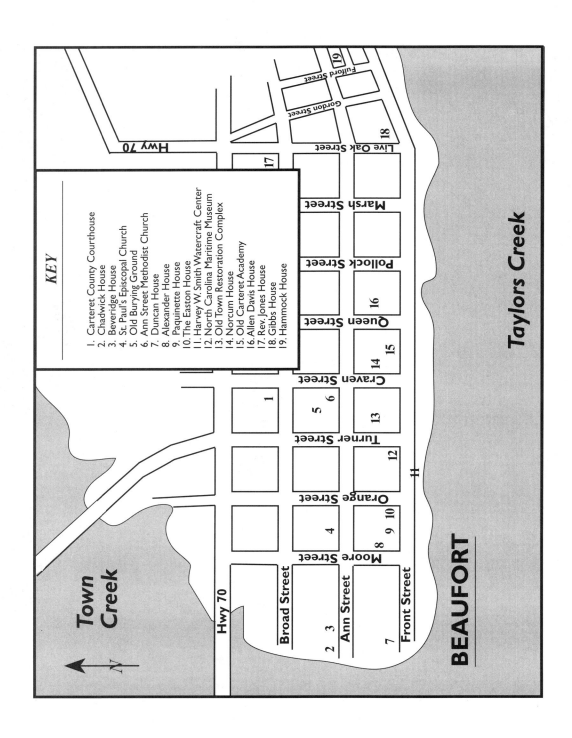

Town Creek

N

Hwy 70

BEAUFORT

Taylors Creek

KEY

1. Carteret County Courthouse
2. Chadwick House
3. Beveridge House
4. St. Paul's Episcopal Church
5. Old Burying Ground
6. Ann Street Methodist Church
7. Duncan House
8. Alexander House
9. Paquinette House
10. The Easton House
11. Harvey W. Smith Watercraft Center
12. North Carolina Maritime Museum
13. Old Town Restoration Complex
14. Norcum House
15. Old Carteret Academy
16. Allen Davis House
17. Rev. Jones House
18. Gibbs House
19. Hammock House

Broad Street

Ann Street

Front Street

Moore Street

Orange Street

Turner Street

Craven Street

Queen Street

Pollock Street

Marsh Street

Live Oak Street

Gordon Street

Fulford Street

The Beaufort Tour

This tour examines the historic district of the old port town of Beaufort, beginning and ending at U.S. 70.

Among the highlights of the tour are the Old Town Restoration Complex, the North Carolina Maritime Museum, the Old Burying Ground, the story of Nancy Manney French, the colorful Beaufort waterfront, the Rachel Carson National Marine Estuarine Sanctuary, the horses of Carrot Island, and the historic homes of Beaufort, including Hammock House.

Total mileage: approximately 4 miles.

This tour begins at the intersection of U.S. 70 and Turner Street in the historic port town of Beaufort. Proceed south on Turner Street to the Carteret County Courthouse, located in the first block.

Beaufort-by-the-Sea, as the town is romantically called, is a place of historic distinction. While most historians have recorded that Beaufort is the third-oldest town in North Carolina, there are some who contend it is the second-oldest. Regardless of its rank, the ageless town has written a captivating history that now spans almost three hundred years.

Records inside the Carteret County Courthouse date back to 1713. The imposing 1907-vintage structure is the fourth courthouse to serve the county. Designed by a New Bern undertaker, it features huge Corinthian porticoes on the southern and western sides, granite arches with keystones, and an octagonal, copper-clad cupola.

In 1983, the Carteret County commissioners considered demolition of the dignified red-brick structure because of age and deterioration. Pressure from historical groups persuaded the governing body to spare the Neoclassic Revival building. A modern annex was subsequently connected to the original structure, marring its appearance.

From the courthouse, continue south on Turner Street.

If you have never been to Beaufort before, it will soon become apparent

Carteret County Courthouse

that this is a rare and special kind of place. Simply put, it is hard for anyone not to like the old port town. Included among its treasures is a magnificent historic district containing one of the finest concentrations of eighteenth- and nineteenth-century homes for a town its size in all of America. Beaufort also boasts a world-class maritime museum, a fully accessible waterfront affording spectacular views of nearby Carrot Island and its herd of wild horses, and a compact business district chock-full of interesting antique and gift shops, ship's stores, and restaurants.

Beaufort residents are proud of their town's splendid ensemble of historic structures. The majority of the old homes of Beaufort are privately owned. Some of the buildings have survived wars and invasions, storms, and pangs of modernity for more than two centuries. This superior collection of more than 120 historic treasures is located in a 3-block-by-11-block area south of U.S. 70.

It is 2 blocks from the courthouse to the Old Town Restoration Complex. Operated by the Beaufort Historical Association, this complex of restored homes, cottages, shops, a jail, and a courthouse provides an opportunity to inspect and appreciate the distinctive architecture of Beaufort. Among the holdings are the Joseph Bell House, considered by many to be the finest house in town. Constructed in 1767, this frame house, painted conch red, was restored in 1966.

The headquarters for the complex are located at the Josiah Bell House. Constructed in 1825, this home contains a number of interesting rooms furnished with Victorian pieces.

The Josiah Bell House

Also located on the beautifully landscaped grounds is the Apothecary Shop/Doctor's Office, constructed around 1859. Authentic medical instruments, bottles, and prescription files used in early country medicine are exhibited inside.

The nearby R. Rustell House, constructed in 1732, houses the Mattie King Davis Art Gallery.

Two former government buildings are also maintained as part of the complex.

The Carteret County Courthouse of 1796 is the oldest existing public building in the county. Prior to that year, the Church of England used the small frame building as a meeting place. During the War of 1812, this old courthouse quartered American troops from Beaufort, Lenoir, and Craven counties. Today, a rare, original thirteen-star American flag is displayed in the building.

Adjacent to the former courthouse is the architecturally perfect building which once served as the Carteret County Jail. Constructed in 1836, the two-story masonry structure now contains several cells, the jailkeeper's quarters, and a small museum.

Guided tours of the Old Town Restoration Complex are available, and special programs and activities are scheduled throughout the year. A tour of the complex provides an excellent opportunity to reflect upon the long, storied history of Beaufort.

Around 1708, the site now occupied by the town was settled by French Huguenots and immigrants from Germany, Sweden, England, Scotland, and Ireland. At their arrival, the place was known to the Indians as Wareiock, meaning "Fish Town" or "Fishing Village." On early maps, the site appears as C. Wareuuock. Archaeological evidence indicates that Indians used the area as fishing grounds.

In keeping with the Indian tradition, the earliest white settlers called their community Fishtown. Beaufort emerged from Fishtown in 1713 when Robert Turner surveyed and platted two hundred acres between the Newport and North rivers. Original plats show that his pattern of streets remains virtually intact today. Henry Somerset (1684–1714), the duke of Beaufort, one of the Lords Proprietors, was the town's namesake.

Although its early growth was sluggish, Beaufort possessed an asset which attracted the attention of the colonial government. Its magnificent harbor along Taylors Creek made the town a natural choice as a port, and in 1722, Beaufort was formally designated a port of entry.

About the same time, there were other indications that Beaufort was coming into its own. Carteret was made a precinct in 1722, and Beaufort immediately became the seat of local government, a distinction that it continues to enjoy today. A year later, Beaufort was officially incorporated by the colonial assembly.

Early residents were constantly alarmed by the failure of the colony to provide coastal defenses against pirates and the ships of foreign navies. On August 21, 1747, Beaufort residents watched in horror as the Spanish fleet sailed into the harbor. After planting the flag of Spain, the sailors occupied and pillaged the town for several days. They were finally chased away by the militia and local farmers.

After the Spanish threat was quelled, Beaufort was able to turn its attention to commercial development. By the middle of the eighteenth century, the town had become the third-largest port in the colony, behind only Brunswick Town and the unnamed port on Albemarle Sound. By the early 1770s, approximately sixty families were living in the town.

Beaufort residents were filled with patriotic fervor at the outbreak of the Revolutionary War. As a consequence, the town played a leading role in the quest for American independence.

To supply the wartime need for salt, several facilities were built in and around the town in 1776 to produce the commodity from boiled seawater.

Through its blockade of the major colonial ports, the British navy sought to choke off vital supplies intended for George Washington's army. By providing a base for privateers and a port for Spanish and French sailing ships, Beaufort made its greatest contribution to the struggle for independence. Both the port town and Beaufort Inlet were unprotected for the duration of the war, but somehow the port remained open to serve as a vital supply line for the American cause.

It was not until after the surrender of Cornwallis at Yorktown that British forces attacked Beaufort. Several British warships sailed through the inlet and docked at the town on April 3, 1782. Landing troops pillaged and burned for several days. Townspeople, enraged by the attack, fought back. Finally, the determined patriots were able to cut off the invaders' supply of fresh water. Discouraged and defeated, the warships sailed for Charleston on August 18. This skirmish has been called the last battle of the American Revolution.

Beaufort entered the nineteenth century as one of the most prosperous commercial and governmental centers in the state. In the early 1800s, wealthy planters began to bring their families to live in Beaufort townhouses to sample the happy lifestyle and enjoy the healthy environment. Thus, the local resort industry was born. Many of the beautiful white homes that now grace the streets of Beaufort were built during the prosperous years of the early nineteenth century.

At the outbreak of the Civil War, Beaufort had a population of more than sixteen hundred. On March 25, 1862, the town fell under Union occupation. For the duration of the war, it served as an important base of operations for the Union offensive in the South. It was from Beaufort that the most formidable naval fleet ever assembled in the history of the world sailed in early January 1865 to deliver the death blow to the Confederacy at Fort Fisher.

One of the great ironies of the Union occupation of Beaufort was that the father of President Lincoln's secretary of war, Edwin M. Stanton, was born on the shores of nearby Core Creek.

Beaufort emerged from the Civil War relatively unscathed, and it quickly positioned itself as an important commercial port and summer resort. A profitable menhaden processing plant began operation near town in 1881. For many years afterward, the port was the home of a large fleet of menhaden boats.

Between the world wars, the town changed very little. By 1940, Beaufort counted almost three thousand residents, but its appearance resembled that of a nineteenth-century seaport, its waterfront dominated by the tall crow's-nests of the menhaden fleet.

Beaufort entered a period of serious decline in the 1960s. Buildings on the ancient waterfront were rotting; shopping centers on the outskirts of town had begun to lure businesses from the downtown area; and suddenly, the once-abundant supply of menhaden was no more.

North Carolina Maritime Museum

At the height of its decline in the 1970s, the town embarked on a path toward a remarkable recovery. Beaufort residents worked tirelessly to beautify and preserve their ancient village. Decaying buildings on the waterfront were removed in order to reveal the splendid beauty of Taylors Creek and nearby Carrot Island. A spacious boardwalk was built along the waterfront. Businesses in the form of gift and antique shops, bookstores, and art galleries returned to Front Street. An active Beaufort Historical Association spearheaded the drive to identify and preserve the 120 historic structures in town. As a consequence of these developments, Beaufort has been able to realize its potential as a tourist attraction without sacrificing its charm.

Continue south on Turner Street from the restoration complex to the waterfront. Turn right, or west, on Front Street to visit the North Carolina

Maritime Museum, located at 315 Front Street. Parking is available to the rear and side.

Beaufort is proud to be the home of one of the fastest-growing maritime museums in the nation. On May 18, 1985, the North Carolina Maritime Museum opened the doors to its new permanent home. Constructed at a cost of $1.5 million, the handsome building is an architectural blend of nineteenth-century Beaufort and the stations of the United States Lifesaving Service. The museum is covered with cedar shakes, a tradition on the Outer Banks, and adorned with a widow's walk.

Though the hundred thousand visitors who tour the facility annually would never suspect it, the museum, long known as the Hampton Mariner's Museum, had a pillar-to-post existence until recent years. It had its beginnings in the late 1930s with a crude collection of fish models and similar items assembled by the United States Fish and Wildlife Service at nearby Pivers Island. In 1951, the state acquired the museum's holdings. Over the next quarter-century, while the collection was growing, the museum was moved to several different locations.

North Carolina yellow pine treated with flame retardants was used throughout the interior of the spacious, new 18,000-square-foot building that now houses the museum. Laminated, exposed heavy-beam construction gives visitors the sensation of being in the hold of a large wooden ship. Ceilings reaching to thirty feet enable the museum to house sailboats.

The exhibits are many and varied. The world-class shell collection is so large that only parts of it can be exhibited at one time. Aquariums filled with sea life are popular with patrons of all ages. In addition to the massive exhibit hall, the museum features a reference library, a bookstore, and an auditorium. Mariners and coastal researchers enjoy the elegantly apportioned library, which offers a wide variety of reference books on marine topics, as well as some rare volumes. Among the treasures are a Dutch book on shipbuilding dating from the 1600s and a century-old copy of "Rime of the Ancient Mariner," illustrated with elaborate woodcuts. Classes and large events are held in the two-hundred-seat R. J. Reynolds Auditorium, the walls of which are decorated with coastal scenes painted by Winston-Salem artist Robert B. Dance.

Located directly across Front Street from the main building is the

Harvey W. Smith Watercraft Center. This unique waterfront facility, dedicated to the preservation of the wooden craft and boat-building techniques indigenous to North Carolina, houses the museum's boat shop and displays restorations and reproductions of traditional wooden boats.

Two annual events sponsored by the museum grow more popular every year.

During the last weekend in September, the museum sponsors the Traditional Wooden Boat Show. The event features a wide variety of activities, including rowing, paddling, and sailing demonstrations. It is recognized as the largest gathering of wooden boats in the Southeast.

Held on the third Thursday in August, the Strange Seafood Exhibition showcases the culinary talents of coastal cooks, who serve seafood dishes ranging from those eaten by Indians and early settlers to experimental delicacies. From its beginnings in 1977, the event has grown from eighteen dishes sampled by 150 persons to more than fifty items served to a crowd of approximately 2,000. Among the dishes featured at past exhibitions were conch salad, sweet and sour stingray wings, sea urchin eggs, shark jelly, and deep-fried silversides. The event, the only seafood festival of its kind in the country, is so popular that the museum staff has found it necessary to limit the number of seafood samplers.

Continue west on Front Street. In the 2 blocks west of the museum, there are several houses of historic note.

Located at 229 Front, the Easton House is one of many Beaufort homes listed on the National Register of Historic Places. Twelve years after the house was constructed, it was purchased by Colonel John Easton, who led the town's defenders against the British invaders in April 1782. Jacob Henry subsequently purchased the house. In 1808, Henry was elected to the North Carolina General Assembly, but a year later, he was challenged, because, as a Jew, he "denied the Divine Authority of the New Testament." Henry's dynamic speech in his own behalf and the ensuing debate drew national attention and became important in the crusade for religious freedom in the United States.

Located at 217 Front Street, the Paquinette House was built by a family of French Huguenots in 1768. Its foundation is made of old ballast stones. This house is of special interest because of its eighteenth-century air-conditioning system: an opening in the attic floor allows the cool summer sea breeze to be carried through the house.

The Duncan House, located at 105 Front near the western end of the street, was built around 1790. It is an excellent example of the Beaufort gable-roof style. Most of the first houses in town were patterned after a style observed by local mariners in the Bahamas and the islands of the West Indies. Local craftsmen quickly modified the style to create the unique architectural style known as the Beaufort gable roof. Nearly seventy-five of the distinctive houses built in this style survive. They are distinguished by their unusual roof, which maintains a relatively steep pitch at the ridge and then breaks to a lesser pitch to cover porches in the front and bays in the rear. Homes built later, primarily in the middle of the nineteenth century, introduced the hip roof, common during the Greek Revival period.

Because of its waterfront location, Front Street boasts some of the most impressive homes in Beaufort. Unlike the large cities on the coast of the Carolinas, such as Wilmington and Charleston, Beaufort cannot claim a large array of sumptuous estates built by planters and wealthy merchants. Rather, much of the Beaufort townscape reflects its early days as a working seaport. The tidy white buildings tightly clustered throughout the original

The Duncan House

street grid of Beaufort present a unique view of the middle and working class of coastal North Carolina.

Retrace your route for 1 block on Front Street and turn north on Moore Street. After 1 block on Moore, turn left, or west, onto Ann Street.

Located at 123 Ann, the Beveridge House reflects the maritime heritage of Beaufort. John T. Beveridge, a native of Scotland, built the house in 1841. A sea captain, Beveridge was considered one of the most skillful navigators of his time. Although the house was moved many years ago from Orange Street to its present site, it is still owned by the Beveridge family. A number of interesting furnishings, including Captain Beveridge's sea chest and a solid-oak bedroom suite brought back from the West Indies by Beveridge's son, are found inside.

The Chadwick House, located at 117 Ann Street, is a stately, pedimented Greek Revival house constructed about 1858. Through the compassion of its former owners, Robert and Mary Chadwick, a young Chinese man was given an opportunity to achieve his true potential in the late nineteenth century.

Robert Chadwick was serving as collector of customs at the port of Wilmington in 1880 when Charles Jones, the captain of a United States revenue cutter, introduced him to the ship's mess boy. Soong Yao-jo, as the eighteen-year-old lad was known, made a favorable impression on the Chadwicks. They adopted him and encouraged him to obtain an education.

Soong converted to Christianity, joined the Methodist Church, and enrolled at Trinity College, now Duke University. Upon his graduation, he studied religion at Vanderbilt University. Once his studies were complete, Soong went home to China in 1885 as a missionary of the Southern Methodist Church.

In China, he married and reared six children, all of whom were educated at colleges and universities in the United States. His most famous children were two of his daughters. One married Sun Yat-sen, the leader of the revolution that resulted in the founding of the People's Republic of China. The other married Chiang Kai-shek, the longtime president of Taiwan.

From the Chadwick House, turn around and proceed east on Ann Street. St. Paul's Episcopal Church, located on the north side of the 200 block, is considered one of the ten architecturally perfect buildings in the state. Much

Chadwick House

of the exterior and interior of the Gothic Revival edifice was constructed by shipbuilders. The most interesting of its exquisite stained-glass windows is the memorial window for Sallie Pasteur Davis, a niece of the famous French scientist Louis Pasteur. The cornerstone of the church is dated April 14, 1857.

On nearby Moore Street, the Alexander House, built around 1856, served as the rectory for St. Paul's from 1890 to 1950. During that period, the rector's daughter married North Carolina native Paul Green, the Pulitzer-winning playwright and author of *The Lost Colony*. The wedding was held in the church, and a reception followed in the garden of the rectory.

Ann Street Methodist Church

Continue east on Ann Street. Two blocks east of St. Paul's, Ann Street Methodist Church stands proudly near the corner of Ann and Craven streets. This stately frame structure was completed in 1854 and remodeled in 1897. Intricately designed stained-glass windows highlight the sanctuary. When lit at night, the window on the Craven Street side radiates its message to passersby.

Of all the historic attractions in Beaufort, none is more interesting than the Old Burying Ground, located adjacent to Ann Street Methodist Church. This picturesque graveyard ranks as one of the oldest and most historically important cemeteries in the state.

Beaufort residents began burying their dead in this hallowed ground in the first quarter of the eighteenth century. Although the cemetery site has always been deemed public property, it was officially conveyed to the town of Beaufort in 1731 by Nathaniel Taylor following an official survey.

Some of the first people laid to rest in the Old Burying Ground may have been hapless victims of the Indian wars in the second decade of the eighteenth century. Scores of the earliest burial spaces are covered with deteriorating cypress slabs, shells, or brick. Burial records were originally maintained by the Anglican Church, but these records vanished after being taken to Canada during the Revolutionary War.

There is no doubt that the oldest section of the cemetery is the northern corner. All of the graves in this section face east, because their occupants wanted to be facing the sun when they arose on "Judgment Morn." Time and the elements have combined to obliterate the dates on some of the

oldest grave markers. An inspection of the graves indicates that 1756 is the oldest legible date. However, that grave is hardly the oldest.

As a visitor to Beaufort in 1853, William Valentine described the Old Burying Ground as "the most beautiful place of the kind I ever saw, by far the choicest beauty spot of Beaufort." Many visitors to the town more than 140 years later would still agree with Valentine. Encircled by three churches and enclosed by a handsomely crafted fence of masonry and metal, the cemetery offers an atmosphere of peace and tranquility. Ancient live oaks provide a canopy of shade over the sandy lanes and the tombstones.

Guided visits to the cemetery are included as part of the tour offered by the Old Town Restoration Complex. Self-guided tours are also permitted.

Almost every grave in the burying ground has an interesting story behind it. One of the most noteworthy persons buried here is the famous privateer and American hero of the War of 1812, Otway Burns. When he died on Portsmouth Island in 1850, his body was transported to Beaufort by boat. On July 4, 1901, Burns's grandchildren unveiled the monument that now stands at his grave. A gun taken from his renowned ship, the *Snap Dragon*, surmounts the tomb.

Grave of Otway Burns

As cruel as it may seem at first, the story behind the thirteen-year-old girl buried in a rum keg in the cemetery is actually a heartwarming tale of parental love.

This girl's father and mother brought her to Beaufort from England when she was an infant. Her father became a prosperous merchant who made frequent trips to London. As the years passed, the child listened intently to her father's stories about the exciting city of London. She longed to accompany him on one of his trips, but her concerned mother would not hear of it until the girl reached her thirteenth birthday.

Finally, the mother relented, but only after receiving assurances from her husband that the girl would absolutely be returned home to Beaufort. In London, the child and her father had a grand time, but on the return voyage, tragedy occurred. Fever killed the little girl. Officers of the ship made preparations to bury the child at sea in customary fashion, but the bereaved father persuaded them to allow him to keep his promise. He purchased a keg of rum from the cargo hold and sealed the lifeless body of his daughter inside. When the ship docked in Beaufort, the keg was buried on the Craven Street side of the cemetery. The impressive home of the little girl and her family, constructed in 1768, continues to grace the Beaufort waterfront at 209 Front Street.

No grave boasts a more touching story than that of Nancy Manney French, who was laid to rest in 1885 shortly after being reunited with her long-lost lover. It is a true story, yet it sounds like a plot conceived by Hollywood scriptwriters. Indeed, the tale of the bittersweet romance of Charles French and Nancy Manney reads like a legend.

Nancy Manney was a Beaufort girl, the daughter of a local physician. Charles French was a Philadelphia law student. Their paths first crossed when Nancy's father lured Charles to Beaufort in 1836 to tutor his children. Nancy was sixteen at the time.

Charles spent two years teaching the Manney children. During that time, he and Nancy fell in love, but they kept their romance secret for fear of incurring the wrath of Dr. Manney. However, when the time arrived for Charles to resume his legal education, he revealed his love for Nancy and asked the physician to allow him to marry her upon completion of his studies. To his dismay, Charles was informed by Dr. Manney that the romance had not been a secret. The physician announced his stern disapproval and ordered Charles to end his relationship with Nancy and to leave town for good.

But as is the way with star-crossed lovers, Charles and Nancy pledged their eternal love. They vowed to marry someday. In the meantime, the couple agreed to write to each other to pass their tormented days of separation.

The infatuated pair faithfully penned love letters, but Dr. Manney made sure that none of the correspondence reached its destination. Determined to keep Nancy and Charles apart, the doctor prevailed upon the Beaufort postmaster to intercept all incoming and outgoing mail between the two. All of the letters were collected, tied in a bundle, and held secretly at the post office.

Days melted into years. Charles eventually stopped writing, assuming that Nancy no longer cared. To the contrary, Nancy's love was unfailing. Though she heard nothing from Charles, Nancy continued to write, clinging to the faint hope that he would come for her someday.

Grave of Nancy Manney French

Her father passed away, taking to the grave his terrible secret. However, when death came calling on the Beaufort postmaster, his years of guilt led him to call Nancy to his bedside. There, he detailed his sordid pact with her father. The letters at long last were given to Nancy, who was by then forty-five years old.

Nancy took the revelation with mixed emotions. Her love for Charles was as strong as ever. Knowing that he had not broken his promise was of great comfort, but she also had to face the realization that he had probably married someone else. She threw herself into the work of ministering to wounded troops during the Civil War.

Twenty years passed. Nancy did not marry. Suddenly, one day in 1885, she received word that the mail clerk at the Beaufort post office wanted to see her. A letter requesting information about the Manney family had arrived. It revealed that the writer had known the family many years before. He expressed a desire to visit Beaufort again if any members of the Manney family were living. The signature affixed to the letter was that of Charles French, the chief justice of the Supreme Court of the Arizona Territory.

Joyously, Nancy wrote Charles urging him to come to Beaufort and saying she still loved him. She was now sixty-five years old and seriously ill with consumption. Charles was a dignified but lonely old man. He had married another long ago after patiently waiting for Nancy's letters. His wife had been dead for years.

Charles hurried to Beaufort. When his ship arrived at the waterfront, old friends greeted him, but Nancy was not there. She was sick in her bed. Her long-lost love hastened to her side. After nearly fifty years of heartbreak, the couple was reunited.

Once again, Charles proposed to Nancy. Once again, Nancy accepted. When their wedding day came, the aged groom knelt beside his ailing bride's bed. He tenderly lifted her into his arms, and they became one.

Their long-awaited happiness ended a few days later, when Nancy died.

To continue the tour, proceed east 1 block on Ann Street, then turn right, or south, on Queen Street. Located on the eastern side of the street at 120 Queen, the Allen Davis House served as the headquarters for General Ambrose Burnside—the man for whom sideburns were named—during the Union occupation of Beaufort in the Civil War. The existing structure, an enormous Greek Revival house, is an enlargement of a small Beaufort cottage constructed in 1774.

Queen Street ends on the waterfront at Front Street. To experience the maritime atmosphere of Beaufort, park in the municipal parking lot on Front. This street is bordered by an interesting ensemble of stores and shops and the incomparable waterfront, which is the focal point of much of the downtown activity during spring, summer, and fall. A modern boardwalk separates the public boat docks from shops, restaurants, and parking facilities. Boardwalk strollers are awed by the luxurious pleasure craft from many distant ports that tie up at the docks on Taylors Creek. Since the waterfront was restored, Beaufort has become a favorite port for Intracoastal Waterway traffic.

Boat tours of the surrounding waterways and islands are available on the waterfront.

A four-foot granite monument erected on the boardwalk in July 1986 memorializes Michael J. Smith, a famous native son. America and the rest of the world watched in horror in January 1986 as the space shuttle *Challenger* exploded, killing the mission commander, pilot, and five-member crew. Smith, the pilot on the ill-fated mission, grew up in Beaufort.

Located across Taylors Creek from the Beaufort waterfront, the complex of small islands comprising Rachel Carson National Marine Estuarine Sanctuary stretches from Beaufort Inlet to the North River. Known nationwide by marine biologists and other scientists, the site is used for research and education. It is equally important to area residents and visitors as a recreation spot.

Carrot Island, Town Marsh, Bird Shoal, and Horse Island make up the western end of the sanctuary—that portion visible from the Beaufort waterfront. Combined, these islands are almost 3.5 miles long, covering 2,025 acres. On the eastern end, Middle Marsh, almost 2 miles long and 650 acres in size, is separated from the other islands by the North River Channel.

Coree Indians are thought to have used Carrot Island and Middle Marsh prior to the arrival of the first European settlers. Early residents of Beaufort built wharves on Carrot Island, from which they shipped lumber, naval stores, and fish and farm products. In the early eighteenth century, Carrot Island was known as Cart Island. Fishermen unloaded their nets on its southern side. A causeway of ballast stones was constructed across Taylors Creek, over which they transported their catches in carts. Mapmakers subsequently misread the name of the island and showed it as Carrot Island.

During the British invasion of Beaufort in 1782, the enemy forces camped one night on Carrot Island. A map produced during the American Revolution shows that Carrot Island was the only existing island among those now part of the preserve. Town Marsh, at that time called Island Marsh, was described as a "bunch of bushes." Although the other islands in the present-day preserve were not yet exposed, the water in the area was extremely shallow.

In the middle of the nineteenth century, Town Marsh was known as Bird Shoal. By that time, it had grown from a mere spot of high ground just above the water line to an island nearly 0.4 mile long. Over the next thirty years, it doubled in length.

Dredging by the Corps of Engineers at the mouth of Taylors Creek in the early part of the twentieth century was responsible for the creation of the other islands in the complex. Continued dredging has built up the island chain to such an extent that it now affords protection for Beaufort during hurricanes.

When a developer announced plans to build resort homes on Carrot Island in 1977, Carteret County residents, civic groups, and environmental groups expressed alarm. To thwart the development plans, the North Carolina Nature Conservancy acquired 474 acres on Carrot Island. By 1985, the state of North Carolina had purchased the entire complex of islands.

The sanctuary can be reached only by boat. Local boating concessions and special boat trips sponsored by the North Carolina Maritime Museum provide transportation to the island during the summer season. Pleasure boaters are permitted to land their craft, but Carrot Island has few safe, sandy landing spots.

Once on the islands, visitors are surrounded by an unspoiled environment of natural beauty and solitude. Recreational activities include primitive camping, swimming, shelling, hiking, bird-watching, fishing, and clamming.

Ecologically, the sanctuary presents a diverse habitat that would not have come about except for the dredging operation. Found within the island system are tidal flats, salt marshes, ocean beaches, sand dunes, spoil areas, shrub thickets, and maritime forests.

At least 161 species of birds have been observed in the sanctuary. Because of its location along the Atlantic flyway, the complex hosts many migratory birds.

Ten species of reptiles, including the endangered Atlantic loggerhead turtle, are represented.

Of the mammal species present in the sanctuary, the feral horses that roam Carrot Island are the most interesting. For decades, visitors to Beaufort have gazed across the waterfront to catch a glimpse of these horses as they graze on the plant growth on the island. These animals are believed to be the descendants of a half-dozen horses left on the island in the 1940s by an area physician who wanted to take advantage of the free pastureland there.

For many years, drinking water was piped from the mainland for the horses. After the pipe failed, the horses had to devise ways to find fresh water, as the island has no ponds, streams, or springs. Since that time, the horses have learned to dig holes to trap the rain runoff that collects between sand dunes. At times, the underground water supply becomes so limited that the animals go to the sand flats, where they can sip thin layers of rainwater lying atop tidal pools.

In 1982, the number of horses on the island peaked at sixty-eight. Concern surfaced in the spring of that year when some of the animals died of starvation, brought about by drought and overbreeding. Attempts by Beaufort residents and state officials to feed the starving horses by boating hay to the island failed to solve the problem. Some observers watched helplessly as the dying horses fell. After falling, the animals struggled to get back on their feet. Ruts as deep as one foot were found around the legs of the fallen animals, evidence of their attempts to stand and defeat death.

Responding to the terrible plight of the horses, the state decided to cull the herd. In October 1988, the number of horses was reduced from fifty-two to fifteen during a state-sponsored roundup. Professional rodeo riders were brought to the island to rope the older, less healthy horses. After the roundup, the captured horses were transported to Beaufort, where they were subsequently adopted by animal lovers from many parts of the state.

Despite the claims of marine ecologists that the continued presence of the horses on the island will cause environmental damage, the state intends to maintain a manageable herd there.

Before returning to the parking lot, walk across Front Street to see two historic buildings in the downtown area.

Carteret Academy

Located at 505 Front, the old Carteret Academy seems a bit out of place in the heart of the commercial district. This unusual three-story house served as a school for girls from the Outer Banks in the nineteenth century. Constructed in 1854, it is one of only two houses in Beaufort with an English basement.

Located just around the corner in the first block of Craven Street, the Norcum House, at 128 Craven, is one of a number of houses used by Federal forces during the Civil War occupation of the town. This large, two-story structure, built around 1850 from cypress lumber shipped from Plymouth, served as an army office building.

Return to the parking lot and drive east on Front Street. This scenic waterfront drive provides an excellent opportunity to view the horses on Carrot Island.

Located near the eastern end of Front Street, the Gibbs House, at 903 Front, is one of the most soundly built homes in Beaufort. It was constructed in 1850 of cypress lumber transported by sailboat from Hyde County. Six layers of wooden shakes were used to cover the hip roof. At one time, the structure housed the first United States Marine Laboratory on the Atlantic coast.

Of special interest is the brick-topped granite wall in the front and side yards, constructed in the early part of the twentieth century. This wall was

Gibbs House

designed to prevent waves from washing under the porch in the days before Front Street was filled in, when the water line in Beaufort was higher than it is at present.

Continue east on Front Street. Two blocks from the Gibbs House, turn left, or north, onto Fulford Street. Hammock Lane, an alleyway on the eastern side of Fulford, is the site of the most mysterious house in Beaufort.

No one knows for sure when or for whom the Hammock House was built. However, it is widely considered the oldest surviving house in Beaufort. Nestled in a grove of live oak, cedar, and yaupon on the highest hill in town, it has served as a guidepost for mariners since the early eighteenth century. On a 1738 chart of the North Carolina coast, the house appears as "The Hammock House." Most likely, this ancient, two-story white house is the oldest man-made landmark used by seafarers on the North Carolina coast.

Hammock House

Estimates of the date of construction range from 1700 to 1735. Sills supporting the house are reported to be stamped with the year 1700. Its foundation is made of ballast stones. Before Front Street was filled in, the waters of Taylors Creek beat against the base of the twelve-foot hill on which the house stands.

Most of the seven-inch heart-of-pine boards used to cover the exterior of the house remain intact. Of the eight columns supporting the double front porches, seven are original. Nails, hand-forged on an anvil, are evident.

For many years, the Hammock House has been shrouded in mystery. Numerous eerie legends and tales about its owners and the goings-on there have evolved over the course of its long history.

The most fascinating of the stories are those involving Blackbeard. There is some belief in Beaufort that the infamous pirate built the house from plans he obtained in the Bahamas. Be that as it may, there is evidence that Blackbeard did call at the house on a number of occasions, particularly during his visits to Core Sound in 1718. He is said to have brought one of his wives to the house, leaving her to be executed after he went to sea again. Following the murder, her body was allegedly buried under nearby live oaks. Some Beaufort residents claim that on nights when the moon is full, her screaming ghost can be observed searching for her pirate husband.

Some members of Blackbeard's crew were reportedly left at the house when the pirate sailed toward his fateful encounter with Lieutenant Robert

Maynard at Ocracoke. After Blackbeard was killed by Maynard and his men, the stranded pirates decided to make Beaufort their home, becoming law-abiding citizens.

A sea captain and his wife occupied the house during the Civil War. During the early stages of the conflict, Confederate troops camped on the grounds. While the captain was away at sea, his wife grew increasingly concerned about living alone. To alleviate her fears, she invited a group of her friends to stay in the house. She took a lover as well.

One night, the captain returned to Beaufort unannounced. With his vessel anchored in the harbor, he made his way ashore in a landing craft and walked up the hill to the house, where a wild party was taking place.

The captain sneaked inside and confronted his wife's lover. A struggle ensued. After chasing his wife's paramour up the attic stairs, the irate husband killed him. Bloodstains from the struggle are said to be visible on the attic floor to this day.

Because of the many weird tales surrounding the Hammock House, some Beaufort parents will not allow their children to play nearby.

After 1 block on Fulford Street, turn west onto Ann Street. Follow Ann Street for 2 blocks, then turn north on Live Oak Street.

Located at the northwestern corner of the intersection of Live Oak and Broad streets, the Reverend Jones House served as a Union hospital during the Civil War. This splendid cypress-covered house was built in 1840. The first telephone in Beaufort had to be installed on a post in the yard of this house, since Mrs. Jones was too afraid of the new contraption to have it indoors.

Continue 1 block north. The tour ends here, where Live Oak Street joins U.S. 70.

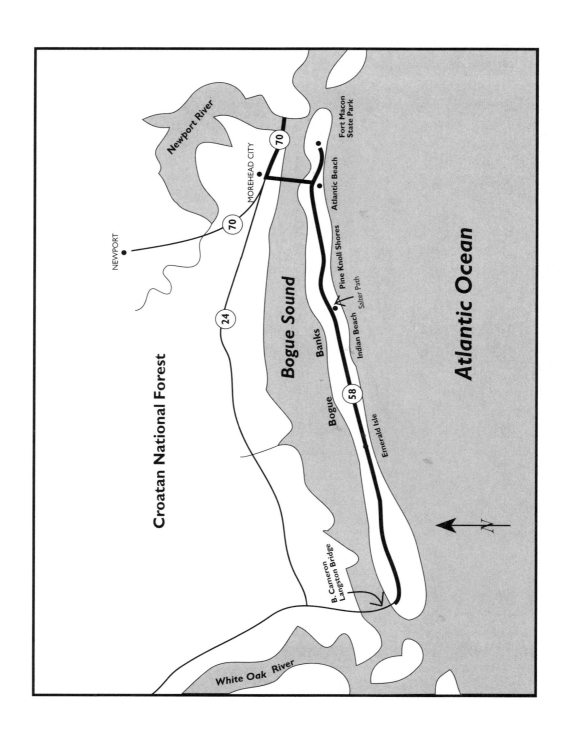

The Crystal
Coast Tour

This tour begins in the historic port of Morehead City and travels across the Newport River to Radio and Pivers islands. It then crosses Bogue Sound to Bogue Banks, where it visits Fort Macon State Park, Atlantic Beach, Pine Knoll Shores, Indian Beach, Salter Path, and Emerald Isle.

Among the highlights of the tour are the North Carolina State Port at Morehead City, the Morehead City waterfront, the story of Old Quawk, historic Fort Macon, Theodore Roosevelt State Natural Area, and the North Carolina Aquarium at Pine Knoll Shores.

Total mileage: approximately 42 miles.

This tour begins at the junction of U.S. 70 and N.C. 24 near the western limits of Morehead City. Proceed east 0.5 mile on U.S. 70 to the K-mart shopping center, on the southern side of the highway.

On this site, a dog-racing track, the Hollywood Kennel Club, successfully operated from 1948 to 1953. An elaborate racing facility complete with grandstands and a press box attracted large crowds on summer evenings. The Miss North Carolina Pageant was once held at the track. When the state legislature made gambling at the track illegal in 1953, it was closed and abandoned. The track was torn down in 1970.

Drive 1.5 miles east on U.S. 70, which takes the name of Arendell Street on its run through Morehead City.

For almost two hundred years, the sun, the sand, and the moderate climate of Carteret County have made the place a favorite resort area for North Carolinians. Over the past several decades, Morehead City and Beaufort, the twin sound-side towns of mainland Carteret, and Bogue Banks, the barrier island lying just across Bogue Sound, have been collectively billed as "the Crystal Coast" by the local tourism industry.

Turn south off U.S. 70 onto Wallace Street at the sign for the Crystal Coast Civic Center. Located at 100 Wallace Street, the Carteret County Museum of History is based in a 1907-vintage frame building which once

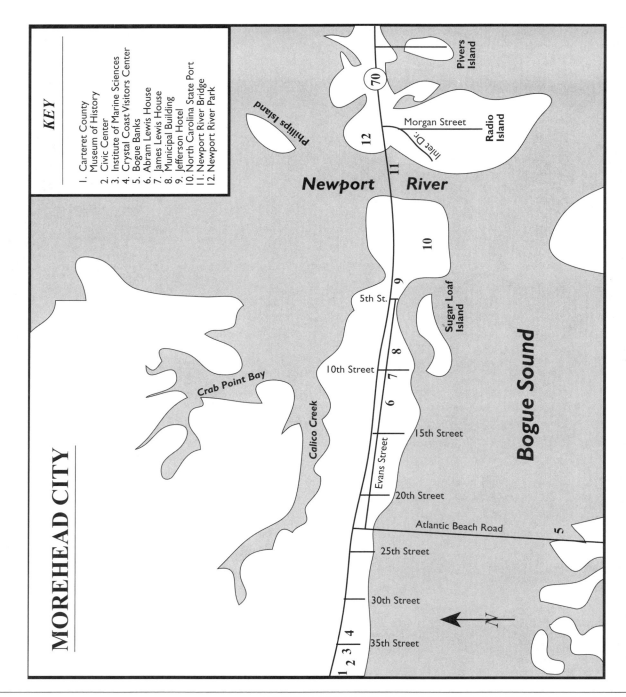

MOREHEAD CITY

KEY

1. Carteret County
   Museum of History
2. Civic Center
3. Institute of Marine Sciences
4. Crystal Coast Visitors Center
5. Bogue Banks
6. Abram Lewis House
7. James Lewis House
8. Municipal Building
9. Jefferson Hotel
10. North Carolina State Port
11. Newport River Bridge
12. Newport River Park

Phillips Island

Newport River

Pivers Island

Radio Island

Morgan Street

Inlet Dr.

Sugar Loaf Island

5th St.

Crab Point Bay

Calico Creek

10th Street

Bogue Sound

15th Street

Evans Street

20th Street

Atlantic Beach Road

25th Street

30th Street

35th Street

N

housed the school for Camp Glenn, a large World War I military encampment. A state historical marker on U.S. 70 describes the camp.

Owned and operated by the Carteret County Historical Society, the Carteret County Museum of History features exhibits dedicated to the study and preservation of local history. Among the displays are old photographs, artwork, seashells, Indian artifacts, quilts, and antique farm implements, furniture, and kitchen utensils. A research library containing materials on local history is available for visitors.

Carteret County Museum of History

Located adjacent to the museum, the civic center is a modern thousand-seat facility owned and operated by Carteret County. Its outdoor plaza provides an outstanding panorama of Bogue Sound and Bogue Banks.

Several marine-research facilities are based in and around Morehead City. One of the most important is the Institute of Marine Sciences, located on the waterfront near the museum and the civic center. This facility is the product of a 1944 project designed to develop a fisheries institute for the University of North Carolina at Chapel Hill. Following World War II, biologists began their work in former naval facilities on the sound shore. The existing building was constructed in 1968. Through its programs of research and instruction, the institute serves the University of North Carolina and other universities, as well as state agencies.

Return to Arendell Street and proceed east. Located on the southern side of the highway just after it widens for the railroad median, the Crystal Coast Visitors Center and the adjacent picnic area and park offer a picturesque sound-side setting. The quiet picnic area shaded by live oaks is located on the former site of Carolina City, a nineteenth-century community that was subsequently swallowed up by Morehead City.

Unlike many coastal towns that developed without specific purpose or design, Morehead City was the product of extensive planning. It was the brainchild of John Motley Morehead, governor of North Carolina from 1841 to 1845. Prior to his service as the state's chief executive, Morehead conceived the idea of developing a deepwater port in the Beaufort area. He envisioned a railroad linking the port to the Piedmont and cities on the Ohio and Mississippi rivers.

Upon completion of his term as governor, Morehead began to survey the Carteret coast for a desirable location for his port town. After much consideration, he concluded that the ideal spot was Beaufort harbor. But the prohibitive cost of a railroad trestle over the Newport River, which runs between Beaufort and Morehead City, forced Morehead to look for a site west of Beaufort. He and his associate, Silas Webb, settled upon a six-hundred-acre site just across the river at Shepard's Point, where they set about developing "a great commercial city." In 1853, working under the name of Shepard's Point Land Company, they purchased the tract for $2,133.33 from the Arendell family, the namesake of the modern thoroughfare.

While Morehead was acquiring Shepard's Point, he was also busy championing plans for the construction of the Atlantic and North Carolina Railroad from Goldsboro to the site of his proposed port. Having laid the groundwork for the railroad during his term as governor, Morehead shrewdly enlisted the support of the state and a coalition of counties, towns, businesses, and citizens to complete the project.

Laid out by Morehead in 1855, Carolina City was to be the terminus of the railroad. However, the town met an early demise in 1857, thanks in part to the boom enjoyed by a new neighbor.

At the time the railroad and port were nearing completion, Morehead decided to subdivide most of his Shepard's Point holdings into 50-by-100-foot lots. This newly laid-out town was located just east of Carolina City.

Preliminary lot sales began in November 1857, and regular railroad service from Goldsboro began on January 1, 1858. Over the next few months, excursion trains hauled thousands of interested North Carolinians to the new development. An official three-day opening celebration in late April brought more than ten thousand visitors to the town which bears Governor Morehead's name. In less than thirty days, every lot in the new town had been sold, earning Morehead $1 million in the process.

A post office was established at Morehead City on February 28, 1859. Prominent families from the rural areas of the county settled in the town, causing it to expand rapidly westward. Pier Number One, as the early port terminal was called, was a beehive of activity. Large shipments of rails were unloaded at the port for use in the construction of the railroad.

Continue east along Arendell Street. The railroad tracks that split the street are reminders of the great enterprise started by Morehead.

Two state historical markers on Arendell call attention to the role that the new town played during the Civil War.

One of them stands fifty yards north of what was the largest Confederate saltworks in Carteret County. In the early stages of the Civil War, the state sought to alleviate the scarcity of salt by extracting the badly needed commodity from seawater. Morehead City was chosen as the site of the first saltworks. In April 1862, when the Union army invaded the area, the salt-processing operation was well under way. It was seized by the invading forces and destroyed.

As the Federal forces began to implement their plans to capture Fort Macon on Bogue Banks, they established a large army camp near the old site of Carolina City. Prior to their arrival, the Confederate army had maintained a large encampment there, covering approximately 1 square mile.

The second historical marker on Arendell Street designates the site of the camp. After Fort Macon fell to Union bombardment, the Federals maintained a sizable force at the camp for the duration of the war.

As you drive through the commercial district of modern Morehead City, you will be hard-pressed to find evidence that the city predates the Civil War.

At 301 Arendell Street stands the Jefferson Hotel, built around 1946. Its predecessor, the famed Atlantic Hotel, towered above the sound at this spot for more than a half-century. Constructed in 1880, the massive three-story frame structure contained 233 rooms. Its architectural design was similar to the famous spas of Victorian America. Throngs of vacationers and distinguished persons enjoyed the hospitality of the grand hotel, which became one of the most popular resort hotels in the state. Its immense popularity helped make Morehead City the unofficial summer capital of North Carolina during the last decade of the nineteenth century. Railroad officials, keenly aware of the value of the hotel to the growing resort economy, purchased it for use as a promotion in rail travel. A fire on April 15, 1933, destroyed the structure. A state historical marker on Arendell Street chronicles the history of the Atlantic.

Located on the waterfront just east of the Jefferson are the facilities of the North Carolina State Port. Motorists get a spectacular vista of the port as they cross the elevated bridge over the Newport River on the eastern side of the complex. Guided tours of the 116-acre port are available to the public. Tour participants enjoy a closeup view of the massive cargo ships that call on Morehead City from ports all over the world. All tours must be scheduled in advance with the ports authority.

Although John Motley Morehead established port facilities on the waterfront in the nineteenth century, the terminal was abandoned in 1904 and soon fell into disrepair. In 1933, the state legislature resurrected the port with the creation of the Morehead City Port Commission. A grant from the Public Works Administration enabled port construction to begin on November 1, 1935. Shortly after completion of the facilities in August of the following year, the SS *Warzaristan* docked at the new terminal with a load of salt from Africa, thereby earning the distinction of being the first ship to unload cargo at the new port. The first ship to be loaded, the SS *Fernwood*, left Morehead City on April 16, 1937, filled with scrap iron and steel bound for Japan.

Unfortunately, Morehead City has never been able to successfully compete with the ports of neighboring states. While a controversy boils over the reasons for this, there is no dispute that the facility has geographic advantages over Norfolk, Wilmington, Charleston, and other Atlantic ports. It is located in a natural harbor connected to the ocean by a 3-mile-long channel. Nearby Cape Lookout provides shelter from the fierce storms of the Atlantic. In nautical terms, Morehead City is closer to the Panama Canal and both South America coasts than most major Atlantic ports, with the exception of the Florida ports. Because of Morehead City's proximity to the Gulf Stream, port traffic is the beneficiary of a temperate climate. Unlike the better-known ports to the north, navigation into the Carteret County port is rarely affected by fog, ice, and snow.

Approximately 130 persons are employed locally by the ports authority. However, almost 1,000 workers from various agencies and companies are involved in the daily operations. Texasgulf, with its expansive facilities in Beaufort County, is one of the largest exporters. Nearly two million tons of phosphate are barged down the Intracoastal Waterway from the town of Aurora each year. Accordingly, Morehead City has become known as a port for bulk cargo. Coal and phosphate, stored in the huge bins located on the northern side of Arendell, are loaded onto waiting ships by conveyor belt.

Scores of tank cars stretching from the port to the central business district are a common weekday sight on Arendell.

Its proximity to the Second Division of the United States Marine Corps, based at Camp Lejeune, has made Morehead City the port of embarkation and debarkation for the marines and equipment from that huge installation. Military activity was particularly hectic at the port in 1990–91 during the deployment of troops and war material for Operation Desert Shield and Operation Desert Storm.

Continue to the eastern end of the port facilities, where U.S. 70 makes its way across the Newport River Bridge. Not only does the tall span provide a bird's-eye view of the port, but it also affords a panoramic glimpse of the Newport River and its extensive marsh islands. This wide, but shallow, river runs 23 miles from central Carteret County to its entry into Bogue Sound near the bridge.

Newport River Bridge

Newport River Park is located at the eastern end of the bridge on the northern side of the U.S. 70 causeway linking Morehead City and Beaufort. Situated on a dredge-spoil site, this new river-access facility features sandy beaches, a pier, picnic facilities, and restrooms. Trails lead to fishing spots on the river, and boardwalks yield splendid views of the port facilities and the river.

Radio Island, created by the Corps of Engineers in 1936 with dredge spoil from the Morehead City channel, is located on the southern side of U.S. 70. Turn south off U.S. 70 onto S.R. 1175 to drive onto the island.

On maps, the 390-acre island, which measures 1.4 miles by 0.7 mile, has the appearance of a miniature South America. It was named by a local radio station, but some locals refer it to as Inlet Island.

Until the North Carolina State Ports Authority recently purchased most of the island, area residents and vacationers used Radio Island as a playground where four-wheel-drive and all-terrain vehicles buzzed over the undeveloped landscape while fishermen, sunbathers, and picnickers crowded its beaches.

Freighter leaving port at Morehead City

A twelve-acre site on the island has now been leased to Carteret County as a day-use public-access area. Divers and marine researchers are attracted to a nearby rock jetty around which teems marine life. Radio Island offers the only walk-in dive beach in the state. Ship watchers are treated to unlimited views of oceangoing traffic from the nearby state port.

North Carolina Division of Marine Fisheries

Return to U.S. 70 and continue east along the causeway to the entrance to Pivers Island. After 0.6 mile, turn south onto S.R. 1208.

Although Pivers Island is much smaller than neighboring Radio Island, it is the center of the growing marine-research industry in the Morehead City–Beaufort area. Its importance is exemplified by the fact that Carteret County currently boasts one of the largest concentrations of marine scientists in the world. Of the six area marine-research facilities, four are located on the island: the Duke University Marine Laboratory, facilities of the National Oceanic and Atmospheric Administration (NOAA), the North Carolina Division of Marine Fisheries, and the North Carolina State University Seafood Laboratory.

In 1988, the Duke University Marine Laboratory celebrated its fiftieth anniversary on Pivers Island. Located on an eleven-acre tract on the southern portion of the island, the Duke campus contains approximately twenty buildings. Its appearance is deceptive. The six cabin-style dormitories housing more than a hundred students resemble a summer camp, rather than a major research facility.

More than 120 employees work at the laboratory, recognized worldwide as an outstanding interdisciplinary research and teaching facility. In addition to the Duke marine-science program, the campus also houses the Marine Biomedical Center, the Duke University/University of North Carolina Consortium, and other public and private research projects.

Chief among the programs of the Duke University/University of North Carolina Consortium is the operation of the 135-foot coastal-zone research ship, R/V *Cape Hatteras*. Since 1982, the consortium, under an agreement with its owner, the National Science Foundation, has operated the large steel-hulled ship for scientific expeditions. It is at sea about 250 days every year on cruises and research trips from Nova Scotia to the Caribbean.

Return to U.S. 70 and retrace your route west to downtown Morehead City. It is 1.9 miles on U.S. 70 to Fourth Street. Turn south onto Fourth, which dead-ends on the water at Evans Street. Turn right on Evans and drive west for a block or so.

Of the jewels in Morehead City's crown, the most precious is the scenic commercial waterfront located on Evans and Shepard streets between Fourth and Tenth streets. Visitors are favorably impressed by the attractive appearance of the waterfront business district, the direct result of a revitalization project inaugurated by the city in 1984. Streetlights and sidewalks of hexagonal stones where installed in a 3-block area. A new bulkhead replaced the old sea wall constructed along Harbor Channel in the early part of the twentieth century.

Park in one of the lots or one of the street spaces along Evans Street. You will be greeted by a picturesque row of fish markets, famous seafood restaurants, and shops offering nautical gifts, books, and crafts.

Though they are indeed competitors for the tourist dollar, the two historic restaurants on the Morehead City waterfront exist harmoniously as matching bookends. The Sanitary Fish Market and Restaurant and Captain Bill's Restaurant, located within sight of each other on Evans Street, are firmly established as institutions on the North Carolina coast.

Tony's, as The Sanitary is popularly known, is the older of the two. Although it has achieved a worldwide reputation for its seafood and is the largest seafood restaurant on the North Carolina coast, it evolved from humble beginnings. A news story in a local newspaper on February 16, 1938, announced the opening of a waterfront fish market by two enterprising

Morehead City waterfront

Morehead City businessmen, Ted Garner and Tony Seamon. Thus began a partnership that lasted forty years until Garner's death on January 1, 1978.

In the early years, Tony and Ted housed their restaurant in a building that rented for $5.50 per week. Total seating in the original facility was twenty—twelve at the counter and eight at the tables. Tony used his party boat to supply fresh seafood for the new business, enabling the restaurant to advertise that its menu selections "slept in the ocean last night."

Almost overnight, the restaurant was a hit. Anxious patrons began to wait in line to enjoy Tony's famous "Shore Dinner." By 1942, the restaurant had become so popular that Tony gave up his boat to devote all of his time to the eating establishment. Finally, in 1949, the ever-growing need for more space resulted in the construction of a new building on the present site. Subsequent additions increased the seating capacity to 650.

When the first Morehead City–Beaufort bridge was completed in 1927, Jesse Lee "Tony" Seamon was the first person to cross it. Thirty-seven years later, he was the first to drive across the replacement bridge. Tony died in Morehead City on May 28, 1985, at the age of eighty-one. Although Ted Garner, Jr., purchased the restaurant in December 1979, Tony's name remains synonymous with the landmark.

Located west of The Sanitary, Captain Bill's Waterfront Restaurant began as the brainchild of Captain Bill Ballou. Prior to World War II, Ballou operated a restaurant on Arendell Street. In 1945, he converted a waterfront officers' club into a restaurant and gave it the name it enjoys today.

At Ballou's death in 1960, Thomas Wade and Ken Newsome purchased the restaurant. After Wade and his wife were killed in a boating accident in 1967, Newsome continued the operation alone for a number of years. Many North Carolinians became familiar with the Wade-Newsome partnership through a popular Pilot Life Insurance Company television commercial during the 1970s.

Visitors to the Morehead City waterfront are fascinated by the fleet of for-hire sportfishing boats docked between The Sanitary and Captain Bill's. From the adjacent boardwalk, pedestrians can share in the joy of happy fishermen as their bounty from the sea is unloaded and weighed. In the late afternoon, as twilight draws near, blackboards appear on boats, detailing the availability of the craft for future fishing expeditions.

Of the festivals and special events that attract visitors to the Morehead City waterfront, the largest and most popular is the North Carolina Seafood Festival. Inaugurated in 1987, the three-day event is held each October to showcase the maritime culture of Carteret County. More than 150,000 people flock to the event annually to enjoy a variety of activities, including historic tours and reenactments, ship tours, music, and local storytelling.

One of most enduring legends of Morehead City involves an old salt who shipwrecked on the sand banks of Carteret County. Where the creature came from, no one could ever ascertain. Local beachcombers called him a South American Indian because of his strange voice and language. His ship veered off course from either South America or Arabia during one of the frequent nor'easters that plague the Outer Banks.

Once ashore, the irreligious, bad-tempered sailor chose to stay in Carteret County. He wore a long pigtail, common to seagoing men of his time, and spoke with a squawking voice that locals could only equate with the guttural sound emitted by the black-crowned night heron. This unusual bird was locally known as a "quawk," and so it came to be that area fishermen referred to this odd fellow as "Old Quawk."

On occasion, the citizens would fish with Old Quawk. They would always end up shaking their heads in disgust at the stranger's foul mouth and bad temper.

One Sunday morning in mid-March, hurricane-force winds lashed the Carteret County coastline with torrential rains and heavy seas. The local fishermen realized that the storm would force them to stay in port. Nonetheless, Old Quawk was determined to fish on that blustery March day. Even though they did not particularly like him, the veteran seafarers urged him not to defy the forces of nature. Rather than heeding their pleas, Old Quawk cursed and shook his fist at the angry sky.

In the midst of the tempest, he put out to sea. A lone night heron took flight after the boat. As man and bird united their voices in an unusual harmony, they disappeared into the storm and became legend forevermore.

In recent years, Morehead City has gained international attention because of its annual Bald Headed Men's Convention.

Since it was founded by local resident John Capps in 1973, the Bald Headed Men of America Club has held its annual convention in the

Morehead City Municipal Building

The James Lewis House

The Kilby Guthrie House

appropriately named Morehead City. Each year, club members from all over the United States travel to Carteret County to enjoy activities dedicated to baldness. In past years, guest speakers have included the likes of nationally syndicated columnist Erma Bombeck. Convention entertainment varies from the "Bald as a Golf Ball" tee-off tournament to the "Most Kissable" and "Sexiest" bald head contests. New members of the Bald Hall of Fame are announced at the convention.

Return to your car and continue in your original direction on Evans Street. West of the commercial waterfront are a number of historically significant buildings. Located at the corner of Evans and Eighth streets, the Morehead City Municipal Building, constructed in 1928, is an excellent example of Florentine Renaissance architecture.

Still farther west, the mainland shore of Bogue Sound is lined with a fine ensemble of beautiful multistory frame houses dating to the first half of the twentieth century. These majestic structures are located along Shepard and Shackleford streets. Interspersed among them are some dwellings that were originally constructed on Core and Shackleford banks and were later moved to their present location. A few of these old "C'ae Banker" houses are identifiable.

From the Morehead City Municipal Building, drive 2 blocks west on Evans to its intersection with South Tenth Street. Located on South Tenth near the intersection is the James Lewis House, which was originally constructed at Wade's Shore on Shackleford Banks. When that community was abandoned, the house was floated to Morehead City on a skiff. A second story was later added with lumber salvaged from a shipwreck. This house is marked with a plaque that identifies it as a "C'ae Banker" structure.

Continue 2 blocks west on Evans. The Abram Lewis House, located at 1205 Evans, was built on Shackleford Banks by its namesake, Thereafter, the home was dismantled, floated across the sound, and reassembled at its current site.

Turn south off Evans onto Twelfth Street and proceed 1 block to Shepard Street. Kilby Guthrie, a recipient of the Congressional Gold Medal for heroism as a member of the United States Lifesaving Service, built the house now located at 1200 Shepard Street. Originally located on Shackleford Banks, it was later floated across the sound.

Turn around and proceed 2 blocks north on Twelfth Street to the intersection with Arendell Street. Turn left, or west, and drive 11 blocks on Arendell to Twenty-third Street. Turn left, or south, onto Twenty-third, which becomes Atlantic Beach Road.

Almost immediately, the road begins to rise as it makes its way across the four-lane high-rise bridge that spans Bogue Sound and connects Morehead City with Bogue Banks. Completed at a cost of $8 million in April 1987, the bridge has alleviated the long lines of summertime traffic that resulted when the old drawbridge was raised.

On the other side of the bridge lies Bogue Banks, generally considered the southern terminus of the famed Outer Banks of North Carolina. A causeway lined with motels, restaurants, and other businesses ushers motorists onto the island, which, at 29 miles, is the longest island on the North Carolina coast south of Cape Lookout.

Atlantic Beach, the popular beach town on the eastern end of the island, is the granddaddy of the resorts on Bogue Banks. When compared to the venerable resorts of the North Carolina coast, such as Nags Head, Wrightsville Beach, and Carolina Beach, Bogue Banks is a newcomer. Yet over the past seventy years, the island has emerged among the most popular vacation destinations on the entire coast.

In Atlantic Beach, at the busiest intersection on Bogue Banks, the causeway junctions with N.C. 58, the only east-west road running the length of the island. Turn east onto N.C. 58 and drive 3.5 miles to the end of the island. En route, N.C. 58 gives way to S.R. 1190.

This drive displays the widespread private resort development that has engulfed much of Bogue Banks. Chief among the reasons for the immense popularity of the island is the beautiful ocean strand stretching almost 30 miles. Not only is the island one of the longest on the North Carolina coast, but it has perhaps the most development potential. Unlike the other sizable islands of the Outer Banks, very little land on Bogue Banks has been reserved for government, military, or public use.

Located at the terminus of S.R. 1190, Fort Macon State Park is an exception.

Each year, more than 1.25 million people visit Fort Macon State Park, making it the most-visited state park in North Carolina. At the park complex, patrons not only enjoy and learn about state history, but about the coastal environment as well. For more than 150 years, Fort Macon has maintained a vigil over Beaufort Inlet, and thanks to the preservation efforts begun by the state more than a half-century ago, it appears much as it did when the first United States Army troops were stationed here in 1834.

Listed on the National Register of Historic Places, the pentagon-shaped fortress is a well-preserved example of the nation's early coastal defenses. Its magnificent architectural design is attributed to General Simon Bernard, a French military engineer who designed a number of forts on the East Coast. More than fifteen million bricks were laid by laborers working under the supervision of master masons.

When the fort was completed in December 1834, it was named in honor of Nathaniel Macon, a North Carolinian who became Speaker of the United States House of Representatives. He was subsequently elected to the Senate. A political favorite of Thomas Jefferson, Macon was dubbed "the last of the Romans" by Jefferson.

Not long after it was garrisoned, the fort began to be plagued by the kind of problems that had spelled the demise of its predecessor, Fort Hampton: erosion and storms. To remedy the problem, the United States Army sent one of its young West Point–trained engineers in the 1840s. While at Fort Macon, Captain Robert E. Lee designed and supervised the construction of a system of stone jetties still in use today.

In open defiance of President Lincoln's request for North Carolina troops to suppress the rebellion of its Southern neighbors, Governor John W. Ellis ordered state troops to seize the coastal installations at Forts Macon, Caswell, and Johnston on April 15, 1861. Little did Ellis know that Fort Macon had been seized by state volunteers a day earlier. Over the next twelve months, Southern forces of about five hundred men garrisoned and fortified Fort Macon.

With Roanoke Island, New Bern, and much of the Outer Banks and the northern coastal plain under Federal control by mid-March 1862, the Union high command sensed that if the North Carolina coast fell, the entire Confederacy would be cut in half. Fort Macon was the logical next step in the quest for complete domination.

On March 22, 1862, General Ambrose Burnside dispatched General

John G. Parke to initiate the preliminary work toward the capture of Fort Macon. Within a week, Union forces secured a beachhead on Bogue Banks. One month later, Lieutenant Colonel Moses J. White, the Mississippian who was in command of the fort, surrendered to General Burnside after the Confederates had weathered an eleven-hour battery from an overwhelming land and sea force.

For the duration of the war, Fort Macon remained under Union control. It was used as a penitentiary and a coaling station. Following the Civil War, the fort remained an active military installation, since there was no other such facility in either of the Carolinas at the time. Additional casemates were converted into prison cells. Visitors to the fort can still observe prison bars.

In the last quarter of the nineteenth century, the federal government changed its national defense policy. It developed a modern navy to command the seas, thereby eliminating the need for many of the existing coastal defense installations. One of the casualties of the new policy was Fort Macon. It was closed as a garrisoned military base on April 18, 1877.

During the Spanish-American War, the fort was briefly manned once again by the army. In 1903, the federal government officially closed Fort Macon. It remained closed during World War I. In 1923, defense officials deemed the fort obsolete and the property expendable. Two years later, the United States War Department conveyed the property to the state of North Carolina under the condition that Fort Macon be maintained as a state park.

Elaborate ceremonies highlighted by a speech by Governor J. C. B. Ehringhaus were held at Fort Macon on May 1, 1936, to celebrate the opening of the second park in the North Carolina's state parks system. The opening was scheduled to coincide with the hundredth birthday of the fort.

Several weeks after the Japanese attack on Pearl Harbor, the park was closed in order that the fort could once again be used for coastal defense. Throughout the war, it was manned by the 244th Division, Coast Artillery, of the United States Army. In June 1946, the last troops departed, and the site was released to the state.

A highly unusual accident took place at the fort during World War II. Troops stationed here found that their only heating system was fireplaces. In 1942, soldiers attempting to warm themselves used some unexploded Civil

War shells as andirons. When they built a fire on the deadly ordnance, which they had mistaken as solid iron shot, the shells exploded, killing two and wounding others. So bizarre was the incident that it made "Ripley's Believe It or Not," a case of Civil War casualties occurring more than eighty years after the battle at Fort Macon was over.

The centerpiece of Fort Macon State Park is the ancient fort, considered by military historians and architectural experts to be one of the best-preserved forts in the nation. At first glance, knowledgeable visitors are impressed by its striking resemblance to Fort Marion in St. Augustine, Florida.

The outer and inner walls are separated by a deep, twenty-five-foot-wide moat. Although now dry and covered with grass, the moat was at one time deeper than it is at present. It was filled with tidal water from nearby Bogue Sound.

More than twenty feet thick, the Covertway, as the outer walls are collectively called, is built of sand and masonry. It affords magnificent views of Beaufort Inlet, Shackleford Banks, Bogue Sound, Bogue Banks, and the Morehead City and Beaufort waterfronts. There are four rooms with cannon placements on the outer walls. Beneath these outer ramparts are dungeons, now filled with water.

Fort Macon State Park

On the northern side of the fort, a wooden walkway located at the site of the old drawbridge crosses the moat to the main entrance—the sally port. Directly through the sally port lies the half-acre parade ground. Surrounding the parade ground are the five-foot-thick inner walls. These walls, of beautiful brick construction, actually form the fort proper. Three handsome staircases, adorned with wrought-iron handrails crafted to resemble the originals, lead to the terreplein—the top platform.

Twenty-six casemates, or vaulted rooms, are situated around the parade grounds. A number of the casemates have been restored since 1977. One of the rooms was restored to represent the quarters of enlisted men, complete with bunk beds. Lieutenant Colonel Moses White's room has been furnished with a bed, chairs, and a table constructed in the shop at the park. Swords, hats, uniforms, and other Civil War memorabilia are also on display. An audiovisual program detailing the unfortunate story of Lieutenant Colonel White is presented in the commanding officer's quarters. White was plagued by epilepsy throughout much of his career. He died at the age of twenty-nine.

Although other casemates have not been restored, most are open to the public. Visitors are free to examine the masterful military engineering which went into the domed rooms, the delicately curved brick arches, and the vaulted stairways. Throughout the fort, you will marvel at the hundreds of bricks that were bent and shaped to fit the unique design of the arches, walls, and floors. Some of the most intricate and unusual brickwork of nineteenth-century America can be observed at the fort. It has been suggested that few modern architects could replicate the arches that have endured here for more than a century and a half.

Attendants on duty throughout the fort answer questions and provide information about the installation. Guided tours are conducted daily, and Civil War reenactments are held on the parade grounds on spring and summer weekends. A museum and a bookstore are located in the casemates.

Although the fort covers only eight acres, the park covers 398 acres. In addition to tours of the fort, a variety of activities is offered at the park. Nature-study programs and beach walks conducted by park rangers cover topics ranging from shells to brown pelicans.

Near the parking lot at the fort entrance, visitors can enjoy the Elliott Coues Nature Trail. Named for the army physician who was stationed at Fort Macon in 1869 and 1870, this easy 0.4-mile loop trail passes through dense shrub thickets to Beaufort Inlet. At the inlet, visitors can observe the jetties constructed by Robert E. Lee. Often found on the jetty rocks are invertebrates such as starfish and sea urchins.

The hiking trail passes near the site of the two military installations that preceded Fort Macon. In response to the Spanish attack on Beaufort in 1747, work began on Fort Dobbs on the eastern end of Bogue Banks in 1756. However, this fort was never completed. In 1808, construction began on Fort Hampton, a small masonry installation at a site three hundred yards east of the present fort. Almost as soon as it was completed, the fort fell prey to erosion.

West of Fort Macon and near the park entrance, a park road takes visitors to picnic grounds, a bathhouse and pavilion, and a public beach. From the bathhouse building, a boardwalk provides access to the beautiful Bogue Banks strand. Dolphins and whales can occasionally be observed in the ocean.

Located adjacent to the state park is the Fort Macon Coast Guard Station, the successor to the old Fort Macon Life Boat Station. This base serves as the command post for the Coast Guard units at Hobucken, Swansboro,

Wrightsville Beach, and Oak Island. In November 1990, the Fort Macon installation achieved a historic milestone when Lieutenant Commander Cynthia A. Coogan was named its commander. She became the first woman to command a Coast Guard group in the two-hundred-year history of America's smallest branch of military service.

Retrace your route to the intersection of N.C. 58 and the causeway in Atlantic Beach.

Although the eastern portion of the island—that lying between Fort Macon and this intersection—falls within the corporate limits of Atlantic Beach, it is referred to locally as Money Island Beach, a name that can be traced to the Civil War.

One of the vital elements of General Burnside's plan to assault Fort Macon was the construction of rafts to float troops and artillery across Bogue Sound. In charge of the raft construction was a cunning Yankee sergeant. Once the crude vessels were built and loaded, the sergeant assembled his soldiers and announced, "Gentlemen, we are going on a very dangerous mission, and we have been instructed not to let anything of value fall into the hands of the enemy, so I want you to bring me all of your money and jewelry. We will bury it here on the banks of Bogue Sound. When the battle is over, we will return here and I will give you back your belongings."

A big cedar tree on Bogue Banks was selected to mark the spot for the burial of the valuables. Each soldier watched intently as his property was carefully placed in a hole dug at the roots of the tree. Although the troops left a mark on the tree to identify it, they took care to leave no evidence of the excavation.

After the swift capture of Fort Macon, the troops whose belongings were buried on Bogue Banks were dispatched to other battlefields, save one. Somehow, the crafty sergeant was able to remain in Beaufort for the remainder of the war. Once the hostilities ceased and he was satisfied that all the others had forgotten the cache, he made his move. He engaged a local fisherman to row him across the sound to retrieve the hidden riches. For his services, the fisherman was promised half the booty.

As fate would have it, about halfway across the sound, the fisherman noticed that the sergeant had taken sick. A closer examination revealed that he was burning up with fever. Immediately, the fisherman maneuvered the boat back toward the mainland. By the time they reached the doctor's office in Beaufort, the sergeant had lapsed into unconsciousness. The physician diagnosed the illness as typhoid fever. Without ever revealing the location of the treasure, the sergeant died. Since his death, many cedar trees on Bogue Banks have been dug up, but no one has ever found the valuables hidden long ago.

At the busy intersection in Atlantic Beach, the name of the causeway changes from Morehead Avenue to Central Avenue. Drive south on Central Avenue to its terminus at Atlantic Avenue, the street that runs parallel to the strand, and park your car. Parking is available on East and West drives, which combine with Central Avenue to form a Y in the heart of the old resort. Amusement parks and beach clubs have come and gone in this area since the 1920s.

A two-story frame hotel was constructed in the fledgling resort in 1923. Prior to that time, this stretch of strand attracted day visitors from Morehead City and other mainland points. Once they were boated across the sound, early beach enthusiasts found little more than a crude bathhouse to accommodate them.

Things began to improve in 1928 with the construction of the first bridge to Bogue Banks. Until 1938, when it was sold to the state, the bridge at Twenty-eighth Street was operated as a toll bridge. Completion of the Atlantic Beach Hotel in 1938 further propelled the resort toward becoming an important tourist destination. Until it was destroyed in 1965, the old hotel stood as a beach landmark.

By World War II, Atlantic Beach, incorporated in 1937, was enjoying widespread popularity. Spread along the strand were numerous cottages and amusement facilities, including a bowling alley and a large pavilion. Following the war, the island began luring so many visitors that the state was forced in 1953 to build a new bridge at Twenty-fourth Street to replace the original structure.

From the parking area, walk to the boardwalk running along the strand. No longer a boardwalk in the true sense of the word, this concrete walkway provides an opportunity to see the numerous half-century-old beach houses that grace the Atlantic Beach oceanfront. To the west, down the strand, the towering hotels and condominiums of Pine Knoll Shores loom on the horizon. Beachcombers will also notice the long sea wall on the strand, evidence of the relentless, costly battle that the town continues to wage against erosion.

Return to the parking area and drive back to the intersection of N.C. 58 and Central. Proceed west on N.C. 58.

Although it was little more than a sandy lane, the first road from Atlantic Beach to Salter Path, 9 miles to the west, was completed during the Depression. Earning $1.25 per day from the federal government, local residents used axes and brush knives to hack their way through the dense maritime forest of live oaks and yaupon. In the 1940s, the state assumed maintenance of the road, and in the process widened and improved it with a clay foundation. The road was not paved until the next decade.

Because of the almost uninterrupted development along N.C. 58, the boundaries of the five resort villages on Bogue Banks are often difficult for visitors to ascertain. Atlantic Beach gradually gives way to Pine Knoll Shores after 2.5 miles.

In appearance, Pine Knoll Shores presents a stark contrast to Atlantic Beach. Newer, fresher, and less densely developed, this resort community of more than a thousand permanent residents contains the most suitable land for development on the island. Remnants of maritime forests are still in evidence along the highway.

A state historical marker on N.C. 58 in Pine Knoll Shores honors famed Florentine navigator Giovanni da Verrazano, who first explored Bogue Banks in 1524.

There remains, however, some dispute as to the origin of the island's name. Most historians believe that it was named for Joseph Bogue, who settled in the area in the early eighteenth century. On the other hand, some writers have noted that "bogue" is a Choctaw Indian reference to a stream or water passage. Along the coast, a bogue is taken to mean a swampy area. There is also some evidence that the word comes from a Spanish term denoting movement to the leeward. Lending credence to the Spanish origin are the incontrovertible facts that Bogue is one of the oldest place names on the North Carolina coast and that Spaniards frequently visited, raided, and were shipwrecked on the Outer Banks in the sixteenth, seventeenth, and early eighteenth centuries.

Iron Steamer Fishing Pier

Regardless of the source of its name, the island was known as Bogue Banks by the eighteenth century, as evidenced in the Moseley map of 1733.

Located on the ocean side of the highway approximately 6 miles from Atlantic Beach, the Iron Steamer Fishing Pier in Pine Knoll Shores marks the site of the wreck of the Confederate blockade runner *Prevensey*, a side-wheel steamer. A Federal warship ran the five-hundred-ton iron ship aground here in 1864.

Park in the pier lot and walk out onto the east wing of the pier. The *Prevensey's* rusting axle and boiler are visible below the surface. Portions of the ship can be seen from the strand at low tide.

Near the pier, turn north off N.C. 58 onto S.R. 1201 for a drive of 0.4 mile to the Theodore Roosevelt State Natural Area and the North Carolina Aquarium at Pine Knoll Shores.

Located on a 297-acre sound-side site, the Theodore Roosevelt State Natural Area preserves one of the few areas of undisturbed vegetation and wildlife habitats on Bogue Banks. This unique remnant of maritime forest was given to the state by the Roosevelt family. Upon its acquisition, it became the state's second officially designated natural area. As such, the site has been subject only to such development as is necessary to preserve the area and to provide interpretive programs.

Although few visitor facilities are provided, visitors may hike through the natural area on the Alice G. Hoffman Nature Trail. This 0.25-mile route offers an excellent overview of the complicated ecosystem of salt marsh, inland freshwater slough, and ancient dunes now stabilized by maritime and shrub-forest communities. At the East Pond Overlook and at other lagoons in the natural area, alligators are commonly observed.

The trailhead for the Alice G. Hoffman Nature Trail is located adjacent to the North Carolina Aquarium at Pine Knoll Shores. Like its sister facilities at Manteo and Fort Fisher, this marine center serves the public and scientific communities. Visitors enjoy attractive displays and artifacts relating to the natural and human history of the North Carolina coast. Special "hands-on" tours on board the trawler *First Mate* are frequently sponsored by the aquarium.

Return to N.C. 58 and continue west. Approximately 2 miles from the turnoff to the state natural area and the aquarium, you will leave Pine Knoll

Shores and enter the eastern portion of Indian Beach. Numerous high-rise condominiums have changed the landscape of this part of the island.

Salter Path, located O.7 mile farther west, presents a sharp contrast to the dense development of the two sections of Indian Beach to the east and west. As N.C. 58 winds its way through the picturesque village, you will pass by white frame dwellings that remain in the possession of the descendants of the original settlers.

In the middle of the nineteenth century, fishermen took up permanent residence on Bogue Banks, fleeing their homes on Core and Shackleford banks. Few, if any, bothered to acquire title to the land on which they settled. By the turn of the century, two settlements started by these squatters had grown into the distinct communities of Salter Path and Rice Path. The word *path* was once part of the vernacular of residents of the southern Outer Banks. It refers to a locality on the island used by people from the mainland for specific activities.

Perhaps they did not bother to obtain deeds to their property because it was considered relatively worthless. Or perhaps they simply could not afford to pay the meager amounts that would have constituted the purchase price. For whatever reason, almost all of the original settlers of the village of Salter Path were squatters.

Although some of the early residents of the village claimed that Salter Path was named for the Salter family, who supposedly lived on the island in the nineteenth century, the actual community dates from 1900. A more likely explanation is that the name was adopted from the dunes-to-saltwater patch of ground on which the settlement grew.

Few, if any, of the early residents of the village bothered to ask the owner of the land for permission to live there. John A. Royal, a native of Carteret County and a Boston resident, owned not only the middle portion of the island, but the eastern portion to Atlantic Beach and the entire western half as well. However, Royal did little to interfere with the lifestyle of the squatters.

In 1917, Royal sold the stretch of property from Salter Path to Atlantic Beach. The squatters were quick to realize that the new owner might not be as lenient as Royal. No sooner had Mrs. Alice Hoffman acquired the property than she announced that she would no longer allow residents to settle where they pleased or to rummage about collecting firewood. Villagers were also told to stop their cattle from roaming.

A bitter controversy ensued. Mrs. Hoffman, a socialite from New York and Paris, ensconced herself at her fine home on Bogue Sound. Finally, irate squatters proceeded en masse to Mrs. Hoffman's estate, where they openly displayed their hostility to her policies. For several days, the protestors marched around her house and fired their guns.

Mrs. Hoffman would not bow to the pressure of the villagers. Determined to bring the controversy to a conclusion, she chose to have the matter litigated in Carteret County Superior Court. At one point, she said, "I'd rather go to court than to the theater."

A judgment rendered by the court in 1953 ended the dispute. Under its terms, the thirty-five squatters were not evicted, but their settlement was restricted to eighty-four acres. A further judicial restriction required that every house had to be handed down from generation to generation and occupied by the descendants of the original owner. Otherwise, the property would revert immediately to Mrs. Hoffman or her estate.

Until her death on March 15, 1953, at the age of ninety-three, Mrs. Hoffman spent much of her time at her estate on Oakleaf Drive in Pine Knoll Shores. Approximately three hundred people were living at Salter

Public beach walkway at Salter Path

TOURING THE BACKROADS OF NORTH CAROLINA'S LOWER COAST

Path at the time of her death. Her holdings of more than 2,000 acres were inherited by the children of Mrs. Theodore Roosevelt, Jr. Subsequently, the Roosevelt family sold or gave away all but 175 acres.

In the heart of Salter Path alongside N.C. 58, Carteret County has developed a picturesque twenty-two-acre site providing access to the strand. From the parking area enclosed by a picket fence, a boardwalk leads through a majestic maritime forest to an undisturbed dune field and the public beach. Picnic facilities, restrooms, and a bathhouse are provided.

Continue west on N.C. 58. The western portion of Indian Beach presents a different appearance from the village of the same name on the eastern side of Salter Path. Its landscape is punctuated by a high density of mobile homes. For many years, it has been a favorite spot for fishermen.

At the western limit of Indian Beach, the island narrows drastically as U.S. 58 carries motorists on a 9.5-mile drive through the resort town of Emerald Isle. A permanent population of approximately twenty-five hundred is spread throughout the town, which extends down the western third of Bogue Banks. Property development here has been characterized by single-family cottages, versus the condominiums and hotels in the Atlantic Beach–Pine Knoll Shores area.

As you drive by the sand dunes and beach houses lining the highway, there is little to distinguish one mile from another in Emerald Isle. Had the early-twentieth-century dreams of one man come true, Emerald Isle might have become one of the premier resorts of the entire Atlantic coast.

Henry K. Fort, a wealthy industrialist from Philadelphia, purchased a 12.5-mile stretch of Bogue Banks from Salter Path to Bogue Inlet in 1918. He acquired an additional tract of 496 acres on the mainland at present-day Cape Carteret six years later. Both parcels were purchased from John Royal.

Fort, a pencil-manufacturing magnate, became interested in the island because of its abundance of cedar trees. However, he soon discovered that the cedar could not be harvested and shipped economically. Soon after his acquisition of the mainland parcel, he dispatched a crew of engineers from New Jersey to Bogue Banks. For several months, the team surveyed Fort's holdings and reduced its findings to maps.

Once the engineers and architects completed their work, an artist painted Fort's conception of a resort comparable to Atlantic City, New Jersey. It depicted streets, summer homes, businesses, fishing piers, and amusement centers. On the mainland portion of the Fort holdings, plans called for year-round homes, businesses, and recreation areas.

Essential to the realization of Fort's dream was the construction of a bridge at the western end of the island. His efforts to persuade state and county officials to provide assistance with the bridge were unsuccessful. Determined to complete his project, Fort proceeded with his plans until the grand dream became one of the many casualties of the Depression.

Fort died in 1943, leaving his vast holdings to his daughter. Ultimately, she sold nearly 10 miles of the land to a group of seven men from the North Carolina communities of Smithfield and Red Springs. Once the deal was consummated, the seven individuals divided the land into two-thou-sand-foot oceanfront sections. It was on this property that the resort of Emerald Isle began to take shape in the 1950s.

The town of Emerald Isle was incorporated in 1957. Its growth was spurred by the establishment of a state-operated toll-free ferry from the western end of the island to the mainland.

Once you have toured Emerald Isle, drive across the B. Cameron Langston Bridge over Bogue Sound. Completed in 1971, this high-rise span affords a magnificent view of the shallow sound and its green marsh islands. To the

The B. Cameron Langston Bridge

TOURING THE BACKROADS OF NORTH CAROLINA'S LOWER COAST

west lies Bogue Inlet, the southern boundary of Bogue Banks. Only three inlets along the entire North Carolina coast are known to have been open continuously since 1585. Two of the three—Bogue and Beaufort inlets—serve as boundaries for Bogue Banks.

The tour ends on the mainland at the far end of the B. Cameron Langston Bridge.

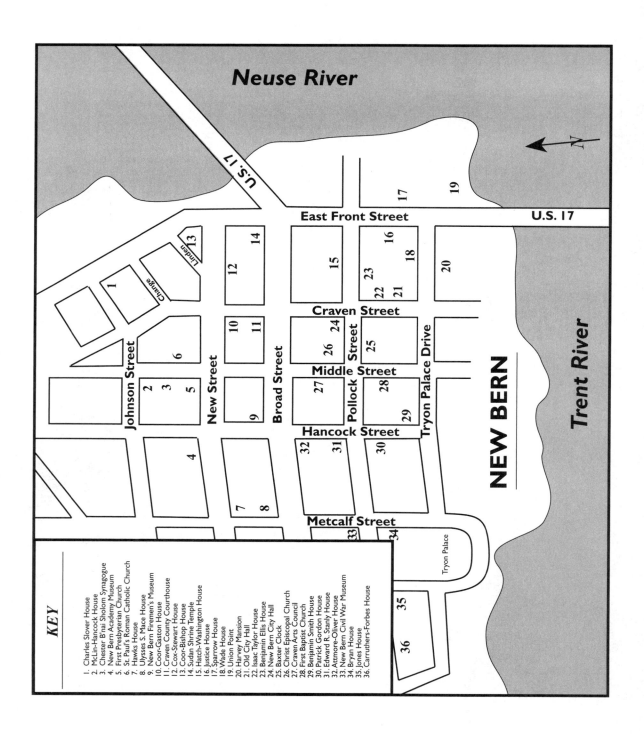

Neuse River

U.S. 17

N

17

19

East Front Street

U.S. 17

13

Linden

14

12

1

Change

16

15

23

18

20

22

21

Craven Street

10

11

26 24

Street

25

6

Johnson Street

2

3

5

New Street

Middle Street

27

28

9

Broad Street

29

Pollock

Tryon Palace Drive

NEW BERN

Trent River

Hancock Street

4

32

31

30

7

8

Metcalf Street

33

34

Tryon Palace

35

36

KEY

1. Charles Slover House
2. McLin-Hancock House
3. Chester B'nai Sholom Synagogue
4. New Bern Academy Museum
5. First Presbyterian Church
6. St. Paul's Roman Catholic Church
7. Hawks House
8. Ulysses S. Mace House
9. New Bern Firemen's Museum
10. Coor-Gaston House
11. Craven County Courthouse
12. Cox-Stewart House
13. Coor-Bishop House
14. Sudan Shrine Temple
15. Hatch-Washington House
16. Justice House
17. Sparrow House
18. Wade House
19. Union Point
20. Harvey Mansion
21. Old City Hall
22. Isaac Taylor House
23. Benjamin Ellis House
24. New Bern City Hall
25. Baxter Clock
26. Christ Episcopal Church
27. Craven Arts Council
28. First Baptist Church
29. Benjamin Smith House
30. Patrick Gordon House
31. Edward R. Stanly House
32. Attmore-Oliver House
33. New Bern Civil War Museum
34. Bryan House
35. Jones House
36. Carruthers-Forbes House

The New Bern Tour

This tour combines a driving tour and a walking tour of historic New Bern, one of coastal North Carolina's great treasures.

Among the highlights of the tour are the New Bern waterfront, New Bern City Hall, the story of Caleb "Doc" Bradham, Christ Episcopal Church, the magnificent Tryon Palace restoration, the John Wright Stanly House, the New Bern Firemen's Museum, the story of Fred the horse, First Presbyterian Church, the New Bern Academy Museum, and New Bern National Cemetery.

Total mileage: approximately 11 miles.

This tour begins at the intersection of S.R. 1004 (Madam Moore's Lane) and U.S. 70 Business just across the Trent River from New Bern. Near the intersection, two state historical markers call attention to Abner Nash, Richard Dobbs Spaight, and Richard Dobbs Spaight, Jr., three North Carolina governors who are buried nearby. Another marker acquaints visitors with the Battle of New Bern on March 14, 1862.

To visit the Spaight Family Cemetery, proceed 2.5 miles south on S.R. 1004.

Among the graves within the brick-wall-enclosed cemetery are those of Governor Richard Dobbs Spaight (1758–1802), a signer of the United States Constitution, Governor Richard Dobbs Spaight, Jr. (1796–1850), and Mary Dorothy Vail Moore (1735–1775). These graves and others of the Spaight family are located on property that once was part of Chermont, a 2,500-acre plantation along the Trent River. An elegant mansion built by Mary Moore graced the plantation.

Moore's daughter was the wife of Richard Dobbs Spaight, whose tomb was desecrated by invading Union forces when they burned the mansion in 1862. The marauders took Spaight's skeleton from its resting place and displayed his skull on a gatepost. The body of a fallen Union soldier was placed in Spaight's metal coffin for shipment north.

Spaight Family Cemetery

Return to the intersection of S.R. 1004 and U.S. 70 Business. Turn north on U.S. 70 Business and proceed across the bridge spanning the Trent River.

Visitors approaching New Bern on any of the several bridges leading into town are treated to one of the most beautiful panoramas in all of coastal North Carolina. The broad, scenic rivers encircling the town, the church spires towering above centuries-old structures, and a living display of North Carolina's proud past converge to welcome visitors to a modern city that retains much of the charm of a bygone era.

Prominently situated on a peninsula formed by the confluence of the Neuse and Trent rivers, the historic city has an atmosphere matched by few others on the Atlantic coast. Bathed in antiquity, yet clothed with the amenities of the modern world, North Carolina's second-oldest incorporated town maintains a graceful and exquisite blend of old and new. Now almost three centuries old, this Craven County town, born of the dreams of Baron Christophe DeGraffenried and John Lawson, has grown into a vibrant commercial center whose citizens have done a commendable job in preserving its heritage.

Without question, the best place to begin a tour of New Bern is on its picturesque waterfront. Union Point, located at the northern end of the bridge over the Trent River, is a small spit of land marking the juncture of the two great rivers. After this historic ground was used for decades as a dumping ground for trash, a local woman's club, in cooperation with the city, developed it into a small municipal park. Located within the park is the Woman's Club Building, constructed in 1932 from concrete curbing that had been dumped at Union Point. Equipped with picnic facilities and a boat landing, Union Point Park is located on U.S. 70 (East Front Street) at Tryon Palace Drive.

Park at Union Point Park.

Thanks to the chronicles of John Lawson, North Carolina's first resident historian, many details of the founding of New Bern survive. When the intrepid Lawson first caught sight of Union Point in the early eighteenth century, he was not only awed by its wild beauty, but also cognizant of its strategic value. Its two rivers and their tributaries, navigable far into the interior, provided access to the Atlantic through Ocracoke Inlet. Long before Lawson's arrival, the future site of New Bern had been a favored spot among area Indians. They called it Chattawka, meaning "where fish are taken."

Somehow, Lawson was able to persuade the Indians to part with some of their prime real estate. He purchased a thousand acres and constructed a cabin approximately 0.25 mile from the nearest Indian village. Impressed by the amicable nature of the Indians, Lawson sent exciting accounts of the Neuse area and its fertile, inexpensive lands back to Europe.

By 1709, he returned to London to oversee publication of his book, *A New Voyage to Carolina*. While in Europe, Lawson extolled the virtues of his New World paradise to three men from Bern, Switzerland. George Ritter was interested in settling a group of paupers and religious dissenters in the American colonies, while Christophe DeGraffenried and Franz Ludwig Michel were looking to obtain mining rights to the vast mineral resources lying just across the ocean.

Lawson was so persuasive that the three men successfully negotiated with the English Crown and the Lords Proprietors to obtain land in the New World. As a result, Ritter and Company acquired 18,750 acres along the Neuse and Trent rivers. DeGraffenried, the head of the company, dispatched an advance team of Lawson and Christopher Gale to select a site for the first settlement.

An attempt to settle the site in 1710 with 650 German Protestants expelled from Baden and Bavaria failed miserably. Land disputes with the neighboring Tuscaroras ensued. Finally, after these initial setbacks, DeGraffenried was able to concentrate his energies toward establishing the town he had envisioned. At the request of DeGraffenried, Lawson laid out the town on the point between the two rivers.

Lawson's engineering genius was evident in the main streets. They were laid out in the form of a cross, one running from river to river and the other running northwest from the confluence of the two rivers. Although this design had religious implications, practical considerations were paramount in Lawson's scheme. Ramparts constructed along the transverse road provided a measure of defense against Indians.

In honor of the capital of his native land, DeGraffenried named his town Bern-on-the-Neuse. Among the early residents, the name quickly became

New Bern. Almost overnight, New Bern achieved a prominence which rivaled that of Bath and Edenton.

Unfortunately, several tragic events in 1711 seemed to lend credence to the belief that DeGraffenried's town was ill-fated.

In September, Lawson cajoled DeGraffenried into making a canoe trip up the Neuse. A few days into the trip, the expedition fell into the hands of a war party of Tuscaroras. In a desperate plea for his life, DeGraffenried threatened the Indians with reprisals by the English Crown, promised them favors and services, and shifted all the blame for the Indians' woes onto Lawson. At the last moment, his life was spared, but Lawson was not so fortunate. Ironically, he died a horrible death by a style of torture which he had witnessed and written about earlier: "Others split the pitch pine into splinters and stick them into the prisoner's body yet alive. Thus they light them, which burn like so many torches, and in this manner they make him dance round a great fire, every one buffeting and deriding him til he expires, when every one strives to get a bone or some relic of this unfortunate captive."

At dawn on the day following Lawson's demise, DeGraffenried was told of a mighty Tuscarora assault which was about to be carried out on white settlers. He was detained as a prisoner and forced to sit by helplessly as the entire area was ravaged. During the first wave of the mayhem, New Bern was spared. However, the gruesome bloodbath was to plague the entire region for the next two years.

A financially ruined, disgusted DeGraffenried mortgaged his holdings to Thomas Pollock, a wealthy planter and acting governor of North Carolina, and moved to Williamsburg, Virginia, where he stayed with Governor Alexander Spotswood for a brief time. Finally, in 1714, DeGraffenried sailed with a group of the surviving Swiss settlers for Europe, never again to return to America.

In the meantime, the Tuscaroras were soundly defeated in March 1713 at Snow Hill, approximately 45 miles to the west, by a band of Indian fighters, white settlers, and friendly Indians. Following the defeat, the Tuscaroras moved from North Carolina to upper New York, where they joined the Five Nations. There, they gave their new land the name of their North Carolina home. Over time, Chattawka became the now-famous Chautauqua, New York.

New Bern witnessed its rebirth around 1720 under the tutelage of Cullen Pollock, the son and heir of Thomas Pollock. He worked diligently to promote the town, and due in large part to his efforts, the settlement by the rivers emerged as an important seaport and seat of government. In 1723, the town was incorporated and made the seat of Craven County, a political subdivision created in 1705 and named in honor of William, earl of Craven, the longest-lived of the eight Lords Proprietors.

As the North Carolina colony grew, choice land on the coast became scarce. Consequently, settlement spread inland and to the south. These new settlement patterns worked to the benefit of New Bern. Suddenly, the town was at the center of the state, rather than on the fringes of the frontier. By 1732, roads connected the town with the Albemarle region to the north and Charleston, South Carolina, to the south. New Bern's central location and increasing prominence within the colony led the colonial assembly to convene here in 1737.

After years of setbacks and ill fortune, DeGraffenried's dream was coming true. Yet events were soon to occur that would forever end his vision of a permanent German-Swiss outpost in America.

None of the original European settlers at New Bern owned their land. Once the Pollock family called in the mortgages and took control of the settlements, few of the German-Swiss colonists had the means to purchase the land on which they lived. Most of them were forced from their original plots in 1749 and dispersed inland. English-speaking settlers rapidly replaced the last of the DeGraffenried colonists, thus sealing the destiny of New Bern as a British American town.

To view the city that John Lawson designed in 1710, proceed west from Union Point Park across East Front Street onto Tryon Palace Drive.

New Bern and Wilmington stand as the two ancient cities of significant size on the North Carolina coast that have taken important steps toward the preservation of their illustrious pasts. Throughout the twentieth century, New Bern has avoided the mistakes of other cities on the Atlantic coast that have, through demolition and urban renewal, deprived future generations of the enjoyment of historic structures. Due to the efforts of various associations and countless individuals, the city possesses a superb ensemble of eighteenth- and nineteenth-century buildings of not only state,

The Wade House

Harvey Mansion

The Isaac Taylor House

but national, importance. More than two dozen of them are listed on the National Register of Historic Places.

As soon as you enter Tryon Palace Drive, you will get a sample of the historic structures of the city.

Constructed in 1843, the Wade House, located at 214 Tryon Palace, is a massive, three-story frame dwelling. When it was remodeled in the Second Empire style in the 1880s, the distinctive mansard roof was added.

Nearby at 219 Tryon Palace stands the Harvey Mansion, a three-story Federal-style edifice erected in 1798 as a residence and office for John Harvey, a prosperous ship owner and merchant. Of particular interest is the elegant Federal woodwork in the interior, considered the finest in the city. Slated for demolition, the imposing building was saved by the New Bern Renewal Commission. It has been meticulously restored as a popular restaurant.

After 1 block on Tryon Palace Drive, turn right, or north, onto Craven Street.

Located on the eastern side of the street at 220–226 Craven, the old city hall exhibits a turn-of-the-century front that masks the original 1817 facade.

Adjacent to the old city hall, the Isaac Taylor House, at 228 Craven, is the oldest brick side-hall-plan townhouse in the city. Built in 1792 for Isaac Taylor, an affluent merchant, planter, and ship owner, the tall structure has three full stories and an attic above a full basement.

After 1 block on Craven Street, turn left, or west, onto Pollock Street. Park in the 300 block of Pollock in the heart of downtown New Bern. Much of the old city can best be explored on foot. Many of the important structures are located within an 8-block area surrounding the current tour stop. Each historic building is identified with a plaque and the Historic New Bern sign. This special area is listed on the National Register of Historic Places as the New Bern Historic District.

Walk east on Pollock to the intersection with Craven. Located on the northwestern corner of the intersection at 300 Pollock, New Bern City Hall is one of the most unusual buildings in the city. This striking Romanesque Revival three-story brick structure was constructed between 1895 and 1897 to house the United States Post Office, Courthouse, and Custom House. Its distinctive clock tower dominates the Pollock Street landscape. This illuminated, four-sided clock tower was added in 1910.

Since 1936, the property has served as the municipal building for the city of New Bern.

Cast-metal black bears, gifts from Bern, Switzerland, guard each entrance to the building. New Bern shares this symbol with it sister city in Europe. Inside the building hangs a framed bear banner, a gift from the Swiss ambassador to the United States in 1896. Visitors will notice the bear on signs, flags, and plaques throughout the city.

A larger-than-life bust of Christophe DeGraffenried was dedicated on the lawn of city hall on April 9, 1989. Representatives from the Swiss and German governments and a descendent of DeGraffenried were in attendance when the monument was unveiled.

New Bern City Hall

Proceed east on Pollock Street. Constructed in 1845 as a brick Federal-style townhouse, the Hatch-Washington House, at 216 Pollock, now houses one of the city's historic restaurants.

Continue east to the intersection with East Front Street. Turn right on East Front and proceed a half-block south, where two impressive antebellum brick townhouses face each other. Located at 221 East Front, the Justice House was constructed in the Greek Revival style in 1843 for local merchant John Justice. Across the street, at 222 East Front, the three-story Sparrow House, built around 1840, is one of only seven brick side-hall houses surviving in the city.

Return to the intersection of East Front and Pollock streets. Walk west on Pollock. The Benjamin Ellis House, at 215 Pollock, has an unusual architectural history. This large, two-story frame dwelling was built in 1845. In 1900, it was cut in half and widened to its present six-bay form. It now serves as a bed-and-breakfast inn.

Cross Craven Street and continue west on Pollock. Located at 323 Pollock, the tall, heavily ornamented Baxter Clock has graced the downtown streets of New Bern since 1920. Believed to be one of only three of its kind still operating in the nation, this four-sided clock was built by Seth Thomas.

A state historical marker near the intersection of Pollock and Middle streets honors Caleb D. Bradham, one of the favorite sons of New Bern. For Americans who are curious as to why Pepsi-Cola advertises its products as the "Pride of the Carolinas," the answer is found at the southeastern corner of Pollock and Middle. A small plaque attached to the outside wall of the corner jewelry store announces to the world that Pepsi-Cola was invented at this very spot.

Caleb D. Bradham acquired the nickname "Doc" because of his ability to fashion remedies in the basement of his pharmacy in downtown New Bern around the turn of the century.

Doc Bradham formulated a soft drink for his customers and began selling it at his soda fountain. His concoction, dubbed "Brad's Drink," was a hit with patrons. Inspired by the local success of his beverage and the growing acceptance of Coca-Cola, Bradham envisioned a larger market for his soft drink. Dissatisfied with its name, he spent a hundred dollars to acquire a registered brand name, Pep Kola, from a New Jersey company. To make his drink more marketable, he modified the name to Pepsi-Cola.

Unfortunately, after launching the enterprise, Bradham was ruined by the collapse of the sugar market following World War I. He had invested heavily in sugar when fears of a shortage had driven up the price. When the price of sugar plummeted, Bradham's company was forced into bankruptcy.

Pepsi-Cola was saved from extinction by a New York company that acquired the rights to the drink and by a few distributors who had hoarded barrels of Pepsi at the time it became apparent that Bradham was going under. Doc Bradham died in 1935 without ever receiving the financial windfall his concoction produced. By that time, Pepsi-Cola was a national brand and a household name.

Continue along Pollock Street. At 320 Pollock, in the heart of the historic commercial district between Craven and Middle streets, Christ Episcopal Church is the first of the magnificent church buildings on this tour. This late Gothic Revival edifice, built around 1875, was constructed over the shell of the previous building, built in 1824.

Christ Church traces its roots to the parish formed here in 1741. Portions of the original church, King's Chapel, built in 1750, are preserved on the grounds. Some of the oldest graves in the city are located around the church.

Open to the public on weekdays, the church holds rare treasures inside. Eight years before his death in 1760, King George II of England gave Christ Church a silver communion service, said to be America's oldest. Created by royal decree, each piece of the service bears the royal arms of Great Britain.

In addition to the service, the church also owns a Bible and a *Book of Common Prayer*, both gifts from King George II.

That the unique silver service has survived to this day is something of a miracle. When Royal Governor Josiah Martin hastily fled New Bern in 1775, he tried unsuccessfully to take the property of the church with him. After protecting the royal gift through the Revolutionary War and the War of 1812, the church almost lost it during the Civil War, despite precautions against plunder. The Reverend A. A. Waters, rector of the church, delivered the set to Wilmington for safekeeping during the conflict. From there, it was transported inland to Fayetteville, where it was placed in the care of Dr. Joseph Huske. Marauding Federal troops subsequently ransacked Dr. Huske's home, but they failed to discover the service, hidden under a pile of rubbish in a closet. Following the war, the service was returned to New Bern.

At the intersection of Pollock and Middle, turn north on Middle. Located at 317 Middle, in the middle of the first block, the Bank of the Arts is housed in an impressive Neoclassical Revival granite building constructed in 1913 for use by Peoples Bank. Now home to the Craven Arts Council, the building features a two-story public gallery with exhibits that change monthly.

Return to the intersection of Middle and Pollock and continue south on Middle for half a block to First Baptist Church. This dignified Gothic Revival structure is the second building constructed by the church, which was organized in 1809. Thomas and Son of New York designed the existing sanctuary. Since the church's completion in 1848, a number of notable ministers have served here. William Hooper, founder of Wake Forest University, and Samuel Wait, the first president of that institution, were two of them. Thomas Meredith and Richard Furman, the men for whom Meredith College and Furman University were named, also pastored the church.

Walk back to the intersection of Middle and Pollock. Turn west on Pollock and proceed to the intersection with Hancock. Now serving as the office for the Neuse River Council of Governments, the Edward R. Stanly House, at 502 Pollock Street, was constructed in 1850 by a wealthy local manufacturer. Of particular interest on the exterior of the two-story, brick Greek Revival structure are the cast-iron window gables, the only such gables in the city.

Turn left and proceed south on Hancock Street. Two noteworthy eighteenth-century homes are located in the 200 block.

At 213 Hancock, the Patrick Gordon House was begun in the 1760s and completed a decade later. This frame Georgian dwelling with Federal elements is one of two pre–Revolutionary War gambrel-roofed houses in New Bern.

Also displaying a mixture of Georgian and Federal elements, the Benjamin Smith House, at 210 Hancock, is a splendid brick townhouse built in 1790. It was once owned by Governor Benjamin Smith, the namesake of Smithville (now Southport) and Smith Island (Bald Head Island). Because of its spectacular view of the river, the tall structure was used by troops from both armies during the Civil War.

Return to the intersection of Hancock and Pollock. Turn west on Pollock and proceed to its intersection with Metcalf. Constructed in 1801, the Bryan House, at 603–605 Pollock, is a stately brick townhouse with exquisitely carved ornamentation. The adjoining frame office was completed in 1820 by John Heritage Bryan, a United States congressman.

Located on the northern side of Pollock opposite the Bryan House, the New Bern Civil War Museum displays one of the most comprehensive private collections of Civil War memorabilia in the nation. Among the holdings are an assortment of weapons, accouterments, uniforms, and camp furniture. Built to preserve the Civil War heritage of New Bern, the museum opened in the spring of 1990.

In the midst of the tree-shaded residences in the 600 block of Pollock Street, visitors are overwhelmed by the visual grandeur that seems to rise from the Trent River, for here is the crowning glory of the city: the Tryon Palace restoration.

Thanks to the generosity of many history-minded North Carolinians, this structure, an exact replica of the palace known as the finest government house in the colonies, claims the honor as the major tourist attraction of New Bern. Since the Tryon Palace restoration officially opened to the public on April 8, 1959, its popularity has grown annually. Now, more than seventy-five thousand people a year tour the palace.

A tour of Tryon Palace begins at the visitor center, where a short audiovisual orientation program is offered in the auditorium. The visitor center is located on the northern side of Pollock Street just across from the palace.

Mighty oaks with limbs arching over a cobblestone drive grace the entrance to the palace. Costumed guides greet visitors as they enter the main building. As they walk over the marble floors of the entrance hall or ascend the wide staircase of mahogany and pegged walnut, guests marvel at the intricate workmanship in this restoration, which has, ironically, stood longer than the original palace.

The story behind the short existence of the original is fascinating. William Tryon, the newly appointed lieutenant governor of North Carolina, arrived in the colony on October 10, 1764, buoyed by assurances from London that Arthur Dobbs, the aged royal governor, was ready to relinquish his job in favor of his native Ireland. Tryon called on Dobbs at his home at Brunswick Town, where, much to Tryon's chagrin, the governor was in good health and spirits. He had apparently fully recovered from a stroke suffered two years earlier, just after the seventy-four-year-old chief executive had married fifteen-year-old Justina Davis.

A year later, the thirty-five-year-old Tryon was en route to New Bern from Wilmington when his servant caught up with him bearing news that Governor Dobbs had died in the arms of his youthful wife. After officially assuming Dobbs's position the following day, Tryon penned a letter to the Board of Trade in London with news of his predecessor's death and his choice of New Bern as the site for the colonial capital.

When the colonial assembly convened at New Bern on November 8, 1765, Governor Tryon presented his request for an appropriation with which to construct a public edifice. This structure would serve as the house of colonial government as well as the governor's residence. On December 1, the assembly overwhelmingly passed legislation providing seventy-five thousand dollars to purchase the land and to construct the necessary buildings.

Tryon had begun plans for his grand building even before he sailed from England. To guarantee that his future government house would be of the highest quality, he had persuaded John Hawks, a talented architect, to travel with him to North Carolina.

A strong hurricane ravaged New Bern in September 1769, destroying two-thirds of the buildings in the city, but Tryon's luxurious masterpiece, which was in the final stages of construction, survived.

A gala was held on December 5, 1770, to celebrate the official opening. Cannon at Union Point fired salutes, music filled the air, and fireworks lit the night sky. For the first time in America, a colonial governor lived in and ran the government from the same building.

Tryon and his family enjoyed the palace less than a year, as he received a rather sudden appointment to the governorship of New York. Given the volatile state of affairs in North Carolina, Tryon was glad to leave.

His successor in North Carolina, Josiah Martin, arrived in New Bern to a hero's welcome on August 11, 1771. Martin was accompanied by his wife and six children. For the next four years, Governor Martin spent much of his time lavishly furnishing the palace, aloof to the momentous events occurring in North Carolina and the other colonies. By the last day of May 1775, Martin found his position tenuous at best, so he and his family fled the town in a coach bound for the Cape Fear region.

After Martin abandoned the palace, it fell into disrepair. But when Richard Caswell, the first governor of the state of North Carolina, took his oath on January 16, 1777, he obtained legislative authority to restore the palace buildings and grounds.

Abner Nash, a Craven County resident living across the Trent River from

New Bern, succeeded Caswell as governor in 1780. His occupancy of the palace was short, due to the threat of enemy invasion during the last years of the Revolutionary War. To sustain the war effort, much of the eight tons of lead used in the construction of the palace was stripped away, to be melted into musket balls.

The victorious conclusion of the Revolutionary War did not signal brighter days for the palace. Ultimately, intruders stripped the once-grand lady of carpets, locks, and panels of glass. Vagrants sought shelter where the affairs of the colony and the state had once been administered. A bayonet fight among drunks left one of their number dead on the kitchen floor.

Governor Richard Dobbs Spaight, who had earlier owned several of the lots on which the structure was erected, took his oath of office in the palace in December 1792. After the legislature held a final session in New Bern in 1794, the building's days were numbered.

For the next four years, New Bern Academy held classes in the council chambers, its schoolmaster residing on the second floor. On the night of February 27, 1798, he sent a young servant to search for eggs in the hay cellar. While on her mission, the servant accidentally set the hay on fire with her torch. Church bells tolled throughout the wee hours of the morning, summoning volunteers to fight the fire. In haste, a hole was cut through the grand staircase to the outside. Flames engulfed the main building. Ashes and smoldering ruins were all that remained of the historic structure the following morning, though the firefighters did manage to save the outbuildings.

Over the next 150 years, the surviving western wing bore little resemblance to the dignified government building that it once represented.

In the 1930s, Governor Gregg Cherry created the twenty-five-member Tryon Palace Commission in response to mounting interest in a possible restoration project. A legislative appropriation of $287,000 allowed the commission to purchase the lots in the original Palace Square, which by that time was covered with fifty-four deteriorating houses slated for demolition.

Were it not for the hard work, dedicated leadership, and philanthropy of the commission chairperson, Maude Moore Latham, the palace would most likely never have been rebuilt. Latham, a New Bern native who had played in the ruins of the palace as a child, established a living trust of $225,000 and bequeathed another $1,116,000 for the restoration she did not live to see completed. She also acquired $125,000 in antiques to partially furnish the new palace. Her daughter, Mrs. John A. Kellenberger, succeeded her as chairperson and steered the project to a successful completion.

William G. Perry, a noted architect from the Boston firm that restored Colonial Williamsburg, began his work in New Bern in 1951. He had the benefit of original copies of the palace drawings by John Hawks. Construction on the restoration commenced in 1953 after years of planning.

Today, virtually every nook and cranny of the palace is visible on the tour. In addition to the two main stories, the tour includes the large attic and cellar. Extreme care was taken in the $3.5-million restoration project to make the entire forty-room structure appear as close to the original as possible.

More than $5 million in period antiques adds to the elegance of the palace interior. Aided by an inventory of William Tryon's original furnishings, the commission has assembled some seven thousand art objects and pieces of furniture to reflect the atmosphere of the palace during the tenure of the royal governor.

On one side of the main building, the eastern wing has been meticulously restored as the kitchen. On the other side, the western wing, with 85 percent of its original brickwork remaining, is the only part of the structure that has survived since 1770. It has been restored as a stable, carriage house, and granary. Among the support buildings around the palace are a smokehouse, a greenhouse, and a crafts demonstration shed. A garden shop adjacent to the eastern wing sells plants to the public.

Not to be missed are the beautifully landscaped grounds and gardens overlooking the river. Most prominent among the half-dozen or so gardens is the Maude Moore Latham Garden. This formal garden of clipped dwarf yaupon in geometric patterns typifies the English garden of Governor Tryon's time. Other nearby flower gardens are ablaze with tulips in the spring and chrysanthemums in the autumn.

Five other houses have been restored as part of the complex.

Located on the eastern front side of the palace, at 609 Pollock Street, the Stevenson House is open to the public. Portions of the two-and-a-half-story, gable-roofed, side-hall dwelling date from 1805. It was constructed on one

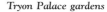

of the original palace lots by a wealthy sea captain. On the inside, visitors are treated to original hand-carved woodwork and rare antiques of the Empire and Federal periods.

Just across the street, at the corner of Pollock and George streets, stands the Commission House (Lehman-Duffy House). Not open to the public, this two-story Italianate-style dwelling was constructed in 1886 on the frame of an earlier home. It now houses the administrative offices of the restoration complex.

From the Commission House, turn right and proceed north to 307 George Street to visit the John Wright Stanly House, the second of the complex's houses open to the public for tours. Built between 1779 and 1783, this massive, two-story frame mansion is considered one of the most elegant late Georgian houses in America. To the rear of the house is the unique, formal Town House Parterre garden, which was a favorite of First Lady Pat Nixon.

Rear of the John Wright Stanly House

Architecture experts have deemed the sumptuous interior of the John Wright Stanly House the most sophisticated in New Bern, save the interior of the palace itself. The antique woodwork, especially the Chippendale staircase, is eye-catching. Historians believe that many of the craftsmen who worked at the original palace also labored at the Stanly mansion.

Not only is the existing structure fascinating, but so, too, are the stories of the Stanly family and the visitors to the house in the late eighteenth century. John Wright Stanly, the man for whom the house was built, was one of America's foremost patriots during the Revolutionary War. Ironically, Stanly traced his lineage to the throne of King Edward I of England. Inscribed upon the Stanly family's coat of arms were words meaning "always loyal."

Stanly settled in New Bern in the early 1770s, after a treacherous storm in the Graveyard of the Atlantic forced him ashore on the North Carolina coast. In the years leading up to the Revolutionary War, Stanly used his business acumen to achieve great success as a shipping magnate. Guided by his longstanding rebellious attitude toward England, Stanly used fifteen of his ships to form a personal privateer fleet, which raided and even did combat with English ships throughout the war.

As one of the most prominent financiers of the American Revolution, he became a marked man, living in constant danger. On Sunday, August 20, 1781, his life was spared only because he was out of town when the enemy came calling. Though Stanly was not harmed physically, his ships, wharves, and home were torched.

In the postwar years, Stanly called on his friend and fellow church member John Hawks to design a mansion to meet the needs of his growing family. Completed at a cost of thirty thousand dollars, the structure was the home of Mr. and Mrs. Stanly until they died of yellow fever within a month of each other in 1789.

Thereafter, the Stanly descendants entertained many famous guests in the home. On his Southern tour in 1791, President George Washington spent two nights in New Bern at the mansion. He described it as "exceedingly good lodgings." A state historical marker on Pollock Street just around the corner from the house notes Washington's visit. General Nathanael Greene and the Marquis de Lafayette also enjoyed the hospitality of the Stanly home.

One of John Wright Stanly's sons, also named John, was a brilliant attorney and a United States congressman who became embroiled in a bitter dispute with Richard Dobbs Spaight, the former governor of North Carolina, over a Senate election in 1802. A duel between the two politicians ensued, resulting in the death of Spaight. Ironically, when descendants of

TOURING THE BACKROADS OF NORTH CAROLINA'S LOWER COAST

the Spaight family moved into the Stanly house in the latter part of the nineteenth century, neighbors reported seeing ghosts in and about the mansion. Stanly County, North Carolina, was named in honor of John Stanly.

Confederate general Lewis Addison Armistead, the grandson of John Stanly and the great-grandson of John Wright Stanly, was born in the house in 1817. Armistead was killed on July 3, 1863, while leading a portion of Pickett's Charge at Gettysburg. Ironically, Union general Ambrose Burnside chose the Stanly mansion as his first headquarters during the occupation of New Bern during the Civil War. It was subsequently used as a hospital for Union troops.

From time to time, the Stanly descendants lend family heirlooms— including fine portraits of John Wright and Ann Stanly, household items used by George Washington when he was a house guest, and the dueling pistol that killed Governor Spaight—for display at the house.

Although it now stands a few hundred yards north of the palace, the Stanly mansion was erected on New Street between Middle and Hancock streets. Around 1935, it was moved to the present location, where it was restored for use as the public library. It was given to the Tryon Palace Commission in 1966.

Return to the intersection of George and Pollock streets. On the western front side of the palace stands the McKinlay-Daves-Duffy House, at 613 Pollock. Built around 1813, this home is owned by the commission but is not open to the public. The two-story, frame, side-hall-plan house was constructed in the Federal style. It was moved to its present site in the late 1950s so the palace gardens could be developed.

Cross Eden Street, the circular drive around the palace, to the 700 block of Pollock. Located at the corner of Pollock and Eden, the two-story, frame Jones House, built around 1808, houses the palace's gift shop. Emeline Pigott, a Confederate spy and heroine of coastal North Carolina, was imprisoned in this house during the Civil War.

Jones House

Continue west on Pollock, away from the restoration complex. Three Georgian-style houses—the John Chadwick House at 712 Pollock, the John Horner Hill House at 713 Pollock, and the Green-Wade House at 726 Pollock—date from 1770 to 1795.

Located at 717 Pollock, the Carruthers-Forbes House features a 1760 cottage

The Anne Greene Lane House

that became the attached wing of a two-and-a-half-story side-hall dwelling built in 1810.

Cross Bern Street to the 800 block of Pollock. At least a half-dozen Federal-style houses of note are located here: the Nathan Tisdale House at 803 Pollock, built around 1800; the Anne Greene Lane House at 804 Pollock, built around 1805; the Osgood Cottage at 807 Pollock, built around 1820; the Bryan Jones House at 812 Pollock, built around 1830; the Elizabeth Thomas House (Silas Statham House) at 816 Pollock, built around 1810; and the John H. Jones House at 819 Pollock, built around 1810.

Three other structures in the 800 block are of architectural significance. The Pendleton House at 815 Pollock, built around 1800, and the Alston-Charlotte House at 823 Pollock, built before 1770, are gambrel-roofed dwellings. Located at 809 Pollock, All Saints Chapel serves as the arts-and-crafts store of the New Bern Historical Society. Constructed in 1895 as a mission chapel of Christ Episcopal Church, the handsome, frame Gothic Revival structure was deconsecrated in the late 1930s.

Return east to the intersection of Pollock and Bern. Turn left and walk north on Bern. Located at 300 Bern, the Thomas Cottage represents an outstanding example of the efforts of New Bern citizens to restore their past. This handsome, frame story-and-a-half Federal cottage was constructed in the early nineteenth century. Its restoration in the late 1970s preserved most of its rich architectural detail.

Continue on Bern Street to the intersection with Broad Street. Turn right and proceed 1 block east on Broad to its intersection with George Street. A state historical marker for Tryon Palace stands at this corner. Located near the marker at 701 Broad, the Joseph L. Rhem House is an elegant Greek Revival and Italianate mansion built around 1855 by the owner of a turpentine distillery. Its present Colonial Revival appearance is the result of a remodeling project in the first quarter of the twentieth century.

Cross George Street and continue east on Broad. Located on a shaded lot at 613 Broad, the William Hollister House is an impressive two-and-a-half-story structure built in 1840. A widow's walk adorns the roof of this dwelling, which combines the Federal and Greek Revival styles.

Cross Metcalf and continue on Broad. Three significant structures are found on this block.

Located at 515 Broad, the Attmore-Wadsworth House is an unusual structure built around 1850 as a combination office and residence. Subsequent additions to the sprawling one-story building have given it a combination of late Greek Revival, Italianate, and Colonial Revival details.

The Attmore-Oliver House

Next door at 513 Broad stands the Attmore-Oliver House, now the home of the Attmore-Oliver House Museum and the New Bern Historical Society. Constructed in 1790 and enlarged in 1834, the stately building features two different facades. Its Broad Street front exhibits exquisite Greek Revival ornamentation, while the rear facade features two-story porches of the late Federal period. Inside, the museum offers antiques of the eighteenth and nineteenth centuries and Civil War artifacts. A state historical marker near the museum chronicles the duel between Governor Spaight and Congressman Stanly.

Located on the northern side of the street at 518 Broad, the two-story Ulysses S. Mace House is one of the finest Italianate structures in the city. It was constructed in 1884 by a local pharmacist.

Walk east on Broad to the intersection with Hancock. Turn left on Hancock and proceed north half a block to the New Bern Firemen's Museum, at 410 Hancock.

More often than not, historic gems are hidden in old cities, waiting for discovery. Housed in an old, one-story building behind New Bern's main fire station, this museum is one such hidden treasure. It was opened to the public in 1957 by the two oldest continuously operating fire companies in the United States: the Atlantic Company, organized in 1845, and the Button Company, organized twenty years later. In 1900, the latter company set two world firefighting records for the production of steam. These records have never been broken.

The New Bern Firemen's Museum

Visitors to the museum enjoy an interesting, unique collection of antique fire engines and other firefighting equipment. Without question, the most sentimental exhibit is that of Fred, the most beloved firefighter in New Bern history. Fred joined the Atlantic Company in 1908 in the days before New Bern had motorized fire engines. This amazing horse was assigned to duty pulling a hose wagon, and he quickly became an invaluable member of the company. As soon as the fire alarm sounded, Fred backed into the wagon stall so his harness could quickly be dropped over his head. Firemen took pride in the special horse that always tried to get to his hose as soon as possible.

By 1915, New Bern obtained two motorized fire engines. Yet Fred's days of service were far from over. When the opportunity presented itself, the animal attempted to race the "horseless carriage" to a fire.

Fred again proved his mettle in 1922, when he was in the thick of the fight against the worst fire in the history of the town.

No matter when a call came, the horse always responded. He dropped dead in his harness in 1925 while answering an alarm from Box 57, at New Banks and North streets. His death in the line of duty proved to be a tragedy when it was discovered that the alarm was false.

To honor Fred's memory, the firemen of Atlantic Company decided to have his head mounted. It was displayed at the fire station until the museum opened. Since that time, it has been preserved and exhibited in a glass display case.

Return to the intersection of Hancock and Broad and turn east on Broad. Cross Middle Street and walk to the Craven County Courthouse, located on the northeastern corner of Broad and Craven streets.

The Craven County Courthouse is the largest Second Empire-style building in the city. Designed by Philadelphia architects Sloan and Balderson, the two-and-a-half-story brick structure was completed in 1883 as the county's fourth courthouse.

A large boulder on the courthouse lawn memorializes the three New Bernians who have served as governor of North Carolina.

On the street in the shadow of the stately courthouse stands a pair of state historical markers that boast of two of the "firsts" for which New Bern is famous. One sign commemorates the First Provincial Congress, held in open defiance of British orders. It convened in New Bern on August 25, 1774, with seventy-one delegates present. The other marker describes the first printing press in North Carolina. This press was set up near the site of the present courthouse in 1749 by James Davis, who published the first book, the first newspaper, and the first pamphlet in the colony.

Because of its significant historical and cultural achievements during the colonial period and the early days of statehood, New Bern acquired the soubriquet "Athens of North Carolina." Among the firsts claimed by this

river town are the following: New Bern was the first town in America to celebrate George Washington's birthday; it was the first town in North Carolina and the third in America, after Boston and Philadelphia, to celebrate Independence Day; it was the site of the first incorporated school in North Carolina and the second private secondary school in English America to receive a charter; it was the site of the first free school for white children and the first public school for blacks in North Carolina; it was North Carolina's first state capital; it was the site of the first inauguration of state officials; it was the site of the first meeting of the state legislature; it was the site of the first post office in North Carolina under the American republic; it was the site of the first public banking institution in the state; it was the site of the first bookstore in North Carolina; and it was the first town in North Carolina to decorate its streets with multicolored electric lights at Christmas.

When you have enjoyed the courthouse, return to your car by turning south off Broad onto Craven and walking to Pollock, where the walking tour started.

Drive north on Craven to its intersection with Broad. Turn right, or east, onto Broad. On the northern side of Broad near its intersection with East

Front stands the Sudan Shrine Temple, the sixteenth-largest Shrine temple in the nation.

Turn left, or north, off Broad onto East Front. Located on the waterfront near the bridge over the Neuse River are two state historical markers. One honors Christophe DeGraffenried, while the other details the Battle of New Bern.

At the outbreak of the Civil War, New Bern was recognized as an extremely significant port by both armies and by President Lincoln. Not only was the town the second-largest city on the North Carolina coast, but its east-west railroad was vital to the state's transportation network.

On March 11, 1862, a month after General Ambrose Burnside captured Roanoke Island, Lincoln and his advisers ordered Burnside to advance on New Bern with three brigades and supporting artillery. A fleet of Union warships and transports made its way down Pamlico Sound, reaching the Neuse River on March 12.

New Bern was defended by four thousand Confederate troops under the skillful command of a native North Carolinian, Brigadier General Lawrence O. Branch. A graduate of Princeton and a former United States congressman, Branch knew that his forces were outnumbered more than three to one.

On March 14, General Burnside led Union naval and marine forces in one of the first combined amphibious assaults in United States history. Hordes of his troops stormed ashore at New Bern. Once the landing was accomplished, the Union troops battled the defenders from seven-thirty that morning until noon, when General Branch ordered his army to retreat.

Fighting valiantly side by side for the Confederates during the fall of New Bern were two young North Carolina colonels whose names would become well known to all New Bernians as the war progressed. Colonel Zebulon B. Vance would be elected governor of North Carolina later that same year, and Lieutenant Colonel Robert F. Hoke, later a general, would return to the city on several occasions in an attempt to liberate it from Union occupation.

Despite the nearly impregnable defense system of ten forts, a cavalry camp, and two blockhouses subsequently set up around the town by the Union occupation forces, the Confederates were anxious to retake New Bern. Expeditions led by Major General Daniel Harvey Hill and Major General

George Pickett in March 1863 and January 1864 failed miserably. However, after his impressive victory at Plymouth in mid-April 1864, Major General Robert F. Hoke laid siege to, and demanded the surrender of, New Bern on May 4. But before he could retake the town, Hoke and his troops were ordered to Virginia, where Lee was being challenged near Petersburg.

The restored cannon on the waterfront walkway near the historical markers is not of Civil War vintage. Rather, it was unearthed in the center of town in the 1920s and is believed to be one of the original cannon from Tryon Palace.

In 1962, President John F. Kennedy visited the area to commemorate the hundredth anniversary of one of the nation's military firsts, the combined amphibious assault on New Bern.

Continue north on East Front Street to its intersection with New Street. This site along the waterfront is known as Council Bluff. It was here that DeGraffenried and his settlers landed in 1710.

Across the street from the waterfront, at 501 East Front, is the Coor-Bishop House. This lavish Georgian mansion, remodeled in the Colonial Revival style, was built between 1770 and 1778 by James Coor, a local real-estate speculator. George Pollock, a subsequent owner and one of the wealthiest men in the state, entertained President James Monroe and Secretary of War John C. Calhoun at the residence in 1819. When the house was remodeled in 1903, it was turned ninety degrees from its original orientation on New Street.

Turn left, or west, off East Front Street onto New Street. Located at 219 New, the Cox-Stewart House was built between 1785 and 1790 in the Georgian style. An addition in 1810 gave the two-story frame structure its Federal touches.

Continue west on New across Craven. Now used as the eastern office of the governor of North Carolina, the Coor-Gaston House, at the southwestern corner of New and Craven streets, was built in 1770 by Colonel James Coor, a prominent politician who served in the North Carolina General Assembly from 1777 to 1792. At the time of its construction, the house exhibited a feature unique among New Bern dwellings: double porches engaged beneath the main gabled roof.

In 1819, the elegant, two-story Georgian townhouse was purchased by

William Gaston, one of the truly great men of nineteenth-century North Carolina. Gaston served in the United States Congress and on the North Carolina Supreme Court. He also wrote the official state song, "The Old North State." Gaston County, North Carolina, bears his name.

Located at the southeastern corner of New and Middle streets one block west of the Coor-Gaston House, Centenary United Methodist Church was the first major church building constructed in the city in the twentieth century. Built in 1904, the appealing Romanesque Revival structure features several turrets, which give it a castlelike appearance.

When the monumental Federal Building was constructed at the southwestern corner of New and Middle streets in 1935, the three-story brick structure was deemed too large and extravagant for a city the size of New Bern. Murals in the courtroom detail important events in the history of the city.

Turn right, or north, off New onto Middle Street. St. Paul's Roman Catholic Church, at 510 Middle, is not only the oldest Catholic church in North Carolina, but also the home of the oldest Catholic congregation in the state. Erected in 1839, the tall, graceful frame edifice has been altered very little since that time. William Gaston, a devout Catholic, inspired the establishment of St. Paul's when he brought Bishop John England to New Bern in 1821 to celebrate the first Catholic mass in the city.

Located just across Middle Street, the Chester B'nai Sholom Synagogue has served as the principal house of worship for Jews in New Bern since 1908. Although it is unclear where they worshipped before this Neoclassical temple-style structure was constructed, there is evidence of a local Jewish community as early as 1824.

Adjacent to the temple, the McLin-Hancock House, built around 1810, is a Federal-style cottage known for its strict symmetry.

Proceed to the intersection of Middle and Johnson streets and turn left, or west, onto Johnson. After 1 block, turn left, or south, on Hancock.

Constructed between 1801 and 1809, St. John's Masonic Lodge and Theater, at 516 Hancock, features a second-floor lodge room with original Federal woodwork and walls painted with symbolic trompe l'oeil Masonic decorations. Presidents Washington and Monroe visited the lodge while in the city. Located on the first floor of the building, the Masonic Theater is the oldest theater in the United States still used for that purpose.

Nearby at 521 Hancock stands the Coor-Cook House, built by James Coor in 1790. This large, two-and-a-half-story frame structure was moved from Craven Street to its present location in 1981 to make room for the expansion of the county courthouse.

Drive to the intersection of Hancock and New streets and park in the parking lot on Hancock. Walk to the northern side of New Street to visit First Presbyterian Church, located at 412 New.

First Presbyterian Church

Of all of New Bern's architectural masterpieces, none, including Tryon Palace, is more awe-inspiring than First Presbyterian. Dignified by its tidy white exterior and tall frontal columns, the majestic wooden structure is considered one of the most beautiful religious edifices in all of America.

An interior like that of First Presbyterian can be found in only one other church in America: the Congregational Church of Litchfield, Connecticut. Both structures were built from plans drawn by Sir Christopher Wren, England's most famous church architect.

New Bern Presbyterians purchased the church site in 1819. Three years later, the building was completed under the supervision of architect Uriah Sandy.

One of the final matters to be attended to prior to the opening of the church was the sale and rental of pews. Depending upon their location, pews were sold to members for prices ranging from $350 for center seating to $150 for side pews. Members who could not afford to buy or rent pews were not denied seating. Instead, a few pews near the front, known as "Stranger's Pews," were free to all.

Since 1822, the exterior of the church has changed little. Visitors marvel at the classic architectural features embodied in the building: a pedimented Ionic portico, a fanlight above the central entrance, and a square tower diminishing in five stages to an octagonal cupola. On the interior, the sloping floor is an extraordinary feature for a structure of its time. A balcony encircles the entire sanctuary except for the raised "swallow's nest" pulpit.

Return to the parking lot and drive west on New Street to the New Bern Academy Museum, at 508 New.

When noted cartographer C. J. Sauthier drew his map of New Bern in 1769, he represented New Bern Academy as a small box on the outskirts of town. The academy was a wooden building erected in 1766 as a result of legislation in 1764 that authorized the incorporation of the first school in North Carolina. After the original school building burned, the academy moved to the vacant Tryon Palace in 1790. Eight years later, the academy was once again without a home when the palace was consumed by fire.

Funds for the existing two-story, cupola-topped Federal-style building came from a state-authorized lottery. The structure was completed in 1810. From the outset, the school enjoyed an excellent reputation. An early visitor from Rhode Island deemed it "one of the best regulated schools of its kind in America."

A second building, the Bell Building, was constructed nearby at 517 Hancock Street in 1884. Fourteen years later, the buildings were merged into the New Bern city school system. Central School, as the combined campus of the old academy and the Bell Building was known thereafter, operated until 1971.

In the fall of 1990, the New Bern Academy Museum opened as a major component of the Tryon Palace restoration. The building contains four large rooms, each filled with exhibits centered around four themes: the general history of New Bern, the architecture of the city, the Civil War in the city, and the history of education in New Bern.

Three houses of historic importance are located near the academy in the 500 block of New Street.

The Cutting-Allen House, at 518 New, was saved from demolition and moved to its present site in 1980. Constructed in 1793, this side-hall house with late Georgian and early Federal elements features a large rear ball-room.

Located next door at 520 New, the Palmer-Tisdale House was built in two sections. Its Georgian front section was constructed in 1767, and the rear section was added in 1800 for Judge John Louis Taylor, who later served as the first chief justice of the North Carolina Supreme Court.

Just across the street at the corner of New and Metcalf, the Hawks House dates from 1769. It was once the home of Francis Hawks, the local customs collector and the son of the architect of Tryon Palace.

Drive west 1 block on New Street and turn right, or north, onto George Street, which becomes National Avenue after 1 block.

Situated on a block bounded by National Avenue and Queen Street, the expansive Cedar Grove Cemetery was begun by Christ Episcopal Church as a response to a yellow-fever epidemic in 1798. Visitors are greeted at the cemetery entrance on Queen Street by a beautiful Roman triumphal arch made of coquina. A legend behind the arch holds that if water drips on a person entering through it, that person will soon die.

Many of the most famous citizens of New Bern, including William Gaston, are buried here. Among the many impressive monuments is the Confederate Monument, erected in 1885 atop the underground Confederate vault.

Continue north on National Avenue for 0.9 mile to New Bern National Cemetery.

In February 1867, the United States Congress authorized the development of this 7.5-acre cemetery on the outskirts of the city. Soon thereafter, the remains of approximately a thousand Union soldiers who died in New Bern of war wounds or yellow fever were moved to the new cemetery from Cedar Grove Cemetery. Four states—Vermont, Massachusetts, New Jersey, and Rhode Island—have erected monuments here to honor their Civil War dead.

One of the bodies reinterred in 1867 was that of Carrie E. Cutter, the only woman buried with the initial group of soldiers. Cutter came to New

New Bern National Cemetery

Bern in 1864 to administer to her fiancé, Charles E. Coolidge, a Union army private from Massachusetts who was suffering from yellow fever. After Coolidge succumbed, his weakened, heartsick girlfriend also fell prey to the disease and died shortly thereafter. Her dying wish was to be buried beside Private Coolidge.

The beautifully landscaped cemetery features one tree of particular interest. A giant redwood brought to New Bern from California just after the Civil War is said to be one of only three such trees on the entire Atlantic coast.

Retrace your route south on National Avenue to the intersection with Queen Street. Turn left and proceed east on Queen for 1 block, then turn right, or east, onto Johnson Street. Proceed 3 blocks to the 300 block, where four houses—the Captain Elijah Willis House at 311 Johnson, the Thomas Jerkins House at 309 Johnson, the John D. Flanner House at 305 Johnson, and the Jerkins-Duffy House at 301 Johnson—date from before 1855.

Continue to the next block. The Brinson House at 213 Johnson, built around 1770, and the Mitchell-Stevenson House at 211 Johnson, built around 1800, display the late Federal style.

Located at the southwestern corner of Johnson and East Front, the Charles Slover House is the oldest Greek Revival house in New Bern and one of the finest in the state. This elegant three-story brick mansion was erected in 1848 and has remained virtually unaltered since its construction. During the Civil War, General Ambrose Burnside used the house as his headquarters. It was purchased in 1908 by Caleb Bradham, the inventor of Pepsi-Cola.

Turn left, or north, on East Front. Located at 607 East Front is the birthplace and boyhood home of the famous Rains brothers. Both men, educated at West Point, were inventors and geniuses in the field of explosives. General James G. Rains invented the land mine and developed naval torpedoes for the Confederate war effort. His brother, Colonel George Washington Rains, was in charge of the procurement of gunpowder for the Confederacy. His powder mills produced 2,750,000 pounds of gunpowder during the war. Their early-nineteenth-century house was moved to its present site from Johnson Street in order to make room for an expansion of the public library.

Turn around and drive south on East Front Street. Built in 1810, the

Jones-Jarvis House at 528 East Front is nearly identical in appearance to the nearby Eli Smallwood House at 524 East Front, built around 1810. Both are among the finest brick Federal side-hall-plan houses in the city.

Constructed in 1885 in the Italianate style, the Samuel W. Smallwood House, at 520 East Front, is best known for the historic trees in its backyard on the Neuse River. A famous cypress tree believed to be between seven hundred and a thousand years old is one of the twenty trees in the Hall of Fame of American Trees. Legend holds that during the Revolutionary War, General Nathanael Greene met under this tree with local patriots to receive a pledge of substantial financial assistance. When he visited New Bern after the war, President Washington asked to see the tree where America's fortunes of war turned.

The Dawson-Clarke House, better known as the Louisiana House, is located at 519 East Front. This home is best known for its most famous resident, Mary Bayard Devereux Clarke (1827–1886). A North Carolina native, Clarke was one of the most famous poets in the state in the nineteenth century. She published a two-volume anthology of North Carolina poetry, *Wood-Notes*, in 1854. Clarke's two-story frame house, built in 1807, was so named because of her stay on a Louisiana plantation prior to the Civil War.

Gull Harbor, a two-and-a-half-story, frame Federal house, was constructed at 514 East Front in 1815. It stands on the site of the birthplace of Elizabeth Shine, the mother of Admiral David Farragut.

Continue south on East Front to its intersection with Tryon Palace Drive. Turn right, or west, onto Tryon Palace Drive and park at Bicentennial Park. The tour ends here, at this expansive park on the Trent River, with its scenic view of the modern New Bern waterfront.

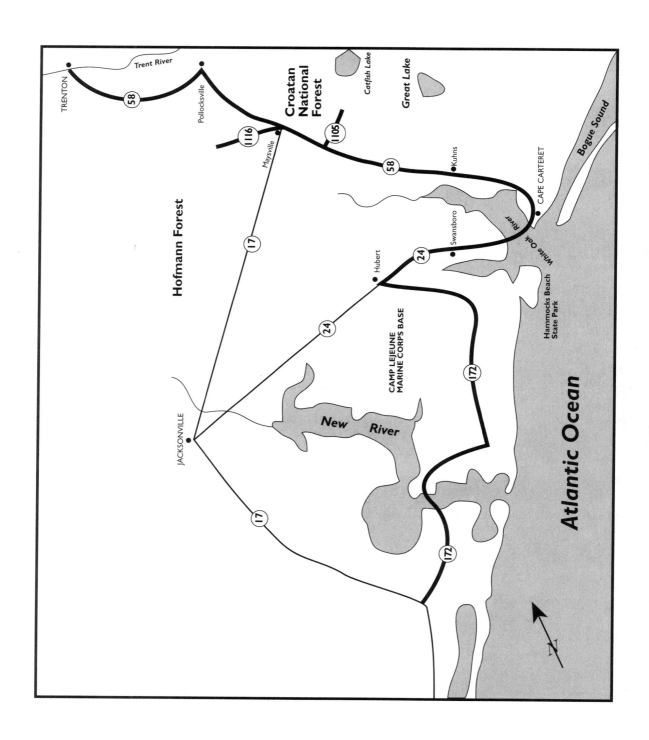

The Onslow Bay Tour

This tour begins in Trenton, the county seat of rural Jones County, and then visits the other two towns in the county, Pollocksville and Maysville. It passes through portions of Hofmann Forest and Croatan National Forest before traveling to the villages of Cape Carteret and Swansboro. Next comes a ferry ride to Hammocks Beach State Park, one of the least visited, but most intriguing, of North Carolina's state parks. The tour concludes with a visit to mighty Camp Lejeune.

Among the highlights of the tour are the riverside towns of Jones County, Croatan National Forest, stories from remote Catfish Lake, historic Swansboro, Hammocks Beach State Park, and Camp Lejeune.

Total mileage: approximately 79 miles.

This tour begins at the intersection of N.C. 58 and N.C. 41 in downtown Trenton, the county seat of Jones County.

Separated from the ocean by Onslow and Carteret counties, Jones County is one of the least-visited counties of coastal North Carolina. Most people who visit do so not by choice, but because their travels on U.S. 17 take them here.

Rural in nature, the county has been blessed with, and influenced by, two coastal rivers: the Trent and the White Oak. Not surprisingly, the three incorporated towns in the county are located near the rivers. A visit to these towns—Trenton, Pollocksville, and Maysville—provides an opportunity to see small tidewater settlements that have changed little over the past century.

Trenton, with a population of five hundred, is a delightful town on the banks of the Trent River. Despite the town's small size, an interesting historic district is to be found on the streets intersecting N.C. 58, the town's principal street. This district, listed on the National Register of Historic Places, offers a variety of architectural styles, including Federal, Gothic Revival, and East Lake.

To enjoy the handsome ensemble of century-old commercial buildings and graceful homes in Trenton, park near the intersection of N.C. 58 and

Jones County Courthouse

N.C. 41 and walk west on N.C. 58. The 4-block section stretching to the old high-school building at School Street contains a good selection of the town's old houses.

After you have enjoyed this 4-block stretch, return to the intersection of N.C. 58 and N.C. 41 and turn right, or south; N.C. 58 and N.C. 41 run conjuctively heading south.

Located on the eastern side of the street, the Jones County Courthouse dominates the first block south of the intersection. Built in 1939, the two-story, rectangular, brick Colonial Revival building is distinguished by its pilastered entrance pavilion and its three-stage polygonal cupola. For many years, this courthouse was one of the few in the state to provide office space for local attorneys.

Located behind the courthouse is an old jail that is believed to be the oldest brick building in town. It was constructed between 1867 and 1873.

One block south of the intersection, turn left on Lake View Avenue. It is 1 block on Lake View to the intersection with Weber Street. Here stands Grace Episcopal Church, a tiny, strikingly beautiful building constructed in 1885. The interior of the gray frame structure still features its original hand-hewn furnishings.

Return to your car and drive south on N.C. 58.

Although not incorporated until 1874, Trenton actually dates from the creation of the county in 1779. Initially known as Trent, the town was renamed Trenton in 1784. The source of the name is subject to dispute, as is the case with many places in coastal North Carolina. Some historians contend that the town was named for Trenton, New Jersey, but a more logical source is the nearby river.

Trenton enjoyed a degree of prominence in its early years, because of its location on the stagecoach road from New Bern to Wilmington. On April 22, 1791, President George Washington stopped at Trenton. The house where he dined vanished long ago.

It is 0.3 mile on N.C. 58 to Brock Mill Pond, the most eye-catching feature of Trenton. This magnificent elongated pond, rimmed by moss-draped cypress trees, serves as a recreational area for boaters and water-skiers. A gristmill has operated on the pond for more than two centuries. The existing mill dates to the 1940s.

Brock Mill

Slave labor was used to construct the dam that created Brock Mill Pond. Early Trenton residents built their homes around this majestic body of water.

Continue following N.C. 58 as it winds lazily for 10 miles through beautiful farmland to the intersection with U.S. 17 approximately 1 mile south of Pollocksville. Turn north on U.S. 17 and proceed to Pollocksville, a picturesque town on the banks of the Trent River.

Considered the most beautiful river in America by its admirers, the Trent is unlike most other coastal rivers in North Carolina in that its banks are high above the water and are thus suitable for development. Accordingly, a number of old houses are visible along the riverbanks of Pollocksville.

The municipal dock in the heart of town affords a spectacular view of the black river. From Pollocksville, the Trent flows southeast to its confluence with the Neuse River in New Bern. In 1709, the intrepid explorer John Lawson gave the Trent its name, most likely for the river of the same name in England.

Brock Mill Pond

Pollocksville is believed to be the oldest town in Jones County. As early as 1779, there was a settlement here called Trent Bridge, and before 1828, a post office by that name was established. Long before U.S. 17 was conceived, the river served as the town's avenue of commerce. A steamboat landing was located on the river before the Civil War.

Turn around and head south on U.S. 17 leaving Pollocksville. It is approximately 7 miles to the junction with N.C. 58 in Maysville, the largest town in Jones County. Situated near the banks of the beautiful White Oak River, the town has maintained a population of approximately a thousand for more than half a century.

Younger than either Trenton or Pollocksville, Maysville grew from a settlement known as Cross Point in 1829. When the Atlantic Coast Line Railroad reached the sleepy village in 1892, its economy received a welcome boost. Five years later, the town of Maysville was incorporated.

Because it is located adjacent to Croatan National Forest and Hofmann Forest, Maysville serves as an area hunting center. Guides for bear and deer hunting are available at Maysville, Trenton, and Pollocksville.

If you are interested in taking a side trip, turn west off U.S. 17 onto S.R. 1116 in Maysville. It is 9.2 miles to Hofmann Forest, located in an area of pocosins commonly associated with the Carolina bays. (For more information on Carolina bays, see The Land of Waccamaw Tour, page 328–30.)

Covering some seventy-eight thousand acres in Jones and Onslow counties, the northern half of the forest lies in the southern midsection of Jones County. The forest bears the name of Dr. Julius V. Hofmann (1882–1965), the first person to earn a Ph.D. in forestry in the United States. Hofmann established the School of Forestry at North Carolina State University. Today, the university uses a portion of the forest for research and instruction in forestry management.

Two particular areas of the forest are of special note. Ancient trees towering seventy-five feet or more thrive in the Pond Pine Area, while cypress trees, some of which are six to seven feet in diameter, thrive in the twenty-seven-acre Cypress Natural Area.

Approximately thirty thousand acres of the forest, managed by the North Carolina Wildlife Resources Commission, have been set aside as a game area. The hunting of fox, deer, and bear is regulated. Hiking in the forest is permitted. The fire roads throughout the forest make excellent hiking routes.

Retrace your route to the junction of U.S. 17 and N.C. 58 in Maysville to complete the side trip.

Leaving Maysville, turn southeast off U.S. 17 onto N.C. 58 as the road enters Croatan National Forest. After 2.6 miles, N.C. 58 intersects S.R. 1105.

Turn east on S.R. 1105 and proceed into the heart of the forest for 6.2 miles to the Craven County line. Note that the road is unpaved for the last 4 miles of the drive. Along this route, you will enjoy a spectacular view of the magnificent forest.

Lying between the Neuse and White Oak rivers, Croatan National Forest is a national treasure that sprawls over 308,234 acres in Jones, Craven, and Carteret counties. Within its boundaries is one of the most extensive pocosins in the state. Highly productive forestland covers the other half of the national forest. Blended within these two natural habitats are the associated swampland and numerous Carolina bays.

Congress passed the Weeks Act in 1911, which authorized the acquisition of the forest. The actual purchase did not occur until 1933, in response to the economic woes of the Great Depression. The tract was to be used for scientific experiments leading to the restoration of cutover and burned forestland. Its name came from the Algonquin word for the Indians' "council town," which was located nearby. Many famous men, including Babe Ruth, have hunted in Croatan National Forest.

Recreational opportunities are provided for the public at three primary sites. Most visitors use the Neuse River Recreation Area, located on U.S. 70 just west of Morehead City. That site offers boating and fishing on a scenic 1-mile stretch of primitive river beach. Camping is also permitted at the site. The other primary access sites—Haywood Landing and Cedar Point Tideland Trail—will be discussed later in this tour.

Of the 157,000 acres of the forest owned by the federal government, 90,000 are pocosin. Most of the remaining acreage is timberland of cypress, oak, gum, and pine. Numerous insectivorous plants are found throughout the forest.

Wildlife abounds in the vast wilderness. Since the forest is managed as a game land, hunters must comply with all local, state, and federal game laws. At least seventy-eight species of reptiles and amphibians thrive here. One of the largest populations of American alligators in the state is found around the bay lakes of the forest. The forest's location along the Atlantic flyway also makes it a habitat for seasonal waterfowl. Egrets, hawks, owls, bald eagles, ospreys, and red-cockaded woodpeckers are permanent residents.

Sadly, the forest is one of the last domains of the eastern black bear, once prevalent all across the coastal plain but now almost hunted to extinction.

In 1982, the black-bear population was estimated to be between 750 and 1,000 in the entire state. Some authorities believe the black bear will become extinct before the turn of the century.

Within the pocosin area of the forest are five enormous Carolina Bay lakes. The largest among them is the 2,600-acre Great Lake. Though this lake measures 2.5 miles by 3.5 miles, it has a maximum depth of only five feet. The other lakes in the forest are also extremely shallow. Most are not noted for their fishing, although 106 species of fish have been recorded. The lakes are known for their large populations of snakes and alligators, some measuring fourteen feet long. These lakes lie in a remote, forbidding wilderness area virtually inaccessible to humans.

When you reach the Craven County line, you will be about as close as it is possible to get by improved road to one of the most significant of these lakes. Every year, thousands of tourists visit Croatan National Forest without knowing of the existence of the thousand-acre lake less than 2 miles due north of where S.R. 1105 hits the Craven County line. Despite its rather unsophisticated name, Catfish Lake provides a natural wilderness setting that is unequaled anywhere along the coast. In fact, it is considered to be among the wildest, most mysterious places in all of North Carolina.

Few people have ever seen Catfish Lake, because it is completely encircled by a peat-filled pocosin that makes road building to the lakeshore here virtually impossible. Near the current tour stop, a forest service road makes its way close to the lake. Throughout much of the year, even foot travel over the pocosin causes the surface of the earth to tremble for several yards in all directions. To further complicate matters, the junglelike undergrowth surrounding the lake makes a hike to this eerie place impossible except in late autumn and early winter, when the underbrush has died off and the ground is dry.

In addition to the hazardous terrain, any attempt to walk to the lake is fraught with danger because of the heavy population of wildlife: poisonous snakes and spiders, wild boar, bears, alligators, and wildcats. Any person desiring to visit should first hire an experienced guide who is thoroughly familiar with the lake and its surroundings.

As there are no well-marked trails leading to the lake, numerous experienced outdoorsmen have been hopelessly lost in the surrounding wilderness.

In the 1930s, a timber estimator entered the forest in the vicinity of Catfish Lake and never returned. Four years later, while constructing a fire road, forest-service workers unearthed a human skeleton believed to be that of the unfortunate man.

The source of the lake's waters has never been discovered.

The lake's name is derived from the bounteous catfish thriving in its waters. A number of legends and stories have evolved concerning the fish in the lake.

It is said that a young Confederate soldier found his way into the lake wilderness after he deserted his company near Maysville. Some years later, a group of hunters found his skeleton near a rotting camp on the lakeshore. A stack of catfish bones large enough to fill a two-horse wagon was located at the camp. Apparently, the deserter had lived near the lake and fed himself with its bounty.

Folks in Maysville tell another tale about the unbelievable quantity of catfish in the lake. According to the story, a group of fishermen entered the lake with a goal of determining whether it was actually filled with fish. Arriving late in the afternoon in order to set their lines before dark, the men were delighted as they took boatload after boatload of fish and deposited them on the banks. As midnight approached, the fishermen, blessed with an enormous pile of catfish, decided to call it quits. To their chagrin, as they attempted to divide their catch among their sacks, they were surrounded by countless pairs of horrifying green eyes glowing in the light of their lanterns. These eyes belonged to dozens of ravenous wildcats attracted to the banks by the smell of the fish. The fishermen had little choice but to toss a portion of their catch to the animals to satisfy their appetite.

As the wildcats fought over the catfish, screaming fiercely, the fishermen gathered as many fish as they could hold and made a run for it. Throwing fish to the pursuing wildcats, they exhausted their supply by the time they finally reached the road and safety.

Retrace your route on S.R. 1105 from the county line back to N.C. 58. Turn south on N.C. 58 and drive 5.3 miles to the first national-forest road leading west. Turn west onto this road for a pleasant 2.2-mile drive under a canopy of towering trees to Haywood Landing, one of Croatan National Forest's recreational sites.

Located on the banks of the White Oak River, this landing provides a delightful spot for fishing, boating, and picnicking. It is also the best place to sample the natural splendor of the White Oak River.

Few rivers in all of North Carolina can compare in beauty with the White Oak. Rising in the black, peaty soil of southern Jones County and northern Onslow County, the river slowly winds for 20 snakelike miles along the Jones County–Onslow County line and the Carteret County–Onslow County line until it empties into the Atlantic through Bogue Inlet. On John Lawson's map of 1709, the river appeared as the Weetock, while on the Moseley map of 1733, it was shown as the Weitock. By 1780, the river was shown as White Oak on the Collett map.

Rich in tannic acid, the White Oak is a black-water river, as distinguished from the brown-water rivers of the North Carolina mountains. It begins as small rivulets flowing from the pocosins within Hofmann Forest. The water changes from fresh to brackish to salty as it nears the ocean. Side creeks flow into the river along its route.

Much of the land along the banks is swampland. Lofty cypress trees mix with lush, exotic vegetation such as wild rice, swamp rose, wild camellias, and duck potatoes. On the bluffs, hardwood forests of oak, hickory, and maple provide a beautiful spectacle during autumn, when their leaves turn from green to various shades of purple, rust, and gold.

Animal life along the river is also varied and interesting. Deer frequently graze quietly on the banks, where raccoons and opossums may also be observed. The summer months bring forth many water snakes and some alligators, although the latter are rarely seen. The riverbanks provide habitat for numerous species of birds. Hawks fly above the forests, and woodpeckers break the silence of this natural paradise as they work on trees. As darkness descends upon the river, numerous owls make their presence known.

Retrace your route to N.C. 58. Turn south on N.C. 58 and drive 2.5 miles to Kuhns, a small crossroads community in the northwestern corner of Carteret County.

National-forest roads leading east from Kuhns make Great Lake the most accessible of the lakes in Croatan National Forest. This rural outpost on the fringe of the forest was named for William Kuhns, a German native

White Oak River

who settled in the area in the distant past and engaged in lumbering along the White Oak River.

Continue south from Kuhns on N.C. 58. After approximately 3.7 miles, turn right, or west, onto S.R. 1106. Proceed 1.7 miles on S.R. 1106 to the Crystal Coast Amphitheater, constructed in 1985 on the banks of the White Oak.

During its premiere season and for one season thereafter, this two-thousand-seat facility was the home of the outdoor drama *Blackbeard's Revenge*. Based on a plot by North Carolina playwright Stuart Aronson, the drama highlighted the early career of Blackbeard. After its second season, the pirate adventure gave way to a religious passion play, *Worthy Is the Lamb*, which continues to run each summer season from mid-June until late August.

Cedar Point Tideland Trail

Return to N.C. 58 and continue 3.5 miles south from the amphitheater, where a sign on the western side of N.C. 58 will direct you to Cedar Point Tideland Trail, another of the recreational areas in Croatan National Forest. One of the two planned camping sites in the forest, Cedar Point has fifty camping spaces, drinking water, and restrooms.

Because Cedar Point is located at the mouth of the White Oak, its interpretive nature trail provides a rare opportunity to see the natural forces at work at an estuary. Winding its way through tidal marshes covered by boardwalks and through hardwood forests, the trail features strategically placed wildlife-viewing blinds.

Observation Platform at Cedar Point Tideland Trail

From Cedar Point, return to N.C. 58. Proceed south on N.C. 58 for 0.8 mile to the intersection with N.C. 24 at the community of Cape Carteret. With a population of nearly fifteen hundred, this town serves as the commercial hub of the resorts just across Bogue Sound on Bogue Banks. Incorporated in 1959, Cape Carteret was established by the developers of Emerald Isle Beach.

Turn west onto N.C. 24. The 5-mile drive from Cape Carteret to Swansboro is a scenic one. Lining the road are numerous antique shops. During the summer months, roadside fruit-and-vegetable stands featuring Bogue Sound watermelons attract large numbers of motorists.

If you care to make a brief side trip, turn off N.C. 24 onto S.R. 1214 approximately 1 mile south of Cape Carteret. Approximately 0.1 mile east of the intersection, an unpaved road leads to an unusual octagonal house constructed in 1856. This house is privately owned and is not open to the public.

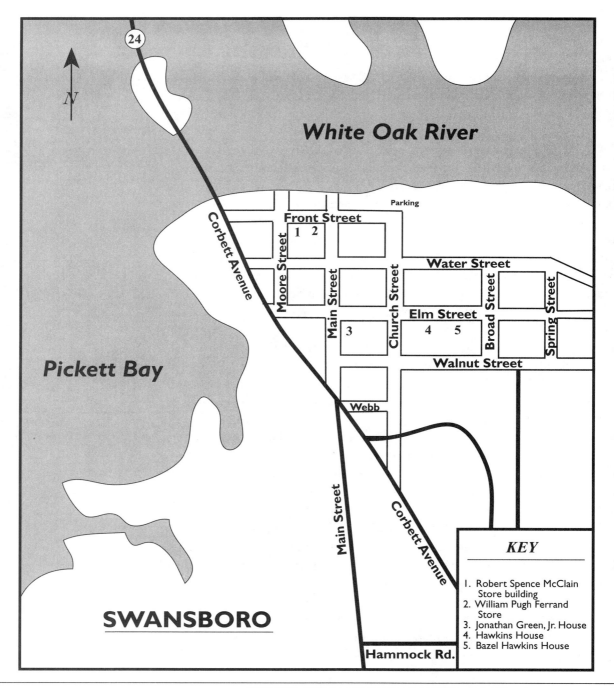

As N.C. 24 nears the White Oak River, the antique shops and roadside markets give way to vacation cottages and fish houses. From the bridge crossing the river, you will be treated to a postcard panorama of the beautiful river and the Swansboro waterfront. You may also catch a glimpse of Russells Island, formerly known as Huggins Island. Located on the waterfront just south of the bridge, the island appeared on early maps as Stones Island. This island has an interesting history.

During the final months of 1861, a Confederate earthwork fort—Fort Huggins—was constructed on the island to guard Bogue Inlet and the access channels to Swansboro. The fort contained underground bunkers and barracks for the two-hundred-man garrison that arrived in January 1862. Two months later, the fort was abandoned when its guns and men were needed for the defense of New Bern.

When Major General Thomas G. Stevenson and his Union forces invaded Swansboro on August 19, 1862, they burned the underground bunkers and barracks. Two months later, in an attempt to impress his superiors, Union naval officer William B. Cushing—who later made a name for himself when he destroyed the Confederate ram *Albemarle* at Plymouth in 1864—boasted that he had destroyed Fort Huggins. However, the fort had been laid to ruin several months before Cushing ever set his eyes on it.

Following the war, the island was used for farming. Despite the years of cultivation, the earthworks were left relatively undisturbed. In 1962, archaeologist Stanley South excavated an underground bunker at the fort. Remains of charred timbers were also found. Although the fort is now overgrown with vegetation, its earthworks are remarkably intact. A state historical marker erected near the bridge commemorates the fort.

Acclaimed by its residents as "the Friendly City by the Sea," the charming port town of Swansboro has greeted visitors to the western banks of the White Oak for more than 250 years.

At Bicentennial Park, located on the northern side of U.S. 58 at the foot of the bridge, a handsome statue of Otway Burns, Swansboro's most famous son, welcomes visitors. Burns was born in the village in 1775. From 1810 to 1819, he operated a shipyard on the eastern side of Main Street between Front Street and the river. It was at that spot that the most historic event in the ancient port town's history took place. In 1818, Burns completed work on the *Prometheus*, thereby giving Swansboro the distinction of being the construction site of the first steamboat built in the state.

To sample the salty atmosphere that pervades old Swansboro, turn left, or east, off N.C. 24 onto Front Street. Park on the street near where Front ends at Church Street after 3 blocks. Swansboro is best enjoyed on foot.

Visitors will be disappointed if they expect to see the site of historic events that shaped the destiny of the state or grand buildings of bygone eras. Swansboro is not Edenton, New Bern, or Wilmington, nor does it pretend to be. Rather, it is an unpretentious fishing village that has preserved its maritime heritage.

Despite Swansboro's small population, estimated at approximately thirteen hundred, few towns provide a better view of what coastal North Carolina must have looked like many, many years ago. As visitors walk along Front and Water streets, located on a bluff just above the river, they travel down lanes that have witnessed more than two and a half centuries of American history. Not only is Swansboro the oldest town in Onslow County, it is also one of coastal North Carolina's oldest communities.

From your car, walk back east along Front Street.

The waterfront has been the focal point of activity in the downtown area ever since the town was founded. Long gone are the large sailing vessels that carried cargo to and from distant ports, but in their place are many commercial fishing boats and pleasure craft that dock on the waterfront and along the causeway of N.C. 24.

Turn right off Front Street onto Main Street, which soon dead-ends at a spot where a municipal wharf existed throughout much of the town's history. Here stood the original wharf where trade flourished during the third quarter of the eighteenth century, and from which the town took its first name, Week's Wharf.

Along the ancient streets of Swansboro are some historic structures little altered over the past two centuries. This treasure trove of commercial and residential buildings is concentrated along four downtown streets. The fine ensemble of commercial buildings now houses an assortment of cafes and quaint antique and gift shops.

Return to Front Street and turn right. Constructed around 1840, the Robert Spence McLean Store building, at 116 Front, is situated on lot No. 5 of the

original town layout. During the Civil War, the Confederate post office was housed in this building. It was raided for tobacco and other items by Union troops on several occasions.

Located just down the street at 122 Front, the William Pugh Ferrand Store, known as "the Old Brick Store," was erected in 1839, replacing a store that burned the year before.

Beautiful, century-old homes lining the quiet streets back of the waterfront help to preserve the "Down East" atmosphere of Swansboro. Most of the houses are two-story, white frame structures with well-tended yards displaying evidence of the seafaring lifestyle of the residents: stacks of crab pots, drying nets, hunting decoys, and small boats.

Return to Main Street and turn right. After 2 blocks, turn left on Elm Street, which boasts an impressive array of homes dating back more than two hundred years.

Located at 114 Elm, the Jonathan Green, Jr., House was constructed by the son of one of the original settlers of the town. Thought to be the oldest house in Onslow County, it is definitely the oldest in Swansboro. Evidence indicates that the house was constructed before the lots in the town were laid out in 1769 and 1770.

The Jonathan Green, Jr., House

The exact date of the first European settlement in the Swansboro area is unknown, but it is certain that the shores of the White Oak at or near the modern town were settled by the first decade of the eighteenth century.

In 1711, the Indians living on the river aided the Tuscaroras in their rampage at New Bern and in the surrounding area, including the site of Swansboro. William Bartram, the father of noted botanist John Bartram, was murdered by the marauding Indians in the morning hours of September 22, 1711, at his home 4 miles east of Swansboro.

Once the threat of Indian violence ended, the White Oak River area was reopened for land grants in 1713. Soon thereafter, settlers from New England, Maryland, Virginia, northeastern North Carolina, and Carteret County began pouring into the region. Two brothers from Falmouth, Massachusetts—Jonathan and Isaac Green—are believed to have been the first white settlers on the exact site of Swansboro. They purchased land here in 1730. Jonathan and his wife, Grace, constructed a plantation house near the mouth of the river. Five years later, Jonathan died. His widow subsequently married Theophilus Weeks.

Theophilus Weeks is known as "the Founder of Swansboro." He was also a native of Falmouth, Massachusetts, and most likely moved with the Greens to the area. After his marriage to Grace Green, Weeks moved to her plantation. In 1757, he was appointed inspector of exports for Bogue Inlet, a position he held until his death in 1772.

In 1769, Weeks began laying out streets and lots after deciding to establish a town on his plantation lands. Although the new town initially grew slowly, it was the only village on the North Carolina coast between Beaufort and Wilmington. Leading citizens of the area became associated with the port as it began to attract a growing trade in naval stores.

In its infancy, the town was known by various names: Week's Wharf, Week's Point, New Town, and Bogue, the most popular name during the American Revolution. As the Revolutionary War was drawing to a close, the North Carolina General Assembly incorporated the town on May 6, 1783, and named it Swannsborough, in honor of Samuel Swann, an early Onslow County statesman. Recognizing the commercial importance of the town, the general assembly enacted legislation in 1786 that created the port of Swannsborough the following year.

According to the 1800 census, forty-nine people lived within the town limits. Trade was brisk. Stores and other commercial facilities were constructed on the waterfront throughout the first half of the century.

However, the port never recovered from the effects of the Civil War. Following the war, much of the ocean shipping traffic shifted to the deepwater ports of the coast.

The local economy was bolstered by area lumbermills, many of which operated until the Great Depression. In the town's charter of 1895, the modern spelling of Swansboro was adopted.

Over the past half-century, commercial fishing, boat building, and tourism have allowed Swansboro to enter the modern age without destroying its character.

From the Jonathan Green, Jr., House, continue west to the 200 block of Elm Street, which offers a couple of interesting historic houses.

Located at 208 Elm, the Hawkins House was built between 1830 and 1840. While home on furlough to visit his parents, a young Confederate soldier was captured in one of the upstairs bedrooms by Union forces during their occupation of the town in 1862.

Constructed in 1826, the Bazel Hawkins House, at 224 Elm, once stood at the corner of Water and Spring streets. This two-story frame structure was moved to its present site when its original location was purchased by a lumber company.

The Hawkins House

Retrace your route to where you parked your car on Front Street to resume the driving tour.

Drive back east on Front Street to Moore Street and turn left. After 2 blocks, Moore merges into Elm. Turn left, or south, off Elm onto N.C. 24 and proceed 1.9 miles through the modern commercial district of Swansboro to the entrance to Hammocks Beach State Park. Turn east on S.R. 1511 for a 2.1-mile drive to the ferry landing.

The adage "Half the fun is getting there" holds particularly true for this state park. Covered pontoon boats, each with a capacity of thirty-six passengers, ferry visitors from the mainland to the park from Memorial Day to Labor Day. Each one-way trip takes approximately twenty-five minutes, as the boats slowly wind their way through a maze of beautiful marsh islands. This ride provides a refreshing opportunity to relax and enjoy the magnificence of the unspoiled North Carolina coast. As with most state-operated ferries, you can expect waiting lines at the mainland ferry landing during peak vacation periods. Because access is limited to watercraft, visitors can reach the island only by private boat during the off-season.

Hammocks Beach State Park
Ferry landing

Squeezed between heavily developed Bogue Banks and bomb-scarred Brown's Island, 3.5-mile-long Bear Island—or Hammocks Beach State Park, as the entire island is called today—is a paradise for conservationists and nature lovers. Upon reaching the ferry landing, you will discover the picturesque landscape of a unique place: a publicly accessible island that remains close to its natural state. Trees, including water oak and cedar, line the sound side of the island.

From the ferry landing, you can reach the ocean strand by taking a 0.5-mile hike through an area of spectacular grass-topped dunes. Many of the dunes are thirty feet high, and some reach sixty feet, providing exceptional views of the sea and sound. The tall dunes on the eastern half of the island are highly visible. Unfortunately, they are smothering the maritime forest there.

Visitors are rewarded for their trek across the sandy backbone of the island. Blessed with more than 3 miles of ocean frontage, Hammocks Beach State Park has been called one of the most beautiful and unspoiled beaches on the Atlantic coast.

Of the wildlife on the island, the most interesting is the endangered loggerhead turtle, which comes ashore to use the beach as a nesting area. Signs have been placed on the strand to warn humans of the nesting grounds. Since the park is considered a prime nesting area for the turtle, it is often closed on summer nights during full moon–high tide periods, the optimum time for egg laying.

The state of North Carolina has done an admirable job of providing visitor amenities on the island while maintaining it as a wilderness area. A large bathhouse designed to blend with the island environment contains shower rooms, restrooms, a refreshment stand, and a shelter that provides refuge from inclement weather. Picnic tables are located adjacent to the bathhouse. Nothing else has been constructed on the island to interfere with its natural state.

A number of activities are available to visitors. One of the prime attractions is a protected swimming beach with seasonal lifeguards. Fishing, shelling, and bird-watching are other popular activities. Primitive overnight camping is allowed, but campers are required to register with park rangers. Hiking is a very popular attraction, with more then 3.8 miles of trail available. Various free nature programs and hikes are offered by rangers.

Before the park opened in 1961, the island, described by a former owner as a place "where every day is Sunday," had a long recorded history. In fact, it was one of the first barrier islands mentioned in the *Colonial Records of North Carolina.*

Tobias Knight, the colony's secretary of state, acquired the entire island by land patent. While it was in his ownership, Knight was alleged to have associated with Blackbeard and other North Carolina pirates. Tales of pirate treasure buried on the island abound to this day.

In addition to being known as Bear Island or Bear Beach, the island is still known locally as Heady's Beach, in honor of Daniel Heady, a former owner. How the name Bear Island came about remains a subject of dispute. Some contend that it came from nearby Bear Creek, while a local legend contends that Daniel Boone's bear-hunting success on the island resulted in the name. Supposedly, the famous trailblazer killed ninety-six bears on the island in one season.

After an attack by Spaniards at Bear Inlet in 1747, the colonial assembly provided a short-lived fort at Bear Island. For the next 150 years, Bear Island was put to various uses by whalers, fishermen, and even a nudist colony.

A noted New York brain surgeon purchased the island in 1914 and in so doing changed the course of its history. Dr. William Sharpe, a pioneer in neurosurgery, owned Bear Island for the next forty-five years.

Sharpe's love affair with the North Carolina coast began in 1911, when he arrived with some friends on a duck-hunting trip. On that expedition, he began a long friendship with a black guide, John Hurst. Dr. Sharpe employed Hurst to locate some land for use as a "retreat that would be beautiful, isolated, and have an abundance of fish and game," as the physician put it.

It took Hurst three years to find a place where Sharpe could escape the rigors of his profession. Known as "the Hammocks," Sharpe's estate consisted of forty-eight hundred acres on a mainland peninsula and Bear Island.

Shortly after he acquired his retreat, the physician named John Hurst and his wife, Gertrude, caretakers. Soon, Sharpe reported receiving unsigned letters containing threats from local residents upset that a black man had been appointed manager of the property. Through a notice in area newspapers offering a $5,000 reward for information leading to the arrest and conviction of any person damaging the island or its occupants, Sharpe ended the threats. Nevertheless, he continued to have his share of troubles with his island paradise.

Near the site of the present-day ferry landing, the doctor built a home secluded from the outside world. Stories circulated about strange operations that Dr. Sharpe was performing. Rumors abounded that he was conducting medical experiments involving the crossbreeding of humans and animals.

A serious threat to the doctor's isolation came in 1937, when the state declared its intent to construct a road to the island. When Sharpe's appeals to Raleigh were unsuccessful, he obtained a personal meeting with his old college roommate, President Franklin D. Roosevelt. After the meeting, the road project was halted.

Sharpe chronicled his ownership of Bear Island in his autobiography, *Brain Surgeon*.

By the late 1940s, he was an old man. Having enjoyed many years at his paradise, he decided to make a gift of the island to the Hursts. Mrs. Hurst, a former schoolteacher, prevailed upon him to donate the land instead to the North Carolina Teachers Association, the segregated black teachers' group in the state. For approximately a decade, the black teachers used the island as a retreat, and other segregated black groups such as the Boy Scouts and the New Farmers of America visited the island for recreation. During that time, Bear Island fulfilled Sharpe's dream of a "refuge and a place of enjoyment for some of the people whom America treated so badly." Indeed, for a number of years, the island was one of the rare places on the coast open to blacks.

Access was always a problem in maintaining the island as a black retreat. Money was not forthcoming for a bridge. As racial barriers began to crumble in the early 1960s, most of the once-segregated associations and groups no longer existed as separate entities. Accordingly, Bear Island was presented to the state on May 3, 1961.

Attendance during the park's premiere season was only four thousand, the lowest of all the parks in the state system. Although attendance has increased steadily since that time, the park remains one of North Carolina's least-visited state parks, due in part to its limited access.

Even though Bear Inlet separates the island from the Marine Corps bombing range on Brown's Island (Shacklefoot Island), the impact of the nearby military activities has been felt and seen at the park. A number of inadvertent bombings of Hammocks Beach have been reported in the past. In 1972, a 250-pound bomb was dropped on the island by a marine plane. Two years later, twenty-eight rockets were fired at the park by an off-course marine helicopter. No injuries resulted from either incident.

After visiting the park, return to N.C. 24 and continue in your original direction for 4.6 miles to the intersection with N.C. 172 at the community of Hubert, located on the boundary of Camp Lejeune Marine Corps Base. For a drive through the sprawling military complex, turn south on N.C. 172.

Four miles south of the intersection, marine sentries guard the entrance to the base. Although this 16.7-mile route follows a state-maintained road, windshield permits, provided by sentries, are required for all nonmilitary through traffic. Take care on the thirty-minute drive to follow the state highway or marked detours. During special maneuvers, portions of N.C. 172 are closed, and the resulting detours give motorists a better view of the installation. Extreme care must be taken to obey all traffic laws on the base, since violations are subject to trial in federal court.

Camp Lejeune stretches from the Atlantic Ocean inland to Jacksonville.

Covering some 110,000 acres (172 square miles), it is known as the world's most complete amphibious marine training base. Home to approximately 41,000 military personnel spread among five marine and two navy commands, the massive complex is used as a training and support base for marine expeditionary and amphibious operations. It also provides specialized engineering and supply schools for the Marine Corps.

With more than 6,000 buildings and 400 miles of roads, the installation is a city in itself. Its 205-bed naval hospital is the largest naval hospital in the South. Among the base holdings are Brown's Island, Onslow Beach, and much of the New River. Brown's Island is approximately the same length as adjacent Hammocks Beach State Park. Subject to repeated target practice, Brown's Island is scarred with craters. Separated from Brown's Island by Brown's Inlet, Onslow Beach is an 11-mile-long barrier island used as a training ground for amphibious landings.

As war clouds were growing in Europe and the Pacific in early 1941, the United States recognized that the Marine Corps had outgrown its facilities at Parris Island, South Carolina, and Quantico, Virginia. As a result, the construction of a new base in Onslow County, North Carolina, was approved in February 1941. Defense Department officials selected the site because it met the needs of the marines: it had isolated surf and beach areas for training, a large, remote, undeveloped tract of land, a good climate, and a strategic location.

Originally known as New River Marine Base, the installation began as a tent city quickly assembled in 1941. Later, the base was renamed in honor of Lieutenant General John Archer Lejeune (1867–1942), commandant of the United States Marine Corps during World War I.

As the nation plunged deeper into World War II, the base played a vital role in training and supplying marines for the European and Pacific theaters. Veterans of the Pacific war zone were brought to Camp Lejeune to instruct new recruits and draftees in ship-to-shore assault. Others who trained here during the war included medics, Seabees, Coast Guard personnel, and women marines. Fittingly enough, Eugenia Lejeune, daughter of Commandant Lejeune, was commissioned at the base in November 1943.

Continue on N.C. 172 to the bridge over the New River, located just past the southern sentry station.

Twisting through the heart of Onslow County, the New River is an exceptionally beautiful coastal river. Approximately 40 miles in length, it rises in the northwestern part of the county. It is the only significant coastal river in the state that has both its headwaters and mouth in the same county.

Local tradition holds that the river was at one time a long lake in a swampy area. It became the New River when it overflowed into the Atlantic as a result of torrential rains.

After it leaves Jacksonville, where it dramatically widens on its course to the sea, the New River and its shoreline are owned almost entirely by the federal government as part of Camp Lejeune, thus depriving the public of enjoying their striking natural beauty. This bridge is one of the best places to view the New River.

The tour ends here, just beyond the boundary of Camp Lejeune.

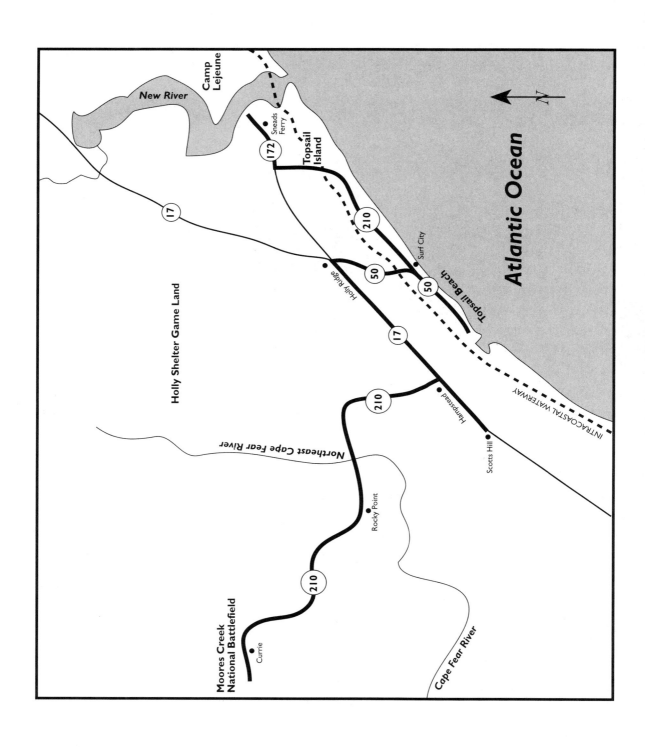

The Topsail Area Tour

This tour begins on the mainland at Sneads Ferry, located on the southern shore of the New River. It then proceeds to Topsail Island, where it examines the entire length of the island from West Onslow Beach to Surf City to Topsail Beach. Back on the mainland, it visits Holly Ridge and skirts Holly Shelter Game Land and Angola Bay Game Land before heading to Hampstead and Scotts Hill. After approaching exclusive Figure Eight Island, it proceeds to Rocky Point and Currie, where it ends at Moores Creek National Military Park.

Among the highlights of the tour are the story of Operation Bumblebee, tales of buried treasure on Topsail Island, the story of Camp Davis, Poplar Grove Plantation, and Moores Creek National Military Park.

Total mileage: approximately 110 miles.

This tour begins on N.C. 172 just across the river from Camp Lejeune, on the southern side of the bridge over the New River. Drive south on N.C. 172. Just east of the highway lies the picturesque sound-side fishing community of Sneads Ferry.

Approximately 1 mile south of the bridge, turn left, or east, on S.R. 1557 (Wheeler Creek Road) and proceed 0.3 mile to the intersection with S.R. 1517 (Fulchers Landing Loop Road). Bear right on S.R. 1517 and follow it as it winds its way south through Sneads Ferry.

Because of its proximity to New River Inlet, Sneads Ferry harbors a large commercial fishing fleet on its scenic waterfront.

The enormous shell mounds visible on the banks of the river are evidence that this area was an important Indian fishing site long before it was settled by people of European descent. Originally known as Lower Ferry, the village was later named for Robert W. Snead, who settled near the mouth of the river in 1760. He assumed operation of the New River Ferry from Edmund Emmett, who had established it in 1725. Snead, an attorney, gained notoriety throughout North Carolina when he shot and killed George W. Mitchell, a hero of the American Revolution, in a political quarrel at the Onslow County Courthouse. Although the cause of the confrontation has been lost to history, a superior-court trial resulted in Snead's conviction.

Fishing fleet at Sneads Ferry

However, he came to his sentencing with a full pardon from Governor Richard Dobbs Spaight.

Sneads Ferry enjoyed a high volume of traffic in colonial times, because it was located on the first post road from Suffolk, Virginia, to Charleston, South Carolina. In 1775, news of the Battle of Lexington reached the area by a post rider galloping down the sandy trail.

Not until 1920 was the river ferry motorized. Nineteen years later, a drawbridge was constructed a short distance from the old ferry operation. In the 1990s, the existing high-rise bridge was constructed to replace the drawbridge.

After 1.4 miles, S.R. 1517 merges with S.R. 1515 (Sneads Ferry Road). Proceed west for 1.1 miles on S.R. 1515 to the intersection with N.C. 172. Turn south on N.C. 172 and drive 1 mile, then turn east onto N.C. 210.

Along this route, you will be greeted by a large variety of billboards advertising the amenities of Topsail Island, located 4.2 miles east. Topsail (pronounced Tops'l) is the first barrier island south of Bogue Inlet subject to commercial development. Twenty-two miles in length, the island is the longest on the North Carolina coast south of the Outer Banks. Despite its length, Topsail is only about 0.5 mile wide and covers only 15 square miles. Its oceanfront is an uninterrupted shoreline of white, sandy beaches.

Portions of the sound side offer various trees, such as live oak, holly, cedar, and pine, along with scuppernong grapevines.

An unusual feature of Topsail is that it is shared by two counties, Onslow and Pender. The county line lies in the southern half of the island, just north of Delmar Beach. Traditionally, the southern portion—the Pender County portion—has been the more developed part of the island. Although touted by local realtors as "the last frontier in North Carolina's coastal development," Topsail has fallen prey to large-scale development in recent years.

N.C. 210 makes its way to the island over a high-rise bridge spanning the Intracoastal Waterway. Once on the island, turn north on S.R. 1568 and proceed to the northern end of Topsail.

Until a decade ago, this 5.2-mile stretch of beach, just north of West Onslow Beach, was virtually undeveloped. Now, condominiums and a towering hotel–conference center complex dot the oceanfront at a place called North Topsail Shores. Despite problems with highway erosion on this part of the island during coastal storms, continued rapid development here is almost a certainty for the future.

The pleasant drive "up" the beach offers an excellent opportunity to contemplate the island's storied past. From the swashbuckling adventures of Blackbeard to a secret government missile-testing project, Topsail Island has had a fascinating history. Its earliest inhabitants, at least on a temporary basis, were Indians. Remains of a prehistoric Indian fishing camp a thousand years old were found during recent archaeological digs near New River Inlet, on the northern end of the island. During these excavations, various artifacts—including arrowheads, charred fire pots, and tools made from shells—were recovered.

As early as the eighteenth century, the island was known as Topsail. Historians have concluded that the name originated during the golden age of piracy. Some of North Carolina's most infamous pirates, including Blackbeard and Stede Bonnet, frequented Topsail during that period. In the sound and the channels behind the barrier island, the buccaneers secreted their ships and lay in wait for unwary merchant ships. After news of their acts of piracy spread up and down the eastern seaboard, pilots gave the island close scrutiny in passing, scouring the western horizon for the sight of the tops of sails over the island dunes. Thus, the name Topsail Island was born.

The first permanent settlers in present-day Pender County arrived in the latter part of the seventeenth century. Onslow County was settled in the early eighteenth century. However, these settlements were confined to the mainland along the rivers and sounds. Topsail Island did not attract a significant permanent population until after World War II.

During the Civil War, Topsail was an important source of badly needed salt. Not surprisingly, the island was the scene of a number of daring raids by Union forces seeking to destroy the saltworks, which processed the scarce commodity from salt water.

Before World War II, the only access to Topsail was by boat. In the early stages of the war, at the nearby mainland community of Holly Ridge, the federal government began constructing Camp Davis, an enormous antiaircraft training facility. As part of the massive installation, the island was considered a vital link in coastal defense and was leased by the government. Topsail was promptly connected to the mainland by a pontoon bridge. Barracks, warehouses, and other military structures were erected on the island.

At the close of the war, Camp Davis was deactivated, but the existing facilities on Topsail were immediately put to another use. The United States Navy selected the island as a testing ground for the nation's early defense-missile project, Operation Bumblebee. Chosen because it offered an isolated area for missile tests, Topsail served as the site for the program from its infancy until it was moved to Cape Canaveral, Florida, and the Mojave Desert in California in 1948.

In 1949, when the military no longer had need of the island, it was released to its owners, who wasted no time in converting the existing structures into resort facilities. Two years later, Topsail Island had its first incorporated town: Surf City.

Although minor residential development began on the island in the 1930s, the early 1950s saw the southern half transformed into a family-oriented coastal resort. Unfortunately, Topsail had the same fate as did most of the other barrier islands along the southern half of the North Carolina coast in 1954, when Hurricane Hazel left her deadly calling card. Before the ferocious storm pounded the island, 230 buildings were standing. In the wake of the hurricane, 210 were completely demolished, while the remainder were

Observation tower
from Operation Bumblebee

damaged. To make matters worse, the storm stripped the island of a vast amount of sand and destroyed the only bridge to the mainland. In subsequent years, two other hurricanes, Diane and Donna, raked Topsail and caused serious damage.

The 1960s brought a much-needed reprieve from devastating storms. In 1963, Topsail gained a second incorporated town when Topsail Beach was chartered on the southern end of the island. Since that time, development has escalated rapidly. Now, "the last frontier"—the island's northern quarter—is considered ripe for development.

From the northern end of Topsail, retrace your route on S.R. 1568 to the point where the island tour started. Here, S.R. 1568 merges into N.C. 210 on its southern route down the island.

Some 1.5 miles south of the junction, a multistory rectangular structure decorated with graffiti towers over the Atlantic on an undeveloped portion of the strand. Over the past three decades, the island's best-known landmarks have been eight of these concrete towers, arranged approximately every 2.5 miles along the strand. Ever since Topsail was opened for resort development, tourists driving the island from West Onslow Beach to Topsail Beach have been puzzled by the unusual structures.

Because the island was off-limits to civilians when the towers were erected, legends have arisen about their original purpose. One theory suggests that the towers were constructed for the observation of enemy submarines during the war. A more glamorous notion that they were part of the nation's early space program also became popular.

In reality, the concrete platforms stand as virtually the only visible reminders of Topsail's greatest secret. Operation Bumblebee remains shrouded in mystery, most of its details buried in military records which are either classified or almost impossible to locate.

The facts that are known about the project are fascinating. As World War II drew to a close, Topsail was selected as the site of the incubation phase of the nation's newest secret project: ramjet propulsion and its application to defense missiles. As a result of the tests conducted on the isolated shores of Topsail, the world's first supersonic missiles, designed to protect an entire fleet of warships, were developed.

Scientists from Johns Hopkins University, working in conjunction with

Jolly Roger Fishing Pier, former launch site for Operation Bumblebee

the United States Navy, first came to the island in the summer of 1945 to assess the suitability of the site. By the following year, electricity, streets, and water and sewer facilities were in place on the island. Personnel, including two hundred workers employed by a defense contractor, lived in old military barracks.

The construction of the missiles took place in a building on the sound side of the island. Dollies then moved the missiles through underground tunnels to launch pads on the oceanfront.

In the fall of 1946, the first test missiles were fired. Ranging in length from three to thirteen feet, they were tracked from the eight now-famous towers. Several underground bunkers were also constructed to provide safer observation areas.

Although some area residents claim that money, politics, and the desire to market the island as a resort forced the project to be moved from Topsail in 1948, it appears that the change was dictated by increased ocean traffic in the firing range, which extended 20 miles in a northeasterly direction.

Over the decades, most of the observation towers have been converted to private residences. Another has become the entrance to a fishing pier. Several others, like the one at the present tour stop, stand as abandoned monuments to the fleeting moment when, unbeknownst to the outside world, Topsail was the place where a prototype weapon that forever changed military strategy was being developed.

There are few structures surviving from the missile project. In the 1980s, a construction crew inadvertently unearthed a hidden reminder of the abandoned testing site. While installing a new sewer line, they discovered a portion of the underground tunnel connecting the assembly area to the oceanfront launching area. The large concrete-block structure on the sound side of the island that served as the assembly building for the missiles was transformed into a nightclub several years ago.

Continue south on N.C. 210. It is approximately 7 miles from the concrete tower to Delmar Beach, located just north of the Pender County line. This small beach town is dominated by a large number of mobile homes in various states of repair.

One mile south of Delmar Beach, at the crossroads where N.C. 210 becomes N.C. 50 near the drawbridge spanning the Intracoastal Waterway, lies Surf City, the commercial hub of the island. With a permanent population in excess of five hundred, the town is the most populous place on the island.

Much of the mystique of the North Carolina coast comes from tales of buried treasure. Topsail Island, and specifically the Surf City area, is believed to be the site of a number of treasures, either ill-gotten booty hidden by pirates or the cargoes of ships that wrecked centuries ago.

Stede Bonnet—"the Gentleman Pirate"—apparently found Topsail to his liking. He sailed from Old Topsail Inlet in 1719 on an adventure that netted him a dozen ships. Speculation about the ultimate disposition of the loot taken on this spree has centered around Topsail Island. Legend has it that Bonnet's treasure was buried on the Pender County side of the island. Two of Bonnet's ships went down in Topsail Sound when he was double-crossed by Blackbeard.

Whether any of Topsail's treasure has ever been recovered is unknown. This century has seen a number of serious and expensive attempts to locate it.

Perhaps the first—and undoubtedly the most extensive—effort began in 1938, when a group of men from New York City formed the Carolina Exploration Company and attempted to recover the riches of an old pirate ship. After leaving the mainland village of Hampstead, the treasure hunters moved their equipment—including a new invention, the metal detector—across the sound by boat. Once on Topsail Island, the group, armed with old maps and charts, put the metal detector to work. Signals from their equipment revealed the presence of metal beneath the sands of Topsail. Excavation rights on the island, which was virtually uninhabited at the time, were obtained from Topsail's owner, Harvey Jones.

From their initial exploration, the New Yorkers ascertained that the ship they were seeking was much deeper under the sand than they first imagined, and that its location was ninety feet inland from the existing Topsail shore. They dug a gigantic, funnel-shaped hole measuring seventy feet across into the island. Sections of sheet metal were installed in the shaft to form a cofferdam around the digging pit.

Gradually, old ship timbers were pulled to the surface by pressure pumps. Whether anything else was raised from the shaft is known only to the explorers, because they, like most treasure hunters, were secretive about their find. By the time the project was abandoned in 1939, it was estimated that fifty thousand dollars had been poured into the venture.

The pit, which thereafter became known to locals as "the Old Pirate Ship Treasure Pit," soon filled with water. Later, a lead weight dropped into the mine revealed that the hunters had probed at least thirty-one feet below the water level.

Located 2 miles south of Surf City, the remains of the excavation site endured for many years.

Spanish galleons laden with gold, silver, and other precious commodities from the New World customarily sailed along the North Carolina coast on their return trip to their mother country. Such was the case on August 17, 1570, when somewhere near Topsail, a Spanish fleet of five ships bearing chests full of valuables encountered a savage hurricane. Driven close to the deadly shoals of the barrier island, the crews fought valiantly to keep their vessels afloat. However, the first of the ships to be lost, the *El Salvadore*, slammed ashore at Topsail with a loss of most of her crew and 240,000 pieces of eight. Within two years, the wreck was covered by more than seven feet of sand.

Approximately 1 mile south of the 1938–39 treasure hunt, a different search subsequently took place on the ocean side of the island. There, metal detectors were used in an attempt to locate the remains of the *El Salvadore*. This event was dubbed "the Old Spanish Galleon Treasure Hunt" by locals.

After the expensive search, the only evidence left at the scene was a round iron caisson embedded deep in the sand. Again, it is not known what the searchers discovered, but a fifty-five-foot sounding line lowered into the abandoned shaft failed to reach bottom.

With the recent development of the island, it appears that any treasure hidden under the sandy surface of Topsail will remain buried there forever.

The 8-mile stretch from Surf City to the southern end of Topsail is the final leg of the island tour. Over the past forty years, cottages of all sizes and shapes, fishing piers, motels, campgrounds, restaurants, and small shopping centers have sprung up along this route.

Follow N.C. 50 to Topsail Beach, which serves as a bookend to Surf City. Topsail Beach has a smaller permanent population than its northern neighbor, but it offers a variety of amenities for vacationers on the southern part of the island.

A tangible reminder of Operation Bumblebee is visible at the Jolly Roger Motel, located on the oceanfront in the heart of Topsail Beach. A close inspection of the motel patio reveals that it was once a concrete launching pad.

Retrace your route to Surf City and leave the island via N.C. 50. It is 6 miles west from Topsail Island to Holly Ridge, located at the intersection with U.S. 17.

Holly Ridge is a small village to which history has not been kind. Every year, untold thousands of coastal visitors pass through this Onslow County town without so much as a second thought about the place. After all, from outward appearances, Holly Ridge, with a population of less than seven hundred, seems to be nothing more than a crossroads settlement with several convenience stores and gas stations.

However, the town is not without its past glory. If you care to take a brief trip around the side roads of the community, you will notice abandoned military buildings dotting the landscape. You may be distracted by numerous paved roads which suddenly disappear into nowhere in nearby forests. Although it may seem that you have entered a twilight zone, these ghosts of the past are remnants of one of the largest military bases ever constructed in the state: Camp Davis.

Holly Ridge was established around 1890 to serve as a wood station for the railroad. The town was named for the holly that once grew in profusion in the area. Holly was once shipped from the town each Christmas season. By 1980, one lone holly tree survived, and it was in sickly condition.

One of Holly Ridge's roads to nowhere

Holly Ridge's claim to fame began in 1940, when the federal government authorized the construction of an antiaircraft training base in the tiny village of twenty-eight persons. An appropriation of $9.5 million was used to begin construction of an initial complex of a thousand buildings. By the time the installation was ready for troops in April 1941, approximately $40 million had been spent on the project.

Only five voters participated in the initial municipal election in Holly Ridge in 1941, but within five months and ten days of that date, the sleepy little village was transformed into a metropolis of over twenty thousand residents.

The Japanese attack on Pearl Harbor in December 1941 brought the first year of operations at the base to a chilling close. Nearly a hundred thousand people were by then living in the area.

Named in honor of a native North Carolinian, Major General Pearson Davis (1866–1937), the camp encompassed 3,200 acres extending from the Atlantic westward. An additional 50,000 acres were used for training and firing practice. The size of the facility was mind-boggling. More than 2,000 buildings were ultimately erected at the base. Among these were a large power plant, water and sewer plants, a laundry that employed 450 workers, and a 2,000-bed, 56-building hospital unit. Two airports, 3 fire stations, 223 fire hydrants, 830 street lights, 50 miles of water mains, and 30 miles of paved streets were included in the complex. To meet the demands of the military personnel, 4 movie theaters and 8 churches were built in Holly Ridge almost overnight.

Almost as suddenly as it came to Holly Ridge, Camp Davis left. As World War II came to an end, there was no longer a need for the enormous training facility. In October 1944, the camp was closed, only to be reopened for a short time during the summer of 1945 as an air-force convalescent hospital and redistribution center. Most of the buildings that once made up the base were subsequently torn down or removed to other locations.

Today, the seemingly endless miles of blacktop that disappear into the wilderness surrounding the village and the unmistakable military buildings on the side streets bear mute testimony to the future which Holly Ridge might have enjoyed.

At the highway intersection in Holly Ridge, turn south on U.S. 17. Two expansive game preserves comprised of pocosins, swamps, and wetlands are located south and west of Holly Ridge. A portion of the larger preserve, Holly Shelter Game Land, borders the western side of U.S. 17 on this portion of the tour.

Approximately 10 miles long and 7 miles wide, Holly Shelter covers more than 48,500 acres. A shrub pocosin virtually devoid of trees dominates the northeastern part of the preserve. In contrast, the southeastern section features higher elevations and longleaf pines. In the northwestern quadrant, Carolina bay plants such as titi thrive near bald-cypress wetlands. A significant, rare stand of Atlantic white cedar grows near Trumpeter Swamp.

To visitors and area residents alike, the Holly Shelter preserve remains a forbidding place. Stories abound about people who have vanished without trace in this immense wilderness. So remote and untouched is it that an 0-47 observation plane from Camp Davis that crashed in 1943 was accidentally discovered in 1978 by a marine colonel in a flight over the area.

Lieutenant Herbert Evans, one of the survivors of the World War II crash, was able to find his way out of the swamp only after walking for six hours through dangerous, snake-infested water that was at times waist-deep. His wife picked thorns out of his body for two months after the ordeal. Evans had this to say of Holly Shelter: "You can't imagine what a beastly place that swamp was." That impression has been shared by many others who ventured into the wilderness.

There is no road access to the smaller of the two preserves, Angola Bay Game Land, which lies some 8 miles north of Holly Shelter. Encompassing 21,134 acres in Pender and Duplin counties, Angola Bay is a remote, primitive area that is almost inaccessible to humans. During dry seasons, the large peat beds underlying this vast expanse are highly combustible.

Some years ago, an attempt was made to build a road through Angola Bay. A canal was dug as part of the process, and the peat and muck extracted from it were piled up to make the roadbed. Before the streams in the vicinity could be bridged, the roadbed caught fire and burned down. When the area was part of Camp Davis, roads were constructed in the great morass. To prevent them from burning, the army kept them soaked with water from dammed-up roadside canals.

Both Holly Shelter and Angola Bay are administered by the North Carolina Wildlife Resources Commission. The lands in the preserves have been set aside for hunting and wildlife management. Deer, bear, and alligators are prevalent in both areas, as are insectivorous plants such as Venus' flytrap, pitcher plant, and trumpet flower.

It is 12 miles on U.S. 17 from Holly Ridge to Hampstead.

"Ocean Highway," as U.S. 17 is called, passes through a number of small, quaint coastal villages as it runs the length of the North Carolina coast from South Mills in the north to Shallotte in the south. None of these villages is more charming than Hampstead. Adorned with huge, ancient, moss-draped oaks along the roadway, this fishing hamlet presents a visual delight to motorists.

The Washington Tree

Although the present population is less than a thousand, Hampstead's roots can be traced to colonial times, when the village was a commercial center for fishermen, planters, and farmers. During the Civil War, salt production was important to the community, with the valuable product bringing as much as fifty dollars a bushel. Due to its proximity to the Atlantic, the Intracoastal Waterway, and Topsail Sound, the community has been able to maintain its maritime flavor in the present era.

One significant part of Hampstead's past is visible on the western side of U.S. 17. On his 1791 tour of the South, President George Washington stopped for a rest under one of the tall, sweeping oaks in the village. That tree, still standing today, has been appropriately marked by the Daughters of the American Revolution as the Washington Tree.

Hampstead hosts an annual festival to celebrate one of the most abundant food fish in North Carolina. The Hampstead Spot Festival, held during the first week in October, offers a variety of activities. Although spots were caught commercially as early as the 1930s, they did not become the largest-selling fish in the South until twenty years later. Because of the popularity of the distinctively marked fish, which have a black spot on each side near the gills, several seafood packing houses have been built in the village. In order to raise money for local projects and to call attention to Hampstead's claim of being "the Seafood Capital of the Carolinas," the festival was inaugurated in 1964.

Continue 4 miles south from Hampstead to Scotts Hill.

Located on the eastern side of U.S. 17 in the village is Poplar Grove Plantation. Purchased in 1795 by James Foy, Jr., the son of a Revolutionary War patriot, this is one of the oldest peanut-producing plantations in the state. At one time, the estate stretched from Topsail Sound to the present route of U.S. 17 and covered more than 835 acres.

After passing through six generations of the Foy family, the plantation manor house and the adjacent fifteen acres have been opened to the public by a nonprofit corporation, Poplar Grove Foundation, Inc. The plantation is listed on the National Register of Historic Places.

Without question, the centerpiece of the plantation is the Greek Revival manor house. Joseph M. Foy built the multistory frame structure in 1850 to replace the original plantation house, which had burned a year earlier. The

Poplar Grove Plantation

wood used in the present house was hand-hewn and pegged, and the bricks in the foundation and chimney were made on the grounds. Situated among stately oaks festooned with Spanish moss, the house boasts many of the features found in fine Wilmington homes of the same period. The furnishings and exhibits in the house date to the early and middle years of the nineteenth century. The three floors contain four rooms each, arranged around a central hallway connected to the next floor by a straight stairway.

Tours of the house and its outbuildings provide visitors with a glimpse of what plantation life was like in the antebellum South. In 1860, the prosperous plantation yielded more than five thousand bushels of peanuts. Raiding Union forces looted horses and food in 1862.

During your tour of the manor house, you may hear the tale of one member of the Foy family who still considers the plantation her home. Aunt Nora, the wife of Joseph M. Foy, is the subject of a colorful ghost story.

Nora moved into the house as a young bride after the Civil War. A windowpane bears her name, along with that of her husband, etched there on their wedding day. Nora later served as the local postmistress. Before her death in 1923, she apparently became a colorful character, prone to cracking jokes and smoking a pipe. Since her death, her presence lingers. She has been heard walking about in her upstairs room. Members of the plantation staff refer to her as Aunt Nora. They have reported tricks she has played on them. Around the Christmas season, a mysterious glow sometimes emanates from the window of her room after all the lights of the house have been turned out.

Complementing the fine manor house and outbuildings are the beautiful gardens and grounds of the estate. Stately oaks, sycamores, and poplars lend their shade to the plantation, while seasonal flowers are ablaze with color throughout the year.

Continue in your original direction on U.S. 17. Three miles south of Poplar Grove, you will notice a sign for Figure Eight Island. Turn east onto Porters Neck Road. After 1.1 miles on Porters Neck, turn south onto Edgewater Club Road, which terminates near the Intracoastal Waterway after 1.4 miles. Across the bridge lies magnificent, 5-mile-long Figure Eight Island. Blessed with maritime forests and high, rolling sand dunes covered with sea oats, Figure Eight Island is one of the most beautiful developed barrier islands on the North Carolina coast.

Guarded entrance to
Figure Eight Island

Unless you are an owner of property on the island or an invited guest, your chance of visiting this, the most exclusive of all the developed barrier islands in the state, is remote at best. Security is tight, and the bridge is manned by tenders around the clock.

Some 250 homes have been constructed on the island, and they are among the most beautiful on the entire coast. Most have been placed well back from the beach in forested areas. Prior to construction, all building and site plans must be reviewed and approved by an architectural review board. The resulting homes are aesthetically pleasing structures that carry price tags upwards of a million dollars. At the elegant Figure Eight Yacht Club, members dine in luxurious surroundings. The island has no hotels.

James Moore, the brother of "King" Roger Moore of Orton Plantation in Brunswick County, was the first recorded owner of the island. In 1755,

Cornelius Harnett, Jr., the famous Cape Fear patriot, acquired it. It is highly probable that neither of these owners ever walked on the island.

In 1795, after Harnett's death, the island was purchased at an auction of his estate by James Foy. Thus, Figure Eight became part of Poplar Grove Plantation. It remained in the Foy family for the next 160 years and was known for a time as Foy Island or Woods Beach. Legend has it that the present name came from mariners who perceived that they were sailing in a figure eight as they navigated their vessels through the channel.

In the mid-1950s, after the devastation caused by Hurricane Hazel, the value of coastal property in the Cape Fear area plummeted. In 1955, Figure Eight was sold by the Foy family and the Hutaff family—who had earlier obtained the southern portion of the island—to two Wilmington businessmen. The purchase price of a hundred thousand dollars pales in comparison with the current price of a single oceanfront lot, which is more than twice that amount. Since 1971, the island has been sold several times to corporate developers.

Retrace your route to Hampstead. Turn west off U.S. 17 onto N.C. 210 for a drive through the Pender County countryside. As is evident from the farmland on both sides of the highway, Pender is an agricultural county. However, much of its land is very flat and poorly drained.

Twelve miles northwest of Hampstead, N.C. 210 crosses the Northeast Cape Fear River at a point called Rocky Point. In 1663, Barbadian explorers gave the place its name in honor of the unusual outcropping of rock in an otherwise flat area. Rocks have been quarried from this massive outcropping for more than 125 years. When New Inlet was closed after the Civil War, stone quarried from Rocky Point was used in the project. (For more information on the closing of New Inlet, see The Wrightsville Beach to Pleasure Island Tour, pages 244–45.)

Continue 2.2 miles to the community bearing the name of the outcrop. Settled in the second half of the eighteenth century, Rocky Point was the home of many distinguished North Carolina families during the colonial period: the Lillingtons, the Swanns, the Ashes, and the Moores.

It is approximately 14 miles from Rocky Point to Currie, the small crossroads village that is home to Moores Creek National Military Park. To reach the eighty-six-acre complex, continue 1 mile past Currie on N.C. 210.

In order to preserve the site of what some experts consider the first decisive patriot victory of the American Revolution, the North Carolina General Assembly purchased the battlefield in 1898 and created a state park. By an act of the United States Congress on June 2, 1926, Moores Creek National Military Park was established when North Carolina donated the site.

Rising in northwestern Pender County, Moores Creek flows in a southeasterly direction until it merges into the Black River, a tributary of the mighty Cape Fear. During the eighteenth century, the creek was also known as Widow Moores Creek, because it flowed past land owned by the widow Elizabeth Moore.

Battlefield monument at Moores Creek National Military Park

On February 27, 1776, a bitterly cold day, this creek was the scene of a short battle that helped determine the fate of the young American nation. The Battle of Moores Creek Bridge was the first battle of the American Revolution fought in North Carolina, and it resulted in a decisive victory for North Carolina patriots over North Carolina loyalists.

Revolutionary fervor in the colony caused Royal Governor Josiah Martin to flee North Carolina in mid-1775. In January 1776, while in exile, Martin formulated a plan to reestablish royal control of the colony. On January 10, he issued a call for loyal subjects to assist in putting down the rebellion.

Within a month, some sixteen hundred Highland Scots, Regulators, and Tories assembled at Cross Creek (present-day Fayetteville). These troops, under the command of General Donald MacDonald and Lieutenant Colonel Donald McLeod, were to march to Brunswick Town on the Cape Fear River, where they would meet up with a British expeditionary force from Ireland and New England. Together, these forces would be of sufficient number to bring the colony back in line.

Months before Martin's call for troops, North Carolina had raised two regiments for the Continental Army, along with several battalions of militiamen. While the loyalists were making their plans upriver, Colonel James Moore, the commander of patriot forces in southeastern North Carolina, was designing a grand strategy to foil the enemy's scheme.

When MacDonald's loyalists began their march toward the coast, their route was blocked by Moore's troops. MacDonald quickly changed his course by crossing the Cape Fear en route to a point known as Corbetts Ferry on the Black River, where he hoped he could slip past Colonel Richard Caswell's militiamen approaching from New Bern. From Corbetts Ferry, MacDonald planned to lead his men over the bridge at Moores Creek and on to Wilmington.

The loyalists reached Corbetts Ferry first, so Moore dispatched Caswell and his patriot troops to Moores Creek. Additional men under Colonel Alexander Lillington were sent to reinforce Caswell's forces.

On the night before the battle, Lillington camped on the eastern side of Moores Creek with approximately 150 men, while Caswell camped on the western side with some 800 men. Colonel Moore and 1,000 troops were located halfway between Moores Creek and Wilmington.

The loyalist force of 1,500 men camped 6 miles from Caswell on the same side of the creek. Cognizant of Caswell's exposed position, General MacDonald convened a council of his officers, at which it was decided that an attack should be launched. When MacDonald suddenly fell ill, command was turned over to Colonel McLeod.

At one o'clock in the morning on February 27, McLeod and his army began their slow march through the swamps in the bone-chilling cold. About an hour before first light, they reached Caswell's camp, which to their surprise was abandoned. During the night, Caswell had withdrawn his forces to the other side of the creek, but campfires had been left burning so as to deceive the enemy. After crossing the creek, Caswell removed the planks from the bridge and greased the girders. At his new position, he threw up a breastwork and placed artillery to cover the road and bridge.

The loyalists regrouped at Caswell's abandoned camp and waited for daylight to pursue the rebels, whom they thought were in retreat. However, approximately a thousand patriots were waiting, anxious to fight, on the opposite side of the dismantled bridge.

At sunrise, musket fire suddenly interrupted the calm. When the attack began, the loyalists yelled, "King George and broadswords!" While 500 men, broadswords in hand, rushed the bridge, bagpipes played in the background. A small contingent of men made their way across the slippery remnants of the bridge, but they were annihilated as they approached the patriot breastwork. Loyalist losses totaled 80 killed or wounded, while the patriots lost one man, who died from wounds four days later. The battle was over in

Reconstructed Moores Creek Bridge

three minutes. Within two weeks, the retreating loyalists were captured, along with 1,600 rifles, 150 swords, and 15,000 pounds in gold.

One immediate result of the victory was the permanent end of royal authority in North Carolina. Even more significantly, the victory prompted North Carolina to become the first colony to direct its delegates to the Continental Congress in Philadelphia to vote for independence.

Because of the loyalist defeat at Moores Creek Bridge, the British invasion of North Carolina was thwarted until the waning stages of the war. Historian Edward Channing summed up the importance of the battle when he wrote, "Had the South been conquered in the first half of 1776, it is entirely conceivable that rebellion would never have turned into revolution. . . . At Moore's Creek and at Sullivan's Island [in South Carolina], the Carolinians turned aside the one combination of circumstances that might have made British conquest possible."

The patriot victory at Moores Creek was a story of heroes.

Richard Caswell was later rewarded for his contribution to the victory when he became the first elected governor of the independent state of North Carolina.

There was also a little-known hero, Private John Colwell. While the patriots were reloading their rifles, the loyalist troops who had made it over the bridge were fast approaching. A wet fuse on the patriot cannon had foiled several attempts at firing. As the enemy neared, Private Colwell pulled a red-hot stick from the campfire and lit the fuse. The resulting cannon blast decided the battle.

There was also a heroine.

As Ezekial Slocumb marched from his farm with eighty men to join Colonel Caswell's forces, he took with him a great wool coat which his young wife, Mary "Polly" Slocumb, had made for him. A terrible dream disturbed Polly's sleep on the second night after Ezekial left. In the nightmare, she saw a bloody body wrapped in the coat she had made. In desperation, she informed her servant, "Something dreadful has happened to Ezekial. Keep the baby, I'm going to find him."

Polly hurried to the barn, where she mounted her fastest horse and sped off into the night. Having covered 30 miles before daylight, she continued until she heard the cannon fire at Moores Creek Bridge. While she paused to rest under a tree, her dream became reality, as she noticed a bloody soldier in a nearby ditch covered with her husband's cloak. When Polly reached the man, she pulled back the cloak and cleaned the blood from the soldier's face. The man was not Ezekial! Still, Polly lingered to provide him water and comfort.

Soon, she was caught up in rendering aid to the wounded soldiers around the battlefield. She obtained water from a nearby stream and fashioned bandages from strips torn from her petticoat. A bloody and battered Ezekial was astonished to find his wife on the battlefield, where she remained into the night. Finally, about midnight, Polly mounted her trusty horse for the 50-mile ride through the swamps to her home.

Today, a monument honoring Mary "Polly" Hooks Slocumb stands in the park.

Monument to "Polly" Slocumb

Tours of the park begin at the visitor center, which offers an audiovisual program covering the historical background of the battle. Interesting exhibits and dioramas are laid out in the museum.

On the battlefield itself, the Battlefield Trail complex begins with the History Trail, located west of the visitor center. This route winds for 1 mile through Spanish moss-laden pines and hardwoods to the bridge, located about 0.4 mile from the trailhead. Numerous historical monuments and markers have been erected along the way. Constructed in 1857, the Patriot Monument, or Grady Monument, is the oldest stone monument in the park. It honors Private John Grady, the only patriot killed in the battle.

Near the bridge, a boardwalk crosses the creek to a trail that leads to Richard Caswell's campsite. This route makes its way through terrain often blanketed with the yellow of Carolina jasmine and the blue of clematis. Pitcher plants, sundews, and Venus' flytraps may also be found along the trail.

Near the visitor center, Tarheel Trail, a circular trail 0.3 mile in length, branches off from History Trail. Along this path, exhibits chronicle the history of naval stores, the chief industry of the Cape Fear region at the time of the battle.

Boardwalk at Moores Creek National Military Park

Although no camping is allowed in the park, there is a sheltered area for picnics on the grounds.

The tour ends here, at Moores Creek National Military Park.

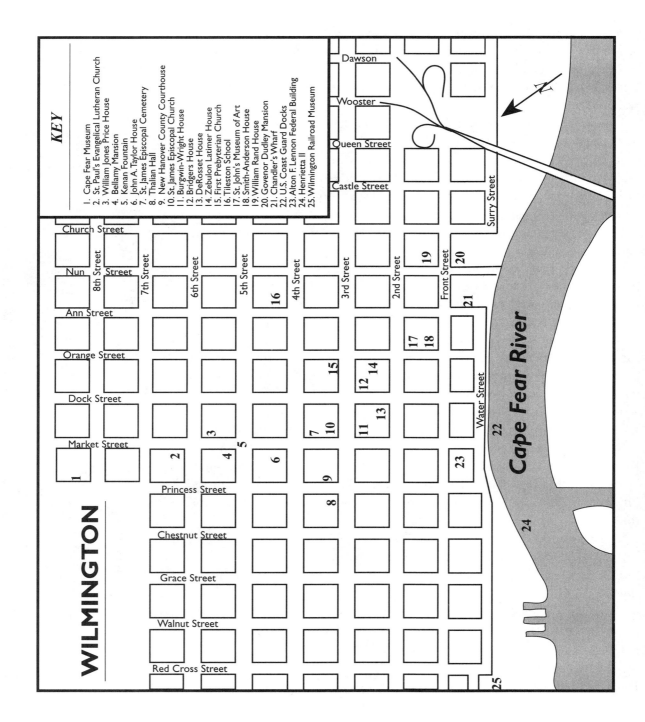

WILMINGTON

KEY

1. Cape Fear Museum
2. St. Paul's Evangelical Lutheran Church
3. William Jones Price House
4. Bellamy Mansion
5. Kenan Fountain
6. John A. Taylor House
7. St. James Episcopal Cemetery
8. Thalian Hall
9. New Hanover County Courthouse
10. St. James Episcopal Church
11. Burgwin-Wright House
12. Bridgers House
13. DeRosset House
14. Zebulon Latimer House
15. First Prebyterian Church
16. Tileston School
17. St. John's Museum of Art
18. Smith-Anderson House
19. William Rand House
20. Govenor Dudley Mansion
21. Chandler's Wharf
22. U.S. Coast Guard Docks
23. Alton F. Lennon Federal Building
24. Henrietta II
25. Wilmington Railroad Museum

Church Street
Nun Street
Ann Street
Orange Street
Dock Street
Market Street
Princess Street
Chestnut Street
Grace Street
Walnut Street
Red Cross Street

8th Street
7th Street
6th Street
5th Street
4th Street
3rd Street
2nd Street
Front Street
Water Street
Surry Street

Dawson
Wooster
Queen Street
Castle Street

Cape Fear River

The Wilmington Tour

This tour begins with a visit to Carolco Studios, on the northeastern side of Wilmington, then heads toward the Wilmington Historic District for a walking tour of the area along the river, which is packed with historical and architectural treasures. The driving tour wraps up with visits to Greenfield Park and the North Carolina State Port at Wilmington.

Among the highlights of the tour are Wilmington National Cemetery, Oakdale Cemetery, the Cape Fear Museum, the William Jones Price House, the Bellamy Mansion, the Wilmington Railroad Museum, Riverfront Park, the Governor Dudley Mansion, the St. John's Museum of Art, the Burgwin-Wright House, the story of the tunnels under Wilmington, St. James Episcopal Church and its cemetery, the Zebulon Latimer House, and Thalian Hall.

Total mileage: approximately 9 miles.

This tour begins at the intersection of U.S. 17/74 and N.C. 132 on the northern side of Wilmington.

Of the many jewels of the North Carolina coast, none sparkles more brightly than the magnificent port city of Wilmington. Strikingly beautiful both naturally and architecturally, historically significant, and economically dominant in the coastal region, Wilmington wears many hats well.

Proceed west on U.S. 17/74 (Market Street) for approximately 2.5 miles to Twenty-third Street. En route, you will glimpse the suburbs and sprawling commercial development of the city that remains the largest on the North Carolina coast. In a state that has been predominantly rural throughout its history, Wilmington has long been a population leader. Until the dawn of the twentieth century, it was the most populous city in the state. While other cities to the west have since surpassed it in size, none has been able to match the unique grace and charm bestowed upon Wilmington by history.

Turn right on Twenty-third Street and drive 8 blocks north to the entrance to Carolco Studios, at 1223 North Twenty-third.

As the undisputed king of commerce in coastal North Carolina, Wilmington boasts a diverse business community. Since the 1980s, the local economy has received a substantial boost from the film industry, which has made Wilmington "the Hollywood of the East."

Located on thirty-two acres, Carolco Studios owns one of the largest movie and television production facilities outside Hollywood. Although the complex is not open for public tours, a cafe adjacent to the lot provides an opportunity for tourists to watch the comings and goings at the studios. Moreover, feature films and television shows are regularly shot in and around Wilmington, thereby giving the public closeup views of the industry. Screen stars can often be seen patronizing local restaurants and businesses.

In 1984, Italian movie mogul Dino De Laurentiis chose Wilmington over Charleston, South Carolina, as the location for his only active permanent studio. He had become enamored with Wilmington while filming Stephen King's *Firestarter* at nearby Orton Plantation in 1983. After De Laurentiis settled on Wilmington, a huge motion-picture complex—complete with more than a half-dozen sound stages, a two-hundred-seat commissary, a gourmet food shop, a cinema, and production facilities—went up almost overnight in the sandy, gray soil just a few blocks from Wilmington International Airport.

From 1984 to 1987, DEG Studios, De Laurentiis's parent company, churned out twenty-five full-length films at the Wilmington facility. On occasion, downtown Wilmington was transformed into New York's Times Square or downtown Boston. Nearby Airlie Gardens temporarily became King Kong's boyhood home in Borneo. However, in late 1987, the sound stages suddenly grew quiet. Financial problems forced DEG Studios into bankruptcy, and for a short period, it appeared that "Hollywood East" would be no more.

Carolco Pictures, the independent production company that brought such blockbusters as *Rambo*, *Total Recall*, *Cliffhanger*, and *Basic Instinct* to the screen, took control of the Wilmington studio in 1989. Since that time, Carolco Studios has become one of the busiest film facilities in the nation. It encompasses eight sound stages, the world's largest backlit blue screen for special effects, and a back lot featuring a three-block-long, four-story-high urban street that has been used to portray New York, Chicago, Detroit, and New Orleans.

More than eighty motion pictures—among them *Betsy's Wedding*, *Sleeping with the Enemy*, *Billy Bathgate*, *Teenage Mutant Ninja Turtles*, *The Crow*, *Date with an Angel*, *Silver Bullet*, *Marie*, *Year of the Dragon*, *The Hudsucker Proxy*, *Maximum Overdrive*, *Super Mario Brothers*, *Amos and Andrew*, *Blue Velvet*, *Loose Cannons*, and *King Kong Lives*—have been produced at the Wilmington studio. Additionally, the television series "Matlock" and "The Young Indiana Jones Chronicles" have regularly been filmed here. This heavy activity at Carolco has helped North Carolina rank third—behind only California and New York—in movie production in the United States.

Return to the intersection of Twenty-third and Market streets. Turn right and drive west on Market to Twentieth Street. Turn right, or north, at the entrance to Wilmington National Cemetery.

Although the two large, historic cemeteries of the city—Wilmington National and Oakdale—are not listed among the museums of Wilmington, they probably should be. Located on a beautiful five-acre tract along Burnt Mill Creek, Wilmington National Cemetery was established in 1867. It was intended for the proper interment of Union soldiers who had been hastily buried near the spots where they fell—along the railroads leading out of the city, along the Cape Fear River, and at Fort Fisher and Southport, near the mouth of the river. Most of the Civil War dead were removed to the cemetery in 1867.

The low brick wall surmounted with ironwork along the Market Street side of the cemetery was constructed in 1934. It allows a spectacular view from the street. This wall replaced the original high wall, which, ironically enough, was fabricated of sandstone from Manassas, Virginia, near the site of the early Civil War battle. The brick walls enclosing the other three sides of the cemetery were built between 1875 and 1878.

Inside the walls, white gravestones, virtually all of them government issue, have been neatly placed in long, straight rows. Each of the stones faces east, in conformity with the belief that the dead should face the rising sun. Most of the stones mark the resting places of American soldiers from every war in which America has been involved, from the Civil War to Vietnam. Nearly sixteen hundred unknown soldiers are interred at the cemetery.

Not all of the people buried here are veterans of the armed services. One of the most famous civilians is novelist Inglis Fletcher. Her funeral in 1969 attracted many well-known authors to Wilmington. She was buried in a grave northwest of the flag circle beside her husband, John A. Fletcher, a veteran of the Spanish-American War.

Return to Market Street and continue west. In the 1700 block of Market, towering, ancient oaks veiled with Spanish moss form a canopy over the relatively narrow highway into downtown Wilmington. Gracing both sides of the street are handsome mansions built in the early nineteenth century, when this area was the streetcar suburb of the city.

Continue west on Market to its intersection with Fifteenth Street, the location of a state historical marker for Oakdale Cemetery. Turn right and drive north on Fifteenth to the historic cemetery, located at the end of the street.

This cemetery is one of the special places in Wilmington that visitors often overlook. Its secluded location deep within a residential section keeps it hidden from many tourists. Still others intentionally leave the ancient graveyard off their itinerary due to the misconception that it is nothing more than an ordinary burial ground.

To the contrary, Oakdale is one of the most peaceful, beautiful spots in all of coastal North Carolina. Considered by some experts to be one of the finest examples of mid-nineteenth-century landscape architecture in the state, the cemetery is situated on high land surrounded on three sides by streams. Since 1855, it has been the burial site of thousands of people, many famous and some unknown.

Oakdale was born in early 1852 at a meeting of prominent Wilmington businessmen who desired to establish a new burial ground outside the town limits. Dr. Armand J. DeRosset, a local physician, was elected the first president of the cemetery company. Ironically, the first burial at Oakdale took place on February 5, 1855, when Annie DeRosset, the doctor's six-year-old daughter, was interred.

During the Victorian era, Oakdale was a popular place for Wilmington residents to socialize on weekends and holidays. To accommodate the crowds, two summer houses were constructed on the grounds in the 1870s. Streetcars ran to the cemetery every ten minutes in the early part of the twentieth century. By 1950, the original 65-acre cemetery site had grown to more than 128 acres.

The beauty of the cemetery is almost beyond description. At first sight, its layout appears to be the product of a Hollywood set designer rather than of dedicated city residents and mother nature herself. Breathtaking live oaks draped in Spanish moss thrive on the hilly terrain and create a cover of shade. Winding paths, old carriageways curving in graceful crescents, and narrow roads wind their way around hundreds of individual family plots. Stone steps inscribed with family names lead to the plots, most of which are bounded by low stone walls or iron fences with elaborate designs. Many sections are furnished with wire chairs and settees cast in iron, with fern and grapevine motifs.

The Victorian-era grave markers in a variety of shapes and sizes are of special interest. Located on the grounds are Egyptian obelisks, simple slabs, rustic logs with flower garlands, Gothic pinnacles, floral bouquets of stone, cast-iron crosses, and imposing Greek Revival mausoleums constructed of stone.

Each spring, the beauty of the cemetery is enhanced when thousands of flowers burst forth in bloom. Many of the plants that now beautify the grounds were planted by descendants of people buried in the cemetery long ago.

In many ways, Oakdale is a history book detailing the story of Wilmington since the mid-nineteenth century. Various sections of the cemetery exhibit the racial, ethnic, and religious heritage of the port city—for example, there is a Masonic section. Some of the finest ironwork in the cemetery is on the arched gate to the Hebrew section, opened on March 6, 1855, by the local Jewish community.

A large plot with few markers is the site where more than three hundred victims of the yellow-fever epidemic of 1862 were buried in unmarked graves. At the time, not one of the ten local physicians had even seen or treated the disease, and as a consequence, none of them could recognize the early symptoms: chills, headache, backache, and fever, followed by a flushed face, nausea, and vomiting. By the time the telltale signs of the disease—the jaundice, the stomach and intestinal hemorrhages, and the terrible "black vomit"—appeared, the doctors were virtually helpless.

Panic struck the city. Many wealthy residents fled upcountry by carriage and railroad, until most towns would no longer accept refugees from Wilmington. For those who could not leave or chose to remain, there was a month of horror to survive. John D. Bellamy, Jr., a future congressman, watched from the steps of his father's mansion on Market Street as wagonloads of corpses were transported to Oakdale.

Throughout the ordeal, which ended in mid-November 1862 with an early cold snap, many stories of self-sacrifice and duty were written. Despite the exodus of many prominent citizens, the physicians and the clergy of Wilmington remained to minister to the suffering city. Dr. James H. Dickinson, one of the finest physicians of the Cape Fear area, spent every waking hour treating those afflicted with the disease. When he realized that he himself had contracted it, Dr. Dickinson wrote out instructions for his patients and returned to his own home to die. Father Thomas Murphy of St. Thomas the Apostle Church, the Reverend John L. Prichard of First Baptist Church, and the Reverend Robert B. Drane of St. James Episcopal Church tended the sick, provided Christian guidance, and worked tirelessly until each clergyman himself became a casualty of the epidemic. Dickinson, Prichard, and Drane are buried in the cemetery.

Confederate Memorial Monument

Of the many monuments gracing the grounds, the most impressive marks the burial site of 467 unknown men. Unveiled on May 10, 1872, the Confederate Memorial Monument consists of a tall bronze statue of a Confederate soldier on a marble and granite pedestal. Bronze likenesses of Generals Robert E. Lee and Stonewall Jackson are on the front and rear faces of the pedestal. Resting under the monument are the remains of Confederate soldiers who died at Fort Fisher in the waning days of the Confederacy.

Much of the fame of Oakdale Cemetery comes from the illustrious individuals buried here.

Perhaps the most famous woman interred in Oakdale is Rose O'Neal Greenhow, the talented, clever Confederate spy who was one of the few women to lose their lives in active service during the Civil War. Her grave is marked by a simple cross bearing the notation "a bearer of dispatches to the Confederacy." Her body was brought to Wilmington after she drowned near Fort Fisher in September 1864 while attempting to avoid capture by Union forces.

Among the other famous Confederate heroes buried in the cemetery are Generals W. H. C. Whiting, Alexander MacRae, and John D. Barry; George Davis, the attorney general of the Confederacy; Captain John Newland Maffitt, naval hero; and Benjamin Beery, Confederate shipbuilder.

Also on the list of honored dead laid to rest in Oakdale are Edward B. Dudley, the first governor of North Carolina elected by popular vote, and Henry Bacon, Jr., the brilliant American architect.

Some graves of the not-so-famous have become noteworthy because of the intriguing stories behind the people buried in them.

A heartwarming tale surrounds a grave marker erected by the citizens of Wilmington in memory of a man and his best friend who gave their lives fighting a fire on February 11, 1880. Captain William A. Ellerbrook, a native of Hamburg, Germany, happened to be in town on that fateful day. When a cry went out along the waterfront for volunteers to assist in fighting a fire at a store at the corner of Front and Dock streets, Ellerbrook responded. From inside the blazing inferno, his cries for help could be heard. Recognizing his master's call, the captain's big Newfoundland dog raced into the burning building.

A day later, after the ruins cooled, the body of Ellerbrook was discovered pinned face-down to the floor by a rafter. Beside him was the body of Boss, his faithful dog. In the dog's mouth was a portion of Ellerbrook's coat, which Boss had torn away while attempting to pull his master to safety.

So moved were the citizens of Wilmington by the heroism of the twenty-four-year-old sea captain and his pet that they donated funds to erect a monument in Oakwood Cemetery, where the two were buried together. On one side of the marker are the details of Ellerbrook's life. On the other is a design of a sleeping dog with the words *Faithful Unto Death*.

Oakdale Cemetery is open daily to the public. Information on specific grave sites and a free brochure giving directions to numbered plots are available at the office, located at the entrance gate.

Return to the intersection of Fifteenth and Market, turn right, and drive west to New Hanover High School, at 1307 Market. Rising two stories over a full basement, the enormous sand-colored building is one of the few structures in the city with an exterior of glazed tile. Construction of the central block was completed in 1922. The two wings were added three years later.

Several Wilmingtonians who have achieved national and international fame in the second half of the twentieth century attended this school.

David Brinkley, the beloved NBC and ABC television journalist and author, was a student here. Born in 1920 in a two-story frame house at the corner of Eighth and Princess streets, he began his career in journalism as a reporter with the local daily newspaper.

Robert Ruark, the noted newspaperman, novelist, and world traveler, also graduated from New Hanover High. Born in Wilmington in 1915, Ruark used his experiences as a child on the Cape Fear as the basis for three of his most famous novels: *The Old Man and the Boy* (1957), *Poor No More* (1959), and *The Old Man's Boy Grows Older* (1961).

Two former superstar quarterbacks of the National Football League, Sonny Jurgensen and Roman Gabriel, began their stellar athletic careers at New Hanover High School.

Continue west on Market Street to the Cape Fear Museum, formerly the New Hanover County Museum of History, located at 814 Market. Since April 1970, the museum has been housed at the present location, but its roots go back to 1897, making it the oldest local-history museum in the state. It was founded by the United Daughters of the Confederacy "to collect and preserve relics and objects of local value . . . relating to the recent war."

The collection was originally assembled and displayed in the John A. Taylor House (Wilmington Light Infantry Building), located farther west on Market Street. Over the years, the holdings were transferred to Raleigh, where they remained until 1925, when the museum was reestablished in the New Hanover County Courthouse on North Third Street.

The present museum building, built in a modified late Gothic Revival style, was constructed as an armory in the mid-1930s by the Public Works Administration. After its acquisition for use as a museum, the expansive brick building was extensively renovated. Numerous additions and modifications have since taken place. Neatly displayed throughout the multilevel exhibition area, the eclectic collection chronicles the cultural and natural history of Wilmington and the surrounding area.

Wilmington was born of a crude settlement that took root on a high bluff on the Cape Fear River in 1732. A year earlier, John Maultsbury had received a grant of 640 acres at the fork of the river, on which he began a village, New Liverpool. About the same time, John Watson obtained a patent for adjoining lands from Governor George Burrington. James Wimble, a Boston mariner, was employed to lay out a town on Watson's grant. By 1733, he was selling lots in the town he called Carthage.

As the community grew, its name was changed to Newton. Its quick rise in stature was accentuated when Governor Gabriel Johnston ordered the county government and court to meet in Newton in 1735.

Legislation was introduced in 1739 to establish the town of Wilmington at the site of Newton. Governor Johnston selected the new name to exalt his patron, Spencer Compton, the earl of Wilmington. In February 1740, the colonial assembly passed an act that incorporated the town of Wilmington and made it the county seat of New Hanover County.

A variety of factors combined to make Wilmington the most important port in the colony soon after it was chartered. Its fine harbor was located upstream from the storms and the pirates of the Atlantic. Of equal importance were the vast forests of virgin pine encircling the town. From these forests came tar, pitch, turpentine, and similar products which were badly needed by Britain and other European powers. From 1720 to 1870, North Carolina led the world in the production of naval stores, and Wilmington was the primary center for their export. Museum exhibits showcase the naval-stores industry.

Wilmington was mostly spared the hostilities of the Revolutionary War until early 1781. Prior to that time, the closest fighting was 20 miles to the north at Moores Creek Bridge.

On April 12, 1781, the battered, demoralized army of Lord Cornwallis straggled into Wilmington after its costly "victory" over the American forces of General Nathanael Greene at Guilford Courthouse. For almost two weeks, the British army rested and took on supplies at Wilmington. Then, on April 25, Cornwallis began his fateful journey north to Yorktown, Virginia.

A fleet horse carrying famous cavalry officer Henry "Light Horse Harry" Lee galloped into Wilmington on November 17, 1781, bearing the jubilant news of the surrender of Cornwallis.

Of all the museum's holdings, the most impressive is the collection of artifacts related to Civil War history. Many of the items were acquired in 1983 from the defunct Blockade Runner Museum at Carolina Beach. Included in the acquisition were two large dioramas—one of Fort Fisher and the other of the Wilmington waterfront during its days of critical importance to the Confederacy.

In the annals of the Civil War, the names of certain Southern cities appear over and over again. By 1864, Wilmington, North Carolina, had become the most important city in the entire South, with the possible exception of the Confederate capital of Richmond.

No sooner had the rumblings of war commenced in early 1861 than Wilmington began its rise to prominence as an industrial center, a supply depot, the chief port of the blockade runners, and "the lifeline of the Confederacy." Over the next four years, the armies of the Confederacy were fed, clothed, and equipped thanks to goods delivered to Wilmington by sleek vessels that had eluded the Federal blockade along the North Carolina coast.

By the second half of 1864, Wilmington was the last major Southern port open to the Confederacy. Just a month after Fort Fisher fell to Union forces in January 1865, Wilmington was abandoned to the approaching blue-clad soldiers. As a result, the fate of the Southern war effort was sealed.

Among the most popular museum exhibits are the displays of memorabilia from hometown sports legends. Exhibited are a number of items that once belonged to favorite son Michael Jordan, the man many observers consider the greatest basketball player ever.

From the museum, proceed west on Market Street toward the waterfront. This route will take you into the heart of the Wilmington Historic District. In a speech before the Historic Wilmington Foundation in November 1975, David Brinkley told his audience, "I'm on the Board of Trustees at Colonial Williamsburg, which is really only a big restoration project. . . . It may be a startling fact, but true, that Wilmington has a greater number of interesting houses than Williamsburg does."

Indeed, Wilmington possesses residential, commercial, and governmental buildings that are the envy of the other historic cities of the Atlantic coast. Bounded by Ninth Street on the east, the Cape Fear River on the west, Harnett Street on the north, and Wright Street on the south, the two-hundred-block Wilmington Historic District has been entered on the National Register of Historic Places. Encompassing the oldest part of the city, it contains buildings dating from the first quarter of the eighteenth century. Within the district are structures representing every major architectural style used in the United States in the eighteenth and nineteenth centuries.

In 1757, a visitor named Peter DuBois provided a glowing account of the city, noting that "the Regularity of the Streets are equal to those of Philadelphia and Buildings in General very good. Many of Brick, two or three stories high with double piazzas which make a good appearance."

Laid out in a style popular in Europe throughout the eighteenth century, the Wilmington grid plan was established in 1739 and modified in 1743. It remains virtually intact. With the exception of Water and Front streets, the north-south streets are designated by numbers. The named streets begin at the river and run east.

A leisurely walk or slow drive along these ancient streets allows visitors to savor the history and architectural heritage of the city. Some of these ancient thoroughfares seem too narrow to allow two lanes of traffic. Paradoxically, others nearby are extremely wide, giving the impression that they were constructed in the modern age to handle vehicular traffic. Three boulevards—Market Street, Third Street, and Fifth Street—measure ninety-nine feet in width, instead of the sixty-six standard for streets. Market and Fifth are decorated with landscaped center plazas and curbside greenery. Some city streets are still paved with brick.

Follow Market Street to St. Paul's Evangelical Lutheran Church, located 2 blocks from the museum at 603 Market. On September 6, 1859, the cornerstone of this handsome Gothic Revival structure was laid by the local German community. Construction was not completed until 1869, and the brick exterior was stuccoed four years later. This church's most striking

William Jones Price House

architectural feature is the square central tower, from which rise four pinnacles and a small spire topped with a cross.

Continue west to the William Jones Price House, at 514 Market.

Wilmington has its share of ghost stories, and one of the most interesting has to do with this two-story brick dwelling, built in the Italianate style in 1855 for a local physician. Before the house was built, the eastern boundary line of the city ran along what is now Fifth Street. The lot on which the house was constructed was situated at the top of a bluff overlooking the city. Known as Gallows Hill, the bluff had previously been the place where criminals were executed. After each execution, if the victim's body was not claimed, it was buried at the site. Legend holds that the unclaimed souls continue to roam the property.

Tales of strange happenings and wandering spirits came from members of Dr. Price's family as soon as they moved in. In the basement, where the physician maintained his offices, and in the twelve large rooms of the upper floors, eerie sounds were heard in the dead of night. Sometimes, after every family member was safely tucked in bed, doors opened and closed. Footsteps were heard on the elegant staircase. The sound of metal on metal emanated from the house.

In 1934, the Gause family came into possession of the property. The reports of the hauntings continued. Experts on the supernatural have been unable to explain the mystery after spending night after night in the house. In recent years, several old brick tombs containing the bones of unknown criminals have been unearthed by workmen laying pipe in the backyard. Some believe that the unexplained occurrences are the work of the condemned men, who are said to be seeking peace.

From the William Jones Price House, proceed to the Bellamy Mansion, located in the same block on the northeastern corner of Market and Fifth streets.

The Bellamy Mansion is one of the last great antebellum houses built in America. Noted architect James F. Post was assisted by Connecticut draftsman Rufus Bunnell in the creation of the splendid twenty-two-room wooden castle, constructed between 1857 and 1859 for Dr. John Dillard Bellamy and family. An ardent supporter of the Confederate cause, Dr. Bellamy allowed Southern soldiers to use the cupola as an observation post throughout the war. When Wilmington fell under Federal control in February 1865, the mansion was used as the headquarters of Union general Joseph Hawley, a native of North Carolina. Accordingly, many slaves were granted their freedom on the steps of the house.

As early as 1903, the magnificent structure made its appearance on post-cards of the city. Later, it was featured in several books and magazines on architecture.

Ellen Douglas Bellamy, one of Dr. Bellamy's daughters, was the last member of the family to live in the mansion. At her death in 1946, the house was inherited by more than fifty relatives. Years passed while the heirs debated what should be done with the house.

In 1971, a potentially destructive fire of suspicious origin spurred the owners to action. Although the fire did only $6,000 worth of damage to the structure, more than $70,000 in antique furnishings were lost. Consequently, in 1972, the heirs formed a nonprofit foundation—Bellamy Mansion, Inc.—to fund the preservation of the house. From 1972 to 1990, the foundation pumped more than $240,000 into the restoration project.

On a cold, windy December afternoon in 1989, more than fifteen hundred people waited in a line that stretched a couple of blocks down Market

The Bellamy Mansion

Street to see the mansion, which was being opened to the public for one day only. It was the first time the mansion had been opened in many years.

Encouraged by the public's interest, and satisfied that the house could be saved for future generations, the Bellamy family donated the mansion and grounds to the Historic Preservation Foundation of North Carolina, Inc. Now operated as the Bellamy Mansion Museum of History and Design Arts, the house celebrated its grand opening in April 1994.

Even though the restoration project continues, the museum offers exhibits related to preservation, decorative arts, regional architecture, and landscape architecture. A glassed-in portion of an unrestored interior wall is used to illustrate the damage sustained in the fire of 1971.

This structure has been unashamedly known as a mansion ever since it was built. Probably the most visually impressive house in the city, the Bellamy Mansion deserves its title. Regarded as an architectural maverick, the enormous white palace is a combination of Greek Revival, Italianate, and Classical Revival styles. The imposing multi-story masterpiece rests on a raised basement. The two-story porch wrapping around three sides of the house features fourteen massive Corinthian columns. Atop the tall, pedimented gable roof rests the ornately decorated cupola.

The mansion's appearance is enhanced by its location on a large corner lot. Giant magnolias and tropical plants grace the front and side yards, which are enclosed by an elaborate cast-iron fence. Several outbuildings, including a two-story slave quarters, a privy, a cistern, and a dairy cooling room, survive in the rear corner of the lot.

Before leaving Market and Fifth, take a moment to enjoy the Kenan Fountain, unmistakable in the center of the intersection.

Wilmington has earned its place as one of the nation's most historic cities. Its citizens have honored significant local events and people with a variety of markers and monuments. Although modern traffic engineers have reduced it in size and splendor, the Kenan Fountain remains one of the most significant monuments of the city.

Erected in 1921, the fountain was given by native son William Rand Kenan, Jr., to beautify the city and to honor his parents. Carrere and Hastings, the firm with such credits as the New York Public Library, the United States Senate Office Building, and the old United States House of

Representatives Building, designed and sculpted this majestic fountain in New York. It was erected there, dismantled, and then shipped to Wilmington in more than thirty boxcars.

Water is sprayed from a limestone bowl and splashes into a circular pool. Secondary fountains featuring sculpted turtles and fish are situated around the pool.

In 1953, a street-level section of the fountain was removed following a recommendation by state highway engineers that the entire intersection be cleared "in the interest of public safety."

William Rand Kenan, Jr., the donor of the fountain, was born in Wilmington in 1872 to parents whose families had already left their imprint on the history of the state. He descended from the famous Kenan family of nearby Kenansville and the Hargrave family, who provided the land on which the University of North Carolina at Chapel Hill was built.

In 1894, Kenan graduated from that school—an institution which would thereafter benefit substantially from his affluence. In Chapel Hill, he gained worldwide attention for his discovery of calcium carbide, the basis for the manufacture of acetylene. From that discovery emerged the Union Carbide Company. As a principal in the company, Kenan made important connections with America's wealthiest industrialists.

His scientific genius caught the attention of Henry Morrison Flagler, a partner of John Rockefeller in the Standard Oil Company. At the time, Flagler was beginning to develop the eastern coast of Florida. He secured Kenan's services as a consultant over all of his Florida enterprises, which included railroads and a chain of resort hotels. In 1901, Flagler married Kenan's sister, Mary Lily, further cementing the relationship between the two men.

Drive west to the 400 block of Market.

Constructed between 1859 and 1870, First Baptist Church, at 421 Market, is little changed from the plans drawn by Samuel Sloan, who later designed the Governor's Mansion in Raleigh. Inside the massive brick sanctuary, the original pews, galleries, and other wooden features—all constructed of heart of pine—survive. Of the exterior architectural features, the most interesting are the double towers, one at either end of the facade. The eastern tower is the taller, stretching 197 feet above the street. At the time it was completed, the tower was the tallest church spire in the United States.

Constructed in 1847 as the residence of a local businessman and ferry operator, the John A. Taylor House (Wilmington Light Infantry Building), at 409-411 Market, is an unusual Classical Revival structure that has been used for a variety of purposes. This sturdy, two-story, pressed-brick building has a marble-veneer exterior. In 1892, it was acquired by the Wilmington Light Infantry and used as an armory until 1951. Wilmington Light Infantry members placed the existing cannon atop the corner of the roof parapet. The building was later used for a time as the public library.

The Harnett Obelisk, set in the center of Market Street just before the intersection with Fourth Street, memorializes Cornelius Harnett, Jr., and the other Cape Fear patriots who offered the first armed resistance to the Stamp Act in the American colonies. From the bottom of the marble base to the tip of the obelisk, the monument rises thirty feet. Its cornerstone was laid in mid-1906.

At the intersection of Market and Fourth streets, turn right on Fourth and drive north to the intersection with Red Cross Street. Turn left on Red Cross and proceed west 4 blocks to the junction with Water Street on the Wilmington waterfront. Turn left on Water Street and park in the on-street spaces just south of the Wilmington Railroad Museum to begin a walking tour of the downtown area.

Located at 501 Nutt Street, near the intersection of Water and Red Cross, the Wilmington Railroad Museum pays homage to an industry that has been an integral part of the city since the first half of the nineteenth century.

In 1835, a meeting of the most influential businessmen of the city at the home of future governor Edward B. Dudley resulted in a revolutionary innovation in the local transportation system: the railroad. Construction of the Wilmington and Raleigh Railroad commenced a year later. However, the failure of Raleigh interests to raise their construction obligations caused the rails to be rerouted to Weldon, near the North Carolina–Virginia border. After four years of arduous labor, the final spike of the Wilmington and Weldon Railroad was driven near Goldsboro on March 7, 1840, completing the 161.5-mile track. At that time, the track was the longest in the world.

During the Civil War, the Wilmington and Weldon Railroad was of ex-

The Wilmington Railroad Museum

treme importance to the Confederate war effort. Weapons, shoes, clothing, and food from the blockade runners at Wilmington were hastily transported via the railroad to the battlefields of Virginia. So vital was the railroad that it was known the world over as "the Lifeline of the Confederacy."

In 1902, the Atlantic Coast Line Railroad, the successor of the Wilmington and Weldon, selected Wilmington as its home office. Until December 10, 1955, when the announcement was made that the general offices of the Atlantic Coast Line would be moved to Jacksonville, Florida—a day still known to many older Wilmingtonians as "Black Thursday"—the railroad shops and buildings dominated waterfront activity. At the time of the unwelcome announcement, the railroad employed 1,350 people locally, and its annual payroll constituted 10 percent of the income in the city.

In the late 1970s, a group of former railroad employees and train buffs, concerned that Wilmington was about to lose a significant part of its history, formulated plans for a museum. Since it opened in 1984, the Wilmington Railroad Museum has been housed in one of the few surviving buildings from the great railroad empire that once flourished here.

Before entering the brick building, visitors are at liberty to examine the steam engine and bright red caboose on the grounds. Inside the museum, the exhibits transport patrons back to the era of the passenger railroad. Among the interesting artifacts displayed are a four-ounce conductor's timepiece, a bar of soap from a Pullman car, and station equipment. Historic photographs line the walls, and model trains fascinate young and old alike.

Adjacent to the museum, the Downtown Area Revitalization Effort has developed the Coast Line Convention Center, a $7-million complex of lodging, dining, meeting, and shopping facilities. Housed in the complex is the Greater Wilmington Chamber of Commerce, thought to be the oldest organization of its kind in the state.

From the museum and convention center, walk south on Water Street.

In accordance with the original town plan, the street on the waterfront was named Front Street, rather than taking its place among the numerically named streets running parallel to the river. A new street named Water Street, located closer to the water, was authorized by the legislature in 1785. Thus, Water Street became the scene of the waterfront activity that has made Wilmington a business and industrial giant for more than two centuries.

Stop at the United States Coast Guard Docks, located 3 blocks from the museum at the foot of Princess Street. Visiting military ships from foreign countries frequently tie up here. Public tours of the vessels are sometimes available.

Just beyond the United States Coast Guard Docks is Riverfront Park. Here, visitors can stand where busy piers and wharves were once located and enjoy the salty flavor of the port city. Just across the river, the once-potent guns of the Battleship *North Carolina* seem to be turned on Wilmington.

This municipal park offers a scenic vista of the Cape Fear River, the very essence of the old city. Although Wilmington is nearly 30 miles upriver from the mouth, the deep Cape Fear has made it an important port of call for ships from all over the world since the middle of the eighteenth century.

From the park, visitors can gaze south down the river to see the Cape Fear Memorial Bridge. When this engineering marvel was completed in October 1969, it was the first lift-span bridge in the state.

Of the many interesting architectural features embodied in the bridge, the 408-foot lift span is the most spectacular. In elevator-like fashion, the span is raised and lowered to allow large ships to clear the bridge. Two enormous support towers rise 200 feet above the river.

A mind-boggling list of materials—including 82,500 pounds of wire rope and cable, 258 railroad cars full of concrete, and 3,000,000 pounds of reinforced steel—were used in the bridge's construction.

Park visitors who wish to see more of the town via the river can use either of two tour vessels that dock on the river at the park.

The *Captain J. N. Maffitt*, a fifty-four-foot World War II launch, operates as a river taxi between Wilmington and the Battleship *North Carolina*. Named for John Newland Maffitt—a Wilmingtonian who acquired the title "Sea Devil of the Confederacy" for his exploits as an officer in the Confederate navy—the boat treats passengers to a panorama of the historic city.

On a much grander scale, the *Henrietta II* offers narrated dinner cruises on the river. When Wilmington native Carl Mashburn brought his new, eighty-six-foot boat to the port city in 1988, the vessel earned the distinction of being the only true sternwheeler in the state. The original *Henrietta*, this ship's namesake, was constructed in 1818 at Fayetteville. The first steam-

The Henrietta II

boat built on the Cape Fear, it made regular trips between Wilmington and Fayetteville for forty years.

Towering above Riverfront Park on the eastern side of Water Street is the massive Alton F. Lennon Federal Building. On December 9, 1916, the cornerstone was laid for this magnificent stone edifice. Designed to house the United States Customs Office, this stately, three-story Neoclassical Revival structure has dominated the Wilmington waterfront since its completion. Few cities of comparable size in the nation can boast such an imposing federal structure.

The Alton F. Lennon Federal Building

James Wetmore, architect of the United States Treasury Building in Washington, D.C., is credited with the design of the building. Rising from an enormous stone base, the central block is adorned with Doric pilasters and engaged columns. Projecting wings on either side add balance to the block, which is capped by a stone balustrade.

Continue 3 blocks south on Water Street to Chandler's Wharf, at the foot of Ann Street. Developed in the 1970s on a site where wharves and warehouses stood in the eighteenth and nineteenth centuries, this five-acre shopping and dining complex features a cluster of restored buildings in a

John Taxis

shady waterfront setting, along with an elegant warehouse mall across the street. Cobblestone streets and nautical antiques spread about the grounds lend a maritime atmosphere. Of special interest on the waterfront is the tugboat *John Taxis*, thought to be the oldest in the United States.

Proceed east for 1 block on Ann Street to its intersection with South Front. Turn right and walk south along the 300 block of South Front. Of the half-dozen or so houses in this block built prior to the Civil War, the Wells-Brown-Lord House, at 300 South Front, is the oldest. Constructed in 1773, the tall, two-story frame dwelling rests on a high bluff overlooking the river.

Cross Nun Street to see the Governor Dudley Mansion, at 400 South Front.

Of the numerous mansions gracing the streets of the Wilmington Historic District, this elegant showplace is the oldest and one of the most beautiful. Constructed around 1825 by Edward B. Dudley, governor of North Carolina and the first president of the Wilmington and Weldon Railroad, the Federal-style mansion was subsequently renovated and enlarged after being damaged by two fires.

Dudley made the house a center for social and political activities. Subsequent owners, including socialite Pembroke Jones, maintained the tradition. As a consequence, the house has hosted more notable people than any other residence in the city. In 1844, during his presidential campaign, Henry Clay stayed in the mansion. Four years later, Daniel Webster was entertained here. Future Union general William T. Sherman attended the wedding of Governor Dudley's daughter in the mansion's dining room. Mr. and Mrs. Pembroke Jones welcomed Cardinal Gibbons and twelve bishops to the mansion in January 1890. Woodrow Wilson, then a professor at Princeton, visited the house in January 1901, while historian James Sprunt owned the mansion. President William Taft breakfasted with Sprunt on his visit to Wilmington that same year. Included in the Taft party was Captain Archibald Butt, who later had the dubious distinction of being the only North Carolinian to die aboard the *Titanic*. When he came to Wilmington to lecture at Thalian Hall, William Jennings Bryan was feted at the Governor Dudley Mansion by Sprunt.

The brick house originally consisted of just the two-story main block. Flanking recessed wings were subsequently added. After he acquired the house in 1895, James Sprunt put a second story on the wings and enclosed the property with the existing brick walls. The tall palm trees growing on the grounds were planted a year later.

At the intersection of South Front and Nun streets, turn east along the 100 block of Nun. There is a fine ensemble of houses, many built in the second half of the nineteenth century, in this block. Of particular interest is the William Rand Kenan House, at 110 Nun. Built in the Italianate style in 1870, the house was the birthplace of William Rand Kenan, Jr., and his siblings. Its present Neoclassical appearance dates from renovations in 1910.

The William Rand Kenan House

Across the street from the William Rand Kenan House, the 1910-vintage dwelling at 117 Nun was the boyhood home of author Robert Ruark.

After 1 block on Nun, turn left onto South Second Street and walk north along the 300 block of South Second. Here, a trio of houses—the Louis Poisson House at 308 South Second, built around 1886; the McRae-Beery House at 303 South Second, built around 1850; and the Walker-Cowan House at 302 South Second, built around 1869—display the classic Italianate style that dominated Wilmington residential architecture throughout much of the nineteenth century.

At the intersection of South Second and Ann streets, turn left and walk west 1 block on Ann. Turn right on South Front and proceed 1 block north to Orange Street. Turn right onto the 100 block of Orange.

Located at 102 Orange, the Smith-Anderson House is thought to be the oldest structure in the city. Erected in 1740, the dignified two-and-a-half-story building stands directly on the sidewalk of an avenue that was nothing more than a narrow, unpaved path when the house was built. Constructed in the Georgian style, the imposing house has been modified on several occasions.

The St. John's Museum of Art is located at 114 Orange in a complex of historic structures that includes the former St. John's Masonic Lodge (1804), the Cowan House (1830), and the former St. Nicholas Greek Orthodox Church. The museum opened its doors on April 5, 1962. Since that time, it has earned a reputation as an outstanding regional art museum.

St. John's Museum of Art

Its permanent collection is housed in the former St. John's Masonic Lodge, one of the most historic landmarks in the city. Constructed as the first permanent home of St. John's Lodge No. 1, the oldest Masonic lodge in the state, it exhibits a Georgian style, even though it dates from the Federal era.

St. John's was one of the few buildings south of Market Street that survived the disastrous fire of November 4, 1819, which destroyed over three hundred buildings in downtown Wilmington. Members of the lodge were able to salvage their meeting house by covering it with wet blankets. They managed to keep the blankets saturated with water from a bucket brigade of members stretching in a long line all the way to the river.

A need for larger quarters led to the relocation of St. John's Lodge to Front Street in 1824. Thomas Brown, a prominent local jeweler, thereafter purchased the property for use as his personal residence. It remained in his family until 1943. Frame additions to the original brick structure were in place before 1849.

James H. McKoy acquired the house in 1943 and converted it into a popular restaurant, St. John's Tavern. For the duration of World War II, the eating establishment proved a favorite of the multitude of armed-services personnel stationed in the area. Following the war, its reputation spread far and wide. By the time it closed in 1955, the tavern had a reservation book that read like a who's who of world-famous personages.

Some of the original English locks and hinges are evident on the doors of the old lodge building. The lamp beside the entrance steps is the only survivor of the first electric streetlights installed in the city in 1886.

On the interior, a map entitled "Plan of the Town of Wilmington" graces the eastern wall. Reproduced from the original drawn in 1810 by J. J. Belanger, a French cartographer, the map depicts the old section of the city and details the nine public buildings in existence when St. John's was erected. Today, only St. John's survives.

The museum maintains the Hughes Gallery at the former St. Nicholas Greek Orthodox Church. Twelve diverse temporary exhibitions are held in this gallery each year.

Art classes, workshops, and other educational programs are conducted in the Cowan House.

The museum's ever-expanding collection features two centuries of North Carolina art. By far the most significant acquisition to date took place in 1984, when the museum received a bequest of a set of original color prints by nineteenth-century American artist Mary Cassatt, who worked with the Impressionist masters of France. Fewer than ten such sets exist in the entire world.

After 1 block on Orange, turn left onto South Second and walk north for 2 blocks.

Located at 23 South Second, the DeRosset House ranks with the Bellamy Mansion as the two finest antebellum homes in the city. The beauty of this enormous, five-bay, two-story frame mansion is heightened by its splendid setting on a brick-terraced hill overlooking the river.

Built in 1841 by Dr. A. J. DeRosset III, the house exhibits a Greek Revival portico supported by fluted Doric columns. Two significant changes were later made to the house. In 1874, the Italianate cornice and the tall cupola, reminiscent of an Italian bell tower, were added. Only three such cupolas exist in the city today. At the same time, an ell was attached to the rear and an enclosed porch was added on the Dock Street side. To enlarge the house, the ell was extended to Dock Street in 1914.

At the intersection of Second and Market, turn right and walk east 1 block on Market.

One of the few historic houses in Wilmington that is open to the public, the Burgwin-Wright House, at 224 Market, affords an opportunity for visitors to appreciate the wealth and prestige of John Burgwin, who built the beautiful house in 1770.

Constructed on the massive stone walls of an old jail that appeared on the Sauthier map of 1769, the two-story frame structure is the most opulent of the few remaining Georgian-style houses in the city. Its most prominent exterior features are its double piazzas, front and back, covered by the overlapping roof. Ionic columns support the porch canopy.

Of special interest is the detached three-story kitchen. Separating the kitchen from the main house is a courtyard surrounded by well-landscaped grounds and a magnificent garden. The garden plan is characteristic of eighteenth-century English gardens. Enormous magnolia trees shade the front lawn.

John Burgwin, an unrepentant Tory who served as colonial treasurer under Royal Governor Arthur Dobbs, found it necessary for his personal safety to flee to England at the outbreak of the Revolutionary War. He remained there until the hostilities ended. In Burgwin's absence, Lord Cornwallis and his staff occupied the house for two weeks in 1781. The house's original floorboards display marks made by British muskets.

An intriguing story that unfolded more than two hundred years ago surrounds the stately house. Before his arrival in Wilmington, one of the young officers on Cornwallis's staff was smitten by a young lady in South Carolina. While sequestered at the Burgwin-Wright House, this officer used his diamond ring to etch his true love's name in a windowpane. The war soon ended, enabling him to return to South Carolina. There, he married the woman of his dreams and took her to England.

Several years later, the young couple sailed to America and took up residence in New York. In 1836, the couple's son visited Wilmington as the guest of Dr. Thomas H. Wright, who had inherited the house. As fate would have it, the visitor was quartered in the bedroom occupied by his father almost a half-century earlier. He noticed the etched pane of glass and at once recognized the name as his mother's.

Forty years later, John W. Barrow, the grandson of the British officer, having been told the story of the windowpane by his father, came to Wilmington in search of it. Calling at the Burgwin-Wright House, he learned from the owner that the house had been remodeled. Barrow and the owner descended to the cellar, where prisoners had once been confined during wartime. There, they found the special pane, which had been put in storage after the renovations. Barrow returned to his home with the prize in his possession.

Every day, thousands of drivers and pedestrians travel the streets and sidewalks of Wilmington without realizing that a mysterious labyrinth of tunnels lies beneath them. Throughout the twentieth century, workmen demolishing buildings and digging utility lines have unearthed ancient, bricked-over tunnels in various parts of downtown. At least four distinct passageways—one of which is evidenced by a bricked-over opening in the northwestern wall of the cellar of the Burgwin-Wright House—are known to exist. This tunnel leads to a second tunnel that connects with the Jacob's Run tunnel, the most famous of the passageways.

While clearing a site at the northeastern corner of Second and Market streets for a construction project in 1958, workers unwittingly smashed a hole in the top of the Jacob's Run tunnel. An examination of the arched passageway disclosed that it ran with the flowing waters of Jacob's Run, an underground stream which originates at springs near the intersection of Fourth and Princess streets and flows west to the Cape Fear. Wooden flooring covers the stream in the tunnel to allow human passage. Constructed of handmade bricks of various sizes, the tunnel measures two feet in width and six and a half feet in height.

Although the origin and initial purpose of the subterranean passages remain a mystery, several explanations have been posited. In colonial times, dark, damp passageways were used to store and cure hides. A more plausible explanation is that the tunnels were escape routes for early citizens of the town, who lived under constant threat of Spanish privateers. Legend has it that during the Revolutionary War, secret passageways allowed American prisoners to escape from the British jail in the subbasement of the Burgwin-Wright House.

Just beyond the Burgwin-Wright House, the George Davis Statue stands in Market Street at its intersection with Third. Erected to memorialize the native son who served as senator and attorney general of the Confederate States of America, the handsome statue depicts Davis with an arm outstretched toward the west. Sculpted by F. H. Packer, it was dedicated on April 20, 1911. In late 1987, the statue was restored to its original beauty by Van Der Stock, an internationally known sculptor from Holland. Fittingly, the northwestern corner of the intersection where the statue stands was the site of the local Confederate headquarters, the nerve center of the "Lifeline of the Confederacy."

Turn right on South Third. Located at 1 South Third, St. James Episcopal Church stands proudly as the oldest church in continuous use in the city. It is actually the second church building constructed by the local Episcopal congregation. Construction of the first church was authorized in 1751, and work commenced on the simple brick building on Fourth Street in 1753. Funds for the construction came from goods recovered when an invading Spanish privateer was sunk in the Cape Fear downriver, near Brunswick Town. One treasure salvaged from the ship—a painting of Christ entitled *Ecce Homo*, "Behold the Man"—hangs in the vestry of the existing church.

St. James Episcopal Church

Nationally known architect Thomas U. Walter, who later gained fame when he designed the cast-iron dome of the United States Capitol, drew the plans for the existing St. James edifice. Its cornerstone was laid in 1839. The most distinctive architectural feature of the Gothic Revival building is its square entrance tower. Accented with octagonal pinnacles at its corners, the bell-and-clock tower rises through the body of the building. Every year since the end of the Civil War, an Easter sunrise service has been conducted from atop the tower.

The Reverend Alfred A. Watson was rector in January 1865. At the height of the second battle at Fort Fisher, amid the sounds of the ferocious bombardment by the Federal fleet, Watson led the Episcopal congregation in a prayer of intercession: "From battle and murder, and from sudden death, Good Lord deliver us."

A month later, upon the surrender of the city to the Union army, Watson was ordered to include the president of the United States in his prayers. He resolutely refused. His open defiance apparently infuriated the invaders, because the 104th Ohio Volunteers halted church services on February 26 and seized the church. After they removed the pews, the Union troops converted the church building into a hospital.

Included among the parade of important houses on South Third Street is a rare residential unit designed by hometown hero Henry Bacon, Jr., architect of the Lincoln Memorial. Located at 15 South Third, the Donald MacRae House represents one of only four residential designs ever drawn by Bacon. Despite its designer's apparent lack of interest in residential architecture, this 1901-vintage dwelling is tangible evidence of the Bacon genius. It is a splendid example of the shingle-style house that became popular in the city in the early part of the twentieth century.

Wilmington and Raleigh are the only cities in North Carolina that possess monuments designed by Bacon. Located in the plaza at South Third and Dock streets, the Confederate Memorial is another of Bacon's hometown masterpieces. He collaborated with sculptor F. H. Packer to produce this monument. Bacon died before it was unveiled in 1924. Set atop the granite pedestal and silhouetted against the fifteen-ton shaft are two bronze soldiers, one representing courage and the other sacrifice.

Continue south to the 100 block of South Third.

Of the mansions built in the city in the first decade of the twentieth century, the most spectacular is the Bridgers House, at 100 South Third. Constructed in 1905, this monumental Neoclassical Revival structure was for many years the pride of Elizabeth Eagles Haywood Bridgers. Mrs. Bridgers

came from a family long distinguished in local, state, and national history. Her father-in-law, Rufus Bridgers, was a nationally known official of the Atlantic Coast Line Railroad. Her grandfather John Haywood was the treasurer of the state of North Carolina. Mrs. Bridgers was also a descendant of Richard Eagles, the man for whom nearby Eagles Island—the site of the Battleship *North Carolina*—was named.

Majestically situated at the top of a hill rising from the river, the two-and-a-half-story structure is constructed of stone quarried in Indiana and shaped in South Carolina. It features a magnificent semicircular portico buttressed by tall Ionic columns.

Nearby at 114 South Third is the Savage-Bacon House, constructed in 1850 as a bracketed and vented Italianate dwelling. Its Neoclassical appearance dates from renovations in 1909. This house is best known for its residents from 1891 to 1899: noted engineer Henry Bacon, Sr., and his family, including sons Henry Jr., the future architect, and Francis, the future archaeologist and furniture designer of national fame.

Among the great churches of Wilmington, First Presbyterian Church, at 121 South Third, has the youngest building. Construction of the late Gothic Revival sanctuary began in December 1926. Designed by noted church architect Hobart Upjohn, the limestone-trimmed building is covered with a gable-roofed basilica and a square, four-story tower from which rises a stone spire. Elegantly designed stained-glass windows punctuate the sanctuary walls. Above the altar is a beautiful rose window.

Among the famous ministers who have preached in the present sanctuary was Peter Marshall, who stood in the pulpit in 1939 and 1940.

Located just north of the sanctuary, the small stone chapel is of Norman and Gothic design. Located to the rear, the educational building was designed in the Tudor style by architect H. L. Cain. All of the handsome buildings blend harmoniously to form a spectacular architectural portrait.

Fire destroyed three sanctuary buildings that preceded the existing church. It was in the third building that the Reverend Joseph R. Wilson preached. He served as minister of the church from November 1, 1874, to April 1, 1885. A splendid memorial plaque honoring the Reverend Wilson's famous son, Tommy, was dedicated in the narthex of the current sanctuary in 1928.

A teenager when he lived in the city, Tommy Wilson spent many hours on the river swimming, watching ships, and chatting with sailors from distant ports. He played shortstop on a local baseball team. He also owned the city's first high-wheel bicycle, a gift purchased by his father to help Tommy gain strength after a digestive disorder.

In preparation for college, Tommy was tutored in Greek and Latin by Mrs. Joseph R. Russell, an outstanding local teacher. She could see that her bright pupil was destined for greatness. His intense interest in government caused her to remark to him on one occasion, "Someday, you are going to be president of the United States."

Soon thereafter, he departed for college, where he dropped the name "Tommy." Although Mrs. Russell died long before her prophetic remark came true, Thomas Woodrow Wilson was elected to two terms as president of the United States.

The Zebulon Latimer House is located at 126 South Third. Zebulon Latimer, the man who constructed this graceful house, was a prosperous Wilmington merchant who migrated to the city in the 1830s from Connecticut. Not only is this stuccoed masonry home an outstanding example of the affluent architecture of the antebellum period, but it also represents a subtle variation on the Italianate style so popular in the city. It is much more ornamented than other houses of the same period.

Built in 1852, the house remained in the Latimer family until 1963, when the Lower Cape Fear Historical Society purchased the property and the home's elegant furnishings. Meticulously restored and furnished, the grand house is open to the public.

Of special interest in the yard of the Zebulon Latimer House is a three-tier cast-iron fountain that was moved from the street plaza when South Third was widened to accommodate modern traffic.

Continue across Orange Street to the 200 block of South Third, where you will see another piece of "street furniture" in the plaza of South Third. This combination cast-iron water fountain and watering trough was installed in the 1880s as part of a beautification project in the city.

At the intersection of South Third and Ann, turn left and walk east on Ann.

Tileston School, located at 400 Ann Street, is a living memorial to the early public-education system in the city. Included on the campus are the original nineteenth-century building, the Ann Street annex of 1919, and later additions. The construction of the school was financed by Mary Tileston Hemenway, a Bostonian, who also underwrote the school's operation for nearly twenty years after it opened as Tileston Normal School in 1872. In 1897, the school became Wilmington High School. It was later converted into a junior high and continues to serve as a public school today.

While attending this school, Woodrow Wilson was a member of its baseball team. His team roster, a diagram of the playing field, and the team cheers were later found inscribed in Wilson's geography book.

Even though much of the original two-story, Italianate brick building is hidden behind the annexes, an examination of the splendid structure reveals windows set in ornate brick arches. Adorning the interior walls of the Classical Revival annexes are more than a half-dozen early-twentieth-century bas-relief sculptures reflecting cultural and patriotic themes.

An ancient live oak stands on the school grounds near the southeastern corner of South Fourth and Ann streets. No one is certain of the exact age of the enormous tree, but it is believed to have served as a boundary marker for the town in the first half of the eighteenth century and as a site of many important political gatherings.

At the intersection of Ann and South Fifth, turn left and walk north along the 200 block of South Fifth.

St. Mary's Catholic Church, at 220 South Fifth, is a majestic Spanish Baroque cathedral built without steel, wooden beams and framing, or nails. Brick and tile were used throughout the structure not only for aesthetic purposes but also for structural strength. The church's exterior is dominated by a pair of tall towers topped with domed cupolas.

When the building was completed in 1911, the St. Mary's congregation moved from a Gothic Revival edifice at 208 Dock Street, which subsequently became the Catholic church for the black community.

In October 1868, Father James Gibbons moved to Wilmington, where he ministered to area Catholics for four years. From Wilmington, he moved to Richmond and then to Baltimore. It was in the latter city that he was notified by the Vatican on May 18, 1896, of his elevation to cardinal.

But Wilmington was the site of his most enduring contribution to his faith and mankind. On an extended visit to the city in early 1876, Gibbons began work on his celebrated *Faith of Our Fathers*. His inspiration came from his dynamic work with converts to Catholicism in North Carolina. Since its publication, the book has become one of the most widely read books on religion in the world. Still in print after more than a century, it has sold nearly three million copies.

Just across the street, at 219 South Fifth, stands the house where Carolina Balestier, the future wife of Rudyard Kipling, lived during a portion of her youth.

At the intersection of South Fifth and Orange, turn left on Orange and walk west 1 block to the intersection with South Fourth. Turn right and proceed north on South Fourth.

Located at 1 South Fourth, the Temple of Israel is the first Jewish synagogue erected in the state. Although the building was not completed until 1876, the Jewish community has played an important role in the life of Wilmington since David David settled here in 1738.

The Moorish-style synagogue features square towers covered with small onion domes. Rabbi Isaac Mayer Wise, the father of American Reformed

Judaism, described the Wilmington house of worship in glowing terms: "For simple elegance, this temple is unsurpassed in the United States." A state historical marker for the Temple of Israel stands on the street near the synagogue.

Located across South Fourth from the Temple of Israel, at the southwestern corner of South Fourth and Market, St. James Episcopal Cemetery is of great historic importance. Some of its ancient gravestones, more than 250 years old, are weathered to the point that they are no longer legible. Begun as a public burying ground in June 1745, the cemetery was conveyed to St. James Parish two years later. When Oakdale Cemetery opened in 1855, some of the graves at St. James were relocated to the new cemetery.

Approximately 125 marked graves remain in the St. James churchyard. They are shaded by massive oaks and cedars. Grave markers range in style from intricately carved upright stones to tabletop designs.

Among the people of note buried in this peaceful setting is playwright Thomas Godfrey. In 1758, Godfrey moved to Wilmington from Philadelphia. Several years after his arrival, he wrote *The Prince of Parthia*, the first play written and produced in America by an American. Godfrey died in Wilmington in 1763, four years before the play was first performed in Philadelphia. A nearby state historical marker calls attention to his grave.

Turn left off South Fourth onto Market and walk west for 1 block. Turn right on North Third and proceed 1 block north to the New Hanover County Courthouse, at the southeastern corner of North Third and Princess.

This structure is the city's only representative of a once-popular national style: Victorian Gothic. Constructed in 1891 and 1892, the symmetrical, two-story brick structure sits upon a full basement. From the second story rises a tall bell and clock tower. The top of the tower is 110 feet above the sidewalk. From its exaggerated pyramidal roof, dormers extend outward to protect the clock faces. Still in working order, the clock and its chimes keep downtown workers and visitors apprised of the time throughout the day. Below the clock hangs the century-old, 2,000-pound bell.

New Hanover County Courthouse

Cross Princess Street to the 100 block of North Third. Located at 102 North Third, the building that houses city hall and Thalian Hall would be an invaluable asset to the largest, most sophisticated city in the United States. That such an imposing structure stands in a city the size of Wilmington is a pleasant surprise to many visitors.

In 1788, the Thalian Association, the oldest amateur theatrical group in the United States, was formed in Wilmington. At the beginning of the nineteenth century, the group used an auditorium that stood on the present site of Thalian Hall. Upon acquisition of the property by the city, plans were announced for a city hall at the same location. However, the Thalians had become such an institution in the city that the citizenry rejected the construction of any building that did not include a theater.

John M. Trimble, the New York architect whose credits included the New York Opera House, was selected to design the combination municipal building and theater building. Local architect James F. Post interpreted the plans, added his creativity to them, and acted as supervising architect. Post had settled in Wilmington in 1849. His previous credits included a residence he designed for millionaire John Jacob Astor in 1840.

Completed in 1858, the original portion of the L-shaped Wilmington masterpiece fronts 100 feet on Third Street and 170 feet on Princess. As originally constructed, city hall measured 100 feet by 60 feet, while Thalian Hall stretched an additional 10 feet. The entire building is 54 feet in height. A gigantic Classical Revival portico supported by four fluted Corinthian columns dominates the Third Street facade. A second floor ballroom runs the length of city hall.

When the theater opened to a performance of *The Loan of a Lover* in the autumn of 1858, it boasted state-of-the-art equipment. A special apparatus raised and lowered the stage curtains. The sound of thunder could be simulated with what was called the "Thunder Run"—a trough through which cannonballs were rolled.

In 1867, the theater was leased to John T. Ford of Washington, D.C., because Ford's Theatre in the national capital had been closed when President Lincoln was assassinated there. Years after the Washington theater reopened, experts restored it to its antebellum splendor using Thalian Hall as their basic source of information.

Throughout its long and storied history, the stage at Thalian Hall has been graced by many of America's most famous actors, orators, and musicians. Included on the list of star performers are playwright Oscar Wilde, dressed in his English walking suit; Maurice Barrymore, father of Lionel, John, and Ethel; James O'Neill, father of Eugene O'Neill; lecturer

Charles Dickens, son of the famous British novelist; Tom Thumb; William Jennings Bryan, who lectured on Prohibition; Buffalo Bill; John Philip Sousa; Lillian Russell; Marian Anderson; and Agnes Moorehead.

Unexplained occurrences have taken place in the theater for many years. Some people claim that James O'Neill haunts the place. Seances have even been held to rid the building of its ghosts. In 1966, actors noticed three figures in Victorian attire watching a rehearsal. By the time crew members reached the balcony, the figures had vanished, but three seats were turned down, as if spectators had been sitting in them.

Upon entering the restored theater building, patrons are awed by the proscenium arch, encrusted with Victorian rosettes and gilded with leaves. Ionic columns are located on both sides of the arch and outside the box seats that flank the stage. Double balconies are located above the main seating area.

As one of the very few surviving antebellum theaters in the United States, Thalian Hall is an extremely important historical and architectural treasure. After visiting the building in 1983, Tony winner Jessica Tandy remarked,

City Hall, Thalian Hall

"I would give anything to act on that stage." However, it was actor Tyrone Power who best summarized the value of the historic theater. In a letter to Governor Luther Hodges dated April 10, 1958, Power wrote, "I wish I could adequately convey to you my surprise and delight upon entering Thalian Hall. It has been years since I have seen anything of its kind in this country. In fact, very few such examples exist anywhere in the world. Upon inquiry, I discovered that many of the greats of the golden age of the theatre had played there. . . . It has atmosphere and a history shared by all too few remaining theatres of its kind in this country."

Continue on North Third to the intersection with Chestnut Street. Turn left and proceed 1 block west on Chestnut. Located at the corner of Chestnut and North Second, the Cape Fear Club stands as a vestige of the port city's past. Housed in the brick Neoclassical Revival building at 124 North Second, the organization was founded in 1866 by thirteen gentlemen who wanted a common downtown meeting place. A plaque on the outside of the two-story structure bears witness to its long-established purpose: "Founded 1866, oldest gentlemen's club in South in continuous existence. Host to many famous men."

Turn left onto North Second and proceed 2 blocks south to the intersection with Market. Turn right, walk 1 block west on Market, and turn right on Front Street. Here, the downtown area showcases 4 blocks of century-old commercial buildings. Among the surviving architectural gems are two cast-iron storefronts.

At 2–4 North Front stands the first of Wilmington's two skyscrapers. Completed in 1912, the Atlantic Trust and Banking Company Building was the first building in the city to rise above five stories. At nine stories, this Neoclassical Revival structure held its title as the city's tallest building for only two years.

Walk 2 blocks north on North Front. In 1914, the eleven-story Murchison–First Union Building, at 201–203 North Front, opened its doors as Wilmington's tallest building, an honor it retains today. Its two-story stone base is highlighted by huge Doric columns and massive windows. Crowning the skyscraper is a two-story entablature ornately decorated with a copper palmetto crown, Ionic pilasters, and other architectural features.

A few doors from the skyscraper is the site of the Bijou Theatre. When a motion-picture theater opened in a tent at 221–225 North Front in 1903, it became the first in North Carolina and one of the first in the South. Eight years later, a theater building was constructed at the site. It was demolished in 1963, but a section of the tile floor of the lobby with the name *Bijou* inscribed on it has been preserved in a pocket park in the busy downtown area.

Continue 2 blocks on North Front to its intersection with Walnut Street. Here, in the 300 block of North Front, the Cotton Exchange occupies the restored turn-of-the-century buildings that once housed the international cotton-exporting firm of Alexander Sprunt and Son. Today, this complex of unique shops and restaurants is connected by a maze of narrow brick walkways and wooden staircases.

Turn left onto Walnut Street and walk west 1 block to Water Street. Turn left on Water to return to your car.

Drive south on Water to its intersection with Market. Turn left on Market and proceed east 3 blocks to Third Street. Turn right on South Third and drive 7 blocks to the junction with U.S. 17/74/76/421.

En route, you will notice a large number of state historical markers lining the street. Of all the historic cities in North Carolina, Wilmington possesses the greatest number of such markers. Many of the signs on South Third honor the long list of famous people who were either born in Wilmington or called the place their home.

Among the people in Wilmington's hall of fame are William Hooper, signer of the Declaration of Independence; Judah Benjamin, the only man to hold three different posts in the Confederate cabinet; Anna McNeill Whistler, the mother of artist James McNeill Whistler; Mary Baker Eddy, the founder of the Church of Christian Science; General Joseph Gardner Swift, the first graduate of the United States Military Academy; Johnston Blakely, naval hero of the War of 1812; Rear Admiral John Ancrum Winslow, Union naval hero during the Civil War; Admiral Edwin Alexander Anderson, winner of the Congressional Medal of Honor; Major Generals William Wing Loring and William Henry Chase Whiting, heroes of the Confederate army; Sammy Davis, Sr., entertainer and father of the legendary star of song, stage, and screen; Charlie Daniels, country-music star; Charles Kuralt, noted television journalist and author; Sugar Ray Leonard, world boxing champion; Luther "Wimpy" Lassiter, billiard champion; Althea Gibson, 1951 Wimbledon tennis champion; Meadowlark Lemon, longtime star of the Harlem Globetrotters, "the Clown Prince of Basketball"; Edwin Anderson Alderman, the only person to serve as president of three major American universities; and James F. Shober, the first known black physician with an M.D. degree in the state.

At the intersection with U.S. 17/74/76/421, South Third becomes U.S. 421 (Carolina Beach Road). Continue south on U.S. 421 across the intersection and drive 9 blocks to Lake Shore Drive. Turn left onto Lake Shore and proceed on a circular, 5-mile route through Greenfield Park.

Considered by some experts the most beautiful municipal park in the nation, Greenfield is the pride of Wilmington. Its centerpiece is a majestic, 180-acre, five-fingered lake. Hundreds of cypress trees festooned with Spanish moss dot the lake and color its placid waters coffee brown. Surrounding Greenfield Lake are more than 20 acres of colorful gardens filled with more than a million flowers, shrubs, and trees.

Greenfield Lake

Prior to the American Revolution, Greenfield was a 500-acre rice plantation. For much of the nineteenth century, a gristmill operated on the lake, which was known at the time as McIlhenny's Mill Pond. Despite its use as a millpond, the lake is not man-made. Rather, it is hundreds of years old, fed by scores of springs that bubble up from the sandy bottom.

During the second decade of the twentieth century, the Greenfield property was converted into an amusement park. Throngs of patrons were attracted by the carnival atmosphere of Lakeside Park. They thrilled to new rides like the roller coaster and chute-the-chute. A motorcycle rider amazed spectators by defying gravity in a large, circular wooden silo with tall walls.

Development of the municipal park began after the property was acquired by the city in 1925. Today, the picturesque grounds and lake offer an outstanding variety of activities and facilities. Picnic tables, shelters, and grills are located around the lake. A playground, an amphitheater, and tennis courts are provided for public use. Wooden walkways, gazebos, and nature trails make it possible for visitors to enjoy the captivating gardens and the lake. On the northern side of the lake, within a few feet of the road, there is an interesting sunken garden of native flowers and Venus' flytraps.

After circling the lake, turn left on U.S. 421 and drive south to the junction with Burnett Boulevard. Turn south on Burnett and drive 3 blocks to Myers Boulevard and the entrance to the North Carolina State Port at Wilmington. Arrangements to watch the loading and unloading of huge cargo ships at the state's largest and busiest port must be made in advance.

More than seven hundred ships dock here annually from numerous countries in Europe, Asia, Africa, and South America. The primary exports that pass through the port are tobacco and tobacco products, textiles, textile machinery, metal and wood products, and poultry. Major imports include bulk chemicals, iron and steel products, burlap and jute, retail items, and lumber.

Over sixty shipping lines connect the port with two hundred ports worldwide.

In 1984, after a twenty-three-year absence, ocean cruise ships began calling once again at Wilmington. These large passenger liners depart throughout the year for Bermuda and other Caribbean ports.

The tour ends here, at the North Carolina State Port at Wilmington.

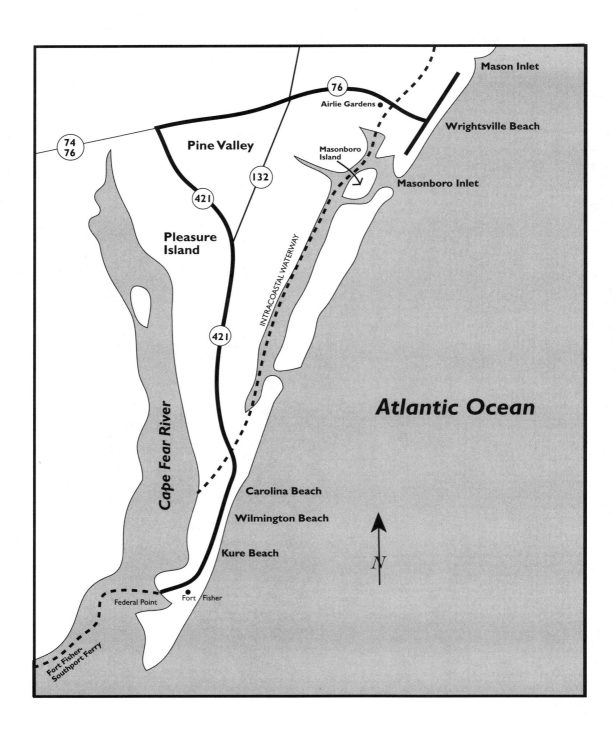

The Wrightsville Beach to Pleasure Island Tour

This tour explores the islands east and south of Wilmington. From its starting point on the mainland east of town, it proceeds to Wrightsville Beach, then returns to the mainland and skirts the eastern edge of Wilmington before exploring the length of Pleasure Island, from Carolina Beach to Wilmington Beach to Kure Beach to Fort Fisher. It ends at "The Rocks," near the southern tip of Pleasure Island.

Among the highlights of the tour are Airlie Gardens, the story of the Lumina, the story of Money Island, Carolina Beach State Park, the famous Carolina Beach Boardwalk, the story of the Ethyl–Dow Chemical facility at Kure Beach, Fort Fisher State Historic Site, the North Carolina Aquarium at Fort Fisher, and the story of the Fort Fisher hermit.

Total mileage: approximately 34 miles.

This tour begins at the intersection of U.S. 74 and U.S. 76, 9 miles east of downtown Wilmington. Proceed south on U.S. 76 for 0.7 mile and turn east on Airlie Road. The entrance sign for Airlie Gardens will come into view after 0.25 mile. Because the gardens are open for public tours for a limited time each spring, be sure to inquire in advance about the schedule.

This magnificent sound-side estate of 155 acres was the country home of Mr. and Mrs. Pembroke Jones during the early years of the twentieth century. Pembroke Jones, a Wilmington native and a Confederate naval officer who served aboard the famed *Merrimac*, parlayed his business acumen into enormous wealth after the Civil War. In the first decade of the twentieth century, Mr. and Mrs. Jones purchased several large tracts east of Wilmington on a heavily wooded, thirty-foot bluff overlooking Wrightsville Sound.

Jones named his new country estate Airlie in honor of the home of his ancestors in Scotland. With the old Sea Side Park Hotel as a nucleus, he constructed a sprawling, multigabled, three-story mansion that contained thirty-three bedrooms and a combination ballroom and theater.

With visions of entertaining the nation's elite, Jones commissioned his son-in-law, John Russell Pope of New York City, to design a palatial lodge nearby. Pope was at that time acquiring a reputation as one of the most able architects in America. It was Pope who collaborated with Henry Bacon of nearby Wilmington in the design of the Mall in Washington, D.C. The overall plan of the Mall and the Lincoln Memorial were products of Bacon's genius, while the Jefferson Memorial, the National Archives Building, and the National Gallery of Art were designed by Pope.

For his father-in-law, Pope created an Italian villa so magnificent that the visiting Italian ambassador once called it "the most perfect note of Italy in America." When completed in 1916, Pembroke Lodge was a spectacular sight. Its two-story main block and adjoining north and south wings were built of cement and covered with a tile roof. Priceless works of art, including tapestries and paintings, adorned the sumptuous interior.

Pembroke Jones lived less than three years after the lodge opened, but during that short time, he entertained the wealthiest people in the United States. Private trains brought the Vanderbilts, the Astors, and other noted families of the Gilded Age.

After the master of the lodge died in 1919, it was used infrequently by the Jones family. Gradually, thieves made their way into the compound. Looting began on a large scale in the 1930s. A fire attributed to vandals caused severe damage to the lodge in 1955.

By 1970, the terraced lawns had become a veritable jungle. Finally, the site was bulldozed for exclusive residential development, with only the three-story mansion left standing. All the while, the adjacent 155 acres of Airlie had been undergoing development as a garden showplace.

After Pembroke Jones's death, his widow, desirous of creating one of the most beautiful flower gardens in the world, employed an internationally known gardener to achieve her goal. R. A. Toppel, a German who had for many years served as gardener to the kaiser, created what one observer called "earth's paradise in all its glory." In the course of his work at Airlie, he developed the Toppel tree, an unusual hybrid created by grafting yaupon to another holly.

Meanwhile, Mrs. Jones married an old friend, Henry H. Walters, a major stockholder in the Atlantic Coast Line Railroad. Inside the palatial home at Airlie, Walters installed a stairway of English oak from the former home of Sir Walter Raleigh in England.

After Mrs. Walters died, her daughter sold the estate to Albert Corbett and wife, Bertha Barefoot Corbett. They demolished the rambling old

mansion and in its place erected a dignified modern residence overlooking the sound.

At their deaths, the Corbetts were buried in the cemetery behind old Mt. Lebanon Chapel, located on the grounds of Airlie. Erected in 1835, the small frame structure is believed to be the oldest surviving church building in New Hanover County.

Mrs. Pembroke Jones' dream becomes a true vision of beauty every spring, when the gardens of Airlie are opened to the public. A winding 5-mile drive enters the estate through a hand-forged gate embroidered with leaves and flowers. Along the route, ancient live oaks draped with Spanish moss shade banks of multicolored azaleas and camellias. Scientists believe one of the ancient oaks, known as the Airlie Oak, to be more than five hundred years old.

The Airlie Oak

Virtually every known variety of azalea is found among the landscaped gardens. Swans swim on tranquil ponds, and lagoons mirror the colors of the seasons in their dark waters. Designed as a natural garden, Airlie has fully matured into a visual masterpiece.

Return to the entrance to Airlie Gardens and continue in your original

---

Pond at Airlie

direction on Airlie Road, which loops around to parallel the Intracoastal Waterway for 1.4 miles until it junctions with U.S. 74/76 at the foot of the drawbridge over the Waterway. This short drive provides a spectacular view of the colorful marinas, where pleasure boats of all sizes and shapes are docked and stored. Wrightsville Beach, located across the bridge from the mainland, has made a name for itself as one of North Carolina's foremost pleasure-boating centers. Since 1853, Wrightsville has been home to the Carolina Yacht Club, one of the oldest such associations in America.

Turn right on U.S. 74/76 at the end of Airlie Road. Once you cross the drawbridge, the panorama of the granddaddy of all the resorts on the lower North Carolina coast will unfold before you. Wrightsville Beach is a 4-mile-long barrier island bounded on the north by Mason's Inlet, on the south by Masonboro Inlet, and on the west by Banks Channel. Geographically, the barrier island is separated from the mainland by the

Intracoastal Waterway, Harbor Island, and Banks Channel, from west to east. Harbor Island, a part of the incorporated town of Wrightsville Beach, is connected to the barrier island by two short bridges spanning Banks Channel.

U.S. 74/76 forks on Harbor Island. Proceed east on the U.S. 74 prong across the Banks Channel bridge to the Wrightsville Beach strand. Turn left, or north, onto North Lumina Avenue and drive 1.9 miles to the end of the paved road at the Shell Island Resort.

This northern portion of the island is known today as Shell Island. Until it was artificially filled in 1965, Moore's Inlet, a highly unstable inlet, separated Shell Island from Wrightsville Beach. Before it was attached to Wrightsville Beach, Shell Island was for many years an uninhabited shell collectors' paradise. Accessible only by boat, its beautiful strand was backed by imposing sand dunes.

Despite its appearance at the time Moore's Inlet was closed, Shell Island was not without a history of human habitation. In fact, on November 15, 1910, the island hosted the flight of the first airplane ever constructed by North Carolinians. Built by two prominent businessmen from Wilmington—M. H. F. Gouverner, vice president of the Tide Water Power Company, and H. M. Chase, manager of the American Chemical and Textile Company—the airplane flew a short distance over the island landscape.

Another group of businessmen from Wilmington took an interest in Shell Island in February 1923, when an exclusive resort for blacks was begun. Before the summer season rolled around, the entrepreneurs had installed a waterworks, sewers, and electric lights. Bathhouses, restaurants, refreshment stands, a large pavilion, piers, a boardwalk, and private beach houses were quickly built. Large numbers of blacks from many states and foreign countries patronized the resort until it was abandoned after a series of fires of unknown origin destroyed many of the improvements.

Today, visitors cannot readily discern where Shell Island and Wrightsville Beach were joined. Over the past quarter-century, Shell Island has been extensively developed. By the summer of 1985, advertisements in North Carolina newspapers announced sales of the last major property to be subdivided on Wrightsville Beach, at a development called South Shell Island.

Turn around and drive south from Shell Island on Lumina Avenue. The Wrightsville Beach Holiday Inn, located 1.3 miles from the northern end of Lumina, is known to coastal geologists as "the Holiday Inlet" because it stands at the exact site of Moore's Inlet. The pool at the hotel was featured in a 1992 episode of the television series "Matlock." Numerous episodes of the series have been filmed in the area.

After reigning for a century as one of the premier resorts on the eastern seaboard, Wrightsville Beach remains among the best-known coastal playgrounds. On the drive down the island, you will not be able to see the ocean because of the uninterrupted hotels, motels, condominiums, cottages, restaurants, and shops that now stretch from end to end and strand to sound on the island.

Because of its long history as a heavily developed resort, the island is lacking in high dunes and maritime forests. Yet Wrightsville Beach has been able to maintain a special charm that has lured tourists here for more than a century. Located just 10 miles from Wilmington, the most populous city in North Carolina until the first decade of the twentieth century, Wrightsville Beach was the logical choice for nineteenth-century Wilmingtonians in their quest for seashore recreation.

By 1888, a steam-operated train transported passengers from Wilmington across a trestle to Harbor Island. Until that time, Harbor Island was an uninhabited island covered with gnarled live oaks. A footbridge over Banks Channel gave visitors access to Wrightsville Beach.

To meet the needs of the public, two bathhouses and a restaurant were built at Wrightsville Beach in July 1888, thus giving the resort its humble beginnings. A year later, the railroad was extended across Banks Channel. Today, South Lumina Avenue runs over the old bed of that first island railroad.

In early 1897, the island's property owners met to formulate an agreement concerning a uniform name for the beach. Since the resort had been advertised as Ocean View for some time, the owners chose that name. Three years later, however, the resort was incorporated under its present name. The name was adopted from the nearby mainland village of Wrightsville and the sound of the same name. At the time the resort was incorporated, more than fifty houses and several rambling hotels stood on the island.

Trolley cars brought their first passengers to Wrightsville Beach on July 25, 1902. An electrified rail line carried passenger cars, each with a fifty-five-person capacity, to seven stations along the strand. Just south of the intersection of Lumina Avenue and U.S. 76 in the heart of the old Wrightsville Beach commercial district, there is a spot still called "Station One," in honor of the first stop on the old trolley line.

Former trolley stop

As facilities were developed, Wrightsville Beach quickly emerged as the premier resort of southeastern North Carolina. In 1902, a 400-seat theater, The Casino, was completed. Fourteen years later, a huge, 2,000-seat auditorium was built on Harbor Island. Until it was demolished in 1936, this massive auditorium, which featured modern conveniences such as gas heating, served as a convention facility.

Once automobile use became widespread, the need for vehicular access to Harbor Island grew acute. A causeway to Harbor Island was constructed in June 1926. When the state purchased the Wrightsville Sound Causeway less than a decade later and announced plans to extend the highway across Banks Channel to the barrier island, the future of Wrightsville Beach as one of the state's premier coastal resorts seemed secure. However, on January 28, 1934, a terrible fire ravaged the island, destroying more than a hundred structures, including the majestic Oceanic Hotel. Twenty years after the great fire, the island lost most of its remaining original structures to the wrath of Hurricane Hazel. Among the losses were the historic Carolina Yacht Club and the old Seashore Hotel.

North Lumina Avenue ends 0.9 mile from the Holiday Inn, at the intersection with U.S. 76 at Station One. Continue south on South Lumina Avenue, the oceanfront road on the southern part of the island. South Lumina Avenue frequently leaves and rejoins Waynick Boulevard (U.S. 76), the main road on the southern end of the island.

Located at 275 Waynick Boulevard, at old Station Three on the oceanfront, the famous Blockade Runner Resort Hotel stands at the site of the old Seashore Hotel, one of the first hotels constructed on the beach. An episode of "Matlock" has also been shot at this location.

The first public pier on the lower coast of North Carolina was a steel pier constructed at this spot as part of the Seashore Hotel complex. It is believed that the seven-hundred-foot, festively lighted metal pier, subsequently destroyed by a storm, was the only one of its kind on this entire portion of the Atlantic coast when it was erected in 1910.

Oceanic Pier

Continue on Waynick Boulevard. Turn left on Nathan Avenue. A second steel pier, the Lumina Steel Pier, was constructed on the strand at 703 South Lumina in 1939. A modern fishing pier, the Crystal Pier—now the Oceanic Pier—was later built at the site.

Underneath and on the southern side of the existing pier are the remains of the *Fanny and Jenny*, one of the many blockade runners that were either destroyed by enemy attack or scuttled by their crews in the waters along the Cape Fear coast during the Civil War. This vessel ran aground and sank in February 1864 after being attacked by the Federal cruiser *Florida*.

Not just an ordinary victim of the Federal blockade of the North Carolina coast, the *Fanny and Jenny* carried a very special cargo that remains buried somewhere in the ship's watery grave. A magnificent cavalry saber laden with gold and precious stones was listed on the ship's manifest. The sword was a gift from the people of England to a man they held in high esteem. On the beautifully engraved blade was inscribed the following message: "To General Robert E. Lee from his British Sympathizers."

Throughout the twentieth century, many divers have attempted to recover the sword, but the waters off Wrightsville Beach have not relinquished the treasure.

The pier and the shipwreck at 703 South Lumina Avenue are not the reasons that this site is considered the most nostalgic on the island. A magnificent structure once stood at this spot on the strand: the incomparable Lumina. Other than the historic lighthouses, perhaps no other structure on the North Carolina coast has achieved more fame than this nightclub, which enjoyed a fabulous sixty-eight-year run from 1905 to 1973.

In February 1905, the Consolidated Railway Light and Power Company of Wilmington decided to build the Lumina to induce visitors to ride the railway to the beach.

Elaborately constructed, the original building had a foundation of pilings driven deep into the white sand. The sills and joists of solid heart pine were of such quality that they were not moved until the building was demolished.

When the Lumina opened on June 3, 1905, it rose two stories above the Atlantic. On the first floor, a broad hallway led to bowling alleys, bathrooms, a ladies' parlor, snack bars, slot machines, and other amusements. A broad stairway in the center of the building led to the second-floor dance hall, which measured fifty by seventy feet. Encircling the dance floor was an area from which seated spectators could watch the dancers. An orchestra balcony was located at the southern end of the dance hall and a restaurant equipped with an open fireplace at the northern end.

From the day the great pavilion opened, it aptly bore the name *Lumina*, a reference to the thousands of incandescent lights that illuminated the building at night. Success was instantaneous. The fame of the fabulous nightclub spread like wildfire throughout southeastern North Carolina. Capacity crowds forced several expansions of the pavilion, the first of which occurred in 1909. Four years later, bleachers were constructed on the beach, from which Lumina patrons could enjoy a spectacular view of the ocean during the day. At night, they could sit in the bleachers and view movies projected on a giant screen that rose on stilts from the Atlantic.

After it was sold to a Wilmington businessman in 1939, the Lumina no longer burned its many outside lights, and its place of dominance on the beach was lost. By the end of World War II, the grand old lady was in the twilight of her storied career, as poor maintenance, a lack of parking, and competing attractions robbed her of her vitality.

With its roof sagging and its once-glittering ballroom covered with mildew, the Lumina met the wrecking ball in May 1973. Suddenly, this palace of lights—where the likes of Tommy Dorsey, Guy Lombardo, Cab Calloway, Louis Armstrong, Kay Kyser, Woody Herman, and Lionel Hampton once performed—was no more.

The lower North Carolina coast has no truer legend than the Lumina. For years, sea captains used its brilliant lights, which could be seen for miles at sea, as a navigational aid. Long known as "the Fun Spot of the South," the Lumina was a topic of conversation all over the world. During World War II, upon meeting a soldier from Wilmington on a remote Pacific island, a soldier from Atlanta asked, "Do they still go to the Lumina?"

From the Oceanic Pier, continue on South Lumina Avenue to the end of the island at Jack Parker Boulevard. Nearby is the dock for the Wrightsville Beach Coast Guard Station. From a vantage point on the strand on the southern end of the island, Money Island, only a few acres in size, looms on the horizon. Despite its diminutive size, this uninhabited island has generated many tales of buried treasure since the golden age of piracy.

Tradition has it that Captain William Kidd, one of colonial America's most infamous pirates, chose the small island at the mouth of Bradley Creek to deposit two chests filled with coins and silver.

Kidd was born in Greenock, Scotland, in the middle of the seventeenth century. By the time he started plundering the North Carolina coast in the last years of the century, he was one of the world's most dreaded pirates.

Upon completion of a particularly lucrative voyage to the Spanish colonies, Kidd returned to ravage the Carolina coast near Wilmington. After he hid some of his riches at Money Island, he sailed to New England, where he was promptly arrested. He was transported to England, where he was tried, convicted, and hanged for murder in 1701.

Whether his treasure has ever been recovered remains an unanswered question. If the chests remain where the pirate buried them, it is not because they have been forgotten. In 1858, the *Wilmington Herald* reported that a fisherman watched one night under the light of a full moon as several men worked on Money Island. Afraid to interrupt their activities, the man waited until the next morning to go to the deserted island. There, he found a pile of fresh earth beside a huge hole under a tree. Lines of rust were apparent on the walls of the pit, perhaps from the metal bands of one of Kidd's treasure chests. To this day, no one knows what the men were doing or what they took that night from the sands of Money Island. Yet it was because of this incident that the island acquired its name.

In the years that followed, Money Island's reputation as a site of hidden pirate's treasure grew. In fact, it became pitted with holes left by treasure hunters.

Two young men from Wilmington were rummaging around the island in 1939 when they discovered a large, badly corroded iron chest with an enormous lock. Inside the chest, the youths reportedly found a rotted wooden interior but no treasure.

Wrightsville Beach

Nonetheless, Money Island continues to be a popular place for treasure hunters. There is probably no spot on the island that has not been subjected to a shovel. It is quite possible that any remaining treasure lies offshore in the waters of Greenville Sound, due to the migration of the island.

Just south of the tip of Wrightsville Beach lies Masonboro Island, the largest undisturbed barrier island on the lower coast of North Carolina. Squeezed between two of the most densely populated islands on the entire coast—Wrightsville Beach and Pleasure Island—the 8.4-mile-long island covers some 5,046 acres. Eighty-seven percent of the total acreage is composed of marsh and tidal flats. The remaining 619 acres make up the island's "firm ground"—beach uplands and spoil islands.

It is one of the great ironies of coastal North Carolina history that what was perhaps the very first stretch of American shoreline to have been visited, explored, and written about by a European explorer remains uninhabited and in a pristine state more than 470 years later. Giovanni da Verrazano, a Florentine navigator in the service of King Francis I of France, caught sight of Masonboro Island in May 1524 and thereafter issued a report to the French monarch detailing what he had seen. His glowing narrative described a land of "faire fields and plains . . . good and wholesome aire, . . . sweet and odiferous flowers . . . [and] trees greater and better than any in Europe."

Until 1991, Masonboro Island was the subject of a battle over preservation. The state of North Carolina, assisted by concerned citizens, has now acquired virtually all of the island so that it might be spared from development. Administered by the North Carolina Division of Coastal Management as part of the National Estuarine Research Reserve system, the island is used by the public for swimming, sunbathing, fishing, shelling, boating, and nature study.

Masonboro is not connected to the mainland by either bridge or ferry. Access is limited to private boat.

From the southern end of Wrightsville Beach, drive 1.8 miles north on Waynick Boulevard, then turn west where U.S. 76 splits off to the left. This route crosses Banks Channel onto Harbor Island and passes the former Saline Water Research Station. This facility was constructed by the federal government after World War II to serve as a world center for research into saline water conversion. The buildings in the complex are now used as municipal offices by the town of Wrightsville Beach.

As you cross the drawbridge to the mainland, you will notice a large, multistory yellow-brick building on the right. This structure once housed the famous Babies Hospital, an institution established by Dr. J. Buren Sidbury in 1920 for the medical care of babies and children. Built in 1928 to replace a building destroyed by fire, the existing Mediterranean-style structure was enlarged in 1956. The facility closed in 1978.

From the Babies Hospital, follow U.S. 76 for 4.5 miles to its intersection with N.C. 132 on the southeastern side of Wilmington. Much of this route is along Oleander Drive, the modern highway that follows the old "Shell Road"—built of crushed shells, rock, and marl—that linked Wilmington and Wrightsville Beach when the resort was in its infancy.

Turn south onto N.C. 132 (South College Road) and drive 1.2 miles to the Pine Valley Estates subdivision. Turn east on Pine Valley Drive. After 0.2 mile, turn south on Robert E. Lee Drive. As this circular road makes its way for 2 miles around Pine Valley Country Club, you may find it hard to imagine that it was here that the Confederate army made its stand to defend Wilmington—the last Southern port open to the Confederacy—in the waning days of the Civil War.

To delay the advance of Union troops making their way up the Cape Fear from Fort Fisher, Confederate forces commanded by Major General Robert F. Hoke fortified a neck of high ground between two swamps at the site now occupied by this sprawling subdivision. On February 20 and 21, 1865, the Southern troops held stubbornly and repulsed the Union forces, inflicting heavy casualties. After the Union troops regrouped and built their own defensive works, General Braxton Bragg ordered the Confederate positions abandoned, thus bringing to a close the Battle of Jumpin' Run.

Today, other than a complex maze of streets named for Confederate heroes, there is little evidence of the final battle for Wilmington. Most of the remaining Confederate entrenchments, located in the southwestern part of the subdivision near Robert Hoke Road, fell prey to the bulldozer in 1993, when the city of Wilmington extended Seventeenth Street.

Leave the subdivision by completing the circle of Robert E. Lee Drive. Turn south on N.C. 132 and drive 3.8 miles to its intersection with U.S. 421 at a place known locally as Monkey Junction. Now a busy intersection dominated by shopping centers, the area received its name many, many years ago when a Mr. Spindle built a simple gas station and grocery store here. Behind the store, the owner kept a rather large monkey in a cage as a way to attract business. Later, he added more monkeys. Despite efforts by state highway officials to rename the intersection Myrtle Grove Junction, in deference to the nearby sound, area residents still refer to it as Monkey Junction.

Proceed south on U.S. 421. Located 1 mile south of Monkey Junction on the eastern side of the highway, the Tote-Em-In Zoo is the largest privately owned zoo in North Carolina. More than 130 different wild animals, reptiles, and birds are exhibited. African animals include a zebra, a tiger, a lion, a camel, and numerous apes. In addition to the live animals, the facility boasts a wide variety of military artifacts and curios from the South Pacific, Africa, and South America. The zoo is the realized dream of George Tregembo, a native of Maine, who came to North Carolina in 1953.

Matteau the elephant

For many years, as motorists drove past the zoo, they got a free glimpse of Tregembo's pride and joy: Matteau. This female Asian elephant, the longtime main attraction at the zoo, could be observed in a shelter near the highway, swinging rhythmically to and fro while munching on bread doled out by zoo patrons. Matteau was by no means an ordinary elephant. When Tregembo acquired the five-ton animal in 1966, she was fifty-five years old, a rather advanced age for an elephant. When she died of a stroke on November 22, 1992, the eighty-year-old elephant was the world's oldest living Asian elephant and one of the oldest ever recorded. She is buried near the zoo on a hill behind Tregembo's home.

Continue south on U.S. 421. The Intracoastal Waterway separates Pleasure

Island from the mainland 4.2 miles from the zoo. Before crossing the bridge over the Waterway, turn west onto River Road (S.R. 1100) and drive 0.25 mile to Snows Cut Park. Located on the northern banks of the Waterway, this twenty-four-acre recreational area, equipped with picnic facilities, restrooms, and a gazebo, is administered by New Hanover County. Park visitors are treated to a scenic view of the Waterway and the massive bridge overhead. Named for the engineer who designed it, Snows Cut is a canal linking the Cape Fear River with Greenville Sound.

Return to U.S. 421 and proceed south over the bridge to Pleasure Island.

Geographically, Pleasure Island has been called a peninsula, as has the whole of New Hanover County. Until its extensive commercial development in the twentieth century, Pleasure Island was known as the Federal Point Peninsula, named for the spit of land at its southern terminus. However, this 7.5-mile-long triangle now qualifies as an island because it is completely surrounded by water—Snows Cut on the north, the Atlantic on the east, and the Cape Fear River on the west.

Pleasure Island's tourism industry—now its *raison d'être*—was born in the last quarter of the nineteenth century. Prior to the Civil War, much of the island was owned by a few planters and wealthy families. All that remains of Gander Hall, one of the magnificent antebellum plantations that thrived here, is a grove of ancient oaks located thirteen hundred feet north of the intersection of Snows Cut and the Cape Fear River.

For many years, the ruins of Gander Hall had an aura of mystery. Rumors of gold hidden at the estate led a number of people to search among the ruins. Local legend has it that when a search was begun on a clear day, the sky would suddenly begin to cloud, the wind would pick up, and cries and groans would be audible over the howling wind.

Carolina Beach, the largest of the three resort communities on Pleasure Island, and one of the oldest beach towns on the lower North Carolina coast, stretches along the northern third of the island. Before visiting the bright lights, the amusements, and the general hustle and bustle of "downtown" Carolina Beach, turn west off U.S. 421 onto Dow Road approximately 0.2 mile from the bridge to Pleasure Island. It is 0.3 mile on Dow Road to the entrance to Carolina Beach State Park.

Encompassing 1,773 acres along the Cape Fear River, this park traces its roots to 1969, when the state purchased a 400-acre tract and developed Masonboro State Park. In 1974, the name was changed to Carolina Beach State Park. Created to save part of the unique natural environment along the river from development and to provide a public recreational area for visitors to the nearby resort beaches, the park continues to fulfill its original mission.

Carolina Beach State Park

The land within the park is an evergreen shrub bog. Preserved within the park's boundaries are a variety of important coastal ecosystems: dune ridges covered with longleaf pine and turkey oak, longleaf-pine and evergreen savannas, pocosins covered with pond pine and evergreen shrubs, swamp forests of gum and mixed hardwood, "limesink" depressions holding freshwater ponds, and brackish tidal marshes along the river. Growing in the bogs and grasslands are a number of carnivorous plants. Venus' flytrap, parrot and trumpet pitcher plants, yellow butterwort, red sundew, and terrestrial bladderwort all thrive in the acidic, mineral-poor soil.

Five distinct hiking trails make up the 5-mile trail system in the park. Sugar Loaf Trail offers an opportunity to visit the island's most historic natural landmark. Sugar Loaf, an ancient, sixty-foot-tall sand dune, has been used as a landmark since early European explorers charted the area. During his exploration of the Cape Fear River in 1663, William Hilton gave the dune its name. However, long before Hilton's exploration, Indians used the Sugar Loaf area for a camp.

In 1730, the only road leading south from the Wilmington area was a sand road called "the Road to Brunswick." It terminated near Sugar Loaf, where a ferry ran across the river to the port of Brunswick Town.

A small community grew up around the dune prior to the Civil War. In the waning months of the war, Major General Robert Hoke's Confederate division made its camp at Sugar Loaf. From its summit, Hoke observed the battle action at Fort Fisher to the south. The entrenchments dug by his men remained in existence prior to World War II. Today, park visitors can climb to the top just as Hoke did more than 130 years ago to enjoy a panoramic view of the mighty river, the adjacent marshes, and the nearby islands.

The amenities in the park are varied. The park office is located just inside the entrance. Camping is permitted at a family campground close to Snows

Cut. An amphitheater near the family campground hosts interpretive programs led by park rangers. Well-equipped picnic grounds are set amid stately oaks towering above the banks of Snows Cut. A marina, located at the end of the park road 1.3 miles from the entrance, looks out on the confluence of Snows Cut and the Cape Fear River. Parking is available at a lot midway between the amphitheater and the marina.

Retrace your route to the intersection of Dow Road and U.S. 421. Proceed south on U.S. 421 for 1.2 miles to the intersection with Harper Avenue. Turn east onto Harper Avenue, which ends after 2 blocks at the intersection with Carolina Beach Avenue in the heart of the old seaside resort. Park near this intersection and walk south to the famed Carolina Beach Boardwalk, still the focal point of local activity.

Recent restoration efforts along the boardwalk, including a $1.6-million project unveiled in 1987, have brought new life to the old taverns and nightspots, the bingo parlors, the amusements, the eateries, and the gift shops, many of which have remained in the same spot for four decades. Generations of tourists have feasted on foot-long hot dogs at The Landmark, played bingo at Red and Eve's, and sampled donuts at Britt's Donuts.

As they have for years, game booths line the boardwalk adjacent to the area once covered by the Seaside Amusement Park. Until it closed several years ago due to competition from Jubilee Park, a newer facility located 1 mile north on U.S. 421, the old amusement park had been a summer fixture since Hurricane Hazel. Though smaller in size, it once rivaled similar facilities at Coney Island and Atlantic City. A chairlift ride named the Skyliner, long since gone, carried passengers over a steel pier that extended well out into the Atlantic.

After visiting the boardwalk, return to your car and drive north on Carolina Beach Avenue for 1.5 miles to the end of the road.

One of the state's oldest coastal resorts, Carolina Beach is a blend of old and new structures. Extending along the strand on the drive to the northern end of the island are countless family-style motels, apartments, condominiums, and private cottages revealing varying degrees of sophistication, and in various states of repair. Most of the structures along this route are less than forty years old, because Carolina Beach suffered cataclysmic damage when Hurricane Hazel struck her deadly blow on October 15, 1954.

More than 362 cottages and other buildings were leveled, and another 375 were severely damaged.

Despite its lack of old buildings, the beach town dates back to the 1880s, when Joseph L. Winner, a Wilmington merchant, envisioned a resort on the island. Winner purchased several tracts comprising 108 acres on the northern end of the island, laid out streets and lots, and named his town St. Joseph. Because of its remote location, St. Joseph never took hold, and only scant traces of the town remain. Within the corporate limits of modern Carolina Beach, St. Joseph Avenue winds through the original tract acquired by Winner. One of the large headboats of the extensive sportfishing fleet harbored at Carolina Beach bears the name *Capt. Winner*.

Although Winner's town was unsuccessful, it took less than a decade for other Wilmingtonians to recognize that his dream was a good one. By 1890, a number of residents from the nearby port city had constructed summer homes at the site of the existing resort town. Several beach hotels were completed over the next two decades.

In 1912, the Southern Realty and Development Company unveiled a five-year plan to create the finest resort on the North Carolina coast at Carolina Beach. To accomplish its goal, the company purchased almost a thousand acres on the island, including 2 miles of oceanfront. After the property was surveyed and divided into lots a year later, hordes of salesmen were dispatched around the South to sell Carolina Beach.

In 1915, an electrical plant was erected to provide the new resort town with its first electric lights. That same year saw the completion of a paved highway linking Carolina Beach to Wilmington. Five highways connecting Wilmington with other parts of the state were in place by 1922. These road projects led to the birth of the modern resort town of Carolina Beach. Motorists eager to enjoy the sand and sun began making their way to Pleasure Island from the interior of North Carolina and nearby states. In 1925, the town of Carolina Beach was incorporated.

Near the northern terminus of Carolina Beach Avenue, the effects of the severe erosion to which this portion of the island has been subjected over the past forty years are evident. There is no beach here. Instead, the shoreline consists of a thousand-foot-long sea wall of granite and rubble constructed in 1970 to control the erosion that threatens the economic vitality of the resort.

To understand the cause of the erosion that has claimed two thousand feet from the northern end of the island, park at the Carolina Beach Fishing Pier and walk onto the pier. To the north, Carolina Beach Inlet is visible. This artificial inlet was created by private interests in 1952 in response to the demands of boaters and local groups for a shorter route to the ocean from the yacht basin at Carolina Beach. At the time, boaters had to make a 12-mile trip to reach the open sea. Almost as soon as the new inlet was proposed, the Corps of Engineers warned that it would disturb the delicate balance of nature by interrupting the southerly flow of sand to the beach.

Dire warnings notwithstanding, the proponents of the new inlet prevailed. Work on the project progressed to the point that on September 2, 1952, a dynamite blast brought the tide through the new, 3,900-foot inlet.

Ten years later, a spring storm swept away an entire block at the northern end of Carolina Beach. Since the inlet was created, more than $10 million has been spent in beach renourishment and shoreline engineering projects to counteract the detrimental effects of the inlet. The battle against erosion continues.

From the pier, proceed south on Canal Drive—which runs parallel to Carolina Beach Avenue 1 block to the west—for 1.4 miles as it makes its way toward the heart of the resort. The body of water on the western side of the street is the southern portion of Myrtle Grove Sound. Located at the foot of the sound, the Carolina Beach Yacht Basin is home to one of the largest recreational fleets north of Florida.

Just north of the Carolina Beach Yacht Basin, Canal Drive intersects Harper Avenue. Turn right, or west, on Harper. After 2 blocks, turn left, or south, on Lake Park Boulevard (U.S. 421).

As you wind your way toward the middle portion of Pleasure Island, the southern section of Carolina Beach blends into Wilmington Beach, now merely an extension of its larger neighbor to the north. Over the past twenty years, numerous condominiums and high-rise towers have been constructed along this mile-long stretch of strand.

The history of Wilmington Beach is another story of shattered coastal dreams. In 1913, the Wilmington Beach Corporation brought forth grandiose plans for a magnificent resort that was to include a pavilion, several ocean piers, tennis courts, a waterworks, and an electrical plant.

The centerpiece of the new vacation spot was to be a large hotel. When The Breakers finally opened to the public in May 1924, the modern, fifty-room building towered three stories above the Atlantic. Unfortunately, this sturdy structure, the first brick hotel erected on the New Hanover County seashore, was no match for the fury of Hurricane Hazel. So severe was the damage to The Breakers that it was demolished several years later. No evidence of the great hotel remains at Wilmington Beach, but bricks and rubble from its ruins were used to line the seaward face of Fort Fisher in the ceaseless battle against erosion there.

Even with the construction of The Breakers, Wilmington Beach never reached the stature envisioned by its developers. Many individual lots were sold, but when the Dow Chemical Company purchased a tract of 310 acres for the construction of a plant near the hotel, the future of Wilmington Beach as a resort was doomed.

Continue south on U.S. 421. Until it was developed with beach cottages in the early 1990s, the 1.5-mile stretch of strand between Wilmington Beach and Kure (pronounced Cure-ee) Beach was a popular public beach that attracted hordes of sun worshipers during the summer season.

Nearby is the site of a federal-government project that draws stares from passing motorists. Located on both sides of the highway are chain-link enclosures containing various metal contraptions that resemble solar panels. For decades on this site, various metals have been exposed to the marine environment to test their susceptibility to corrosion. In recent years, a national magazine advertisement has spotlighted this federal project.

Kure Beach

Other than a marker erected by the state south of the metal-testing area, modern Kure Beach gives no hint of the vital, unique, and successful scientific experiment that took place here more than a half-century ago. In 1931, the Dow Chemical Company and the Ethyl Corporation pooled their resources to begin construction of the world's first installation for the extraction of bromine from seawater.

Several important developments in the 1920s led to the need for the facility. During that decade, not only were more automobiles being built and sold in the United States, but the new vehicles were bigger and better than those of previous years. Ordinary gasoline was no longer satisfactory for the high-performance needs of the newer engines. The discovery of tetraethyl lead fostered the development of "high test" gasoline, or ethyl, as it was known in the trade. When added to gasoline, tetraethyl lead increased the antiknock capacity of an engine, thus improving its performance. When the new gasoline product was introduced in 1923, it was enthusiastically accepted by the motoring public, but the concern of health officials over its lead content resulted in a federal ban of the sale of ethyl gasoline for two years.

Meanwhile, intensive research showed that the addition of ethylene dibromide, of which bromine is a major component, made the fuel safe. When ethyl was once again made available for public use in 1926, sales skyrocketed. The industry was thus forced to search for a source of bromine, because supplies of the mineral were rapidly being depleted. Laboratory tests convinced officials from Dow Chemical and the Ethyl Corporation that the critical need for bromine could be satisfied by its extraction from seawater.

Experiments conducted on a floating laboratory in the continental waters of the United States convinced officials from both companies that bromine could be extracted from water close to shore with minimal difficulty. After considering a number of sites for the location of a revolutionary plant, the newly formed Ethyl-Dow Chemical Corporation selected Kure Beach as the ideal spot.

In 1933, some fifteen hundred workmen were employed in the construction of the massive facility. Seawater first entered the intake valves in January 1934. For eleven years thereafter, much of the nation's bromine was supplied by the facility on the northern side of Kure Beach. The plant, a complex network of pipes and towers, captured scientific attention as the first of its kind in the world. By conclusively proving that the riches of the oceans could be mined in a practical way, the installation came to be considered one of the scientific marvels of the twentieth century.

Expansions at the plant allowed scientists to discover a wealth of by-products in the bromine extraction process. Among the riches contained in the massive quantities of water processed at the plant were enough gold to make a five-inch ball; enough silver to make a twenty-five-inch ball; enough epsom salts to supply every American with nine pounds each; enough potassium chloride to fertilize a million acres of farmland; enough copper to fabricate

1,120 miles of twenty-gauge wire; enough aluminum to make sixty-eight thousand automobile pistons; and enough common salt to put down pavement one foot thick and twenty-six feet wide from New York City to Washington, D.C.

Security was given the highest priority during World War II, because of the facility's vulnerable coastal location and the vital product it produced. Patrol squadrons flying out of Elizabeth City provided twenty-four-hour surveillance. Nonetheless, the plant was the target of a U-boat attack in the wee hours of a Saturday morning in 1943. An army pilot spotted a German submarine 5 miles offshore just as it was firing its deck gun at the plant. Five shots were fired, all of them errant, either landing in the Cape Fear River or beyond in Brunswick County.

Once the submarine was sighted, the pilot dispatched a radio report which resulted in an air-raid alert in the Wilmington area. As sirens pierced the night, the entire area was blacked out while American warplanes searched in vain for the U-boat.

Shortly after the war, the decision was made to phase out operations at the Kure Beach facility, due to the construction of a large, modern plant in Texas. By January 1946, the plant that pioneered the production of bromine from seawater was closed forever. Finally, on February 1, 1956, a demolition crew from Florida began a complex, nine-month job of dismantling the facility. Once that task was completed, the site of one of the great experiments in the history of science was given back to nature.

On the 1.6-mile drive south from Wilmington Beach to Kure Beach, you will notice a marked change in the age and sophistication of structures on the strand highway. Kure Beach is dominated by family vacation cottages and mom-and-pop motels, restaurants, and businesses, much as it has been since its birth in the last decade of the nineteenth century.

Though not as large and well known as Carolina Beach, Kure Beach is almost as old. In 1891, Hans Kure, a native of Barnholm, Denmark, was fishing with a group of Wilmington businessmen near the wreck of the blockade runner *Beauregard* when he conceived the idea of a commercial enterprise at the place which today bears his name.

As a young sea captain, Kure had become familiar with the North Carolina coast when his ship wrecked near Beaufort in the early 1870s. After recuperating in a Beaufort hospital, he returned to his native land, but he could not forget the excellent care and genuine friendship extended to him by the people of the North Carolina coast. By 1879, he settled in Wilmington, where he operated a ship chandlery and a stevedoring business.

Immediately following his 1891 fishing trip to Pleasure Island, Kure acquired oceanfront property 2 miles south of Carolina Beach in an area of rolling sand dunes, beach grass, and scrub oaks. By early summer, his beach holdings included a bowling alley and a saloon.

More than a century later, Kure's resort remains a small, unpretentious vacation town. Missing from Kure Beach are the bright lights and amusements that have made Carolina Beach one of the state's most popular resorts.

To sample the easygoing atmosphere of Kure Beach, park near the traffic light on U.S. 421 in the heart of town and walk to the Kure Beach Fishing Pier, the resort's claim to fame.

Not only is the 950-foot pier the oldest on the coast of the Carolinas, but it is also believed to be the oldest on the entire Atlantic coast. Constructed of untreated wood by L. C. Kure in 1923, the original pier was 120 feet long and 12 feet wide. After only a year, it succumbed to the elements, but Kure rebuilt. In the process, he substantially enlarged the pier and strengthened it with concrete posts reinforced with railroad iron.

Since that time, the pier has been rebuilt eleven times. When Hurricane Hazel struck Kure Beach, the concrete pilings were not broken by the savage wind and waves. Instead, they were knocked over. They now lie on the ocean floor near the pier.

After visiting the pier, continue south on U.S. 421. Much of the land on Pleasure Island south of Kure Beach is owned by the state and federal governments. Consequently, the southern end of the island has been spared widespread commercial development. The only exception is a strip of oceanfront property just north of the old Fort Fisher Air Force Base. Here, the resort village of Fort Fisher has fallen prey to condominium construction.

To the south of the former base, the northern limits of which are marked by two imposing concrete pillars on the shoulder of U.S. 421, the government holdings are put to various uses: a recreational retreat for military personnel from North Carolina bases; Fort Fisher State Historic Site; Fort Fisher State

Recreation Area; the North Carolina Aquarium at Fort Fisher; the Fort Fisher–Southport Ferry; and "the Rocks."

One of coastal North Carolina's newest museums opened on the grounds of the former air-force base in August 1991. Housed in a National Guard building on the western side of U.S. 421 approximately 1 mile south of Kure Beach, the North Carolina Military History Museum offers exhibits of uniforms, firearms, and other military memorabilia. It was founded by the North Carolina Military Historical Society.

Fort Fisher State Historic Site Visitor Center

Continue to Fort Fisher State Historic Site. The combination visitor center and museum is located on the western side of U.S. 421 south of the old air-force base.

In spite of a constant struggle for funding since it was established in 1961, Fort Fisher State Historic Site remains the most-visited state historic site in North Carolina. And although the visitor center–museum was never completed as designed—the architect envisioned a structure that would give visitors the feeling of entering a bunker—it remains one of the focal points of the mighty Civil War fortification. The visitor center–museum offers information about the history of the fort, the famous battles fought here, and the preservation of the remaining earthworks. Without this information, unwary visitors who expect to see a stone or cement fortification might pass right by the remains of the fort without noticing them.

Bunker at Fort Fisher

Inside the museum, a short audiovisual presentation documents the vital role that Fort Fisher played in protecting the Cape Fear area and local blockade runners, which successfully ran the Federal blockade 1,835 times out of 2,054 attempts. Interpretive exhibits display letters, maps, and charts concerning the fort, as well as artifacts recovered from the area. Shells and cannonballs are grim reminders of the massive sea-to-shore bombardment that took place here.

To the rear of the building is all that remains of the once-massive fortification, a complete model of which was used for study in classrooms at West Point after the Civil War. Even though a road and an airstrip were constructed through the fort during this century, a significant portion of its land face remains. To preserve the half-dozen or so mounds that still exist, the state has seeded them with grass. A palisade similar to the one that protected the land face has been constructed.

A trail winds around to the other side of the mounds and leads to the end of the earthworks near the Cape Fear River. It is here that visitors can best visualize how the interior walls of the fort looked, thanks to the work of state archaeologists and site officials.

In the late 1970s, archaeologists unearthed the "bombproof" nearest the river. From the information gained in that project, a bombproof has been reconstructed, the entrance to which is on the side of the mounds opposite the museum.

Just north of the museum and adjacent to the parking lot is the Underwater Archaeology Laboratory, operated by the North Carolina Division of Archives and History. The laboratory, with its five-person staff, is an outgrowth of the centennial celebration of the Civil War and the attendant activities at Fort Fisher. Its curator promptly took steps to salvage some of the forty blockade runners that had been lost just offshore.

Since the facility's opening, divers from the lab have located and explored more than three hundred shipwrecks in North Carolina waters. In addition to preserving Civil War artifacts, the lab has preserved twenty-six dugout canoes used by the prehistoric Indians of Lake Phelps.

The cannon that greets visitors at the museum entrance was discovered by the Fort Fisher laboratory. It came from the USS *Peterhoff*, which went down in nearby waters in 1864 after colliding with another United States Navy vessel.

Several years ago, the laboratory was honored as one of the top five of its kind in the nation. Today, it may very well be the best. Throughout the past quarter-century, its staffers have pioneered many of the processes now in widespread use to protect iron after long periods of exposure to seawater.

Directly across U.S. 421 from the visitor center–museum and the parking lot is a picnic area, located in a majestic oceanfront setting under a canopy of live oaks gnarled by the wind blowing off the sea.

Just south of the picnic area, and within walking distance, stands the Fort Fisher Monument. Since 1932, this tall stone shaft has towered above the ever-encroaching Atlantic. Surmounted by a large eagle atop a sphere, the monument is located at a spot known as Battle Acre. At its unveiling, the Confederate flag flew over Fort Fisher for the first time since its surrender.

Proudly displayed at the United States Military Academy at West Point,

Fort Fisher Monument

New York, is the magnificent, 150-pound, mahogany, carriage-mounted Armstrong gun presented to the officers and men of Fort Fisher by Jefferson Davis, the Confederate president.

In the not-too-distant future, that gun and other relics like it may be all that remain of the old fort. Nothing man has tried over the past six decades has halted the onslaught of erosion. More than three-quarters of the original fort has been eaten away by the sea. Nonetheless, from the parking lot at Battle Acre, visitors can gaze up and down the beach and imagine how the sprawling fortress must have looked.

Named for Colonel Charles Fisher, a North Carolina hero who died at First Manassas, the fort was constructed and enlarged throughout the four years of the Civil War. Major General William H. C. Whiting, the adopted North Carolinian who had the highest grades at West Point prior to the matriculation of Douglas MacArthur, and Colonel William Lamb, a young newspaper editor and attorney from Virginia, were the geniuses behind this coastal citadel, which quickly earned the nickname "Gibraltar of America." Embracing a sea face of more than a mile (1,898 yards) and a land face of more than a third of a mile (683 yards), the L-shaped fort was enormous. Stretching down the long sea face were seventeen heavy gun emplacements.

The earthwork walls rose twenty feet above the sea. They were constructed with a forty-five-degree slope to make it difficult for an assaulting land force to gain entry. As a cushion against heavy gunfire from enemy ships, the walls of the parapet were twenty-five feet thick.

Fort Fisher earthworks

At the southern end of the sea face stood the imposing Lamb's Mound Battery. Towering sixty feet, this gun emplacement was armed with long-range guns for the defense of New Inlet, the primary river entrance used by blockade runners en route to Wilmington. Farther to the south, at the tip of the island, was a tall, oblong fortification called Battery Buchanan, an auxiliary part of the fort.

Many of the thousands of treatises written on the Civil War have failed to relate the extreme importance of the Union capture of Fort Fisher to the ultimate demise of the Confederacy. Six months before the war ended, General Robert E. Lee warned, "If Fort Fisher falls, I will have to evacuate Richmond." Indeed, half the supplies for Lee's Army of Northern Virginia were flowing through the port of Wilmington at that time.

In retrospect, Alexander H. Stephens, vice president of the Confederate States of America, commented, "The fall of this Fort was one of the greatest disasters which had befallen our cause from the beginning of the war—not excepting the loss of Vicksburg or Atlanta."

Fort Fisher fell to combined Union forces on January 15, 1865. General Lee surrendered at Appomattox less than three months later.

The Confederate garrison of fewer than two thousand men did not surrender the Cape Fear installation until it exhausted its entire supply of ammunition. Those men waged a three-day battle against the largest war fleet ever assembled to that time and an invading land force of some ten thousand Union soldiers, sailors, and marines. During the struggle, the guns of the fleet hurled more than fifty thousand shells at the fort. After Fort Fisher capitulated, the federal government excavated a thousand tons of iron from the battle site. Yet after three days of the heaviest sea-to-land bombardment the world had ever witnessed—and since surpassed only by the assault on Normandy eighty years later—not one of the fort's bombproofs or magazines was damaged.

Just south of the Fort Fisher Monument, the state has established the Fort Fisher State Recreation Area, a 237-acre tract along the undeveloped strand. First-time visitors to the shore in this area are surprised, and often alarmed, to see huge chunks of concrete and riprap which have been deposited at the edge of the embankment running along the shore in the vicinity of the old fort. This rubble fortification has been put in place to stem the tide in the constant battle against erosion.

Rocks are abundant in this area, both in the tidal zone and submerged in the shallow waters. However, these rocks are not remnants of an earlier fight with erosion. They are coquina outcrops—the only natural rock exposures on the entire North Carolina coast.

Coquina is a combination of shells and estuarine fossil fragments cemented together in a natural process by calcite. Most of the rock formations are now submerged at high tide. At low tide, much of the rocky area is exposed, disclosing potholes and cracks filled with various sea creatures and algae.

Continue south to the North Carolina Aquarium at Fort Fisher, located on the ocean side of the highway 0.2 mile from Fort Fisher State Recreation Area.

The North Carolina Aquarium at Fort Fisher is the southernmost of the state's three public marine centers. Housed in a modern multilevel building, the center features aquariums, exhibits, conference rooms, research laboratories, and offices. On the lower level, the 20,000-gallon shark tank, the largest aquarium in the state, is the most popular exhibit at the facility. Films and programs dealing with many aspects of coastal life are offered by the aquarium. Off-site excursions are offered as well.

The several hiking trails developed on the twenty-five-acre oceanfront complex afford visitors an opportunity to enjoy the coastal habitat in its natural state. One of the nature trails leads to the former home of one of the most colorful residents of the area. Throughout the year, the aquarium offers guided hikes to the structure where the Fort Fisher hermit once lived. From 1955 until his death in 1972, Robert Edward Harrell called Fort Fisher home.

When he arrived at Fort Fisher at the age of sixty-two, Harrell lived in a tent near the Fort Fisher Monument. As to why he left his hometown of Shelby, the native North Carolinian would only say that he came to write his book. That he did. However, *A Tyrant in Every Home* was never published.

In Shelby, Harrell had earned a living as a newspaper typesetter and itinerant jewelry salesman. His wife and children had left him in the 1930s.

Regardless of what led him to the Cape Fear area, Harrell never wanted to leave after he arrived. He quickly exchanged his tent home for an abandoned World War II bunker in the desolate salt marshes in the vicinity of the present aquarium. Both the federal and state governments were displeased with Harrell's use of the bunker as a dwelling, but the man used his wit, charm, and personality to dissuade all agencies from evicting him.

Harrell lived alone except for a pack of mangy dogs which kept him company. He kept his few worldly possessions hidden in piles of debris around the bunker. His diet consisted primarily of berries, shrimp, oysters, fish, and other seafood caught at nearby Buzzard's Creek. To supplement his diet, he cultivated a small garden. He drank rainwater coffee. Island residents brought food to him on occasion, and he made trips to Carolina Beach to shop at the nearest supermarket.

Except in extremely cold weather, the hermit's dress was nothing more than an old bathing suit and a floppy straw hat. Only on the coldest days did he don an overcoat and shoes. His hair and beard were untrimmed, and he bore a striking resemblance to Ernest Hemingway. Years of exposure to the sun toughened his skin to the point that he did not even feel the bite of coastal deer flies, which bring pain to most people. As he grew older, his hunched back made him look shorter than his five-foot-three-inch height.

As his presence became known, hordes of visitors descended upon his domain. Harrell claimed that as many as seventeen thousand people visited him in a year. His visitors almost always left highly impressed with the hermit's intelligence. He often engaged those invading his solitude in conversation about politics, religion, and the coast. Visitors were required to sign a register maintained by Harrell, who did not object to being photographed.

The hermit was not only well read, but shrewd as well. When visitors called, they were greeted by an old frying pan outside the bunker. In the pan, Harrell put "seed money"—a half-dollar, a quarter, a dime, a nickel, and a penny. By doing so, he said he was using psychology on people. When they saw the penny, they knew that a penny was welcome, and likewise a nickel, a dime, a quarter, or a half-dollar. In return for a donation, the hermit always gave his visitors something, whether it be a piece of shrapnel or a seashell.

On June 4, 1972, some boys ventured to the bunker to call on the hermit. They found his dead body, his raincoat bunched around his neck. His legs were bloody. Shoe prints in the sand seemed to indicate that his body had been dragged.

A coroner's report concluded that Harrell died of natural causes. His body was taken back to Shelby for burial. Harrell's son, Ed, was not convinced that his father's death was natural. At his request, the body was exhumed in 1984 for an autopsy. Once again, no evidence of foul play was found.

To those who knew him on the island, Harrell had expressed his desire to remain at Fort Fisher. He told people not to worry about burying him—he advised them to leave his body for the crabs to eat.

On the seventeenth anniversary of his death, friends and relatives reburied the hermit in a grave on the island he had affectionately called home. The grave is covered with shells and a tombstone, which prophetically reads,

Grave of the Fort Fisher hermit

> Robert E. Harrell
> The Fort Fisher Hermit
>
> "He Made People Think"
> February 2, 1893
> June 4, 1972

Continue south on U.S. 421. It is 1.3 miles from the aquarium to the Fort Fisher–Southport Ferry landing, located near the tip of the island, known as Federal Point. From this point, a state-operated ferry carries passengers and vehicles across the Cape Fear River to Southport, thereby avoiding a 50-mile trip by road.

Two historic sites are located adjacent to the ferry landing. Within walking distance is the last point of rendezvous for Confederate forces during the final assault on Fort Fisher: Battery Buchanan. A small sign erected by the state directs visitors to this rather tall, grassy mound, where the sun set on the Confederacy. A parking lot and a public boat-access area are located at the site.

Located on the riverfront just south of Battery Buchanan, "The Rocks" is a popular recreational spot. Hordes of people fish, swim, picnic, and sightsee on or near the dam that saved the port of Wilmington. Yet few visitors who walk atop this architectural masterpiece realize the magnitude of the dam below them.

"The Rocks" closed New Inlet, which had been opened by a raging storm in 1761. The inlet was used by countless ships during the Civil War. Anna McNeill Whistler, better known as "Whistler's Mother," made her way through New Inlet during the conflict to join her famous artist son in Europe.

In order to maintain a navigable river channel to the port of Wilmington, the Corps of Engineers recommended in 1874 that New Inlet be closed with a dam. Captain Henry Bacon, an engineer from Wilmington, was the mastermind of the project.

To construct the dam, large rafts of logs and brush weighted with massive quantities of stone were sunk for almost a mile from Federal Point to Zekes Island. When the base of the dam was completed, it was 90 to 120 feet wide. Sufficient quantities of rock were barged in and dumped onto the base to raise the dam to the water level—a height of 20 to 25 feet. Since

"The Rocks"

TOURING THE BACKROADS OF NORTH CAROLINA'S LOWER COAST

the dam's completion, engineers have determined that the rock used in the project would build a stone wall 8 feet high, 4 feet thick, and 100 miles long.

Few engineering feats in American history have surpassed "The Rocks." Recognized internationally as an engineering landmark, the project has been designated one of the twelve "Best Ever" projects completed during the two-hundred-year history of the Corps of Engineers.

The tour ends here, near the southern tip of Pleasure Island.

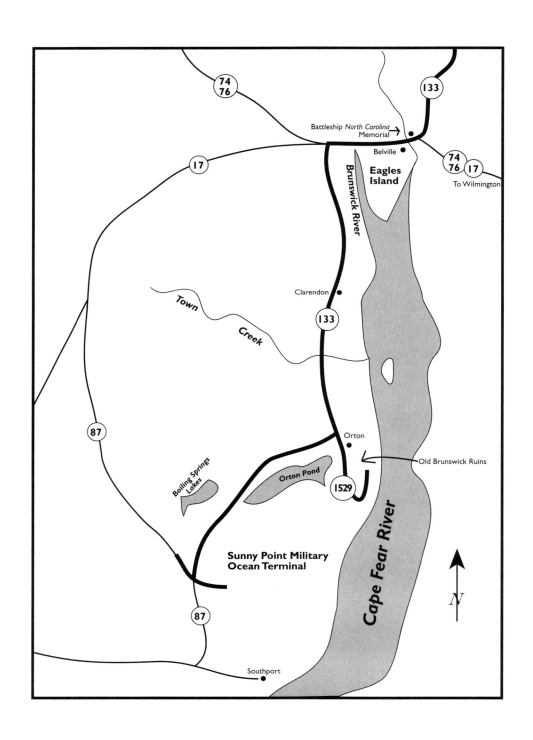

The Cape Fear Riverfront Tour

This tour begins at Eagles Island, home of the Battleship *North Carolina* Memorial, then follows the course of the Cape Fear River to Belville, Orton Plantation, and Brunswick Town State Historic Site before ending near Boiling Spring Lakes.

Among the highlights of the tour are the legendary Battleship *North Carolina*, the story of "the Ghost Fleet of Wilmington," the story of the Cape Fear plantations—chief among them Clarendon, Old Town, Pleasant Oaks, and Orton—and the story of Brunswick Town and Fort Anderson.

Total mileage: approximately 37 miles.

This tour begins on U.S. 421 just north of the intersection with U.S. 17/74/76 on the western side of the Cape Fear River, 2 miles from downtown Wilmington. Follow the giant red and blue sign for the Battleship *North Carolina*, which directs you down S.R. 1352 to Eagles Island.

Eagles Island is the home of one of the most captivating sights in all of coastal North Carolina. Three decades have now passed since a Southport river pilot, Captain B. M. Burris, skillfully guided the USS *North Carolina* (*BB-55*) into the Cape Fear River en route to its permanent berth here, on the New Hanover County–Brunswick County line.

Named for Richard Eagles of Bristol, England, an early planter in the region, the island was linked to Wilmington in pre–Revolutionary War times by a causeway built of large ballast stones and sacks of soil thrown overboard from ships from all over the world. Almost 250 years later, flowers and plants foreign to North Carolina, including the bonny bluebells and thistle of Scotland, thrive on the marshy, semitropical island. Known as "the Granary of the Commonwealth," the island produced abundant quantities of rice in the eighteenth century. Eagles Island helped make Carolina rice world-famous.

At the end of the short, scenic drive looms the enormous warship, moored in the shadow of the Wilmington waterfront. A green picnic area and a spacious parking lot shaded by live oaks laden with Spanish moss greet the

The Battleship North Carolina
Photo by Conrad Lowman

250,000 visitors who annually walk the teakwood decks, climb onto the once-potent guns, and examine the bowels of one of the most battle-tested, highly decorated ships in the history of the United States Navy.

Still emblazoned on the hull of the *North Carolina* is the number *55*, signifying that the ship was the fifty-fifth battleship laid down for the navy. Of the fifty-four that preceded her, two bore the proud name USS *North Carolina*.

The first *North Carolina*, launched in 1820 and commanded by Master Commandant Matthew C. Perry, quickly became the envy of the navies of the world. Much like her namesake now berthed at Eagles Island, the original *North Carolina* was the "show ship" of her day. She was invited to call at ports all around the world, where dignitaries and heads of state marveled at her beauty and power.

The keel for the second *North Carolina* (*BB-52*) was laid in 1919. Had this ship been completed, it would have been the largest, mightiest, and most modern battleship in the world. But the post–World War I "Five Power" treaty called for a ten-year period during which no new warships could be completed. Thus, the hull of the second *North Carolina* was sold for scrap in Norfolk in 1923.

On June 9, 1940, four days before the hull of the current *North Carolina* slid down the ways at the Brooklyn Navy Yard, German troops entered Paris.

When the United States Navy commissioned this, the mightiest naval vessel in the world, at an elaborate ceremony ten months later, on April 9, 1941, correspondents from all over the world were on hand to witness the unveiling of the first modern battleship. The $77-million ship was the first to incorporate new shipbuilding technology with heavy armament, strong protection, and speed.

Stretching more than 728 feet, the 45,000-ton battleship was more than 200 feet longer than World War I battleships. When she was launched, no ship in the world could match the *North Carolina* in firepower. The main battery of nine 16-inch guns could accurately fire armor-piercing, 2,700-pound projectiles up to 22 miles.

The main battery of the Battleship North Carolina

As the forerunner of the mighty battleships to follow, it was the *North Carolina* that wrestled with new equipment, ironed out wrinkles, and generally set the standard for future ships in the American fleet. Chosen to be a class leader, the awesome battleship wore its crown well.

In the course of her six-month shakedown cruise, the dreadnought made her way back to the Brooklyn Navy Yard many times for technical conferences and adjustments. New Yorkers, including radio-newspaper personality Walter Winchell, grew so accustomed to seeing the graceful ship entering and leaving New York Harbor that they nicknamed her the "Showboat," after the riverboat in the Edna Ferber novel and the subsequent musical of stage and screen.

The *North Carolina* and her sailors were in port at New York City when the Japanese struck Pearl Harbor on December 7, 1941. Less than six months later, the ship was ready to take her place as one of the greatest fighting vessels in world history.

On May 29, 1942, the *North Carolina* put in at Hampton Roads, Virginia, to take on ammunition. From there, she sailed for the Panama Canal Zone on June 4. Six days later, the Showboat earned the distinction of being the first battleship to pass through the Panama Canal during World War II. On June 24, the ship arrived in San Francisco, where she spent ten days while final plans were formulated for her entry into the war for the control of the Pacific. Departing from San Francisco under the guise of a training cruise on July 5, the battleship received orders at sea a day later to proceed to Pearl Harbor.

After the virtual destruction of the American fleet in the Pacific, the aged, battered remnants of the United States Navy struggled valiantly for survival against an overwhelming opponent, the Imperial Navy of Japan. The news from the Pacific in the early days of the summer of 1942 painted a bleak picture. Against this backdrop, the United States prepared to unleash the mightiest ship the world had ever known.

On the afternoon of July 11, 1942, the sailors of the beleaguered fleet at Pearl Harbor witnessed a sight they would never forget. Looming on the horizon, under the escort of a carrier and several cruisers, appeared the largest, mightiest, and most modern ship on the seas. Tumultuous cheers rang out all along the harbor as the Showboat made her way past the twisted wreckage of the USS *Arizona*.

Fleet Admiral Chester Nimitz, the commander of the United States Navy in the Pacific, reflected upon the arrival of the *North Carolina*: "I well remember the great thrill when she arrived in Pearl Harbor during the early stages of the war—at a time when our strength and fortunes were at a low ebb. She was the first of the great new battleships to join the Pacific Fleet, and her presence in a task force was enough to keep our morale at a peak. Before the war's end, she had built for herself a magnificent record of accomplishment."

Soon after her arrival at Pearl Harbor, she went on the offensive, becoming the first American battleship to fire into Japanese territory. During the three and a half years that followed, the *North Carolina* spent more than forty months in combat zones. In the long history of the United States Navy, only a handful of ships have served longer stints in the face of the enemy.

Her most significant contribution to the war effort was the protection she provided for aircraft carriers. With cover from the *North Carolina*, thousands upon thousands of bombing missions were successfully flown by carrier-based airplanes against enemy targets.

Her long Pacific tour covered some 307,000 miles. Along the way, the mighty warship was the only American battleship to take part in all twelve major naval offensives in the Pacific theater. Her unsurpassed fighting ability and the bravery and savvy of her crew earned the battleship twelve battle stars, covering operations from Guadalcanal to the Japanese islands.

Ironically, the war that the *North Carolina* helped win produced the technology that spelled doom for virtually all battleships. At the Battle of Leyte Gulf and other struggles in the Pacific, the fallibility of big battle wagons was apparent. Aircraft from modern carriers could swiftly strike devastating blows against the relatively slow ships.

With her obsolescence as a weapon of war assured, the life expectancy of the *North Carolina* diminished rather quickly after World War II. On June 27, 1947, the proud warship was decommissioned. For the next fourteen years, she swung at anchor in relative obscurity as one of the many fighting vessels in the "Mothball Fleet" at Bayonne, New Jersey.

Concern grew in North Carolina over the future of the battleship when on June 1, 1960, naval officials confirmed rumors that the vessel would be scrapped. Exactly five months later, the ship was stricken from the official United States Navy list.

Working against time, state officials, public-minded citizens, and schoolchildren all over North Carolina rallied to raise money to save the ship from the blowtorch. By September 12, 1961, people from all walks of life had contributed nearly $236,000 to acquire the ship, to prepare the site at Eagles Island, and to transport the ship to the berth. More than seven hundred thousand schoolchildren brought nickels and dimes to school in a herculean effort that raised a third of the necessary funds.

On October 14, 1961, the dream of many North Carolinians came true when the Showboat welcomed visitors to its decks for the first time as a battleship memorial.

In March 1986, the memorial was designated a National Historic Landmark. Later that year, the name was changed from the USS *North Carolina*

Battleship Memorial to the Battleship *North Carolina* Memorial amid speculation that there might one day be another USS *North Carolina* in the active service of the United States Navy.

Since the ship was first opened to the public, additional portions of its interior have been made accessible to visitors. Among the areas now open are the teakwood decks, the engine rooms, the cobbler shop, the ship's store, the laundry, the print shop, the crew's mess and quarters, the officers' quarters, the sick bay, the combat information center, and the pilothouse. Several of the turret chambers of the 16-inch guns are open. Audio stations provide messages of interest along the self-guided tour.

Prominently displayed on deck near the stern is a restored OS2U Vought Kingfisher airplane. Three of the aircraft were carried by the ship during the war. These low-wing monoplanes were launched from two sixty-eight-foot catapults on the stern. The planes were used for observation of long-range gunfire, antisubmarine patrol, message drop, sea rescue, aerial photography, and shore liaison. Upon returning from a mission, they landed in the water near the battleship and were hoisted from the water by a deck crane.

Only fifteen hundred of the special aircraft were built during World War II, and very few remain in existence. In 1968, the wreckage of the craft featured aboard the battleship was discovered by the Royal Canadian Air Force in the rugged mountain wilderness of Alaska, where it had crashed in 1942. After the plane was salvaged, it was shipped to Dallas, Texas, where retired workers of the Vought Aeronautical Company volunteered to restore it. After the painstaking task was completed, the wings and fuselage were trucked to Wilmington for assembly.

Inside the Battleship Memorial Museum, located aboard the ship, are many photographs and artifacts related to the history of the *North Carolina*. One of the prominent exhibits is the "Roll of Honor"—a list of every North Carolinian who died during World War II in the service of the United States.

In the late 1980s, a new visitor facility—which includes an orientation center, a ticket office, a gift shop, a snack bar, and restrooms—was completed adjacent to the ship.

No summertime tour of the battleship is complete without an appearance by the resident alligator, Charlie, who often swims in the waters alongside the vessel.

Not one cent of government money—state or federal—has ever gone toward the operation of the battleship memorial. Managed by a sixteen-member commission appointed by the governor, the ship is maintained with funds generated from admissions, gift-shop and snack-bar revenues, and gifts.

The great battleship at Eagles Island is one of the premier attractions on the North Carolina coast and a significant landmark of American history. Except for the *New Jersey*, which served the nation for a much longer period of time, the *North Carolina* is the most-decorated vessel in the history of the United States Navy.

From the grassy picnic area at the battleship, visitors can enjoy the spectacular beauty of one of America's greatest rivers. Of all the historic rivers in eastern North Carolina, none has been more important in the settlement, development, and economic growth of the coastal plain than the mighty Cape Fear.

The only river in the state that offers a direct deepwater outlet to the Atlantic, the Cape Fear has dominated the history of southeastern North Carolina. Its wide, deep channel welcomed the first settlers to the area, served as a primary avenue of transportation and communication before the swampy lowlands along its banks were made accessible by bridges, opened the fertile farmlands and vast forests of the region, provided North Carolina with its first artery of maritime commerce, supplied the Confederacy with munitions and a variety of goods until the waning days of the Civil War, and gave the state its only modern, world-class port: Wilmington.

Its silt-laden waters begin their meandering, 320-mile run at the junction of the Deep and Haw rivers on the Chatham County–Lee County line. As it flows southeast through Harnett, Cumberland, and Bladen counties, the Cape Fear gains strength. Its high banks gradually flatten into marshy wetlands once the river makes its way into New Hanover and Brunswick counties.

It is at Eagles Island that the river gains its great power. Here, at "The Forks," the waters of the Northeast and Northwest Cape Fear join forces to provide a deep, wide river for the Wilmington port facilities, located across the river from, and just south of, the battleship. The Cape Fear is the only coastal river in the state that is significantly affected by lunar tides far upstream. At Eagles Island, the tides average three to five feet.

Over the course of its long run, the Cape Fear drains more than 5,275 square miles. Its oblong basin is 200 miles long and as much as 60 miles wide. Had the river carved a course due east from its headwaters, it would empty into the Atlantic north of Cape Hatteras. However, geologic forces at work more than twenty-five thousand years ago and the rotation of the earth forced the river into its southeasterly route. It is the only river on the East Coast between the Hudson in New York and the Savannah in Georgia that reaches the Atlantic without being intercepted by a sound.

At Eagles Island, the majestic river begins its 30-mile final leg, widening up to 3 miles as it prepares to empty into the ocean. Although the balance of the tour parallels this course, the river will be mostly hidden from view.

To continue the tour, return to the intersection of U.S. 421 and U.S. 17/74/76 and proceed west on U.S. 17/74/76.

After 2 miles, you will cross the Brunswick River, a 5-mile-long branch of the Cape Fear. South of the bridge, this lazy tributary appears to be devoid of modern use, with only rotting pilings to mar its pristine appearance.

Yet few motorists who made their way into Wilmington in the 1950s and early 1960s will ever forget the spectacular sight they saw from this bridge. On the banks of the Brunswick River—where rice plantations once prospered—many of the survivors of America's World War II cargo fleet were tied up as part of the nation's postwar reserve fleet. For as far as the naked eye could see and beyond, hundreds of vessels—mostly aging Liberty ships, each measuring up to five hundred feet in length—stretched down the river. At its peak, the ghost fleet contained 649 ships and extended 2.5 miles along both banks, making it the second-largest merchant-ship graveyard in the world.

From August 8, 1946, when the SS *John Boyce* became the first ship towed to the basin, to February 27, 1970, when the SS *Dwight Morrow* was the last of the ships to leave the river, the massive reserve fleet was anchored within sight of the place where many of the ships were constructed: the North Carolina Shipbuilding Company at Wilmington.

Although the long, gray line of ships in the Brunswick River is nothing more than a memory now, those who saw it often catch themselves craning their necks as they drive along the river bridge, hoping they might catch one more glimpse of the spectacle known as "the Ghost Fleet of Wilmington."

Just beyond the bridge over the Brunswick River, turn off U.S. 17/74/76 onto N.C. 133 at the small community of Belville. From Belville, N.C. 133 runs roughly parallel to the Cape Fear for a distance of approximately 10 miles. Until the early 1950s, when the military shipping installation at Sunny Point was built downriver, the ancient road linking Wilmington and Southport ran adjacent to the river. To accommodate the needs of the Sunny Point complex, N.C. 133 was moved inland, to the west.

Approximately 0.2 mile south of Belville, N.C. 133 offers a view of the Brunswick River. Through the trees, the dark, shimmering waters yield no clue that they once floated the great mothball fleet of Liberty ships. On the shoulder of the road opposite the river, a long row of eight historical markers erected by the North Carolina Division of Archives and History commemorates many of the significant events and persons in the long history of the Cape Fear.

The road makes its way past several modern subdivisions, then winds through forested savannas and swampy lowlands. Nearly a half-dozen large antebellum plantations once graced the banks of the river in this area.

Some of the old plantations vanished when they were consumed by larger plantations. For example, Lilliput, once held by Royal Governor William Tryon, and Kendall, the home of Major General Robert Howe—the highest-ranking American general of the Revolutionary War born south of Virginia—were absorbed by Orton Plantation. Nevertheless, sizable portions of four of the most historic of the river plantations are still intact.

Located 6.2 miles south of Belville, Clarendon remains one of the finest colonial rice plantations in the state. The plantation is situated on the eastern side of N.C. 133 but is not visible from the highway.

Established in 1730 on the site of the old Charles Towne settlement of the seventeenth century, the Clarendon grounds hold a wealth of historically significant artifacts. A powder magazine built in 1666 by early Cape Fear settlers is believed to be one of the oldest buildings in the state. Two canals on the property are of extreme importance. One, running a distance of several hundred yards through the ancient rice fields, is the only survivor of the numerous river canals once found on the plantations. The other canal, a fifty-foot-wide waterway along the river, was dug by Indians as a time-telling device. It is so perfectly oriented that the sunrise at the summer solstice still ascends dead center in the canal. Some historians and scientists contend that this canal represents the first calendar ever used in the Cape Fear region.

Clarendon was acquired after the Revolutionary War by Governor Benjamin Smith. In 1834, the Watters family came into ownership of the plantation and erected a magnificent two-story plantation house, which still stands on a high bank at the end of a magnificent lane of yaupon and silver maples. It was in this house that renowned author Inglis Fletcher penned her famous historical novel *Lusty Wind for Carolina.*

Unfortunately, Clarendon is not open to the public.

Town Creek, a long, scenic waterway which flows from the center of Brunswick County into the Cape Fear, intersects N.C. 133 approximately 1.5 miles south of Clarendon. On the northern banks of the creek are the ruins of perhaps the oldest plantation of the Lower Cape Fear: Old Town Plantation.

Colonel Maurice Moore was granted this thousand-acre site in and around the mouth of the creek in 1725. The massive plantation house was constructed several years later. Located near the mouth of the creek, the Old Town graveyard contains some tombs of the colonists who settled the area in the 1660s.

A private, unpaved road leads from the highway into the heart of Old Town Plantation.

One of the most majestic colonial plantations in all of America lies on the banks of the Cape Fear 0.3 mile south of Town Creek, at the intersection of N.C. 133 and S.R. 1518. Pleasant Oaks, originally named The Oaks, was established from a 1725 land grant to the Moore family. Its stately entrance—magnificent wrought-iron gates enclosed by white brick facades—is similar in appearance to, and often confused with, that of Orton Plantation, the famous plantation next door.

From the entrance to Pleasant Oaks, a mile-long lane winds through a wooded area of white oaks, then crosses a dam that forms an artificial cypress lake. Beyond the lake, the road makes its way up a slight hill to the

Entrance to Pleasant Oaks

TOURING THE BACKROADS OF NORTH CAROLINA'S LOWER COAST

antebellum plantation house, located at the junction of Town Creek and the river.

The fields and gardens of Pleasant Oaks have long enjoyed a reputation for their productivity and beauty. In the decade before the Civil War, the plantation earned the distinction of producing the finest and largest-grain rice in the world. Its camellia gardens later came to be considered among the most beautiful in the nation.

Today, a 2-mile avenue of live oaks, still regarded as one of the most picturesque lanes in all the South, leads to the gardens. Several decades ago, the plantation was open to the public, but it is now closed.

Continue 5.3 miles south from Pleasant Oaks to see one of the best-known colonial-era showplaces in the United States. Orton, that ancient estate of the pre–Revolutionary War era, has survived the ravages of time, war, and economic change to emerge as a magnificent historic portrait of coastal North Carolina.

To reach Orton, turn off N.C. 133 onto S.R. 1529. The entrance is marked by massive gray stone pillars surmounted by eagles with outspread wings. This splendid 10,000-acre estate boasts the only surviving colonial mansion on the Cape Fear River and some of North Carolina's most beautiful gardens.

Orton was born of the efforts of the Moore brothers—Maurice, James, Roger, and Nathaniel—who settled in the area in the first quarter of the eighteenth century, after leading efforts to suppress uprisings by local Indians. In 1725, Roger Moore was granted an enormous tract of land along the river just north of the site of Brunswick Town. There, he established a lavish plantation, which he named Orton for the village of the same name in the Lake District of England, the ancestral home of the Moore family.

Roger Moore wasted no time in erecting a plantation house, choosing a site on a bluff separated from the river by picturesque meadows and marshland. Indians subsequently attacked and destroyed the original structure. Moore rebuilt in 1730, and it was from this second plantation that the existing mansion emerged.

Because his estate was located in the northernmost section of the lucrative rice-growing region, Moore built dikes to flood the fertile marshes for

rice cultivation. His leadership, wealth, penchant for opulent living, and hospitality brought him a large measure of fame. Consequently, he became known far and wide as "King Roger."

By 1880, the estate lay in virtual ruin. The great domain of King Roger was about to be reclaimed by the coastal wilderness.

Colonel Kenneth M. Murchison, a Confederate veteran, stepped forward in 1884 to purchase the plantation house and grounds. He promptly set out to recapture Orton's former grandeur.

Orton entered the modern age in 1905 at the death of Colonel Murchison. Dr. James Sprunt purchased the estate for his wife, Luola Murchison Sprunt, Murchison's daughter. Through the vision and imagination of Mrs. Sprunt, work on the majestic, colorful gardens—enjoyed by thousands of visitors each year—began in 1910. She was also responsible for adding the wings on either side of the plantation house.

When Dr. Sprunt died in 1924, Orton passed to his son, James Laurence Sprunt. At that time, the plantation was accessible only via the river. Sprunt promptly opened the Colonial Road to Wilmington, thereby setting the stage for the birth of the tourism industry at the plantation. In the late 1920s, the grounds and gardens were opened to the public.

Visitors to the estate may be able to hear the thunder of the mighty

Atlantic on tranquil days, as waves culminate their 3,000-mile journey by crashing upon the beaches just across the river.

Countless tides have rolled in since Roger Moore rebuilt his home on the river bluff. Despite extensive modifications and additions in 1840 and 1910, critics have acclaimed the house as one of the finest examples of Greek Revival architecture in the country. Listed on the National Register of Historic Places, the mansion at Orton is one of the few houses on the North American continent that has been continuously occupied since 1730. At present, the house is the private residence of the Sprunt family. Nonetheless, visitors strolling the gardens and grounds are treated to a splendid closeup view of the exterior of the magnificent structure.

Orton gardens

Its classic lines and postcard-perfect appearance have made the mansion one of the most recognizable landmarks in the state. It is little wonder why artists, moviemakers, and writers have used Orton as a setting for their work. In 1954, the mansion was selected as the subject of a mural in the dining room of the famous Blair House in Washington, D.C. Orton also served as a backdrop for the Stephen King movie *Firestarter*, in which a fake facade was used to give the illusion that the house was being consumed by fire. Renowned novelist James Boyd set his classic work, *Marching On*, at Orton.

Of the historic plantations of the Cape Fear region, only Orton opens its grounds and gardens to the general public.

Your drive down the entrance avenue of towering, ancient oak trees festooned with Spanish moss leads past an expansive, dark lake rimmed by dogwoods, Indian azaleas, and shrubs to the storybook gardens. Park in the lot adjacent to the ticket office, just south of the mansion.

Near the parking lot, a brick path flanked by white pines leads to Luola's Chapel, a gleaming white chapel designed as a memorial to Luola Murchison Sprunt, who died in 1916. Simple yet beautiful in design, this private house of worship seats 150.

Interior of Luola's Chapel

From the chapel, a walking tour leads to the Radial Garden, the first of many gardens on the estate. Spread about the sweeping green lawns and shaded by stately live oaks, magnolias, and pines, these gardens showcase some seventy-five species of ornamental plants.

At various points along the garden tour are man-made structures of special interest. Two white, frame belvederes look out over the old rice fields,

Chinese bridge at Orton

now leased to the North Carolina Wildlife Resources Commission as a wildlife refuge, and over a slate-blue lagoon. North of the belvederes, a bridge crosses the water and offers a spectacular view of Orton's northwestern lagoon. This lovely vista is known as "the Water Scene." During the heat of the summer months, alligators can often be observed swimming in the lagoon or sunning on its banks.

On the western side of the gardens, an unusual Chinese bridge zigzags its way over the fringes of the lake and a waterway leading to the lagoon. It was Robert Swan Sturtevant, the famed landscape architect who laid out the modern gardens at Orton, who tackled the problem of getting garden visitors from one side of the lake and waterway to the other. The builders of this unusual bridge have long claimed that its design prevents evil spirits from crossing, since spirits can only walk in a straight line.

The path loops around the northern edge of the gardens to the colonial-era cemetery where King Roger Moore is buried. Moore's tomb dominates the ancient family burial ground.

Once you have enjoyed your walk through Orton Plantation, return to your car and continue driving in your original direction on S.R. 1529. After 0.8 mile, turn left, or east, on S.R. 1533 for a 1.1-mile drive to the ruins of Brunswick Town, on the banks of the Cape Fear.

Museum artifacts and the foundations of eighteenth-century buildings scattered about the riverside landscape are the only tangible reminders of the ancient port that was once the leader in colonial North Carolina. Brunswick Town was the setting for the first armed resistance to British colonial rule in the American colonies, yet by the time independence was won fifteen years later, it was virtually a ghost town. Eighty years later, when the South fought to end the union born of the American Revolution, a mighty earthwork fortress, Fort Anderson, was constructed on the old town site as part of the defense system for the Cape Fear region.

Now a state historic site, Brunswick Town affords visitors an opportunity to walk among the stone foundations of dwellings where royal governors once lived and climb upon the well-preserved mounds of the Civil War fort.

Brunswick Town was the creation of the enterprising Moore family, who in 1726 set aside a 320-acre parcel for the establishment of a town to handle the export of vast quantities of naval stores. In 1731, the fortunes of the fledgling town received a boost when Brunswick Town was declared one of the five official ports of entry in the province. Over the next century, Brunswick Town was one of the leading seaports in North Carolina. For a portion of that period, more than 70 percent of the world's naval stores were shipped from the harbor here. Mariners from the world over called at the Cape Fear port, giving the town a cosmopolitan atmosphere.

Cape Fear River

But even as the port was enjoying commercial success, there were clouds on the horizon. In 1740, the town lost its status as county seat to an upstart river village to the north: Wilmington. Eight years later, the vulnerability of Brunswick Town to foreign attack was made evident when, during the War of Jenkins Ear—which started when Spanish soldiers captured the brig *Rebecca* and cut off the ear of an Englishman named Jenkins—three Spanish sloops invaded and plundered the town.

When Brunswick County was created in 1763, Brunswick Town again became a county seat. And although the port never had a population of more than four hundred, it was home to men whose names are etched on the honor roll of early North Carolina history. Among its residents were three Revolutionary War generals, three royal governors, and a justice of the United States Supreme Court.

On the morning of February 21, 1766, less than four months after the Stamp Act went into effect, Brunswick was the setting of one of the most dramatic moments in the years leading up to the American Revolution. Cornelius Harnett, a local leader who grew up in Brunswick Town, and some 150 armed citizens known as "the Sons of Liberty" encircled customs officials and other agents of the Crown at Brunswick Town and watched triumphantly as each took an oath to refrain from issuing any stamped paper in North Carolina.

George Davis, the gifted nineteenth-century statesmen from Wilmington who served as attorney general of the Confederate States of America, lamented the lack of significance accorded the confrontation at Brunswick in 1766: "This was more than ten years before the Declaration of Independence and more than nine before the Battle of Lexington, and nearly eight before the Boston Tea Party. The destruction of tea was done at night by men in disguise. And history blazoned it, and New England boasts of it, and the fame of it is world wide. But this other act, more gallant and more daring, done in open day by well-known men, with arms in their hands, and under the King's flag—who remembers it, or who tells of it?"

On May 24, 1768, St. Philips Church, planned as far back as 1745, was consecrated in a dignified ceremony at Brunswick Town. Its thirty-three-inch-thick exterior walls, containing four slender, arched windows on each side, still stand today.

As the winds of war began to sweep over the Cape Fear region in the 1770s, most of the inhabitants of Brunswick Town—already dispirited by the destructive hurricanes that frequently hit the area, the high humidity, and the malaria-infested swamps—abandoned the port. On the heels of this exodus, the British attacked in 1776, and in a cruel twist of fate, the town that provided the initial spark of the American Revolution was razed.

A few families returned after the war to live among the ruins, but for all intents and purposes, Brunswick Town was finished. On a visit to the area in 1804, Bishop Francis Asbury, the renowned Methodist circuit rider, noted that Brunswick Town was nothing more than "an old town, demolished houses, and the noble walls of a brick church, there remains but four houses entire."

By 1832, the town was completely devoid of humanity. Title to the site reverted to the state. In 1845, the late, great port of Brunswick Town was conveyed to the owner of Orton Plantation for the sum of $4.25.

Fifteen years later, as the nation stood on the precipice of the Civil War, the ruined buildings of Brunswick Town were hidden in a veritable jungle. To protect the vital port of Wilmington, the Confederate government constructed an earthwork fortress on the ruins of Brunswick Town in 1862. The fort consisted of two five-gun batteries and numerous smaller emplacements set along the giant sand banks, which towered as high as twenty-four feet. Its original name, Fort St. Philip, was quickly changed to Fort Anderson, in honor of General Joseph Reid Anderson, an early commander of North Carolina coastal defenses during the Civil War. Fort Anderson remained in Southern hands until the waning days of the Confederacy.

For almost 90 years after the war, Fort Anderson and Brunswick Town were abandoned to the forces of nature. In 1955, the 119-acre tract was dedicated as a state historic site. Following extensive archaeological work, ground was broken for a combination visitor center and museum in 1963.

With archaeologists assigned to the site on a permanent basis, important research and excavations have been carried out on a daily basis over the past thirty years. The visitor center/museum features interesting displays of many of the artifacts extracted from the ruins.

More than sixty excavated foundations can be seen during the pleasant walking tour of the historic site. Stop at the visitor center to pick up a printed tour route.

From the visitor center, the walking tour proceeds across the parking lot to the most identifiable ruins of the site—those of St. Philips Church. Within the church's roofless walls are twelve graves, including those of Royal Governor Arthur Dobbs, Justice Alfred Moore of the United States Supreme Court, and the infant son of Royal Governor William Tryon.

From the ruins of the church, the walking tour proceeds south along old Second Street and veers sharply east toward the river, passing the ballast-stone foundations of a number of dwellings erected in the first half of the eighteenth century.

Near Brunswick Pond, the walking tour divides. The northern route follows Front Street to the well-preserved remains of Fort Anderson, where the path runs along the top of Battery B. Near the parking lot, this path intersects Brunswick Town Nature Trail, a short route that winds its way

Brunswick Town State Historic Site Visitor Center

Ruins of St. Philips Church

Brunswick Town ruins

Brunswick Pond

along the banks of Brunswick Pond. During the summer months, this pond, covered with green vegetation, often resembles a swamp. It is the remnant of a spring-fed swamp located in the heart of the town during colonial times.

Admission to Brunswick Town State Historic Site is free. A public picnic area is located north of the visitor center/museum.

After you have enjoyed the historic site, retrace your route to Orton Plantation and turn west onto S.R. 1530, the 0.3-mile connector road to N.C. 133. Turn south onto N.C. 133 for a 7.3-mile drive that runs parallel to the Military Ocean Terminal at Sunny Point, the nation's largest shipper of weapons, tanks, explosives, and military equipment. This lifeline for the defense of the free world is situated on an 8,502-acre site.

When the decision was made to construct the nation's only military terminal devoted entirely to ammunition, experts conducted a meticulous search for a relatively isolated spot close to inland transportation. The site at Sunny Point was determined to be ideal, and in 1951, the $26-million, four-year project was commenced.

To minimize the effect of a potential explosion at the facility, a maze of bunkers as high as forty feet has been constructed around the area where hazardous cargo is held and handled. Because of the dangerous and confidential nature of the activities here, access to the installation is highly restricted. The base entrance is located at the junction of N.C. 133 and N.C. 87.

At the entrance to Sunny Point, turn north off N.C. 133 onto N.C. 87 for a 2-mile drive to Big Lake, located in the heart of Boiling Spring Lakes, the youngest of the towns on the tour.

More than fifty crystal-clear spring-fed lakes in a variety of sizes and shapes dot the sixteen thousand acres of pinelands encompassed by this sprawling, sparsely populated community. Since two enterprising businessmen purchased the enormous tract thirty-five years ago with a dream of creating a large resort and retirement development, an assortment of modest residential dwellings, retirement homes, and vacation cottages has been constructed along the 110 miles of roads that weave their way through the forests and around the lakes and ponds.

Unlike most of the lakes, three-hundred-acre Big Lake, the town's centerpiece, is man-made, having been constructed in 1961. Fifteen years later, the Corps of Engineers threatened the vitality of the town when it drained the lake to prevent damage to the railroad supplying Sunny Point and the Brunswick Nuclear Plant at nearby Southport. The lake has since refilled.

Long before the first white settlers arrived in the area, Indians made their way to the site of Boiling Spring Lakes, where they refreshed themselves with the water from the springs. Although the waters were neither curative nor hot, they provided an oasis for the Indians on their annual hunting and fishing pilgrimages to the sea. From the days of the Indians, a popular local legend evolved that whoever drank from the effervescent springs would always return.

In the 1950s, Bill Keziah, noted Southport journalist and self-styled publicist for the Cape Fear area, "discovered" a spring long known to some locals as Bouncing Log Spring, which spews forth 42 million gallons of water every day. To enhance the beauty of the bubbling spring, the developers of Boiling Spring Lakes decided to construct a four-foot-high wall around Bouncing Log Spring. No sooner had the wall been built than the natural fountain stopped flowing. Within a few hours, however, a full flow of water began bubbling forth from the ground fifteen feet from the well.

A railroad bridge constructed in 1988 closed the only paved road leading to Bouncing Log Spring. Now, the fountain bubbles forth in a junglelike thicket of scrub oak and ivy accessible only by a maze of unpaved roads. Pesky biting flies swarm about the site, which is marked by a wooden sign.

Retrace your route from Big Lake to the junction of N.C. 87 and N.C. 133, where the tour ends. Southport is located 4 miles south.

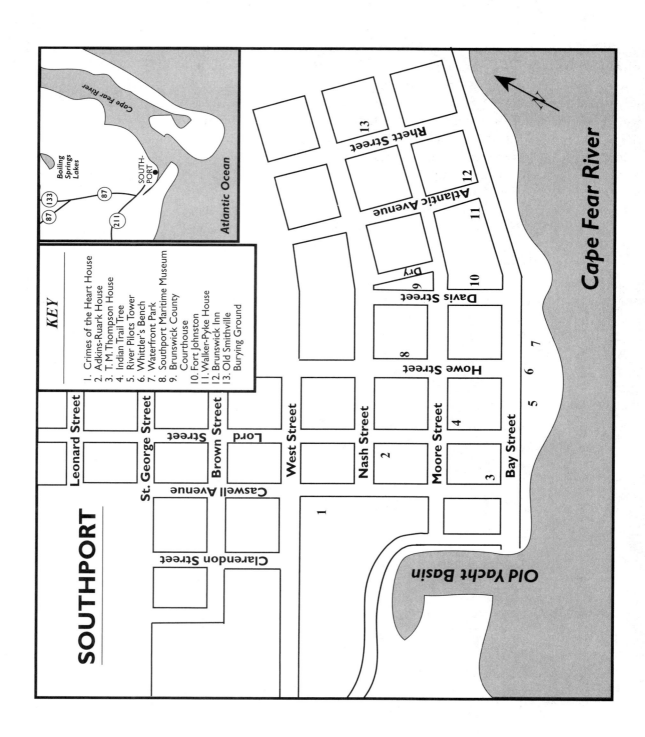

SOUTHPORT

KEY

1. Crimes of the Heart House
2. Adkins-Ruark House
3. T. M. Thompson House
4. Indian Trail Tree
5. River Pilots Tower
6. Whittler's Bench
7. Waterfront Park
8. Southport Maritime Museum
9. Brunswick County Courthouse
10. Fort Johnston
11. Walker-Pyke House
12. Brunswick Inn
13. Old Smithville Burying Ground

Cape Fear River

Boiling Springs Lakes

SOUTH-PORT

Atlantic Ocean

133
87
87
211

Leonard Street

St. George Street

Brown Street

Lord Street

Clarendon Street

Caswell Avenue

West Street

Nash Street

Moore Street

Bay Street

Howe Street

Davis Street

Dry Street

Atlantic Avenue

Rhett Street

Old Yacht Basin

Cape Fear River

N

The Cape Fear Delta Tour

This tour begins by exploring Southport, then travels by private ferry to Bald Head Island, where it ends with a walk to legendary Cape Fear.

Among the highlights of the tour are the Nuclear Visitor Center outside Southport, Waterfront Park on the Cape Fear River, the story of Fort Johnston, the homes of the Southport Historic District, "The Grove," the story of Tony the Ghost, Old Baldy on Bald Head Island, the story of Stede Bonnet's buried treasure, and the story of the disappearance of Theodosia Burr Alston.

Total driving mileage: approximately 10 miles.

This tour begins at the intersection of N.C. 133 and N.C. 87 at Boiling Springs Lakes. Proceed south on N.C. 87 for 2.1 miles to the Nuclear Visitor Center.

In the 1970s, Carolina Power and Light Company completed construction of a two-unit nuclear power plant on the outskirts of Southport. Unit 2 began commercial production of electricity in 1975, and Unit 1 went on line two years later. The plant towers over the sleepy, historic village. Each night, its lights cast an eerie yellow aura in the sky over Southport.

Even before the Brunswick County plant was completed, its safety and security were challenged by various environmental groups. And since it began production of electricity, the facility has been plagued by equipment failure and safety mishaps. Concern over plant safety has forced a series of reactor shutdowns.

Despite the controversy surrounding the plant, Carolina Power and Light Company has attempted to be a good corporate citizen in the Southport area. In an effort to educate the public about nuclear energy and to allay some of the fears and misconceptions about it, the company opened the visitor center in 1972, before either of the two reactor units was completed. Each year, some ten thousand visitors tour the center, which features numerous colorful exhibits on a variety of energy-related subjects.

Nuclear Visitors Center

A model of the Brunswick County plant holds a prominent spot in the center. Although the actual plant is not open for tours, a videotaped tour can be viewed in the small theater at the center. Visitors can get a good look at the exterior of the massive facility from the observation deck.

Proceed 1.2 miles south on N.C. 87 to its intersection with N.C. 211 just north of the corporate limits of Southport. The nuclear plant on N.C. 87 and the shopping center at this intersection combine to present the deceiving appearance that Southport has exchanged its historic treasures for symbols of the modern age. Yet the real Southport will soon reveal itself. Turn left, or south, on N.C. 211 (Howe Street) and follow it for 1.6 mile to its terminus at the parking lot on the picturesque waterfront.

Southport has never been a pretentious town. Never mind that its ancient streets and its waterfront have been witness to numerous events of historic significance. Never mind that its scenic harbor is considered among the most beautiful in America. And never mind that, in recent years, the town has been consistently rated by Rand McNally among the top twenty places to retire. Life goes on for Southport's thirty-eight hundred residents without flair or flamboyance.

The town's beautiful waterfront is a working harbor where commercial fishing boats dock every afternoon from expeditions into the open sea, and where river pilots await calls to gently usher oceangoing vessels into the Cape Fear channel, just as their predecessors did for more than two centuries.

Southport has refused to trade its charm, its heritage, and its maritime flavor for uncontrolled growth. Visitors who come to town after a fifty-year absence will find it little changed today. A majority of the houses that line Howe Street, the main north-south thoroughfare, and Bay Street, the panoramic waterfront avenue, look much as they did a half-century ago. Moore Street, the old commercial district, remains a viable place of commerce.

From the foot of Howe Street, the waterfront is a breathtaking sight. Few coastal towns anywhere are blessed with a waterfront that can compare in charm and beauty to that of Southport, located where the waters of the mighty Cape Fear River meet the Atlantic.

Waterfront Park, a municipal park located adjacent to the Howe Street parking lot, overlooks the Cape Fear and affords visitors an opportunity to enjoy the splendor of the river. Its grassy banks and pavilions are ideal for picnics. Tall palm trees lining nearby Bay Street lend a tropical flavor to this riverfront oasis.

Whittler's Bench

A popular fixture of Waterfront Park is historic Whittler's Bench. For as long as anyone can remember, a wooden bench has been nestled under the shade of several old trees at this spot. While gazing upon the waterways of Southport, countless generations of local residents have rested here, whittled, and swapped tall tales.

Another popular attraction at the park is the City Pier. Though not as long as the ocean fishing piers on the barrier islands, this municipally owned pier is an excellent place from which to view the riverscape and the wide assortment of water traffic passing into and out of the river. On the horizon looms Bald Head Island, where Old Baldy, the oldest lighthouse in the state, towers above the island landscape. To the west, the remains of Fort Caswell and the Oak Island Lighthouse, the newest lighthouse in the state, are visible on the eastern end of Oak Island.

From large ocean liners making their way to and from the port at Wilmington to pleasure yachts plying the Intracoastal Waterway, the traffic on the Southport waterfront is always heavy. Park visitors may first notice an approaching ship as it looms over the buildings of Oak Island. As the ship makes the turn into the Cape Fear, visitors may sense that it is on a collision course with Battery Island in midriver, until it suddenly makes a course adjustment into the well-defined shipping lane.

Located along the waterfront between the picnic area and the pier is an old, crumbling rock wall now covered with masonry and debris. This wall is all that remains of the original fortifications of Fort Johnston, the first fort authorized by the colonial assembly of North Carolina. Now reduced to six acres, old Fort Johnston may well be the smallest military installation in the nation.

Ruins of Fort Johnston

There is one significant reminder of the old fortress: the much-altered commandant's house and officers' quarters, constructed around 1800 and located across East Bay Street from the City Pier. From its commanding position on East Bay Street overlooking the river, the large brick building is one of the most imposing historic structures in Southport. Its two-story central block is joined on either side by one-story wings.

In 1990, a group of influential Southport citizens began a movement to have Fort Johnston returned to the state as a historic site, yet the old building continues to be used as living quarters for the commander and other officers of the military installation at nearby Sunny Point. At present, the public can walk upon the grounds of Fort Johnston, where several historical markers have been erected.

Southport celebrated its bicentennial in 1992. However, its roots can be traced back almost 250 years, to the construction of Fort Johnston. Although the British Crown ordered the fort's construction in 1730 to protect the Cape Fear from attack by Spanish privateers and pirates, work did not actually commence on the fortification until 1745, under the administration of Royal Governor Gabriel Johnston. Within a decade, the project was virtually complete. By that time, a small community of merchants, river pilots, and fishermen had settled in the shadows of the fort. Southport emerged from this early community.

Because the Cape Fear region was a hotbed of revolutionary fervor, Fort Johnston played a prominent role in the events leading up to the war for American independence. The culmination came on the morning of July 18, 1775, when Josiah Martin, the exiled royal governor of North Carolina, scrambled from his berth and watched in horror from the deck of the British man-of-war *Cruizer* as a band of patriots led by Cornelius Harnett and John Ashe raided and burned the fort.

In the years following the war, the community surrounding the ruins of the fort served as the base of operations for a new generation of river pilots, who sailed out into the ocean in search of ships bound for the Cape Fear. Once a bargain was reached for their services, the pilots guided the ships safely around the hazardous shoals and other dangers in the river.

Efforts to incorporate the community around Fort Johnston succeeded in 1792, when 150 acres were set aside for the establishment of the village of Smithville. Named for Benjamin Smith—a notable soldier, statesman, and governor—the new town became the county seat of Brunswick County.

Even though congressional authorization to reconstruct Fort Johnston was obtained in March 1794, the new fort was not completed until 1816. Twenty years later, the dire need for manpower during the Seminole uprising in Florida forced the federal government to remove the garrison from the fort.

All the while, the primary occupation of Smithville residents remained river piloting. To govern themselves, to ensure the orderly dispatch of pilots, to train future pilots, and to care for the families of deceased pilots, the Pilots' Association—the forerunner of the modern organization in Southport—was formed.

In the decade preceding the Civil War, the town began exhibiting the trappings of a well-to-do resort. Wealthy and refined people made their way to the riverfront hotels and boardinghouses that had begun to flourish. Approximately seven hundred permanent residents were living in the town on the eve of the war.

John W. Ellis, the governor of North Carolina, ordered Confederate forces to seize Fort Johnston on April 15, 1861. Until Fort Fisher surrendered on January 15, 1865, Fort Johnston and Smithville remained under Southern control. Throughout the four years of the conflict, the river town served as a vital link in the "Lifeline of the Confederacy." Time and time again, sleek blockade runners under fire from Union warships blockading the North Carolina coast found safety in the tiny harbor at Smithville after harrowing escapes.

In the decades that followed the war, hopes ran high that Smithville would develop into a commercially important seaport. In anticipation of newfound greatness, the town changed its name to Southport in 1887. Enthusiasm for its potential as a port waned after efforts to build a railroad to the town were abandoned in the late 1880s. Nevertheless, by the turn of the century, Southport was an oasis of sophistication and modernity in an area heavily dominated by rural hamlets, farmsteads, and swamps. The town of fourteen hundred residents boasted many conveniences, such as telephone service, then reserved only for major cities.

Completion of the Intracoastal Waterway in the 1930s led to a rebirth of the tourism industry, as Southport became a favorite stopover for north-south water traffic during the summer and winter months. Over the succeeding decades, the town has reaped economic benefits as the supply town for the beach communities on nearby Oak Island.

On July 19, 1975, the reign of Smithville and Southport as the county seat of Brunswick County came to a close, when a hotly contested, sometimes bitter referendum ended in a vote to move the seat to the hamlet of Bolivia, on U.S. 17.

River Pilots Tower

To continue the waterfront tour, leave the parking lot and drive west on Bay Street. Towering above the waterfront is the River Pilots Tower, a tall, skeletal structure resembling a forest tower, without the cabin at the top. This structure was built in the early 1940s to replace a wooden tower located near the foot of Howe Street. Before the advent of modern ship-to-shore communication, the tower was used as an observation post for the river pilots. As soon as a ship was spotted on the horizon, the watchman dispatched a pilot to meet the incoming vessel.

Two distinct harbors grace the Southport waterfront.

Located at the foot of West Bay Street and around the bend of Brunswick Street is the Old Southport Yacht Basin. This ancient port facility, which looks more like a painting by a coastal artist than a working harbor, traces its roots to pre–Revolutionary War times. Despite extensive damage suffered during Hurricanes Hazel and Diane in the 1950s, it has changed little in appearance over the years. On sunny spring days, the calm, smooth waters act as a huge mirror, casting reflections of the wide variety of boats tied to posts and piers. Few visitors disagree with travel experts who have described the yacht basin as one of the most beautiful harbors in all of coastal America.

Southport's large commercial fishing fleet docks here. Daily catches of fish and shrimp are unloaded at the fish houses built over the water on the eastern side of the basin. A wooden boardwalk and a system of piers and walkways connected to the fish houses and the other harbor buildings offer a spectacular view of the harbor.

Of all the vessels moored at the yacht basin, the most identifiable are the pilot boats owned and operated by the Cape Fear Pilots Association. These steel-hulled vessels, painted black and white, are the latest in a line of pilot boats that have been a fixture on the Southport waterfront for about as long as the Cape Fear River has been an important artery for oceangoing traffic.

The abundance of modern navigational aids available to ship captains notwithstanding, no large ocean vessel enters or leaves the river without the assistance of one of the veteran river pilots of Southport. When a ship is ready to make its way up the river to Wilmington, one of the pilot boats carries a pilot out to meet the ship.

To reach Southport's second harbor, follow Brunswick Street to Short Street. Turn right onto Short, then left onto West Street. Long known locally as the Small Boat Harbor, the larger of the two harbors is located at the end of West West Street.

State funds realized from a 1959 bond issue were used to build this expansive facility. Constructed for the State Ports Authority in 1965, the marina complex was operated by the state for some fifteen years. Now privately leased and operated as Southport Marina, the Small Boat Harbor is one of the largest marinas in North Carolina. It provides a wide array of services for pleasure boaters making their way up and down the Intracoastal Waterway.

From the marina, turn around and drive east on West West Street to begin a tour of the Southport Historic District.

In 1981, following three years of arduous work by the Southport Historic Society, this district—roughly equivalent to the original city limits—was listed on the National Register of Historic Places. Most of the historically significant structures within the district are Victorian buildings constructed from 1885 to 1905. Southport is considered by many architectural experts to be the best example of a Victorian coastal town in North Carolina.

Virtually all of the historic buildings lie along streets that have changed little over the past two centuries. These streets bear the names of historic figures who left their imprint on the Cape Fear area and North Carolina in general. For example, Moore Street is named for Colonel James Moore, Revolutionary War hero; Howe Street for General Robert Howe, patriot *extraordinaire* of Brunswick County; Rhett Street for Colonel William Rhett, the man who sailed into the Cape Fear River in 1718 and captured Stede Bonnet; Caswell Street for Richard Caswell, Revolutionary War hero and governor; and Clarendon Street for the earl of Clarendon, one of the eight Lords Proprietors of the Carolina colony, and the man for whom the early British settlement in the Cape Fear region was named.

At the intersection of West Street and Caswell Avenue, turn right, or south, onto Caswell. Ironically, the magnificent Victorian house you will see on Caswell is a product of the arrival of Hollywood in Southport.

During the summer of 1986, Southport was transformed into Hazelhurst, Mississippi, as film stars Diane Keaton, Sissy Spacek, Jessica Lange, and

Crimes of the Heart *House*

Adkins-Ruark House

Sam Shepard arrived in town for the filming of the blockbuster movie *Crimes of the Heart*. More than two hundred thousand dollars and five months of labor were necessary to convert the dilapidated early-twentieth-century house on Caswell into a showplace replete with towers, a cupola, and stained-glass windows. It was pictured in the movie as the McGrath House, the home of the central characters.

From Caswell, turn east onto Nash Street, then south onto Lord Street. At 119 North Lord Street, at the corner of Nash and Lord, stands the Adkins-Ruark House. This immaculate two-story multigabled structure, built in 1890 by river pilot E. H. Adkins, is best known for another former resident. Adkins's grandson, Robert Ruark, the world-renowned author from Wilmington, spent much of his youth at the Southport house and visited often after he was an adult. His early years in Southport formed the basis of his widely acclaimed novel *The Old Man and the Boy*.

Turn right, or west, off Lord Street onto Moore Street. Keziah Park features a tranquil, well-shaded area along one of the busiest avenues of the city. Among its beautiful trees is the legendary Indian Trail Tree, reputed to be more than three hundred years old. When it was very young, this unusual live oak was bent by Indians to mark their line of travel to fishing grounds. Its unusual shape led to its listing in "Ripley's Believe It or Not,"

TOURING THE BACKROADS OF NORTH CAROLINA'S LOWER COAST

which reported that it is one of only five such trees in the United States.

Turn south off Moore onto Caswell Street, then east onto Bay Street. One of the most spectacular homes overlooking the waterfront is the T. M. Thompson House, at 216 West Bay Street. Built in 1868 by a blockade runner for his family, this striking two-story frame dwelling features a widow's walk surrounding the cupola atop the hip roof.

Indian Trail Tree

Turn north off Bay onto Howe Street. Located at 116 North Howe, the Southport Maritime Museum opened in 1992. This museum is the realization of the dream of many civic-minded individuals and history lovers in the lower Cape Fear region.

During the early 1970s, Southport flirted with such a facility when an ill-fated museum operated on the deactivated *Frying Pan Lightship*. From 1967, when the city of Southport acquired her from the United States Navy, until 1981, when the deteriorating hulk was unceremoniously pulled away by tugs, the 133-foot *Frying Pan Lightship* was moored at the foot of Howe Street.

The new museum treats visitors to twelve attractive exhibits linked to each other through a story line. Included are displays concerning the area's first inhabitants, early white explorers, the first area settlements, the American Revolution, the birth of Southport, the Civil War, navigational aids, shipwrecks, and fishing.

Historic Franklin Square, located on Howe Street just north of the museum, is known to many locals as "The Grove." Stone walls constructed more than a century ago from the ballast rock used by sailing ships enclose this town green, which is shaded by a canopy of beautiful live oaks. Some of the trees, including one named "Four Sisters," were in existence at the time the park was established for public use in 1792.

Franklin Square is the focal point of the activities associated with the North Carolina Fourth of July Festival. Now recognized as the state's official observance of Independence Day, this annual four-day celebration dates from 1795, when officers at Fort Johnston and residents of Smithville joined forces to commemorate America's political independence.

An interesting ensemble of late-nineteenth-century public buildings is clustered around Franklin Square. Located on the northern side of the square, the Franklin Square Gallery is housed in a massive two-story frame building constructed in 1904 as a school building. On the southern side of the square

Former Brunswick County Courthouse

St. Philips Episcopal Church

at 203 East Nash Street, across the green from the gallery, the Masonic Lodge is a handsome two-story building erected after the Civil War. Located just across East Nash from the Masonic Lodge, the former Brunswick County Courthouse was the second courthouse located on this site. Listed on the National Register of Historic Places, the building, which fronts on Moore Street, was constructed in the early 1850s. It served as the house of county government until the county seat was moved to Bolivia in 1975.

Proceed to the front side of the courthouse, at 133 East Moore. The old central business district in the 100 block of East Moore contains an interesting collection of late-nineteenth- and early-twentieth-century commercial buildings.

Southport is proud of its old church buildings. For almost 150 years, Episcopalians have worshiped in the church located on East Moore adjacent to the old courthouse. Erected around 1860, the white, frame St. Philips Episcopal Church was used as a hospital and school during the Civil War and Reconstruction. Thereafter, significant repairs and alterations were made on the structure. Some of the fixtures, including the altar rail and baptismal font, are more than 250 years old and were inherited from the church's namesake, the ancient church at Brunswick Town. Wooden collection plates, altar cloths, and other items were also transferred from the original St. Philips. Because of their rarity, the baptismal font and the altar cloths are locked in a vault and are used only on ceremonial occasions.

Return to Howe Street and turn south, then turn east onto Bay Street. Located at 239 East Bay, the Walker-Pyke House is believed to be the oldest home in the city. Built between 1800 and 1820, this graceful two-and-a-half-story structure features three dormer windows on its front and back sides.

The sumptuous Greek Revival house at the corner of East Bay Street and Atlantic Avenue has come full circle in its 140-year history. Now a private residence, it is still known by its former name: the Brunswick Inn.

Built by a Wilmingtonian as a summer residence, the two-story house was enlarged and converted into a resort hotel in 1882. When the Brunswick Inn closed in 1917, the original structure was returned to residential use. In recent years, it has been restored to its early elegance.

There have long been tales that ancient tunnels run beneath this house. The passageways are rumored to have been used to store the loot of pirates and the valuables of local citizens during the Civil War. Pieces of eight unearthed in the backyard of the house are evidence that the tunnels may indeed exist.

The home's current owners, guests who have spent the night in the house, and many Southport residents are familiar with the building's most famous link to its past: Tony the Ghost. Tony, last name unknown, was one of three musicians who lived and performed here when the building served as an inn. His harp brought great pleasure to the patrons.

The musicians saw a tragic end, drowning when a storm came up during a Cape Fear fishing trip. According to local legend, Tony's spirit returned to the inn in search of his harp. Since that time, his beautiful music has been heard throughout the house by many people. On occasion, the music lasts all day, while at other times, it is of short duration. News reporters from Raleigh once visited the house and listened to Tony play.

Tony's presence has been detected in other ways as well. One of the previous owners felt the ghost pass her in a doorway and heard a *whoosh* as it passed. Doors that mysteriously open and close are attributed to Tony. While seeking a place to live, the new Brunswick County planning director was a guest in the house for eight weeks. During his stay, he heard doors opening and closing in the middle of the night.

Another former Brunswick County official, the county manager, stayed at the house when he first arrived in town in 1979. It was on a March night during his three-month stay that he had an eerie encounter with the benevolent ghost. At the time, he was taking prescribed medications, one of which had to be consumed at night. After falling asleep in his room, he was suddenly awakened by someone shaking him. He crawled out of bed, turned on the light, and remembered he had not taken his pill. The county manager related the strange occurrence to his hostess, who then acquainted him with the story of the resident ghost.

Continue 1 block on Bay Street, turn north onto Rhett Street, proceed 1 block, and turn east onto Moore Street.

The Old Smithville Burying Ground is located at the northeastern corner of this intersection. When this shaded spot was consecrated as a burial ground in 1792, there were already numerous graves on the site, some more than thirty years old.

This ancient cemetery is graced with a wide variety of interesting, time-worn headstones, statues, and monuments. The most fascinating grave site features a monument erected in memory of the young sea pilots who drowned in two successive storms in the 1870s. Only two of the bodies were recovered. They were interred in the cemetery beneath the monument, which was purchased by the families of all the lost seamen.

Proceed east on Moore Street to Bonnet's Creek, a historic waterway leading to the Cape Fear. In the second decade of the eighteenth century, Stede Bonnet secreted his famous pirate vessel, *The Revenge*, in this creek.

If you care to take a side trip aboard the Southport–Fort Fisher Ferry, continue 1 mile on Moore Street to where it intersects S.R. 1534, an 0.7-mile road leading to the ferry landing. Note that if you choose this side trip, you will also have to take a return ferry ride to Southport to complete the present tour. (For information on Fort Fisher, see The Wrightsville Beach to Pleasure Island Tour, pages 237–45.)

While waiting for ferry departure, many motorists leave their vehicles and walk to the extensive marsh area adjacent to the landing. During spring and summer, a resident alligator can often be observed swimming or sunning in the streams that meander through the marsh.

Aboard the ferry, passengers are treated to a panorama of historic sites and interesting landmarks. This ferry provides the best opportunity to see one of the least-known historic sites in the area. Few people are able to visit Price's Creek Lighthouse, for it stands on private property owned by the Pfizer Corporation on the banks of the Cape Fear. Though the squat, unpainted brick lighthouse has long been dark and is missing its light, it is of great historic significance, as it is the only survivor of the chain of range lights constructed in the antebellum period to aid in the navigation of the river from its mouth to Wilmington.

When it was equipped with a beacon, the lighthouse stood sixteen feet tall, and its light cast rays twenty-five feet above the water. Until a direct shell hit left a gaping hole near ground level and rendered the light inoperable in early 1865, the lighthouse was a strategic Confederate signal station.

At present, access to the site is extremely limited. Permission should be obtained from its corporate owner before an on-site inspection is attempted.

During the thirty-minute trip across the river, the ferry often passes large ocean liners and other traffic from the port of Wilmington. Several spoil islands—nesting grounds for pelicans, gulls, and other coastal birds—are visible along the route.

There are no bridges across the mighty Cape Fear south of Wilmington. In February 1956, a High Point businessman filed application with the North Carolina Utilities Commission to establish a ferry service between Fort Fisher and Southport. However, nothing came of the proposal, and another ten years passed before the state inaugurated the existing ferry.

During its quarter-century of service, the southernmost ferry on the North Carolina coast has steadily increased its ridership and shrugged off its image as a seasonal tourist attraction. With the exception of a temporary state budgetary crisis that threatened to halt or severely restrict the Cape Fear crossings, the viability of the ferry has never been questioned.

From Bonnet's Creek in Southport, retrace Moore Street all the way to Howe Street. Turn right on Howe, proceed to Ninth Street, turn left, and follow Ninth to where it ends at Maple. Turn left on Maple, then right on Indigo Plantation Drive. Follow Indigo Plantation Drive to the marina on the waterfront, where Bald Head Island, Ltd., provides ferry service to Bald Head Island. Because there are no bridges to this semitropical island, access is limited to water transportation. Private boat owners can make their way to Bald Head from any of the local harbors and marinas. If you plan to take the ferry, be sure to inquire about departure times in advance.

Once visitors set foot on Bald Head Island at the large, modern marina, they marvel at the unspoiled beauty of this masterpiece of nature.

While stationed at Fort Holmes on Bald Head during the Civil War, Captain David A. Brice wrote, "Bald Head is one of the most beautiful places on the coast. . . . It would be murder for me to attempt a description so I will leave its beauties for you to picture."

When Kent Mitchell, a member of the current island ownership group, first saw the island in the 1980s, he was likewise impressed: "What took my breath away was its beauty, a sense of natural wilderness."

There is perhaps no other barrier island on the North Carolina coast that could be described in almost identical terms nearly 120 years apart.

Bald Head Island's name remains a subject of debate for geographers, cartographers, historians, and coastal authorities. Some experts limit their use of the name *Bald Head* to the small area of several hundred acres on the extreme southwestern portion of the complex of islands shown on many maps as Smith Island. But for area residents and most North Carolinians, *Bald Head* means Cape Fear, Middle Island, Bluff Island, and a long strip of barrier beach known as East Beach.

Bounded on the south and east by the Atlantic Ocean, on the north by marshlands and Corncake Inlet, and on the west by the Cape Fear River, Bald Head is a beautiful collage of beaches, dunes, maritime forests, freshwater ponds, tidal creeks, salt marshes, estuaries, and mud flats. Shaped like a triangle, the island complex contains between twelve thousand and seventeen thousand acres, depending on the height of the tide. Only about three thousand acres are highlands—the remains of a series of ridges and forested dunes. Separating these ridges and dunes are large expanses of marsh interwoven by meandering tidal creeks.

East Beach, a sea face of white, sandy beach extending 14 miles from Corncake Inlet to the mouth of the river, is by far the longest expanse of beach. West of the point of land called Cape Fear and extending to the mouth of the river, the southern beach is high and broad. It is from this beach that the island takes its name.

Transportation on Bald Head is one of the most unusual and interesting aspects of the island. With the exception of a few service vehicles, no gasoline-powered vehicles are allowed. Instead, traffic is limited to electric golf carts. The thoroughfares are not called streets, roads, or avenues. Rather, they are *wynds*. Although most have been paved—at great expense to the current and previous island owners—they are narrow. The speed limit on the island is eighteen miles per hour.

Since Bald Head offers no facilities for the public other than those at the marina complex, it is recommended that you tour the island by golf cart, rather than on foot. Golf carts are available for rent at the marina.

The tour of Bald Head Island begins at the Island Chandler, a large, modern complex built near the marina to meet the basic shopping needs of visitors and residents. From the Island Chandler, proceed east on North Bald Head Wynd to the Bald Head Island Lighthouse.

Affectionately known as "Old Baldy," this lighthouse holds the distinction

Bald Head Island Lighthouse

of being the oldest in the state. It was completed in 1817 to replace the island's original lighthouse, which was erected in 1794 as the first lighthouse on the North Carolina coast.

Located on a bluff a hundred feet from the Cape Fear River, Old Baldy towers over the island as it has for more than 175 years. The final retirement of the beacon came in 1958, when the Oak Island Lighthouse was put in service just across the river.

Old Baldy is octagonal in shape, its six-story walls standing ninety feet tall and varying in thickness from two to five feet. On the exterior, the masonry covering has broken away in a number of spots, exposing the underlying brick construction. Windows are located on each story. Inside, the wooden steps have been rebuilt from top to bottom. A spectacular view awaits visitors who climb the 112 steps to the platform at the top of the lighthouse.

Because Old Baldy is located on property owned by the island developer, permission must be obtained before entering or attempting to climb the structure.

Near the lighthouse stands an old oil-storage house, located adjacent to the former site of the multistory keeper's quarters, which vanished long ago.

View of Bald Head Island from atop the lighthouse

Concern over the deteriorating condition of Old Baldy prompted admirers of the lighthouse to form the Old Baldy Foundation in 1985. Since that time, the foundation, in conjunction with the North Carolina Division of Archives and History, has commissioned work on the eroding exterior of the structure.

Proceed west from the lighthouse complex on North Bald Head Wynd to the intersection with South Bald Head Wynd just north of the Island Chandler. Follow the latter wynd as it makes its way along the banks of the Cape Fear River.

It was along this route that the Confederate government constructed a massive earthwork fortification in 1863. Some five hundred slaves, many recruited from nearby plantations, were used to finish the project. When completed, the fort extended more than 1.5 miles from the junction of the river and the ocean to a bluff east of the lighthouse.

Named Fort Holmes for Lieutenant General Theophilus Holmes, North Carolina's highest-ranking Confederate officer, the installation was charged with three important duties: keeping the Cape Fear open to Confederate shipping, preventing enemy landings, and lending assistance to friendly ships that encountered trouble on nearby Frying Pan Shoals.

Upon the fall of Fort Fisher in January 1865, the Southern troops abandoned Fort Holmes after destroying its guns and supplies. The fort served the war effort for a total of only 411 days.

A significant portion of the earthworks is still discernable along South Bald Head Wynd and North Bald Head Wynd. A legend handed down for generations tells of a large brass cannon that was dropped in the deepest part of Bald Head Creek by the garrison of Fort Holmes so that it would not be captured by the enemy. It has never been found.

As South Bald Head Wynd winds its way around the southwestern bend of the island at the mouth of the river, visitors come face to face with history. It was to this very place that many of the great European explorers of the sixteenth century came on their visits to the New World.

Only thirty-two years after Christopher Columbus made his historic voyage, Giovanni da Verrazano became the first European to sight the island and to sail into the mouth of the river.

In 1526, Luis Vasquez de Ayllon, a wealthy citizen of the island of

Hispaniola in the West Indies, attempted to colonize the Bald Head Island area, having obtained a land grant between the Cape Fear and Savannah rivers from King Charles V of Spain. Ayllon's greeting at Cape Fear was anything but pleasant, as the largest ship in his fleet wrecked at Bald Head—the first known shipwreck in the coastal waters of the United States. His men fabricated a replacement vessel while at Cape Fear. This ship is believed to have been the first ship constructed by Europeans in what is now the United States.

The British experience at Bald Head began with the Sir Walter Raleigh expeditions of 1584–1587. On the 1585 expedition, which brought the first colonists to the North Carolina coast, the treacherous shoals at Cape Fear almost changed the history of North Carolina and English America. When the fleet arrived on July 16, 1585, Simon Ferdinando, the captain of John White's flagship, almost ran the ship aground at Cape Fear. Had the flagship wrecked here, it is quite probable that the first English colony in America would have settled at Bald Head Island.

South Bald Head Wynd runs parallel to the strand on the southern half of South Beach.

Sometime before 1840, Bald Head Island received its name from the Cape Fear River pilots, who put a tall dune on this part of the island to good use. To earn the honor of bringing a ship into the river, the pilots began the custom of racing to the incoming vessel. They sought the highest spot on the outermost reach of land as a vantage point from which they might glimpse the sails of approaching ships. The continued use of the tall dune as a lookout spot gradually wore down the sea oats and vegetation until the dune began looking like a big, bald head.

At the intersection of South Bald Head Wynd and Stede Bonnet Wynd, turn north onto the latter road. Though this route passes through the island's golf course and reveals other evidence of resort living, don't be deceived. Bald Head is one battleground where conservationists have actually won the war against future development.

Almost a century has passed since the first plans were announced for the commercial development of Bald Head. In the 1890s, an attempt by a Pennsylvania congressman to build a resort spa comparable to Atlantic City, New Jersey, never got off the drawing board.

Thomas Franklin Boyd, a native of the North Carolina foothills, made the next serious attempt to develop the island, which he renamed Palmetto Island for its profusion of palm trees. In the mid-1920s, he constructed the Boyd Hotel on a high bluff just south of the lighthouse. Boyd's dream for the island turned into a nightmare during the Great Depression. The hotel was abandoned in the 1930s and reduced to rubble by a fire in 1941. A marker near a pile of old bricks on the roadside is all that remains of the old hotel.

For decades thereafter, the future of the island was a subject of heated controversy. Not until the 1970s, when the state of North Carolina acquired title to ten thousand acres—including extensive marshland, 6 miles of shoreline on the eastern side of the island, and numerous small islands—did conservationists and naturalists believe they had won the battle to preserve much of Bald Head in its natural state. Administered as a natural area under the auspices of the North Carolina Division of Parks and Recreation, the North Carolina Division of Coastal Management, and the North Carolina Wildlife Commission, the extensive state holdings became a "day-use only" park in 1986.

Approximately two thousand acres of the island are in private ownership and are subject to development. Fortunately for conservationists, the island's developer has proven sensitive to environmental issues and is seeking to promote orderly development.

At the intersection of Stede Bonnet Wynd and Edward Teach Wynd, turn east on Edward Teach Wynd. These two avenues bear testimony to the time when Bald Head was a pirate haven. That the island was a favorite hangout for pirates is undisputed by experts. Francis L. Hawkins, a nineteenth-century historian, concluded that the Cape Fear region was a haven for pirates "second only in importance to Providence."

It is estimated that during the first two decades of the eighteenth century, a thousand men were using Bald Head as a base from which to launch pirate attacks on unwary ships. In a two-month period in 1718, thirteen ships fell prey to pirates operating from the island. Blackbeard used Bald Head on occasion, but it was Major Stede Bonnet who was most at home at Cape Fear.

No pirate had a stranger story than Bonnet. He was born into a respectable

English family and received a good education. After a successful military career, he retired to Barbados, where he purchased a sugar plantation and assumed a place of stature in Bridgetown society. For reasons never fully explained, Bonnet, who had never been a sailor, forsook his life as a highly respected gentlemen and went a-pirating. Some historians have maintained he changed his lifestyle to escape a nagging wife.

After legitimately purchasing a ship, which he named *The Revenge*, Bonnet recruited a crew of seventy men from the grog shops of Bridgetown. Initial successes at sea were followed by a 1717 cruise with Blackbeard that ended when Bonnet was double-crossed by his partner in crime. This incident etched a streak of cruelty in Bonnet. No longer were his ways those of a refined gentleman. Instead, torture became his modus operandi. Unfortunate victims "walking the plank" have long been a stock scene in Hollywood pirate films. It is believed that Bonnet was the only pirate of the golden age of piracy to actually force prisoners to walk the plank.

Not only did Bonnet take on a vicious nature, he also changed his name to Captain Thomas. Likewise, he gave his vessel a new name: the *Royal James*. About this time, he began making Bald Head Island—with its meandering waterways, dangerous shoals, and complex of small islands—a favorite hiding place.

All the time Bonnet was frequenting the Cape Fear region, the citizens of South Carolina, particularly those from the Charleston area, were clamoring for action against him. Colonel William Rhett, the receiver general of South Carolina, volunteered to command an expedition to eradicate the menace at Cape Fear.

No sooner had Rhett's two vessels attempted to negotiate entry into the Cape Fear River on September 25, 1718, than they both ran aground on sand bars. To Rhett's relief, the ships were not damaged. All he had to do was stay put until midnight, when the two ships would be refloated by the high tide.

While waiting for the tide, the South Carolinians saw several pirate ships in the river, one of them the *Royal James*. Bonnet's ship and the two other vessels in his fleet had been in the river since early August. Bonnet had sought refuge on an island in the river and gone about repairing his leaking vessel. He had found the sandy beach an excellent place to careen his sloop—

a process whereby the ship was lifted to one side as the tide went out, allowing the pirates to effect repairs below the water line.

It is believed that when Rhett's vessels were refloated, they caught Bonnet in a vulnerable position. After Bonnet and Rhett maneuvered their ships for hours trying to achieve an advantage, Rhett gained the upper hand. Unwilling to fight to an almost certain death, Bonnet surrendered unconditionally.

Bonnet was transported back to Charleston, where he was executed on December 10, 1718, thereby ending the unfettered reign of pirates on the North Carolina coast.

Since his demise, Bald Head Island has been rumored to be the site of one of the richest buried treasures in history. According to legend, Bonnet ordered his chief mate, a man named Herriot, to bury some three million Spanish milled dollars and pieces of eight on Bald Head before his execution. After the death of Bonnet and his fellow pirates, no person alive knew the location of the treasure.

Numerous efforts have been made to find it. A Wilmington newspaper ran a story on May 15, 1888, that told of a Southport river pilot who had discovered a substantial number of Spanish coins on Bald Head. A nor'easter the previous winter had apparently exposed the coins, one of which bore the date 1713. Because of corrosion, the dates on the other coins could not be determined. Quite possibly, the pilot may have found some of Bonnet's treasure.

If it ever existed, most of the treasure at Bald Head probably remains buried somewhere on the island. As development continues and sand is dug and moved, workers, residents, or visitors may one day discover a cache hidden on the island for more than 275 years.

Edward Teach Wynd merges into Muscadine Wynd just north of the former site of a Coast Guard station erected on the island in 1914. The maritime forests that line Muscadine Wynd and the other roads cover much of the island. Teeming with unusual plants and animals, these forests, unlike any others in North Carolina, are dominated by live oak, loblolly pine, and sabal palmetto. One live oak measures seventeen and a half feet in circumference and is estimated to be more than three hundred years old. The palm trees grow naturally nowhere else in the state. They attest to the semitropical climate of the island.

It was one of these ancient forests that provided the setting for one of the most bizarre tales from the long history of Bald Head. More often than not, the fine distinction between truth and legend is blurred by time. And thus it is with one of coastal North Carolina's greatest mysteries: the disappearance of Theodosia Burr Alston.

This intriguing mystery remains a significant part of the history of two distinct areas of the coast: the Outer Banks and Bald Head Island. While both places lay claim to the site of the mystery, there are certain uncontroverted facts related to the incident.

Theodosia Burr Alston was the wife of Joseph Alston, the governor of South Carolina, and the daughter of Aaron Burr, the third vice president of the United States. She was known as a woman of great beauty, intelligence, and refinement. On the last day of 1812, she boarded a small pilot ship, *The Patriot*, at Georgetown, South Carolina, on a trip to New York for a reunion with her father, who had recently returned from self-imposed exile in England after his famous duel with Alexander Hamilton. Whether because of storm or piracy, *The Patriot* never arrived in New York. Rather, it drifted ashore at Nags Head in early 1813, devoid of passengers and crew.

At this point, truth meets legend. Exactly what happened to Theodosia continues to be a source of dispute.

Some have speculated that pirates killed Theodosia and plundered *The Patriot* while the ship was off Nags Head. To substantiate their claim, they point to a portrait of a young woman that now hangs in a private gallery in New York. The painting was taken off *The Patriot* by Outer Bankers after the vessel drifted ashore at Nags Head. In 1869, this oil portrait was given to Dr. William G. Pool, an Elizabeth City physician, as compensation for medical treatment rendered to a Nags Head woman. News accounts of the intriguing painting subsequently brought a descendant of the Burr family and the daughter of the portraitist to Elizabeth City. They concurred that the portrait was that of Theodosia Burr Alston.

Yet another piece was added to the puzzle in 1910, when J. A. Elliott of Norfolk uncovered a story concerning the body of a young woman of obvious refinement that had washed ashore at Cape Henry, Virginia, in early 1813. The farmer who discovered the unidentified body buried the woman on his farm.

Adherents of the Bald Head legend claim that *The Patriot* became stranded on the shoals of the Cape Fear region. While the helpless ship foundered, the pirates of Bald Head moved in. After plundering the ship, the raiders threw the crew and passengers of *The Patriot* overboard, save the beautiful Theodosia Burr Alston. Her striking beauty apparently led the cutthroats to spare her life.

Sometime later, the ransacked and abandoned ship was set adrift by the tides, only to be carried to its final resting place at Nags Head. Meanwhile, Theodosia was carried to the pirate leader in the forests at Bald Head. He recognized her to be the first lady of South Carolina and realized her enormous ransom potential.

Until arrangements could be made to contact Governor Alston for a payoff, Theodosia was placed in the custody of three pirates. Rum being their weakness, they were soon intoxicated, and Theodosia escaped into the night. One tale contends that after she committed suicide, her lifeless body was found by a search party of pirates. Outraged by the incompetence of his subordinates, the pirate chieftain ordered the threesome beheaded. A divergent tale has it that the search party found Theodosia alive and returned her to the pirate camp, where she died in captivity.

Yet another twist to the Bald Head story was given credibility by two men who were hanged in Norfolk after the ill-fated voyage of *The Patriot*. At their trial, the men testified that they were members of the band of pirates responsible for the pillaging of *The Patriot* at Bald Head. They bore witness to Theodosia's death.

Regardless of how Theodosia may have met her demise at Bald Head, various accounts of her ghost persist to this day. Before the development of Bald Head, the apparition was seen roaming over the island in a relentless search for a way to escape. In more recent times, her ghost, attired in an elegant emerald-green dress, has been observed walking on the island.

Old Coast Guard building

Not only has the ghost of the beautiful lady continued to haunt the island, but so have those of the trio of pirates assigned to guard her. In the distant past, their headless ghosts were observed pursuing the ghost of the young woman. When the Coast Guard manned a station on the island, guardsmen often walked the beach on single-man patrols each night. More than once, stunned sentries returned to the station with tales of headless pirates joining them on patrol.

Many years have passed since the last guardsmen patrolled the beaches of Bald Head, but sightings of the headless pirates have continued. Lovers strolling on the moonlit beaches or through the magnificent maritime forests have been startled by ghosts, who often tap young women on the shoulder in hopes that they might be the elusive Theodosia.

Like many other fascinating mysteries of the North Carolina coast, that of Theodosia Burr Alston may never be explained.

Muscadine Wynd ends at Federal Road, an extension of North Bald Head Wynd. Proceed east on Federal Road as it makes its way to the southeastern tip of the island: Cape Fear. This ancient route was cut through virgin stands of oak, palmetto, pine, and yaupon at the turn of the twentieth century to provide a straight path for a tramway, which supplied materials for the construction of the Cape Fear Lighthouse, formerly located near the southeastern tip of the island.

Even though Old Baldy was constructed on one of the highest parts of the island, its usefulness was limited to guiding traffic into and out of the Cape Fear River. Accordingly, navigational assistance was needed for ocean traffic plying the Atlantic shipping lanes off Bald Head Island. Because of the great expanse of Frying Pan Shoals, which begin at the southeastern tip of the island and extend 30 miles into the Atlantic, navigational experts reasoned that a lighthouse should be located at Cape Fear.

To meet this critical need, a tall, skeletal structure was erected near the point in 1903. In stark contrast to the romantic, dignified sentinels that guard the coast at Cape Lookout, Cape Hatteras, Bodie Island, and Corolla, the Cape Fear Lighthouse was not a thing of beauty.

After more than a half-century of continuous service, the 161-foot lighthouse was retired on May 15, 1958—not because it was inadequate, but because a new, more efficient lighthouse had been constructed at Oak Island. After defying a demolition team's effort to reduce it to rubble, the tower succumbed to sixty-two sticks of dynamite on September 12, 1958. Nothing remains of the structure except its foundation.

A short side road leads from the foundation to three white frame dwellings known as Captain Charlie's Complex. Named for Captain Charles Norton Swan, the longtime keeper of the Cape Fear Lighthouse, the houses were built for the families of the keeper and his two assistants. Two of them

are available for vacation rental. The entire complex is listed on the National Register of Historic Places. A number of paintings by well-known North Carolina artist Bob Timberlake have featured these venerable structures.

Federal Road ends at a gazebo on East Beach. Continue down the beach to the point. This is Cape Fear, an awe-inspiring sight. So terrifying, so menacing, so forbidding is the place that it could have no other name. No one before or since has more eloquently described Cape Fear than George Davis, native son and attorney general of the Confederacy:

> A naked, bleak elbow of sand jutting far out into the ocean. Immediately in its front are the Frying Pan Shoals pushing out still farther twenty miles to the south. Together they stand for warning and woe. . . . The kingdom of silence and awe, disturbed by no sound save the seagull's shriek and the breaker's roar. . . . Imagination cannot adorn it. Romance cannot hallow it. Local pride cannot soften it. There it stands today, bleak and threatening, and pitiless. . . . And its nature, its name, is now, always has been, and always will be the Cape of Fear.

The tour ends at Cape Fear. Were it possible to make your way here at both sunrise and sunset on the same day, you would be rewarded with a breathtaking experience: due to its unique geographic orientation, Cape Fear allows visitors to see the sun both rise and set on the Atlantic.

Retrace your route to the ferry landing on Bald Head to return to Southport and your car.

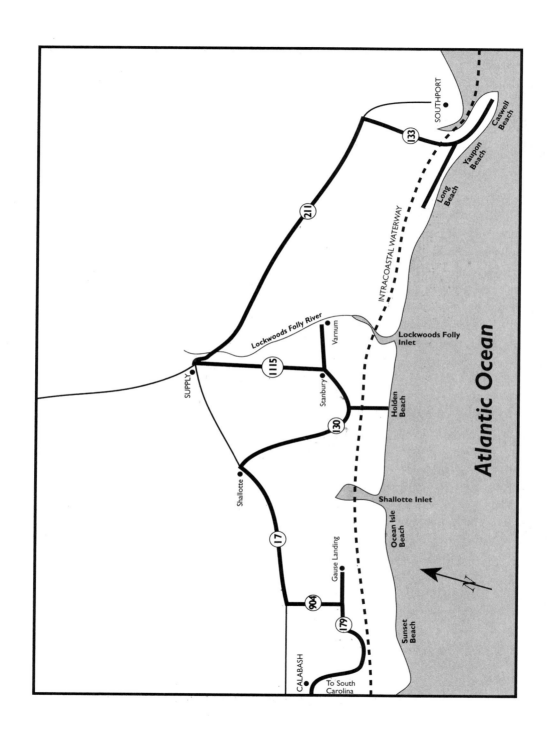

The Brunswick
Islands Tour

This tour begins with a visit to Oak Island and its three resort communities: Yaupon Beach, Long Beach, and Caswell Beach. It then threads its way back and forth between mainland villages and the remaining Brunswick Islands, moving from Varnum to Holden Beach, from Shallotte to Ocean Isle Beach, and from Gause Landing to Sunset Beach. Back on the mainland, it visits Calabash before ending near the former site of historic Boundary House.

Among the highlights of the tour are the story of Hurricane Hazel, the shipwrecks in Lockwoods Folly Inlet, the Oak Island Lighthouse, Fort Caswell, the healing waters of Shallotte Inlet, and the story of Mrs. Calabash.

Total mileage: approximately 93 miles.

This tour begins at the intersection of N.C. 133 and N.C. 211 approximately 2 miles west of Southport. Drive south on N.C. 133.

As you make your way toward the Atlantic, you will pass a variety of businesses and service facilities that have proliferated over the past several decades in response to the burgeoning tourism industry on Oak Island, the largest of the Brunswick County islands on this tour.

After 2.8 miles on N.C. 133, the mainland ends at the Intracoastal Waterway, located just south of the Brunswick County Airport, a small airfield with paved, lighted runways.

When the $3.6-million bridge to Oak Island was completed over the Waterway in 1975, it was one of the first modern high-rise bridges constructed to replace the romantic, but antiquated, drawbridges that once linked most of the barrier islands to the mainland. At the crest of the 5,000-foot, arched span, you will have a magnificent panorama of the Intracoastal Waterway, Oak Island, and the Cape Fear River. A night crossing offers the comforting beam of the Oak Island Lighthouse.

Erroneously described as a peninsula by some geographers, Oak Island is the western landmass at the mouth of the Cape Fear River. Separated from Bald Head Island, to the east, by the Cape Fear, separated from Holden Beach, to the west, by Lockwoods Folly Inlet, separated from Southport and the Brunswick County mainland, to the north, by the Elizabeth River, and bordered on the south by the vast Atlantic, Oak Island is truly an island. As early as 1770, it was shown as such on the Collet map of North Carolina.

Apparently named for the live-oak trees that grow abundantly on its 14-mile-long landscape, Oak Island was relatively free of human habitation until well into the nineteenth century. Except for a handful of farmers, fishermen, shipwreck victims, and fugitives from justice, there were no permanent residents on the island until Fort Caswell was completed at the extreme eastern end of the island in 1838. Even then, the fort maintained a relatively small garrison until the Civil War.

Despite its strategic location at the mouth of the Cape Fear, the island saw limited action during the war. Three island forts were garrisoned by Confederate troops. Fort Caswell was wrested from Union control once North Carolina joined the Confederacy. To supplement Caswell, the Southern forces put up two small earthwork fortifications—Forts Campbell and Shaw—farther down the island. Nothing remains of those two makeshift outposts.

Following the Civil War, Fort Caswell was manned during irregular periods through World War II. Nonetheless, Oak Island did not begin to attract a significant population until the latter stages of the Great Depression. A pontoon bridge was put in place in the 1930s, thus providing a direct connection to the mainland for the first time. Improved access aided in the development of a vacation resort in and around Fort Caswell in the years preceding World War II. About the same time, E. F. Middleton of Charleston, South Carolina, purchased much of the island west of the Fort Caswell development as part of vast Brunswick County land acquisitions by a pulpwood concern. His employers found the island to be of little value to their business, so Middleton arranged to take title to the Oak Island property for speculative purposes. The beach towns of Long Beach and Yaupon Beach were subsequently built on this property in the 1950s.

Immediately prior to World War II, the first bridge to the island was replaced by a concrete drawbridge. Unfortunately, the war intervened before the island's resort potential could be realized. The drawbridge succumbed to a runaway barge on September 7, 1971. The old road approaches to that bridge are visible from the modern bridge.

Yaupon Beach, squeezed between Caswell Beach and Long Beach, begins where the bridge ends and serves as the gateway to the island. Although it plays second fiddle to Long Beach in area and population, Yaupon Beach boasts approximately a thousand permanent residents.

From the southern end of the bridge, proceed 0.7 mile south to where N.C. 133 ends at the traffic light. Continue south on Caswell Beach Drive for 0.3 mile, then turn west onto Ocean Drive.

Yaupon Beach pier and eroding shore

Here, the Yaupon Beach oceanfront offers visible evidence of the erosion to which many of the barrier islands of the North Carolina coast are exposed. Coastal geologists contend that *erosion* is a layman's term for the natural migration of barrier islands toward the mainland. The strand at Yaupon Beach is scarred by numerous tree stumps—graphic reminders of a time when ancient maritime forests stood where beachcombers now frolic.

One of the landmarks on Ocean Drive is the Yaupon Beach Pier, the newest and tallest ocean fishing pier on the North Carolina coast. Completed in 1993 at a cost of half a million dollars, the pier replaced a 1955 structure damaged beyond repair by Hurricane Hugo. The pier is located at the end of Womble Street after 6 blocks on Ocean Drive.

After 0.5 mile on Ocean Drive, turn north on Crowell Avenue. A drive along this short residential street reveals the abundant forest canopy that distinguishes Oak Island from most of the other barrier islands of North Carolina. Although trees reach the strand only at Yaupon Beach, where the island is just over 2 miles wide, pine forests cover much of the northern half of the island.

Turn west off Crowell Avenue onto Yaupon Drive, which becomes Oak Island Drive as it makes its way to Long Beach and the western end of the island.

Tourists who come to Oak Island and its sister Brunswick Islands in search of the glitz of Myrtle Beach are disappointed. On these heavily developed barrier islands, the rush to modernity has been tempered by an abiding respect for a slow-paced lifestyle. During the peak of each summer season, upwards of fifty thousand vacationers flock to Oak Island each week in search of sea, sun, and fun at a resort lacking high-rise hotels, posh restaurants, large shopping complexes, and sprawling amusement parks.

After 4.5 miles, turn south off Oak Island Drive onto Middleton Street in Long Beach. Named for the man who was instrumental in the development of this resort community, the road is the only sound-to-sea street on the western quarter of the island.

It is 0.3 mile on Middleton to the Long Beach strand. Midway, a bridge spans Big Davis Canal, a wide, scenic tidal creek that runs the length of the western half of Oak Island, thus splitting the island into two distinct bodies. When viewed from the air or from a map, the island resembles the head of a giant alligator.

Long Beach scenic walkway

Middleton Avenue ends at Beach Drive, a long oceanfront road lined with rows of brightly painted beach cottages of all shapes and sizes. Turn west onto Beach Drive.

Although Long Beach is in its infancy compared with the historic settlements of the Cape Fear area, it has a year-round population of thirty-three hundred, making it the second-most-populous town in Brunswick County. Most of the permanent residents do not live in the oceanside retreats on Beach Drive. Rather, they live on the sheltered northern side of the island.

On the 3.5-mile drive on Beach Drive to the western end of the island, you will notice several tall, vegetated sand dunes. These survive as mute reminders of the numerous dunes and sand hills that dominated the island landscape prior to resort development. Before the bulldozer leveled most of them, these tall dunes were used as navigational guides and landmarks.

After World War II, Oak Island seemed destined to take its place as the state's newest barrier-island resort. In the early 1950s, E. F. Middleton and his associates began selling lots on the strand at the future sites of Long Beach and Yaupon Beach. When the town of Long Beach was incorporated as the first municipality on Oak Island in 1953, there were at least a dozen families living permanently on the island.

But the development of Oak Island was temporarily blocked by a catastrophe of immense proportions. In the early-morning hours of October 15, 1954, the North Carolina coast experienced the ultimate storm when Hurricane Hazel unleashed her devastating power on the Cape Fear coast. On that fateful day, North Carolina lost every one of its fishing piers.

No North Carolina coastal community was spared the wrath of Hazel, but the most complete destruction occurred at Long Beach. On October 14, 1954, the infant resort boasted 357 houses.

One day later, only 5 were left.

The Capel House, one of the two frame houses that survived, is still visible today high atop Folly Hill. Easily identifiable as the tallest sand dune on the island, Folly Hill is located on the northern side of Beach Drive approximately 2 miles west of Middleton.

The sheer terror of a storm of the magnitude and intensity of Hazel has not often been recorded, because few people who stay to "ride out" hurricanes survive. Two such people survived Hazel on Long Beach.

Connie Ledgett, a seventeen-year-old newlywed, and her twenty-one-year-old husband arrived at Long Beach for their honeymoon in the early-evening hours of Thursday, October 14, 1954. Although they had heard news reports of a hurricane in the Bahamas, they did not give the storm much thought.

During the wee hours of the next morning, the newlyweds were awakened by a howling wind. From their third-row cottage, they could see the ocean rising above the high dunes. As conditions worsened, they realized that they had to leave the island.

By the time their car was loaded, the ocean had breached the dunes and spilled onto the road. When water reached the fenders of the car, they abandoned the vehicle and made it back to their cottage. From there, they waded in waist-deep water to a two-story apartment house and forced their way into the structure.

They survived the first half of the hurricane in a second-floor apartment. Gradually, the raging ocean reached their second-story window, and waves broke against the building. Their temporary place of refuge rocked like a boat. Connie Ledgett could hear it breaking up below her.

Recognizing that their best chance for survival was to get out of the building, the newlyweds attempted to float a chest of drawers out the window, but a wave carried it away. Finally, they put a mattress out the window, and Connie, who could not swim, lay on it while her husband held onto the straps. They also used a piece of house wall that floated by to increase their buoyancy.

Wind and water carried the couple to the tops of some scrub oaks that were twenty feet high. From their vantage point, they saw the kind of sights few people have lived to tell about. Floating houses crashed into each other. They saw several other people but could not reach them or communicate with them because of the fury of the storm. They could see nothing of the landscape, as Oak Island was completely inundated with water.

Finally, the storm began to diminish and the water receded. The terrified newlyweds climbed down and made their way off the island. Their cottage had been destroyed, but the apartment which had provided temporary refuge was one of the five surviving buildings. However, it had been moved some seventy-five feet, and the second floor had given way.

Days later, Connie's parents found the refrigerator from their daughter's cottage in a marsh, where it had floated during the storm. Inside was the newlyweds' wedding cake.

Although the storm cut an inlet through the island near Folly Hill, it did not dampen the enthusiasm of developers and potential property owners. Very little time passed before work was under way to re-form dunes that had been leveled by the storm surge. Bulldozers closed the inlet; streets were cleared of sand and debris and were repaved; lots were surveyed and boundary lines were reestablished; and the basis of the modern resort towns of Oak Island was created.

Beach Drive forks near the western end of the island. Take the right fork and drive to the parking lot at the end of the road. This road once circled around the end of the island, but in the late 1970s, Hurricane David and other coastal storms destroyed such a large portion of it that repairs were never effected.

Many visitors leave their vehicles at the parking lot and take the short walk across the sand flats to Lockwoods Folly Inlet, which separates Oak Island from Holden Beach. Shell collectors, beachcombers, and fishermen are attracted to this scenic, undeveloped spit of land, known locally as "The Point."

From The Point, Holden Beach is easily visible to the naked eye. Although the two islands are separated only by a relatively narrow inlet, the distance between them by roadway is more than 20 miles.

The name Lockwoods Folly first appeared on the Ogilby map of 1671. It is said to have originated with a man named Lockwood who built a boat up what is now Lockwoods Folly River, only to discover that it was too large to float downriver. Ultimately, the vessel was abandoned and fell to pieces.

Four Civil War shipwrecks have been discovered in the shallow waters of Lockwoods Folly Inlet near The Point. Two of them—the *Ranger* and the *Bendigo*—are visible above the surface at low tide. When the water level is extremely low, intrepid swimmers from Long Beach and Holden Beach wade to the wrecks. Both ships were steamers that were pressed into service as blockade runners.

Built on the famous Clyde River in England, the five-hundred-ton *Bendigo* was set afire in the inlet on January 4, 1864, to avoid capture by pursuing Union naval forces. The inlet floor around the wreck is littered with the hull, the engine, and some machinery.

A week after the *Bendigo* met her demise, the double side-wheeler *Ranger*, loaded with Austrian rifles and carpentry tools, was set afire by Confederate ground forces at Oak Island to prevent it from falling into the hands of the enemy.

Wreckage of a third blockade runner, the wooden-hulled steamer *Elizabeth*, lies below the surface 1,250 feet south of the *Bendigo*. Also nearby and hidden below the waters is the wreckage of the USS *Iron Age*, one of the few Union vessels sunk while engaged in blockading activities during the entire war.

From "The Point," turn around and drive east on Beach Drive.

From time to time, shifting sands reveal the wooden skeletons of several unknown ships on the Long Beach shoreline near Thirteenth Place West and Third Place West. Farther east, the Long Beach Scenic Walkway, located just off Beach Drive at Twentieth Place East, offers unspoiled vistas of Davis Canal as it winds its way through cordgrass and marshes.

After 7 miles on Beach Drive, turn left, or north, onto Fifty-eighth Street. Follow Fifty-eighth to Oak Island Drive and turn right, or east. Oak Island Drive changes to Yaupon Drive along the 3-mile drive to the traffic light at Caswell Beach Drive back in Yaupon Beach. Turn southeast onto Caswell Beach Drive and proceed 2 miles to the final stop on Oak Island—Caswell Beach, the smallest and youngest of the three resort municipalities.

Incorporated in 1975, Caswell Beach has several hundred permanent residents. It is the home of two of the most historic landmarks on Oak

Oak Island Lighthouse

Island—the Oak Island Lighthouse and Fort Caswell, both located at the eastern end of the island near the mouth of the Cape Fear River.

Located adjacent to the entrance to Fort Caswell, and towering over the Oak Island Coast Guard Station, the Oak Island Lighthouse is the newest and southernmost lighthouse on the North Carolina coast. Constructed in 1958 to mark the entrance to the Cape Fear River, the 169-foot tower was the first lighthouse to be constructed in the Fifth Coast District—which includes Maryland, Virginia, and North Carolina—in fifty-four years. Due to technological improvements in navigation since World War II, this lighthouse is likely to be one of the last constructed along the coast of the United States.

In appearance, the Oak Island Lighthouse is the ugly stepsister of the romantic old lighthouses standing guard over the North Carolina waters to the north. It resembles a tall, slender silo decorated in drab colors. Designers sacrificed aesthetics for utility and economy when drawing the plans for the tower at Caswell Beach.

When construction began in 1957, the builders were forced to excavate 125 feet underground to find a rock foundation strong enough to support the tower. In order to eliminate the need for future painting, colors were mixed into the wet concrete of the three sections. Gray was used for the bottom section, white for the middle, and black for the top. Now, a third of a century later, the harsh coastal elements have caused the colors to fade.

On May 15, 1958, the light was put into operation. For many years thereafter, the 1,400,000-candlepower beacon was rated the second most brilliant in the world, with only a French lighthouse on the English Channel having a more powerful beam. At present, the main light features a four-light rotating fixture working in conjunction with twenty-four-inch parabolic mirrors and quartz bulbs. Visible up to 19 miles at sea, the light flashes four times every ten seconds. So intense is the heat it generates that Coast Guard personnel who maintain the facility must wear protective clothing while working in the aluminum-frame beacon room.

The lack of eye appeal of the concrete tower can be partly attributed to its uniform diameter of eighteen feet. Despite its relatively narrow base, the lighthouse is a sturdy structure. By design, it sways as much as three feet in a sixty-mile-per-hour wind.

Although the lighthouse is a favorite of painters and photographers, only authorized personnel are allowed inside the tower, which has 134 steps and a narrow ladder leading to the beacon. The grounds are open to the public from four o'clock in the afternoon to sunset Monday through Saturday, and from noon to sunset on Sunday.

Located behind a cottage between the lighthouse and the entrance gate to Fort Caswell is the brick foundation of an old lighthouse, one of two constructed on the island by the United States Treasury Department in 1849 to aid ships entering the river. Rebuilt in 1879, the rear beacon operated until 1958, when its wooden tower burned.

On the oceanfront directly across from the old lighthouse, a former United States Lifesaving Station has been converted into a private residence.

Fort Caswell

Fort Caswell, that ancient military bastion built when the nation was a half-century old, survives on the extreme eastern end of Oak Island. Even though this outpost was considered one of the strongest fortifications in the nation at the time of its construction, it never saw extensive military action during its 140 years of service as a vital link in America's coastal defense system.

The War of 1812 exposed the extreme vulnerability of the American coast to attack by foreign invaders. In an attempt to fortify the major coastal inlets, the federal government initiated the postwar construction of sea fortifications. From this building program came Forts Caswell, Macon, Moultrie, and Sumter in the Carolinas.

In 1824, the government purchased 2,755 acres on the eastern half of Oak Island for a military reservation to protect the entrance of the Cape Fear. A year later, on March 2, 1825, Congress appropriated funds for the project. However, plans were not drawn until 1826, and actual construction did not begin until 1827.

By the time the project was completed in 1838, numerous cost overruns ballooned the final price tag to $473,402, almost four times the original estimate. Twelve years of work culminated in an enclosed pentagonal fort with a two-tiered escarpment flanked by gun galleries providing fire down the moat. It also featured sixty-one guns bearing on the channel, as well as a few small guns for land defense. The inner citadel contained barracks, officers' quarters, storerooms, and an armory.

On April 18, 1833, in the midst of the laborious construction project, Fort Caswell was named in honor of Richard Caswell (1729–1789), the hero of the Battle of Moores Creek Bridge and the first governor of the independent state of North Carolina.

Following World War I, the entire reservation—save fifty-seven acres reserved for Coast Guard use—was declared government surplus and was sold to a group of North Carolina and Florida businessmen. But with the Great Depression and World War II waiting in the wings, the elaborate plans for the development of a port and resort town at Fort Caswell never came to fruition.

Less than a month before the Japanese attack on Pearl Harbor in December 1941, the federal government reclaimed the 248.8 acres containing Fort Caswell for use as a submarine patrol base. After the war, the site was once again declared surplus property. Plans to include the fort in the state parks system never got off the drawing board.

On September 17, 1949, following their abandonment by the military, the buildings and grounds were acquired by trustees of the North Carolina Baptist Convention for the sum of eighty-six thousand dollars. Since then, the Baptists, while cognizant of the historic significance of Fort Caswell, have been hard at work turning swords into plowshares at this time-honored spot, using it as a spiritual retreat and recreational center. A security station is located at the retreat entrance on Caswell Drive. Visitors interested in seeing the site are permitted to enter the grounds.

The most visible remains of the fort are the inner walls. There is scant evidence of the foundation of the cross-shaped citadel which stood inside the walls. One of the three entrances into the rooms under the fort is preserved.

All of the gun emplacements and much of the concrete that made up the seven batteries constructed between 1896 and 1905 survive. Most of the buildings on the grounds are former military structures constructed to meet the needs of troops during the two world wars.

After you have enjoyed Fort Caswell, retrace your route on Caswell Beach Drive to its junction with N.C. 133 in Yaupon Beach, then follow N.C. 133 back to where this tour started at the intersection with N.C. 211 near Southport. Proceed northwest on N.C. 211 for a 13-mile drive through a rural, relatively undeveloped, forested section of Brunswick County. Throughout the eighteenth century and until the Civil War, these pine forests fueled the area's naval-stores industry, which was a world leader.

Visitors and residents alike are mystified by the strange, rumbling booms that shake cottages and other buildings along the beaches of southeastern North Carolina. No one is sure what causes them, where they come from, or when they will come again. Residents say that while the sounds bear a similarity to thunder or a sonic boom, they are different from both. It is almost universally agreed that they emanate from the ocean. The booms last two or three seconds and are strong enough to rattle windows and shake articles off shelves. Most often, the mysterious rumblings occur in the fall and spring. On occasion, they shake the coast more than once a day. Sometimes, they strike several days in a row, while at other times, weeks pass without a single one.

There is no record of how long this weird commotion has been going on. Grandparents in the area claim that their grandparents, who lived long before the advent of airplanes, remembered the booms, so the sonic-boom theory has been thoroughly discounted.

Because all attempts to unravel the mystery have failed, many residents of the Brunswick coast are satisfied to explain the phenomenon with the legend of the "Seneca Guns." According to this legend, the Seneca Indians, who were driven from the area by white settlers, are now returning with the white man's own weapons for revenge.

Legend aside, seismographic instruments have indicated that the reverberations are not caused by earthquakes. Conventional wisdom is that they have a military connection. Despite denials by officials at nearby Sunny Point Ocean Terminal and other military personnel, many area residents compare the sounds to the thunder of artillery or depth charges. Some scientists believe that it is more than coincidence that the booms seem to take place when there is military traffic in the area.

Twelve miles into your 13-mile drive through the Brunswick County countryside, you will cross the black waters of the Lockwoods Folly River, one of the most beautiful rivers in southeastern North Carolina.

Just north of the river bridge at the village of Supply, turn south onto S.R. 1115.

Were there not a modern county hospital located nearby, Supply would be little more than a crossroads village scattered along U.S. 17 on the southern fringes of the Green Swamp. Indeed, its sleepy appearance belies its historic past. From 1805 to 1810, Supply was the county seat of Brunswick County, and a courthouse stood in the village.

After 5.4 miles on S.R. 1115, turn south onto S.R. 1231 and proceed 0.5 mile to the community of Stanbury. At Stanbury, turn east onto S.R. 1122 for a 1.5-mile drive to Varnum.

This village of fewer than three hundred inhabitants is one of those out-of-the-way places that give the North Carolina coast its charm. It is at coastal communities like Varnum, which are not shown in guidebooks or glossy chamber-of-commerce brochures, that the character of the coast can best be appreciated.

Located on the banks of the Lockwoods Folly River, this fishing community is also known as Varnam, Varnumtown, and Varnamtown. Locals tend to prefer the latter two names, although the state spells it Varnum on county maps.

Whatever the spelling, the settlement traces its origin to Roland Varnum, who migrated from Maine to the Lockwoods Folly area in the early eighteenth century. Many of the current residents are Varnams or Varnums. Even though their brotherly disagreement over the spelling of their last name continues, they are all descendants of the original Varnum family.

On the docks of the picturesque hamlet, visitors can purchase fresh seafood as it is unloaded from the boats and chat with fishermen whose families have known no other way of living. During the winter months, the local shrimpers fish the Florida Keys, but by springtime, they return to the Brunswick coast to trawl the local waters.

Of special interest dockside is the marine railway used for pulling the large fishing vessels from the water for cleaning. This facility is one of the few marine railways in Brunswick County, one of the biggest commercial seafood producers in North Carolina.

Begin retracing S.R. 1222 from Varnum. Turn west onto S.R. 1120 halfway to Stanbury. After 2 miles, S.R. 1120 intersects N.C. 130. Turn south on N.C. 130. It is 1 mile to Holden Beach, the second-largest island on this tour.

A twisting high-rise bridge, completed by the state in 1986 to replace an antiquated drawbridge that caused massive traffic jams in the summer, affords a spectacular view of the island and the numerous shrimp boats that make it their home port. Eleven miles in length, Holden Beach is bounded by the Atlantic Ocean on the south, Lockwoods Folly Inlet on the east, Shallotte Inlet on the west, and the Intracoastal Waterway on the north.

Once on the island, turn east onto Ocean Boulevard, the oceanfront road that runs the length of Holden Beach. The island's eastern end—from which Long Beach can be seen across the inlet—is less than 1.5 miles distant. It is from the beach near the end of the road that beachcombers make their way to the exposed Civil War shipwrecks in the inlet.

Retrace your route west on Ocean Boulevard and drive to the guard house for the private development on the western end of the island.

Along the way, it will become evident that the island has been developed almost to the saturation point. More than seventeen hundred vacation cottages not only crowd the oceanfront, but also the leeward side of the island, where numerous concrete finger canals have been built to provide access to the Intracoastal Waterway. Though the island has a permanent population of less than seven hundred, upwards of ten thousand sun worshippers and fishermen crowd its landscape during the summer months.

It has not always been this way. When Hurricane Hazel tore into the island with winds in excess of 150 miles per hour, just twelve of its three hundred cottages remained on their foundations. The hurricane made landfall at the worst possible time: high tide during a full moon. The storm surge created a gaping inlet that severed the island. Federal funds were used to fill the inlet nearly a year later.

References to "Holden's Beach" date back as far as 1785. The island was named in honor of Benjamin Holden, who received a land grant from the king of England that included the island and much of the mainland as far back as the present U.S. 17. Thereafter, the island was handed down through the Holden family from generation to generation. Today, the Holdens continue to maintain significant property interests on the island.

Resort development at Holden Beach began in 1925, when a creek separating the island from the mainland was bridged. A year later, the first hotel, a ten-room structure on pilings, was erected by John Holden, Jr. The

Great Depression hampered further development. As the 1930s drew to a close, the island boasted fifteen cottages and a pavilion. The modern resort emerged from the devastation of Hurricane Hazel.

Much like Oak Island, its sister island to the east, Holden Beach is recognized as a family-oriented vacation spot. John F. Holden proudly proclaimed in 1988 that Holden Beach "is the only incorporated town in Brunswick County that does not have an ABC store, liquor by the drink, beer sales, or night clubs."

The western end of the island overlooks Shallotte Inlet, which separates Holden Beach from Ocean Isle Beach. Thousands of vessels of all sizes and shapes ply the mouth of the Shallotte River on their travels along the Intracoastal Waterway. Little do most of the mariners realize that the waters of the inlet are reputed to have curative powers.

For many years, reports have flowed out of the area that people who bathe in the inlet near a place called Windy Point are mysteriously cured of infections. Such tales have brought visitors from as far away as Canada to avail themselves of the waters and take supplies of it home.

The most plausible explanation for the curative powers concerns a peculiar type of reed that grows in the inlet and nowhere else. Found in the center of the reed is a breadlike substance, on which a mold develops when the reed is inundated with salt water. As the mold is washed off, the water turns a milky color. It is in these milky waters that the miraculous cures have reportedly taken place.

Some who believe in the curative powers assert that these are the same healing waters of which Ponce de Leon wrote. Indians told him that healing waters were located to the north at the end of a journey of many moons' duration, but the famed Spanish explorer—more interested in gold and the Fountain of Youth—apparently never searched for them.

Although the scientific community has expressed skepticism about the curative powers of the waters, a number of documented cases exist. Perhaps the best-known incident occurred in 1945, when Joseph Hufham, a newspaperman from nearby Whiteville, was fishing from a boat anchored in Shallotte Inlet. Hufham was suffering from an eye disease which was gradually worsening despite constant medical care, special glasses, and medication. At times, his pain was so excruciating that he even rubbed alcohol into his eyes to obtain temporary relief.

On this occasion, the sun's reflection on the waters of the inlet hurt his eyes to the point that he could not keep them open long enough to bait his hook. To soothe the pain, Hufham decided to go for a swim. As soon as he resurfaced from his dive, the pain was gone, and it never recurred.

For several years thereafter, Hufham collected and published reports of the unusual cures that had occurred at Shallotte Inlet. One involved an eighty-one-year old Indian who had lived in the area all of his life and had heard tales of the waters since his youth. Hufham witnessed the cure of a twelve-year-old boy whose grotesquely swollen arm was returned to normal after it was dipped in the waters of the inlet.

He issued invitations to scientific and medical organizations to study the waters, but he was consistently turned down. In the 1950s, when the American Medical Association warned him that he would be prosecuted for practicing medicine without a license if he persisted in extolling the virtues of the waters, Hufham fell silent.

Nonetheless, the mystery persists. People continue to seek the healing powers of the waters. Science has yet to prove them wrong.

Holden Beach bridge

Shallotte River

From the guard house, retrace your route to N.C. 130 and proceed over the bridge to the mainland. It is drive of 9 miles to Shallotte. Along this route, the local boat-building industry is very much in evidence. Local craftsmen, often working without blueprints, fabricate large, seaworthy fishing boats in their yards using methods that have been handed down for generations.

Until the late 1980s, when a multilane bypass was constructed around "downtown" Shallotte, the two lanes of U.S. 17 carried a heavy volume of traffic through the heart of the town of some fifteen hundred residents. Over the past forty years, a heavily developed 2-mile commercial strip has grown up along the old "Ocean Highway."

Entering Shallotte, N.C. 130 merges with U.S. 17 Business and follows the old route through town. From the bridge, you will enjoy a spectacular view of the Shallotte River, which rises near the town and provides at least two feet of water here, with three more feet at high tide. As the river flows from Shallotte, it broadens significantly until it reaches the ocean at Shallotte Inlet.

A settlement named Shallotte has been located in Brunswick County for many years. According to the *Pennsylvania Gazette* of April 29, 1731, there was a Shelote as early as 1729, but the exact location of the place is unknown. The year 1840 saw an unsuccessful attempt to establish a village at the mouth of the river. Finally, in the last quarter of the nineteenth century, the community of Shallotte was settled at its present site. By 1899, when the town was incorporated, its population was 149.

It is believed that the town received its name from the wild onions, or shallots, that grow in local fields and on the banks of the river. For the past four decades, Shallotte has served as the commercial hub for the beach resorts on the nearby barrier islands.

At Shallotte, turn south onto N.C. 179 and proceed 6 miles to N.C. 904. Turn south on N.C. 904 and drive across the high-rise bridge that spans the Intracoastal Waterway to 7-mile-long Ocean Isle Beach. Just after crossing the bridge, turn left on Second Street and proceed 1 block east to the Ocean Isle Museum of Coastal Carolina.

In January 1988, a group of local property owners organized the Ocean Isle Museum Foundation. Three years of hard work and fund-raising culminated in the Ocean Isle Museum of Coastal Carolina, which opened in the spring of 1991 in a handsome 7,500-square-foot building. Designed to make a significant contribution to the coastal Carolinas as both an educational and cultural facility, the museum offers a wide variety of interesting exhibits, including historic artifacts, native shells, mounted wildlife of the local marshes and swamps, and displays of wave and tidal action.

Ocean Isle Museum of Coastal Carolina

Return to N.C. 904. Turn south on N.C. 904 and drive 1 block to First Street, the oceanfront boulevard. Turn left, or east, onto First and proceed 3 miles to the eastern end of the island for a tour of the local landscape.

Ocean Isle Beach is considered the most upscale of the Brunswick Islands. Virtually all the land here that is suitable for development has been sold. Some lots have been sold on land that is nothing more than filled-in marsh.

The development of the island began in 1950 as a dream of Odell Williamson, who subdivided the sparsely inhabited island into lots and began constructing concrete finger canals, now prevalent on the eastern half of the island.

Few places on the North Carolina coast suffered the wrath of Hurricane Hazel more than Ocean Isle. The storm completely destroyed thirty-three of the thirty-five structures on the island, and the two buildings that survived were found more than a mile from their original sites. Ocean Isle also sustained the highest loss of life of any place in the Carolinas. When Hazel moved northward, the grim totals at Ocean Isle were eleven dead and seven missing.

Turn around and follow First Street for 5 miles toward the other end of the island.

Particularly noticeable on the western end are two fifteen-story condominiums, the first such structures in Brunswick County. They stand incongruously on the island landscape, perhaps foreshadowing an invasion of development from the nearby South Carolina Grand Strand. The public road ends in the shadow of the tall structures.

When you are ready to leave Ocean Isle Beach, retrace your route to N.C. 904 and head back across the Intracoastal Waterway. At the intersection of N.C. 904 and N.C. 179, turn west onto N.C. 179. Less than 0.5 mile from the intersection, turn left onto S.R. 1159. Here lies a majestic place where the simple beauty of the North Carolina coast can be enjoyed in its pristine state.

Set amid a backdrop of live oaks festooned with Spanish moss, Gause Landing is a tranquil fishing village just across the waterway from Ocean Isle. Its quiet streets are shaded by trees equal in size and beauty to those at Orton Plantation and other showplaces of the Cape Fear region.

Visitors might be surprised to learn that in the distant past, this village was a thriving center of water commerce.

Upon their arrival in the North Carolina colony from Bermuda in the eighteenth century, the Gause family established temporary roots at Town Creek in northeastern Brunswick County. However, the prevalence of yellow fever there caused the Gauses to move 40 miles down the Brunswick coast, where they founded the community of Gause Landing. In his diary, President George Washington noted that he visited Gause Landing and stayed a night as the guest of the Gause family during his famous Southern tour.

Without question, the most famous local historic site is the Gause Family Cemetery, located on the grounds of the ancient plantation built by William Gause on a bluff overlooking the modern Intracoastal Waterway.

Gause Landing

TOURING THE BACKROADS OF NORTH CAROLINA'S LOWER COAST

Within the cemetery is a brick burial vault constructed in 1836 under the terms of the will of John Julius Gause. Several decades ago, after vandals had broken into the tomb, a family member had it resealed. Vandals struck again by removing an inscribed stone over the door of the tomb. After the second episode of desecration, the Gause descendants removed the remains of their ancestors and reinterred them at an undisclosed location.

Although it is not readily apparent, there are eight to ten graves surrounding the tomb. Since tombstones were not easily available in the area at the time these graves were filled, small cedar trees were planted to mark the graves. Some of the trees remain today.

From Gause Landing, return to N.C. 179 and continue west for 4.5 miles to Sunset Beach, the southernmost developed barrier island in the state. This 3-mile-long island has been termed the most beautiful in Brunswick County. Located just northeast of the South Carolina line, Sunset Beach is separated from Ocean Isle Beach, located to the east, by Tubbs Inlet. It is separated from uninhabited Bird Island, to the west, by Mad Inlet.

When Hurricane Hazel struck Brunswick County, property losses at Sunset Beach were less than at the nearby barrier islands, thanks to the island's light development. In 1955, the year after Hazel, the entire island was purchased by Mannon Gore for sixty thousand dollars. During the next three years, Gore busied himself constructing roads and a bridge to the island. In 1961, the state took over responsibility for the maintenance of this unique pontoon bridge, which is the center of a great controversy today.

Within the next few years, this coastal landmark will be nothing more than a pleasant memory. It is slated to give way to a 65-foot high-rise span. Technically known as a "steel barge swing span," the existing bridge is a single-lane, 13.5-foot-wide structure with a tender's office in the middle. Unlike traditional drawbridges, which are raised or turned laterally on a support, the movable portion of the Sunset Beach bridge floats on a pontoon barge. The last of its kind not only in North Carolina but on the entire eastern seaboard, the bridge has been a significant part of the island's charm since its initial development.

Turn east onto Main Street, the oceanfront road running the length of the island. You will notice that the Sunset Beach oceanfront features a wide zone of sand hills covered with beach grass and sea oats. The oceanfront

Sunset Beach bridge

structures here are set back much farther from the Atlantic than at any other beach on the North Carolina coast.

On the eastern end of the island, just south of Tubbs Inlet, the wreckage of the blockade runner *Vesta*, a five-hundred-ton, double-propeller vessel, is exposed at low tide. On January 10, 1864, the ship was en route to Wilmington from Bermuda when she ran aground while being chased by three Union ships. She was subsequently set afire by her crew.

Turn around and drive to the western end of the island. Bird Island, a small, undeveloped barrier beach which lies partly in South Carolina, is visible across Mad Inlet. The island can be reached only by boat or by wading or swimming across the inlet from Sunset Beach at low tide. Visitors considering making the trip should pay close attention to the tide, because the inlet is too deep to cross when the tide comes in.

For many years, Bird Island has been a popular place for picnics and shelling. Less than 2 miles in length, and too small to support large-scale development, the 1,150-acre island may nevertheless soon be overrun by bulldozers. In 1992, the longtime owner of the island began the application process to bridge the inlet and to develop 150 acres of land.

Calabash waterfront

TOURING THE BACKROADS OF NORTH CAROLINA'S LOWER COAST

From the western end of Sunset Beach, return to N.C. 179. Proceed northwest on N.C. 179 for 4.2 miles to Calabash. At the traffic light on N.C. 179 in Calabash, turn south onto River Road, the road leading to the historic waterfront.

Few place names on the North Carolina coast are more nationally and internationally known than Calabash. For more than four decades, this tiny town nestled on the banks of the Calabash River has been a seafood lover's paradise. No town its size anywhere can boast more seafood restaurants. Some 1,300 people call Calabash home. There is a seafood restaurant for every 75 or so of them. Strung along U.S. 179 and River Road, these restaurants serve seafood to more than 1.25 million patrons each year.

Not only has the abundance of restaurants put the town on the map, but so has the method of preparation of Calabash seafood, imitated all over the South and in other parts of the country. Restaurants that claim to cook their seafood "Calabash-style" are spread well beyond the boundaries of Calabash itself.

For most of the day, Calabash is a slow-paced, one-stoplight community. However, after four o'clock in the afternoon, automobiles bearing license plates from all over the United States and Canada begin pouring into town, bearing hungry diners to the place acknowledged by the food editor of the *New York Times* as "The Seafood Capital of the World." By six o'clock, many of the waterfront restaurants have long lines of patrons.

The town had its beginnings in colonial days, when a settlement emerged on the riverbanks where planters brought their peanut crops for shipment. Over time, the village became known as Pea Landing. By 1873, when the name was changed to Calabash—a name taken from a variety of gourd, samples of which hung outside local wells—the community was a flourishing trade center.

Fifty years later, the town was fast becoming a ghost town. Had it not been for the seafood industry, Calabash might not have survived.

In 1935, a rustic wooden shed with a sawdust floor became the first seafood restaurant in the village. Five years later, Vester Beck opened an indoor restaurant. After learning Beck's special preparation technique for shrimp, his sister-in-law, Lucy Coleman, opened her own restaurant nearby. Yet on a leisurely drive through modern Calabash, it is easy to become confused as to which of the restaurants was the original. Signs claiming that particular restaurants are the "Original" or the "First and Only" are visible throughout the town.

Before newspapers made Calabash a well-known place name throughout the country, one of America's best-loved entertainers mentioned the town's name at the close of his shows. Few Americans over the age of thirty will ever forget Jimmy Durante's famous closing line: "Goodnight, Mrs. Calabash, wherever you are."

There is little doubt that "the Old Schnozzola" was referring to the seafood town when he ended his shows. However, there are two theories about the person to whom he was speaking.

Durante dined often at Coleman's Restaurant in the 1940s. There, he joked with Lucy Coleman and called her Mrs. Calabash. Thus, some locals contend that Durante was referring to the restaurant owner in his closing line.

Another explanation concerns a woman who once performed with Durante. This woman moved to Calabash to live near her father, who had a small house near the South Carolina border. Atop the house was an antenna, and the woman's father was implicated in a scheme to send messages to German ships off the North Carolina coast. Jimmy Durante begged this "Mrs. Calabash" to resume her work with him, but she refused, insisting on remaining with her father. Both she and her father later disappeared.

From the Calabash waterfront, return to N.C. 179 and proceed west. It is 0.4 mile to S.R. 1168 (Country Club Road). Turn north on S.R. 1168.

Nearby is a six-hundred-pound granite post erected by surveyors in 1928 to mark the former site of Boundary House. Standing astride the state line, this house was an important landmark in the boundary survey between the two Carolina provinces in 1735.

At one time, Boundary House was the home of Isaac Marion, brother of General Francis Marion, the famed "Swamp Fox." On May 9, 1775, the people of South Carolina learned of the Battle of Lexington when an express horseman from Wilmington delivered the message to Boundary House.

At the outbreak of the Civil War, only the chimney of the house was standing.

When the line between the two states was last surveyed in 1928, the exact location of the house had to be determined in order to achieve an accurate survey.

Continue 1.2 miles on S.R. 1168 to the intersection with U.S. 17, where the state of North Carolina has erected a historical marker for Boundary House. The tour ends here, 0.9 mile from the South Carolina line.

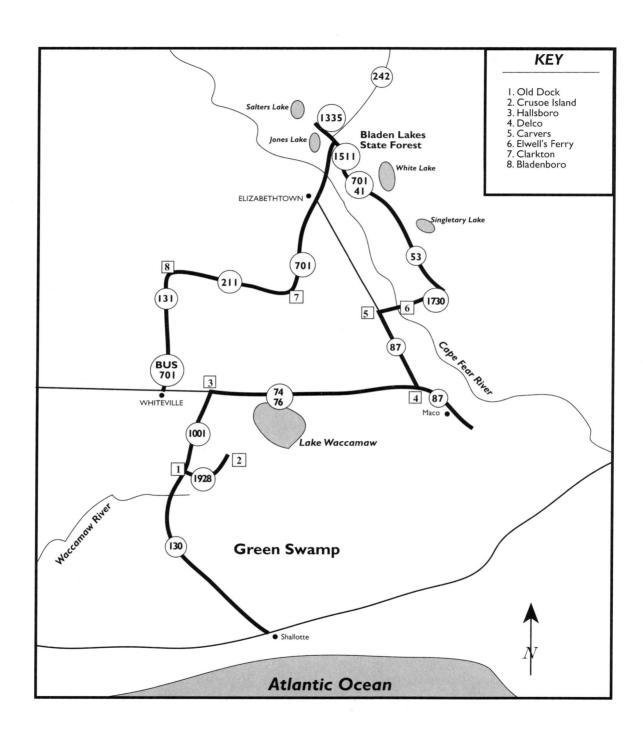

KEY

1. Old Dock
2. Crusoe Island
3. Hallsboro
4. Delco
5. Carvers
6. Elwell's Ferry
7. Clarkton
8. Bladenboro

242

Salters Lake

1335

Jones Lake

Bladen Lakes
State Forest

1511

White Lake

701
41

ELIZABETHTOWN

Singletary Lake

53

8

211

701

131

7

5   6   1730

87

Cape Fear River

BUS
701

3

74
76

4   87

WHITEVILLE

Maco

1001

1   1928   2

Lake Waccamaw

130

Green Swamp

Waccamaw River

Shallotte

N

Atlantic Ocean

The Land of Waccamaw Tour

This tour begins with a drive through the Green Swamp and visits to Old Dock and mysterious Crusoe Island. It then travels to Lake Waccamaw, Maco, Bladen Lakes State Forest, Singletary Lake State Park, White Lake, Jones Lake State Park, Elizabethtown, Clarkton, and Bladenboro before ending near Whiteville.

Among the highlights of the tour are some of the most famous of the Carolina bay lakes, the story of headless Joe Baldwin, the story of Battle Royal, the two-vehicle Cape Fear River Ferry, the story of Anna McNeill Whistler, the story of the Beast of Bladenboro, and the story of Mille-Christine McCoy, the world-famous Siamese twins.

Total mileage: approximately 175 miles.

This tour begins at the intersection of N.C. 130 and U.S. 17 on the outskirts of Shallotte. Proceed northwest on N.C. 130 as it twists its way into and through the Green Swamp, a 140-square-mile wilderness of pocosins, wetlands, and pine savannas.

Although farming and timber production have greatly reduced the size of the Green Swamp over the past two hundred years, it still covers an enormous 20-mile swath of land in Brunswick and Columbus counties between U.S. 17 and U.S. 74. Within this forbidding jungle—portions of which have never been seen by the eyes of man—are stands of ancient cypress, impenetrable thickets of vines, and meandering creeks and streams.

Named for John Green, the man to whom the expanse was granted by the Crown, the swamp was considered worthless until the twentieth century.

Patrick Henry of Virginia once owned land here. Today, most of the swamp is owned by Federal Paper Board Company of Montvale, New Jersey. In 1977, three years after the swamp was declared a national natural landmark by the Department of the Interior, Federal Paper Board donated 13,850 acres to the North Carolina Nature Conservancy for the establishment of the Green Swamp Preserve. Subsequent acquisitions by the Nature Conservancy have increased the size of the preserve, making it one of the largest and most significant wetland areas in the state.

Much of the preserve is open to the public, but venturing into the swamp without an experienced guide is ill-advised. Numerous dangers—such as quicksand, peat holes, dense undergrowth, poisonous snakes, alligators, black bears, and bobcats—have swallowed up unwary explorers in the past.

Thirteen miles from Shallotte, N.C. 130 crosses the black, snakelike Waccamaw River. Park near the bridge for a panoramic view of the river and the surrounding swamp.

Considered one of the most picturesque and unspoiled waterways in coastal North Carolina, the Waccamaw River rises at Lake Waccamaw and flows into South Carolina, where it empties into the Atlantic. At many places within the Green Swamp, the course of the river is indistinguishable from the adjoining swamp.

The river is named for the earliest known inhabitants of its banks, the Waccamaw Indians. Although the Waccamaws aided Carolina colonists in their reprisals against the Tuscaroras in 1712, the tribe was gradually decimated throughout the eighteenth century by hostile encounters with white explorers and settlers and exposure to new diseases. Ultimately, the surviving members of the tribe fled to join the Catawbas in the western Carolinas and the Seminoles in Florida.

Permanent white settlement along the river took place in the mid-eighteenth century. Over the next hundred years, immense quantities of naval stores were brought forth from the dense swamp forests bordering the banks. Vast stands of cypress trees led to the development of a significant cypress-shingle industry in the nineteenth century.

Approximately 6 miles past the bridge over the Waccamaw River, you will reach the tiny village of Old Dock, once a key port on the river for the shipment of cypress shingles and lumber. When Old Dock was settled in 1800, and during the entire nineteenth century, the river was much wider and deeper than it is now, making it navigable for deep-draft vessels. As late as 1895, a steamer ascended the river from Georgetown, South Carolina, to Lake Waccamaw, some 8 miles north of Old Dock.

During its long-forgotten heyday, Old Dock, originally known as Pleasant View, was a bustling place, with turpentine distilleries turning out thousands of barrels of product for waiting barges and rafts, which were poled down the river by crews of up to fifteen men.

In the first quarter of the twentieth century, Old Dock was relegated to its present status as a crossroads community when the construction of a dam ended the Waccamaw's days as a navigable river.

At Old Dock, turn right off N.C. 130 onto S.R. 1928 and head deeper into the swamp for a visit to one of the most mysterious communities of coastal North Carolina: River View. It is 2.7 miles to the intersection with S.R. 1930. Turn left and drive 2.3 miles along River View's "Main Street."

Old house at Crusoe Island

A quick glance at the homes and gardens in this isolated community gives the impression that it is no different from the hundreds of other rural settlements throughout coastal North Carolina. However, Crusoe Island, as River View was officially known until 1961, is an ancient place. It was home to white people long before other white settlers took up residence along the banks of the nearby river.

Why and how people of European descent came to settle deep inside one of the most remote and impenetrable swamps in the United States is one of America's most enduring mysteries. Over the years, a wide variety of theories have been proposed. Some historians contend that the colony in this snake-and-alligator-infested wilderness was established by pirates who fled into the swamp after an unsuccessful raid on the nearby river. Others claim that the first residents were Indians and Europeans who intermarried and mixed. Still others believe that the original Crusoe Islanders were coastal residents who fled inland after being attacked by pirates. Crusoe Island has also been posited as the ultimate destination of the Lost Colonists of Roanoke Island.

Perhaps the most logical and satisfying explanation involves a group of French refugees who fled their mother country during the French Revolution. Among the refugees was a young French army surgeon, Jean FormyDuval. After being put ashore near Cape Fear, FormyDuval led his group into the Green Swamp in order to avoid being discovered by the authorities. In the heart of this jungle, the French settlers built a secret enclave so remote that few outsiders knew of its existence.

Though that theory has never been proved, and though some current residents of the swamp community doubt its validity, there are facts that lend credence to it. Traces of French heritage were discernible in natives of the village well into the twentieth century. Speech patterns, intonations, and conversational gestures of longtime residents hinted of a French background. Likewise, there is architectural evidence to support the theory. Chimneys that once stood at Crusoe Island were constructed of mud and sticks and covered with smooth white clay from the swamp. Old photographs reveal that the chimneys resembled those of cottages in Normandy.

Early national census records reveal other evidence. They disclose that a Dr. FormyDuval settled in the area just south of Lake Waccamaw between 1790 and 1800. Indeed, as you drive past the homes lining the road, you will notice last names on mailboxes—such as FormyDuval, Clewis, and Sasser—hinting of a French background. The last two names appear to be Anglicized versions of Cluveries and De Saucierre.

Local residents who discount the French-refugee theory contend that their ancestors were early English settlers of southeastern North Carolina.

Regardless of their origin, many of the first Crusoe Islanders obtained land grants from the state in the first half of the nineteenth century.

For more than a century, Crusoe Island was virtually hidden from the eyes of the outside world. Few residents emerged from their jungle settlement. Rather, the hardy settlers and their descendants developed a self-sufficient lifestyle. Men hunted and fished the swamp. Bountiful vegetable crops were produced from the dark, fertile soil. Home-grown cotton yielded thread, and hand-made looms produced cloth.

Likewise, only on rare occasions did outsiders make their way into the secluded colony before the twentieth century. In fact, Crusoe Island was not "discovered" until large timber companies sent engineering crews and loggers into the Green Swamp. From their initial contact with the Crusoe Islanders, the timber workers emerged to tell the world of an unusual people with a dialect totally unlike that spoken anywhere else.

It was not until the first bridges and roads to Crusoe Island were completed in the 1920s that the village was made accessible to the public. Prior to that time, the swamp residents forded the rivers and creeks on rare trips to Old Dock and other nearby towns.

Even though improved access to the outside world afforded children in the swamp an opportunity to attend public school at Old Dock and Whiteville, village residents were reluctant to give up their traditional ways of doing things. Outsiders who made their way to the community were shocked to find oxcarts rumbling down the unpaved roads. Reports of harsh treatment of visitors and strange occurrences in the village added to its mystery.

In the late 1950s, the state paved the road to Crusoe Island, but the community remained an isolated outpost in the jungle.

Crusoe Islanders successfully petitioned the state legislature to change the name of their community following an unflattering wire-service story that termed local residents "ignorant." Despite the change, the village is still best known by its original name.

No one knows how this village of approximately five hundred residents came to be known as Crusoe Island. Most likely, it was named for Ben Crusoe, an early settler in the area. However, there are some who maintain that it was named for Daniel Defoe's fictional adventurer, Robinson Crusoe.

After surviving more than seventy-five years of incursions by outsiders in this century, Crusoe Island remains a homogeneous community. Yet time and outside influences have taken their toll on the unique speech of the villagers. Even for residents who were born and have lived in the swamp all of their lives, the pattern of speech is not as pronounced as it once was. Nonetheless, some old-timers maintain the ancient drawl, which elongates the pronunciation of short words. Described as pleasant to the ear, this sing-song speech is almost impossible to imitate.

Surrounded by the jungle that protected its privacy for centuries, the village rests on one of the largest "islands" of high ground in the Green Swamp.

The drive along S.R. 1930 dead-ends at the fringe of the swamp wilderness. Just beyond the terminus of the road is the wild splendor of the Waccamaw River.

Retrace your route to Old Dock. Turn right on N.C. 130 and proceed 1.8 miles to its intersection with S.R. 1001. Turn right onto S.R. 1001 for a scenic drive along the northwestern edge of the Green Swamp. Bridges cross many of the lazy creeks that twist through the pristine wilderness.

After 10 miles on S.R. 1001, you will reach the small village of Hallsboro. Turn right onto U.S. 74/76 for a 4.5-mile drive to Lake Waccamaw.

When viewed from the air, this portion of coastal North Carolina reveals a spectacular pattern of elliptical depressions spread over the landscape. Deriving their name from the area of their greatest concentration and from the place where they were first studied, the "Carolina bays" number more than half a million lakes along the Atlantic seaboard from New Jersey to Florida.

John Lawson, the early explorer of much of coastal North Carolina, first wrote about these peat-filled swamps, which range in size from four acres to thousands of acres.

Scientists have long debated the origin of the Carolina bays. The most plausible theory was espoused by Dr. W. F. Prouty, the former head of the Department of Geology at the University of North Carolina at Chapel Hill, who postulated that a large meteorite shower smashed into the coastal plain during the late Pleistocene era.

Most scientists theorize that all of the bays were once filled with water. Many are now only peat-filled bogs. The tour route passes the greatest concentration of bay lakes in the world.

At the town of Lake Waccamaw, turn right off U.S. 74 onto N.C. 214, which stretches 2.5 miles along the northern shore of one of the most beautiful bodies of water in the world.

Measuring 5 miles long and 3 miles wide, and covering 8,938 acres, Lake Waccamaw is one of the largest natural lakes in North Carolina. It is little wonder that John Bartram, the famed Philadelphia botanist, fell in love with it during a visit in 1734. Its stately cypress trees, draped with Spanish

Lake Waccamaw

moss and mirrored by shimmering waters, led Bartram to call the lake "the pleasantist place I ever seen in my life."

There is no conclusive proof of the origin of the lake, although many geologists believe it to be a Carolina bay. If so, Lake Waccamaw is one of the largest bay lakes in existence. It differs from other local bay lakes in that it is not sterile. A limestone outcrop on the northern shore reduces the acidity of the adjacent swamp, and the lake therefore teems with fish and plant life.

John Powell, who moved here from Virginia around 1745, is thought to have been the first white settler on the lake. According to some historians, Osceola, the famous half-breed chief of the Florida Seminoles, was born on the southern shore of the lake. Tradition says that Powell was his father. The young Indian moved to Georgia as a child when the federal government removed the local Indians.

In 1852, Josiah Maultsby began development of the northeastern shore of the lake. By 1869, a small village known as Flemington had taken root, but it was not until the arrival of the railroad at the turn of the century that the lake became a summer tourist attraction. Pavilions and bathhouses sprang up along the northern shore to serve the large numbers of visitors who made their way here by train.

N.C. 214, which becomes Lake Shore Road, passes the lakeshore residential development that began after World War II. Paralleling the road is a portion of the 5-mile-long canal constructed in 1952. Though the dark waterway has a serene appearance, it is not unusual to spot an alligator basking in the sun nearby.

Follow the northern shore for an additional 3 miles by turning right off N.C. 214 onto S.R. 1947. Development on Lake Waccamaw, primarily in the form of permanent homes and summer cottages, has been limited to the northern and western shores.

Lake Waccamaw State Park, located just off S.R. 1947, remains one of the least-developed parks in the state system. Established in 1976, the park now includes the entire lake and 1,509 acres of land, primarily on the wild southern shore. As late as the 1950s, bear hunters killed as many as fifteen bears on regular hunts on the southern side of the lake, portions of which have never been fully explored.

The centerpiece of the park, the majestic lake, is an exquisite work of nature. A scenic park road extends almost a mile from the entrance to a parking lot. From there, a trail leads to the lake.

With an average depth of seven feet and a maximum depth of eleven feet, Lake Waccamaw is not very deep. Its water has a rich, dark hue but is remarkably clear. A person of average height can see the bottom of the lake when the water is up to his or her shoulders.

From the park, retrace your route to the junction with N.C. 214. If you are interested in taking a brief side trip to the southwestern shore of the lake, where the dam on the Waccamaw River is located, proceed west on N.C. 214, then follow S.R. 1900 and S.R. 1967 for approximately 5 miles.

Otherwise, turn right, or north, onto N.C. 214 for a 1.3-mile drive back to U.S. 74/76. Turn east on U.S. 74/76 for a 15-mile drive through the small communities of Bolton, Freeman, and Delco. Each of these settlements grew up alongside the railroad in the last quarter of the nineteenth century. Although the ancient railroad running to Wilmington was abandoned and the rails removed more than fifteen years ago, the bed still runs parallel to the highway in the fringes of the swamp.

From Delco, U.S. 74/76 runs conjunctively with N.C. 87 for 5 miles to Maco, the home of the most famous ghost of coastal North Carolina. At Maco, follow N.C. 87 to the right when it splits off U.S. 74/76. Park near the old railroad bed after approximately 0.3 mile.

Although the railroad crossing has been paved over, the old railroad bed is visible nearby. If you visit on a warm, dark night, there is a possibility that you will encounter the spirit of Joe Baldwin, or so the legend goes.

About midnight on a rainy spring night in 1867, Joe Baldwin was working as the conductor on a freight train bound for Wilmington. Near the station at Maco, then known as Farmers Turnout, the rear car—the one in which Joe was riding—became separated from the rest of the train. Hoping to avert a disaster, Joe raced to the rear platform and waved his lantern from side to side to warn a fast-approaching train.

Despite the frantic warning, a terrible collision ensued, and Joe Baldwin was decapitated. His lantern was thrown into a nearby swamp by the force of the impact, but it continued to burn brightly. Authorities never found Joe's head, and his body was buried without it.

Old railroad track bed at Maco

Not long after the crash, local people began to notice an unusual light on the railroad tracks in the vicinity of the disaster. Appearing at fifteen-minute intervals, the light would make its way down the tracks, growing brighter and swinging up and down, until it came within seventy-five feet of the witnesses. Suddenly, it would take on a bright glow and speed away into the night. Eyewitnesses said it looked like someone was using a lantern to search for something on the ground. No other explanation being available, area residents concluded that the apparition was Joe Baldwin looking for his head.

Reports of the ghost spread far and wide. Soon, the curious were attracted to the site, especially on dark nights. Six years after the tragedy, railroad employees added credibility to the ghost story when they reported seeing the eerie light.

President Grover Cleveland was on board a train as it rumbled into the depot at Maco on a warm, muggy night in 1889. While the train was stopped, the president took a stroll to stretch his legs and to say a few words to the assembled crowd. During his brief layover in the tiny Brunswick County community, Cleveland was bewildered by a signalman holding red and green lanterns. Once the train got under way again, railroad employees related the Joe Baldwin story and explained that the dual lanterns were used to prevent confusion with the ghost light. According to some accounts, the president actually saw the light on his visit.

Over the years that followed, many trustworthy railroad men filed reports that they had seen the mysterious light. On many occasions, cautious engineers, confused by the light, brought their trains to an abrupt, unscheduled stop to avoid what they thought was going to be a collision.

Scientists have studied the phenomenon throughout the twentieth century, but no one has been able to conclusively explain the origin of the light. Foxfire, swamp gas, St. Elmo's fire, and automobile headlights have been cited as causes. Adherents of the ghost story are quick to point out that the light is seen only on the railroad and not in the nearby swamp. Moreover, the light was observed long before the advent of automobiles.

On one occasion, a machine-gun company from Fort Bragg camped near the scene to solve the mystery. Attempts to shoot the light were unsuccessful.

Though the tracks on which the horrible accident occurred are now gone, visitors still peer up and down the empty railroad bed in hopes of seeing the phantom light that has mystified people for more than 125 years. Until a better explanation comes along, the notion that Joe Baldwin continues to search for his head is as plausible as ever.

Maco is located on the northeastern edge of the Green Swamp. Much like the community of Crusoe Island in the western portion of the swamp, an isolated, mysterious settlement existed near Maco until the first decade of the twentieth century. Known to its residents as Battle Rial or Batterial, Battle Royal was isolated from the outside world. Outsiders who braved the jungle to visit the place found "Over Creek People" whose ancestors had lived there since pre–Revolutionary War times. These people spoke Elizabethan English until the community was assimilated into the modern world in the first quarter of the twentieth century, when a public road was opened to the nearby community of Malmo.

One aged native of Battle Royal reported that his family had passed down the tradition that their ancestors "were Roe Noakers, from an island in the sea." Perhaps this long-vanished settlement in the swamp held the answer to the mystery of the Lost Colony of Roanoke Island.

From Maco, retrace your route to Delco. When N.C. 87 splits back off U.S. 74/76 in Delco, turn right on N.C. 87, which parallels the Cape Fear River on its run to Fayetteville. It is 14 miles from Delco to Carvers, a small Bladen County community on the western side of the Cape Fear.

For a unique river crossing, turn right off N.C. 87 onto S.R. 1730. The road ends at the riverbank 3 miles to the east. No bridge crosses this isolated stretch of the river. Rather, the state operates the tiny, two-vehicle Cape Fear River Ferry, known locally as Elwell's Ferry.

For almost ninety years, a small ferry has transported vehicles and passengers across the river at this spot. Though small and quaint when compared with the ferries that ply the North Carolina sounds, the river ferry is a modern bargelike vessel pulled along a cable by a diesel engine. Nearly seventy-five vehicles squeeze onto this free ferry every day. As one of only two river ferries in the state, the Cape Fear River Ferry is a remnant of a romantic bygone era of coastal history.

The upper stretch of the Cape Fear River in Bladen County was the site of many plantations that predated the Revolutionary War or the Civil War.

Most of the plantation homes that overlooked the river from the high bluffs disappeared long ago. For example, all that remains of Owen Hill is an ancient burying ground which contains the unmarked grave of a servant, Omar Ibm Said, who penned his autobiography in Arabic in 1831.

After you cross the river, continue 1 mile on S.R. 1730 to its intersection with N.C. 53. Turn left onto N.C. 53 for a pleasant drive through rural Bladen County. It is 8.5 miles to the southern limits of Bladen Lakes State Forest. Named for the large, picturesque bay lakes within its boundaries, the 40,000-acre wilderness preserve is the result of one of the most comprehensive land-reclamation projects in American history.

Following the Great Depression, the forest was comprised of little more than pocosins and worn-out farmland. The federal government set about reclaiming the wasteland by relocating its owners and using the Civilian Conservation Corps to plant trees. In 1939, the land was turned over to the state and became a state forest.

Over the past half-century, this has evolved into one of the finest state-managed forests in the nation. It not only preserves rare ecological communities and offers outstanding recreational opportunities on the bay lakes, but also provides income for the state from pulpwood sales. Of even greater significance, the forest is an outstanding outdoor teaching laboratory. More than two dozen scientific research projects are being conducted within the forest at any given time.

Bladen County is the fourth-largest of North Carolina's hundred counties. Within its massive boundaries are in excess of twelve hundred Carolina bays—more than in any other county in the nation. Singletary, White, Jones, and Salters lakes are large bay lakes within the state forest.

Continue 2.7 miles on N.C. 53 to Singletary Lake, the featured attraction of the state park of the same name.

Park roads circle most of the 572-acre lake, named for Richard Singletary, an early pioneer in the county. Hiking, swimming, fishing, boating, and camping are popular activities here and at the nearby state parks at Lake Waccamaw and Jones Lake.

Singletary Lake State Park features extensive camping facilities, including a group camp with an infirmary and dining facilities for a hundred campers, built by the federal government as a recreational demonstration project. Campers and day visitors alike are enchanted by the picturesque lake, which is framed by huge pond cypress trees and surrounded by rare plant communities which include insectivorous sundews and Venus' flytraps. Reaching a maximum depth of twelve feet, Singletary is the deepest of the Bladen lakes.

From Singletary Lake, proceed north along N.C. 53 for 3 miles to White Lake. Turn right onto U.S. 701/N.C. 41, then right onto S.R. 1515 for a circular drive around the 1,068-acre lake.

Like the other bay lakes of five hundred acres or more in Bladen County, White Lake is owned by the state. However, in sharp contrast to the other lakes, the shore of White Lake is privately owned and has been subjected to resort development.

Without question, the most distinguishing feature of the majestic lake is its beautiful, clean water, enhanced by the white, sandy bottom. Although its average depth of 7.5 feet makes White Lake one of the deepest of the Bladen lakes, the water is so clear that the bottom can be seen even where the depth reaches 10 feet near the southeastern corner.

White Lake has no inlets or outlets, other than drainage ditches that maintain the water at sixty-six feet above sea level. Instead, it is fed by

White Lake

rainwater and artesian wells, some of which are visible to boaters. As a result, it never loses its clarity.

Scientists as well as visitors have long been fascinated by the crystal-clear water. Chemists have found it to be purer than that produced by municipal water systems.

Botanist William Bartram studied and wrote about White Lake in the last quarter of the eighteenth century. Originally known as Granston Lake, the lake was subsequently renamed Bartram's Lake for either the botanist or his uncle, a resident of the Cape Fear region. Since 1886, it has been known by its present name.

Despite White Lake's recreational potential, the public did not begin to use the lake as a resort until 1907, when Ralph Melvin opened a public beach. A hotel, cottages, and a bathhouse were added in subsequent years as Melvin Beach grew in popularity. Roads were constructed in the early 1920s to link the lake with other parts of the state, thereby throwing the door open to widespread development. Within ten years, more than a half-dozen public beaches—including Goldston's Beach and Crystal Beach, which are still in operation—were attracting vacationers from North Carolina and adjoining states.

Over the past half-century, the 4.5-mile lakeshore has been almost completely developed, with motels, campgrounds, summer homes, and various amusements. A number of public beaches offer bathhouses for visitors who want to enjoy the gentle beaches and special lake water, the carnival rides and arcades, the gift shops, and the refreshment stands.

While the resort has taken on a more pronounced local flavor in the past decade, the beaches and parking lots remain crowded with visitors from all over the state at the peak of the summer season.

After circling White Lake, you will reach the junction of N.C. 53 and U.S. 701/N.C. 41. Turn left onto U.S. 701/N.C. 41, drive 1.6 miles, and turn right onto S.R. 1511 for a 5.2-mile drive through the Bladen countryside to Jones Lake, located at the junction of S.R. 1511 and N.C. 242.

Named for Isaac Jones, the man who provided the land upon which the nearby town of Elizabethtown was built, Jones Lake is the smaller of the two bay lakes located within 2,208-acre Jones Lake State Park. Visitor facilities and the park's headquarters are located at Jones Lake, a beautiful, tree-lined, 224-acre lake whose sandy beaches and calm waters are popular with swimmers. Extensive hiking trails around the lake offer an excellent opportunity to view the flora and fauna of the Carolina bay environment.

After visiting Jones Lake, turn left, or north, onto N.C. 242. After 1.5 miles, turn left onto unpaved S.R. 1335. Salters Lake, the larger of the two lakes in the state park, lies just south of the road after approximately 1.2 miles on S.R. 1335. This 315-acre lake, managed as a natural area, is an outstanding example of a water-filled Carolina bay. A small boat landing and a parking lot are located here, but visitors must obtain advance permission from park personnel for access to the lake.

Return to N.C. 242, turn right, or south, and proceed 4.5 miles to the junction with U.S. 701. Drive south on U.S. 701 for 1 mile to the bridge over the Cape Fear River. On the southern side of the bridge, turn right at the entrance to Tory Hole Park. This waterfront park offers picnic facilities, hiking trails, and a boat landing in a beautiful, forested setting along the river. It is named for the deep gully into which fleeing Tories leaped after a Revolutionary War battle at nearby Elizabethtown in August 1781.

Tory Hole Park

From the park, proceed south on U.S. 701 for 0.2 mile to Elizabethtown, the county seat of Bladen County. Located on a 125-foot bluff above the Cape Fear River, the town was created by the colonial assembly in 1773. It was named either for the girlfriend of Isaac Jones, the man on whose land the town was established, or for Queen Elizabeth I. Today, Elizabethtown is a bustling place—the largest town in Bladen County.

In the heart of town, at the intersection of U.S. 701 and N.C. 87/41, stands the Bladen County Courthouse. Completed in 1965, this large, multistory brick building is the fourth courthouse to stand in Elizabethtown.

A monument on the courthouse grounds honors Mrs. Sallie Salters, who became the heroine of the Battle of Elizabethtown during the Revolutionary War when she hurried into town, innocently bearing an egg basket, to gain valuable intelligence about the location of the Tories. Salters Lake is named in honor of Sallie Salters and her husband, Walter.

Turn east off U.S. 701 onto N.C. 87/41 (Broad Street) and drive 3 blocks to Trinity Methodist Church, the most prominent of the historic buildings in the downtown area. This tall, frame church building, erected in 1836, towers over Broad Street at its intersection with South Lower Street.

From the church, retrace your route to the courthouse. Turn left onto U.S. 701 and follow it south from Elizabethtown on a 10.5-mile drive to the thriving agricultural town of Clarkton, on the southern border of Bladen County. Be sure to follow U.S. 701 Business when the highway divides 9.3 miles south of Elizabethtown.

Settled by Scotch Presbyterians almost 250 years ago, Clarkton was the home of the subject of one of the most recognizable paintings in the world. For a number of years prior to the Civil War, Anna McNeill Whistler, born in Wilmington in 1804, made her home at Oak Forest Plantation, just north of downtown Clarkton. The historical marker at the intersection of U.S. 701 Business and S.R. 1760 in Clarkton stands approximately 0.75 mile west of the plantation site.

At the outbreak of the war, Mrs. Whistler, by that time a widow, left North Carolina, fearing reprisals because her husband, a West Point engineer, had been an officer in the United States Army. She sailed out of the Cape Fear River on board a blockade runner, heading to Europe to join her first-born son, whom she addressed as Jamey.

Her son, an artist, persuaded his mother to pose for a painting, which he officially titled *Arrangement in Gray and Black No. 1*. When he completed the masterpiece in Paris in 1881, James McNeill Whistler sold it for $620. Now known the world over as *Whistler's Mother*, it is the only painting by an American artist to hang in the Louvre in Paris.

Built in 1737, Mrs. Whistler's plantation home in Bladen County was gutted by fire in 1933, some fifty years after her death.

Turn right off U.S. 701 onto N.C. 211 in Clarkton. It is 8 miles to Bladenboro, a textile town of fifteen hundred people.

Forty years ago, this community was in the national spotlight when reports came to light that a vicious, bloodsucking monster was loose in the swamps surrounding the town. The Beast of Bladenboro soon became a part of North Carolina folklore.

On the night of December 29, 1953, a young Clarkton housewife reported seeing a monster resembling a big cat in the darkness outside her house. A day later, Lloyd Clemmons of Bladenboro claimed the monster had dragged a dog into a nearby swamp. When the unfortunate animal was found, the blood had been drained from its body, though its flesh had not been devoured. Similar reports poured into the Bladenboro Police Department. The mayor telephoned the information to the Wilmington newspaper, which informed its readers in a front-page story that "a mystery killer beast with a vampire lust" was stalking the Bladenboro area.

Search parties organized by the Bladenboro police scoured the nearby swamps, but they produced only one piece of tangible evidence: large tracks the size of half-dollars, with one inch claws. Soon, reporters and curiosity seekers poured into Bladenboro. As interest in the story grew, so did wild rumors. Reports that a rabbit had been found with its head bitten off and that two beasts might be roaming the area sent panic through the townspeople.

To complicate matters, the mayor, who operated the local movie theater, rented a grade-B movie, *The Big Cat*, which played to a packed house. Things got completely out of hand when hordes of gun-toting, homemade-whiskey-drinking hunters and armed fraternity brothers from as far away as Raleigh took to the streets to find the beast.

When the police chief threatened to call in the National Guard to quell the widespread panic, the mayor ended the nightmare almost as quickly as it had begun. He prominently displayed a bobcat recently killed by a local hunter. Photographs of the dead "monster" were dispatched to the press.

To this day, no one knows what kind of creature the Beast of Bladenboro was. Some say it was a coyote or a feral dog, while others say it never existed at all. Some residents of Bladenboro claim that the cries of the beast can still be heard in the darkness of the swamps.

Turn left off N.C. 211 onto N.C. 131 in Bladenboro. It is approximately 9 miles to the intersection with U.S. 701 Business. Turn right onto U.S. 701 Business and drive 6 miles to Whiteville, the county seat of Columbus County.

In Whiteville, U.S. 701 Business intersects U.S. 74/76 Business at the Columbus County Courthouse. Constructed in 1914 and 1915, this handsome, two-story, brick Neoclassical Revival building was designed by J. F. Leitner, a prominent architect who settled in Wilmington in 1895.

In 1810, two years after the formation of Columbus County, Whiteville was authorized to be laid out on land owned by James B. White, a local planter and politician.

Yet long before this bustling town in the heart of tobacco country was established, a true love story had its happy ending here. Duncan King, a privateer in the service of the Crown, made port at the mouth of the Cape Fear River in the fall of 1752. With him was a five-year-old girl he had rescued in the Caribbean after pirates attacked her ship and killed her French

Columbus County Courthouse

parents. King located some French-speaking residents and left little Lydia Fosque with them. Shortly thereafter, he sailed away.

While Lydia was growing into a beautiful young lady, King was serving with distinction in the British army in Canada.

In 1761, Lydia's guardian decided that she and her ward should move to Savannah. As they waited for their ship near Fort Johnston, at modern-day Southport, Lydia's long-vanished hero, Duncan King, walked down the gangplank. He was taken by her beauty. The two soon fell in love, and they were later married.

Duncan King used the wealth he had accumulated during his service to the Crown to purchase several thousand acres in Columbus County. There, he and Lydia lived in happiness until he died in 1793. From this Columbus County romance came many noteworthy King descendants, including Civil War heroes, the founder of Kings Business College, and a vice president of the United States, William Rufus King.

Turn east off U.S. 701 Business onto U.S. 74/76 Business in Whiteville. After 3.3 miles on U.S. 74/76 Business, turn left onto S.R. 1700. Drive 3.1 miles on S.R. 1700, then turn left onto S.R. 1719. It is 0.9 mile to Welches Creek Community Cemetery.

A granite grave monument here reads, "A soul with two hearts. Two hearts that beat as one." Interred at this site are the remains of Mille-Christine McCoy, the world-famous Siamese-twin girls.

On July 11, 1851, on the Columbus County plantation of Jabe McCoy, the twins were born joined at the hip to slaves of African descent. Sold when they were one year old, they were exhibited in Europe, where physicians concluded they could not be separated because their spines were fused. Pearson Smith, a subsequent owner, successfully promoted them on a world tour. They were received by the royalty of many nations, including Queen Victoria, who presented them with gifts. She enjoyed their singing and requested return visits.

Following their liberation during the Civil War, the twins retained Pearson Smith as their manager. Their success continued when they performed for President Lincoln. Highly intelligent, they spoke five languages fluently. Through their world travels, Christine acquired a love of Shakespeare.

By 1892, the twins had tired of touring and retired to Columbus County.

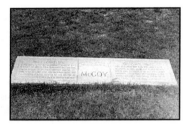

Grave of Mille-Christine McCoy

Back home, they were generous with the wealth they had acquired. Not only did they build homes for family members, but they also constructed a church and a school for black children in the county. Their generosity benefited a number of schools of higher learning, including Johnson C. Smith University, Shaw University, and Bennett College.

The twins requested that they be referred to as one. Often, they spoke in unison. They walked on two of their four legs.

When Mille died of tuberculosis on October 8, 1912, Christine told of her death before those in attendance could detect it. The surviving twin lingered another day, calmly singing hymns and praying.

From the cemetery, retrace your route to U.S. 74/76 Business, where the tour ends. A state historical marker honoring Mille-Christine stands nearby.

Appendix

Federal Agencies, Parks, and Historic Sites

**Cape Lookout
National Seashore**
131 Charles Street
Harkers Island, N.C. 28531
919-728-2250 or 919-240-1409

**Cedar Island National
Wildlife Refuge**
Star Route 78
Cedar Island, N.C. 28520
919-225-2511

Croatan National Forest
141 East Fisher Avenue
New Bern, N.C. 28560
919-638-5628

**Moores Creek National
Military Park**
200 Moores Creek Drive
P.O. Box 69
Currie, N.C. 28435
910-283-5591

State Agencies, Parks, and Historic Sites

**Bald Head Island
State Natural Area**
P.O. Box 475
Carolina Beach, N.C. 28428
910-458-8206

Battleship *North Carolina*
P.O. Box 480
Wilmington, N.C. 28402
910-251-5797

Bladen Lakes State Forest
Route 2, Box 942-A
Elizabethtown, N.C. 28337
910-588-4161

**Brunswick Town
State Historic Site**
Route 1, Box 55
Winnabow, N.C. 28479
910-371-6613

Carolina Beach State Park
P.O. Box 475
Carolina Beach, N.C. 28428
910-458-8206

**Coastal Reserve Coordinator
North Carolina National
Estuarine Research Reserve**
7205 Wrightsville Avenue
Wilmington, N.C. 28403
910-256-3721

Fort Fisher State Historic Site
1610 Fort Fisher Boulevard
P.O. Box 68
Kure Beach, N.C. 28449
910-458-5538

**Fort Fisher State
Recreation Area**
P.O. Box 475
Carolina Beach, N.C. 28428
910-458-8206

Fort Macon State Park
P.O. Box 127
Atlantic Beach, N.C. 28512
919-726-3775

Hammocks Beach State Park
Route 2, Box 295
Swansboro, N.C. 28584
910-326-4881

Jones Lake State Park
Route 2, Box 945
Elizabethtown, N.C. 28337
910-588-4550

North Carolina
Aquarium at Fort Fisher
P.O. Box 130
Kure Beach, N.C. 28449
910-458-8257

North Carolina
Aquarium at Pine Knoll Shores
P.O. Box 580
Atlantic Beach, N.C. 28512
919-247-4003

North Carolina Division
of Archives and History
Historic Sites Section
109 East Jones Street
Raleigh, N.C. 27611
919-733-7862

North Carolina Division
of Coastal Management
P.O. Box 27687
Raleigh, N.C. 27611
919-733-2293

North Carolina Division
of Marine Fisheries
P.O. Box 769
Morehead City, N.C. 28557
800-682-2632

North Carolina Division
of Parks and Recreation
512 North Salisbury Street
Raleigh, N.C. 27611
919-733-4181

North Carolina Ferry Division
113 Arendell Street
Morehead City, N.C. 28550
919-726-6446 or 800-BY-FERRY

North Carolina
Maritime Museum
315 Front Street
Beaufort, N.C. 28516
919-728-7317

North Carolina Travel
and Tourism Division
430 North Salisbury Street
Raleigh, N.C. 27611
919-733-4171 or 800-VISIT-NC

North Carolina Wildlife
Resources Commission
512 North Salisbury Street
Raleigh, N.C. 27611
919-733-3393 or 800-662-7350

Singletary Lake State Park
Route 1, Box 63
Kelly, N.C. 28488
910-669-2928

Theodore Roosevelt
State Natural Area
P.O. Box 127
Atlantic Beach, N.C. 28512
919-726-3775

**Museums and Other
Historic Attractions**

Airlie Gardens
Airlie Road
Wrightsville Beach, N.C. 28480
910-763-9991

Attmore-Oliver
House Museum
511 Broad Street
New Bern, N.C. 28560
919-638-8558

Bank of the Arts
317 Middle Street
New Bern, N.C. 28560
919-638-2787

Beaufort Historic Site
100 Turner Street
P.O. Box 1709
Beaufort, N.C. 28516
919-728-5225

**Bellamy Mansion Museum
of History and Design Arts**
503 Market Street
P.O. Box 1176
Wilmington, N.C. 28402
910-251-3700

Burgwin-Wright House
224 Market Street
Wilmington, N.C. 28401
910-762-0570

**C P & L Nuclear
Visitor Center**
N.C. 87
Southport, N.C. 28461
910-457-6041

Cape Fear Museum
814 Market Street
Wilmington, N.C. 28401
910-341-4350

**Carteret County Museum
of History and Art**
100 Wallace Drive
Morehead City, N.C. 28557
919-247-7533

**Core Sound
Waterfowl Museum**
Harkers Island Road
Harkers Island, N.C. 28531
919-728-1500

New Bern Academy Museum
P.O. Box 1007
New Bern, N.C. 28653
919-638-1560

New Bern Civil War Museum
301 Metcalf Street
New Bern, N.C. 28560
919-633-2818

New Bern Firemen's Museum
410 Hancock Street
New Bern, N.C. 28560
919-636-4087

**Ocean Isle Museum
of Coastal Carolina**
Third Street
Ocean Isle Beach, N.C. 28469
910-579-1016

Orton Plantation
Route 1
Winnabow, N.C. 28479
910-371-6851

Poplar Grove Plantation
10200 U.S. 17 North
Wilmington, N.C. 28405
910-686-9989

Southport Maritime Museum
116 North Howe Street
P.O. Box 11101
Southport, N.C. 28461
910-457-0003

St. John's Museum of Art
114 Orange Street
Wilmington, N.C. 28401
910-763-0281

**Thalian Hall/
Wilmington City Hall**
310 Chestnut Street/102 North
Third Street
Wilmington, N.C. 28401
910-343-3660

**Tryon Palace Restoration
and Gardens Complex**
P.O. Box 1007
New Bern, N.C. 28560
919-638-1560

Wilmington Railroad Museum
501 Nutt Street
Wilmington, N.C. 28401
910-763-2634

Zebulon Latimer House
126 South Third Street
Wilmington, N.C. 28401
910-762-0492

Chambers of Commerce and Information Centers

**Bald Head Island
Information Center**
P.O. Box 3069
Bald Head Island, N.C. 28461
910-457-5000 or 800-234-1666

**Cape Fear Coast Convention
and Visitors Bureau**
P.O. Box 1810
Wilmington, N.C. 28403
910-341-7815 or 800-222-4757

**Carolina-Kure Beaches
Chamber of Commerce**
201 Lumberton Avenue
Carolina Beach, N.C. 28428
910-458-8434 or 800-228-8434

**Carteret County Tourism
Development Bureau**
P.O. Box 1406
Morehead City, N.C. 28557
919-726-8148 or 800-SUNNY-NC

**Craven County Convention
and Visitors Bureau**
219 Pollock Street
P.O. Box 1413
New Bern, N.C. 28563
919-637-9400 or 800-437-5767

**Elizabethtown–White Lake
Chamber of Commerce**
P.O. Box 306
Elizabethtown, N.C. 28337
910-862-4368

**Emerald Isle Merchants
Association**
P.O. Box 4862
Emerald Isle, N.C. 28594
919-393-3100

**Greater Topsail Area
Chamber of Commerce**
P.O. Box 2486
Surf City, N.C. 28445
910-328-4722 or 800-626-2780

**Onslow County Tourism
Department**
P.O. Box 1226
Jacksonville, N.C. 28541-1226
910-455-1113 or 800-932-2144

**South Brunswick Islands
Chamber of Commerce**
P.O. Box 1380
Shallotte, N.C. 28459
910-754-6644

**Southport–Oak Island
Chamber of Commerce**
4841 Long Beach Road, SE
Southport, N.C. 28461
910-457-6964 or 800-457-6964

Southport 2000, Inc.
107 East Nash Street
Southport, N.C. 28461
910-457-7927

Town of Ocean Isle Beach
3 West Third Street
Ocean Isle Beach, N.C. 28469
910-579-3469 or 800-248-2504

Bibliography

Alexandria Drafting Company. *Salt Water Sport Fishing and Boating in North Carolina.* Alexandria, Va.: Alexandria Drafting Company, 1981.

Alford, Michael B. *Traditional Work Boats of North Carolina.* Harkers Island, N.C.: Hancock Publishing, 1990.

Allcott, John V. *Colonial Homes in North Carolina.* Raleigh, N.C.: Carolina Charter Tercentenary Commission, 1963.

Ashe, S. A. *History of North Carolina.* 2 vols. Raleigh, N.C.: Edwards and Broughton Printing Company, 1925.

Bache, Ellyn, et al. *What Locals Know about Wilmington and Its Beaches.* Wilmington, N.C.: Banks Channel Books, 1993.

Barrett, John G. *North Carolina as a Civil War Battleground, 1861–1865.* Raleigh, N.C.: North Carolina Department of Archives and History, 1960.

———. *The Civil War in North Carolina.* Chapel Hill, N.C.: University of North Carolina Press, 1963.

Bedwell, Dorothy Byrum. *Portsmouth: Island with a Soul.* New Bern, N.C.: IES Publications, 1984.

Biggs, Walter C., Jr., and James F. Parnell. *State Parks of North Carolina.* Winston-Salem, N.C.: John F. Blair, Publisher, 1989.

Bishir, Catherine W. *North Carolina Architecture.* Chapel Hill, N.C.: University of North Carolina Press, 1990.

Bledsoe, Jerry. *Carolina Curiosities.* Charlotte, N.C.: East Woods Press, 1984.

Blee, Ben W. *Battleship North Carolina (BB-55).* Wilmington, N.C.: USS *North Carolina* Battleship Commission, 1982.

Brickell, John. *The Natural History of North Carolina.* 1737. Reprint, Murfreesboro, N.C.: Johnson Publishing Company, 1968.

Brown, Joseph Parsons. *The Commonwealth of Onslow: A History.* New Bern, N.C.: Owen G. Dunn Company, 1960.

Burke, Kenneth E., Jr. *The History of Portsmouth, North Carolina.* Washington, D.C.: Insta-Print, 1976.

Burns, Robert P., ed. *100 Courthouses: A Report on North Carolina Judicial Facilities.* Vol. 2, *The County Perspective.* Raleigh, N.C.: North Carolina State University, 1978.

Butler, Lindley S. *North Carolina and the Coming of the Revolution, 1763–1776.*

Raleigh, N.C.: North Carolina Department of Cultural Resources, 1976.

Cashman, Diane Cobb. *Cape Fear Adventure: An Illustrated History of Wilmington*. Chatsworth, Calif.: Windsor Publications, 1982.

Cheatham, James T. *The Atlantic Turkey Shoot: U-boats off the Outer Banks in World War II*. Greenville, N.C.: Williams and Simpson, Inc., Publishers, 1990.

———. *Sailing the Carolina Sounds: Historical Places and My Favorite People*. Charlotte, N.C.: Delmar Printing and Publishing, 1993.

Clay, J. W., et al, eds. *North Carolina Atlas*. Chapel Hill, N.C.: University of North Carolina Press, 1975.

Cleary, William J., and Paul E. Hosier. *The New Hanover Banks: Then and Now*. Raleigh, N.C.: UNC Sea Grant Program, 1977.

Corbett, John Richard. *Ships by the Name of North Carolina*. Wilmington, N.C.: Corbett Publications, 1961.

Corbitt, David Leroy. *The Formation of the North Carolina Counties, 1663–1943*. Raleigh, N.C.: North Carolina Department of Archives and History, 1950.

Corey, Cindy. *Exploring the Seacoast of North Carolina*. Raleigh, N.C.: Provincial Press, 1969.

———. *Exploring the Lighthouses of North Carolina*. Chapel Hill, N.C.: Provincial Press, 1982.

Davis, Maurice. *History of the Hammock House and Related Trivia*. Beaufort, N.C: 1984.

Day, Jean. *Cedar Island: Past and Present*. 2 vols. Havelock, N.C.: The Print Shop, 1986.

———. *Wild Ponies of the Outer Banks*. Havelock, N.C.: The Print Shop, 1988.

———. *Cedar Island: Fisher Folk*. Golden Age Press, 1994.

de Hart, Allen. *North Carolina Hiking Trails*. Boston: Appalachian Mountain Club, 1982.

Dill, Alonzo T. *Governor Tryon and His Palace*. Chapel Hill, N.C.: University of North Carolina Press, 1955.

DiNome, Bill, and Carol Deakin. *The Insiders' Guide to North Carolina's Wilmington and the Cape Fear Coast*. Beaufort, N.C.: By the Sea Publications, 1994.

Doughton, Virginia Pou. *The Atlantic Hotel*. Raleigh, N.C.: 1991.

Edmunds, Pocahontas Wight. *Tales of the North Carolina Coast*. Raleigh, N.C.: Edwards and Broughton Printing Company, 1986.

Evans, W. McKee. *Ballots and Fencerails: Reconstruction on the Lower Cape Fear*. Chapel Hill, N.C.: University of North Carolina Press, 1967.

Farb, Roderick M. *Shipwrecks: Diving the Graveyard of the Atlantic*. Hillsborough, N.C.: Menasha Ridge Press, 1985.

Furr, Gene. *Images: The Outer Banks*. Chapel Hill, N.C.: Cinehaus Productions, 1981.

Fussell, John O., III. *A Birder's Guide to Coastal North Carolina*. Chapel Hill, N.C.: University of North Carolina Press, 1994.

Gannon, Michael. *Operation Drumbeat*. New York: Harper and Row, 1990.

Gentile, Gary. *Shipwrecks of North Carolina from Hatteras Inlet South*. Philadelphia: Gary Gentile Productions, 1992.

Gleasner, Diana, and Bill Gleasner. *Sea Islands of the South*. Charlotte, N.C.: East Woods Press, 1980.

Goldstein, Robert J. *Pier Fishing in North Carolina*. Winston-Salem, N.C.: John F. Blair, Publisher, 1978.

———. *Coastal Fishing in the Carolinas: From Surf, Pier, and Jetty*. Winston-Salem, N.C.: John F. Blair, Publisher, 1986.

Gorrell, Dick, and Bruce Roberts. *USS North Carolina: The "Showboat."* Charlotte, N.C.: Heritage Printers, 1961.

Graetz, Karl E. *Seacoast Plants of the Carolinas for Conservation and Beautification*. Raleigh, N.C.: UNC Sea Grant Program, 1982.

Gragg, Rod. *Confederate Goliath: The Battle of Fort Fisher*. New York: HarperCollins Publishers, 1991.

Hall, Lewis Philip. *Land of the Golden River*. 3 vols. Wilmington, N.C.: Wilmington Printing Company, 1975, 1980.

Herring, Ethel. *Cap'n Charlie and Lights of the Lower Cape Fear*. Winston-Salem, N.C.: Hunter Publishing Company, 1967.

Herring, Ethel, and Carolee Williams. *Fort Caswell in War and Peace*. Wendell, N.C.: Broadfoot's Bookmark, 1983.

Hickham, Homer H., Jr. *Torpedo Junction*. Annapolis, Md.: Naval Institute Press, 1989.

Hill, Michael, ed. *Guide to North Carolina Highway Historical Markers*. Raleigh, N.C.: North Carolina Division of Archives and History, 1990.

Hill, Mrs. Fred, ed. *Historic Carteret County, North Carolina, 1663–1975.* Beaufort, N.C.: Carteret Historical Research Association, 1975.

Holden, John F. *Holden Beach History.* Wilmington, N.C.: New Hanover Printing and Publishing Company, 1988.

Holland, F. Ross, Jr. *A Survey History of Cape Lookout National Seashore.* Washington, D.C.: National Park Service, 1968.

———. *America's Lighthouses: An Illustrated History.* New York: Dover Publications, 1988.

———. *Great American Lighthouses.* Washington, D.C.: Preservation Press, 1989.

Howell, Andrew J. *The Book of Wilmington.* Wilmington, N.C.: 1930.

Jones, S. M. *A History of the Tri-County Area—Craven, Pamlico, and Carteret Counties—from Their Earliest Settlements to the Present.* New Bern, N.C.: Owen G. Dunn Company, 1981.

Junior League of Wilmington. *Old Wilmington Guidebook.* Wilmington, N.C.: Blake Printing and Graphics, 1978.

Kaufman, Wallace, and Orrin H. Pilkey. *The Beaches Are Moving: The Drowning of America's Shoreline.* Garden City, N.Y.: Anchor Press/Doubleday, 1979.

Kell, Jean Bruyere. *Historic Beaufort, North Carolina.* Greenville, N.C.: National Printing Company, 1977.

———. *The Old Port Town: Beaufort, North Carolina.* Beaufort, N.C.: 1980.

Kell, Jean Bruyere, ed. *North Carolina's Coastal Carteret County during the American Revolution, 1765–1785.* Greenville, N.C.: Carteret County Bicentennial Commission, 1975.

Kellam, Ida Brooks, ed. *Wilmington: Historic Colonial City.* Wilmington, N.C.: Carolina Printing and Stamp Company, 1954.

Kelly, Richard, and Barbara Kelly. *The Carolina Watermen: Bug Hunters and Boatbuilders.* Winston-Salem, N.C.: John F. Blair, Publisher, 1993.

Kraus, E. Jean Wilson. *A Guide to Ocean Dune Plants Common to North Carolina.* Chapel Hill, N.C.: University of North Carolina Press, 1988.

Lamb, William. *Colonel Lamb's Story of Fort Fisher.* Carolina Beach, N.C.: Blockade Runner Museum, 1966.

Lane, Mills. *Architecture of the Old South: North Carolina.* New York: Abbeville Press, 1985.

Lawson, John. *A New Voyage To Carolina*. 1709. Edited by Hugh T. Lefler. Chapel Hill, N.C.: University of North Carolina Press, 1967.

Lee, Lawrence. *The Lower Cape Fear in Colonial Days*. Chapel Hill, N.C.: University of North Carolina Press, 1965.

———. *New Hanover County: A Brief History*. Raleigh, N.C.: North Carolina Department of Cultural Resources, 1977.

———. *The History of Brunswick County, North Carolina*. Bolivia, N.C.: Brunswick County Commission, 1979.

Lefler, Hugh T., and Albert Ray Newsome. *North Carolina: The History of a Southern State*. 3rd ed. Chapel Hill, N.C.: University of North Carolina Press, 1973.

Lefler, Hugh T., ed. *North Carolina History Told by Contemporaries*. Chapel Hill, N.C.: University of North Carolina Press, 1948.

Leland, Elizabeth. *The Vanishing Coast*. Winston-Salem, N.C.: John F. Blair, Publisher, 1992.

Lemmon, Sarah McCulloh. *North Carolina's Role in World War II*. Raleigh, N.C.: North Carolina Division of Archives and History, 1969.

———. *North Carolina's Role in the First World War*. Raleigh, N.C.: North Carolina Division of Archives and History, 1975.

Lewis, Taylor, and Joanne Young. *A Tryon Treasury*. Norfolk, Va.: Taylor Lewis Associates, 1977.

Little, Ann Courtney Ward. *Columbus County, North Carolina: Recollections and Records*. Whiteville, N.C.: Columbus County Commission, 1980.

Lounsbury, Carl. *The Architecture of Southport*. Southport, N.C.: Southport Historical Society, 1979.

Manning, Phillip. *Afoot in the South: Walks in the Natural Areas of North Carolina*. Winston-Salem, N.C.: John F. Blair, Publisher, 1993.

McDiarmid, Kate R. *Whistler's Mother: Her Life, Letters and Journal*. 1989.

Merrens, Harry Roy. *Colonial North Carolina in the Eighteenth Century*. Chapel Hill, N.C.: University of North Carolina Press, 1964.

Meyer, Peter. *Nature Guide to the North Carolina Coast*. Wilmington, N.C.: Avian-Cetacean Press, 1991.

Miller, Helen Hill. *Historic Places around the Banks*. Charlotte, N.C.: McNally and Loftin, Publishers, 1974.

Mobley, Joe A. *USS North Carolina: Symbol of a Vanished Age*. Raleigh, N.C.: North Carolina Division of Archives and History, 1985.

————. *Ship Ashore! The U.S. Lifesavers of Coastal North Carolina*. Raleigh, N.C.: North Carolina Division of Archives and History, 1994.

Morehead City Woman's Club. *A Pictorial Review of Morehead City: History through 1981*. Greenville, N.C.: Highland Press of Greenville, 1982.

Morris, Glenn. *North Carolina Beaches*. Chapel Hill, N.C.: University of North Carolina Press, 1993.

Nadeau, Noah. *An Island Called Figure Eight*. Wallace, N.C.: Wallace Enterprise, 1991.

Nance, Tabbie, and Joan Greene. *The Insiders' Guide to North Carolina's Crystal Coast and New Bern*. Beaufort, N.C.: By the Sea Publications, 1992.

New Hanover County Planning Department. *Historic Architecture of New Hanover County, North Carolina*. Wilmington, N.C.: 1986.

Paul, Mary, and Grayden Paul. *Carteret County, N.C.: Folklore, Facts and Fiction*. 1975.

Payne, Roger L. *Place Names of the Outer Banks*. Washington, N.C.: Thomas L. Williams, Publisher, 1985.

Pilkey, Orrin H., Jr., et al. *From Currituck to Calabash: Living with North Carolina's Barrier Islands*. Research Triangle Park, N.C.: North Carolina Science and Technology Center, 1978.

Pilkey, Orrin H., Jr., Orrin H. Pilkey, Sr., and Robb Turner. *How to Live with an Island: A Handbook to Bogue Banks, North Carolina*. Raleigh, N.C.: North Carolina Department of Natural and Economic Resources, 1975.

Pohoresky, W. L. *Fort Macon, North Carolina, during the Civil War*. Havelock, N.C.: The Print Shop, 1979.

————. *Captain Cottineau and John Paul Jones*. Havelock, N.C.: The Print Shop, 1986.

Powell, William S. *The North Carolina Gazetteer: A Dictionary of Tar Heel Places*. Chapel Hill, N.C.: University of North Carolina Press, 1968.

————. *North Carolina through Four Centuries*. Chapel Hill, N.C.: University of North Carolina Press, 1989.

Price, Steve. *Wild Places of the South*. Charlotte, N.C.: East Woods Press, 1980.

Puetz, C. J., ed. *North Carolina County Maps*. Lyndon Station, Wis.: Thomas Publications, Ltd.

Puterbaugh, Parke, and Alan Bisbort. *Life Is a Beach: A Vacationer's Guide to the East Coast*. New York: McGraw-Hill Book Company, 1986.

Rankin, Hugh F. *The Pirates of Colonial North Carolina*. Raleigh, N.C.: North Carolina Department of Cultural Resources, 1976.

Rawlinson, Fred. *Brad's Drink: A Primer for Pepsi-Cola Collectors*. New Bern, N.C.: Bern Bear Gifts, 1992.

Rights, Douglas L. *The American Indian in North Carolina*. 1947. Reprint, Winston-Salem, N.C.: John F. Blair, Publisher, 1957.

Roberts, Bruce, and Ray Jones. *Southern Lighthouses: Chesapeake Bay to the Gulf of Mexico*. Chester, Conn.: Globe Pequot Press, 1989.

Roberts, Nancy. *Blackbeard and Other Pirates of the Atlantic Coast*. Winston-Salem, N.C.: John F. Blair, Publisher, 1993.

Robinson, Blackwell P., ed. *The North Carolina Guide*. Chapel Hill, N.C.: University of North Carolina Press, 1955.

Robinson, Melvin. *Riddle of the Lost Colony*. New Bern, N.C.: Owen G. Dunn Company, Publishers, 1946.

Roe, Charles E. *A Directory to North Carolina's Natural Areas*. Raleigh, N.C.: North Carolina Natural Heritage Foundation, 1987.

———. *North Carolina Wildlife Viewing Guide*. Helena, Mont.: Falcon Press Publishing Company, 1992.

Ross, Malcolm. *Rivers of America: The Cape Fear*. New York: Holt, Rinehart and Winston, 1965.

Russell, Anne. *Wilmington: A Pictorial History*. Norfolk: Donning Company, 1981.

Salter, Ben B. *Portsmouth Island: Short Stories and History*. 1972.

Sandbeck, Peter B. *The Historic Architecture of New Bern and Craven County, North Carolina*. New Bern, N.C.: Tryon Palace Commission, 1988.

Savage, Henry, Jr. *The Mysterious Carolina Bays*. Columbia, S.C.: University of South Carolina Press, 1982.

Scheer, George, III. *North Carolina: A Guide to the Old North State*. New York: Burt Franklin and Company, 1982.

Schoenbaum, Thomas J. *Islands, Capes, and Sounds: The North Carolina Coast*. Winston-Salem, N.C.: John F. Blair, Publisher, 1982.

Schumann, Marguerite. *The Living Land: An Outdoor Guide to North Carolina*. Chapel Hill, N.C.: Dale Press, 1977.

———. *Tar Heel Sights: A Guide to North Carolina's Heritage*. Charlotte, N.C.: East Woods Press, 1983.

Sharpe, Bill. *A New Geography of North Carolina.* 4 vols. Raleigh, N.C.: Sharpe Publishing Company, 1954–65.

Sharpe, William. *Brain Surgeon: The Autobiography.* New York: Viking Press, 1952.

Simpson, Bob. *When the Water Smokes: A Peltier Creek Chronicle.* Chapel Hill, N.C.: Algonquin Books, 1983.

Simpson, Marcus B., Jr., and Sallie W. Simpson. *Whaling on the North Carolina Coast.* Raleigh, N.C.: North Carolina Division of Archives and History, 1990.

Snow, Edmund Rowe. *True Tales of Buried Treasure.* New York: Dodd, Mead and Company, 1966.

South, Stanley A. *Indians in North Carolina.* Raleigh, N.C.: North Carolina Division of Archives and History, 1965.

Sprunt, James. *Chronicles of the Cape Fear River, 1660–1916.* 2nd ed. Raleigh, N.C.: Edwards and Broughton Printing Company, 1916.

Stallman, David A. *A History of Camp Davis.* Hampstead, N.C.: Hampstead Services, 1990.

Stephens, Kay Holt Roberts. *Judgment Land: The Story of Salter Path.* Cape Carteret, N.C.: Bogue Sound Banks, 1989.

Stick, David. *North Carolina Lighthouses.* Raleigh, N.C.: North Carolina Department of Cultural Resources, 1980.

———. *Bald Head: A History of Smith Island and Cape Fear.* Wendell, N.C.: Broadfoot Publishing Company, 1985.

Taggart, John, and Kathryn Henderson. *A Field Guide to Exploring the North Carolina Estuarine Research Reserve.* Raleigh, N.C.: North Carolina Division of Coastal Management, 1988.

Taylor, H. Braugh, ed. *Guide to Historic New Bern, North Carolina.* New Bern, N.C.: New Bern/Craven County American Revolution Bicentennial Commission, 1974.

Taylor, Walter K. *Wild Shores: Exploring the Wilderness Areas of Eastern North Carolina.* Asheboro, N.C.: Down Home Press, 1993.

Thompson, Virginia, and Jack Willis, eds. *Fact, Faith and Fiction: Carteret County Reflections.* Morehead City, N.C.: Herald Printing Company, 1988.

Todd, Virginia H., ed. *Christoph von Graffenried's Account of the Founding of New Bern.* Raleigh, N.C.: Edwards and Broughton Printing Company, 1920.

Toops, Connie. *National Seashores: The Story behind the Scenery.* Las Vegas, Nev.: KC Publications, 1987.

Trotter, William. *Ironclads and Columbiads. The Civil War in North Carolina: The Coast.* Winston-Salem, N.C.: John F. Blair, Publisher, 1989.

Waddell, Alfred Moore. *A History of New Hanover County and the Lower Cape Fear Region, 1723–1800.* Wilmington, N.C.: 1916.

Walser, Richard. *North Carolina Legends.* Raleigh, N.C.: North Carolina Division of Archives and History, 1980.

Walser, Richard, ed. *The North Carolina Miscellany.* Chapel Hill, N.C.: University of North Carolina Press, 1962.

Watson, Alan D. *Society in Colonial North Carolina.* Raleigh, N.C.: North Carolina Department of Cultural Resources, 1982.

———. *A History of New Bern and Craven County.* New Bern, N.C.: Tryon Palace Commission, 1987.

———. *Wilmington: Port of North Carolina.* Columbia, S.C.: University of South Carolina Press, 1992.

Wetmore, Ruth Y. *First on the Land: The North Carolina Indians.* Winston-Salem, N.C.: John F. Blair, Publisher, 1975.

Whedbee, Charles Harry. *Legends of the Outer Banks and Tar Heel Tidewater.* Winston-Salem, N.C.: John F. Blair, Publisher, 1966.

———. *The Flaming Ship of Ocracoke and Other Tales of the Outer Banks.* Winston-Salem, N.C.: John F. Blair, Publisher, 1971.

———. *Outer Banks Mysteries and Seaside Stories.* Winston-Salem, N.C.: John F. Blair, Publisher, 1978.

———. *Outer Banks Tales to Remember.* Winston-Salem, N.C.: John F. Blair, Publisher, 1985.

———. *Blackbeard's Cup and Stories of the Outer Banks.* Winston-Salem, N.C.: John F. Blair, Publisher, 1989.

Wheeler, John Hill. *Historical Sketches of North Carolina from 1584 to 1851.* Baltimore: Regional Publishing Company, 1964.

Whitney, Dudley. *The Lighthouse.* New York: Arch Cape Press, 1989.

Williamson, Sonny. *Unsung Heroes of the Surf: The Lifesaving Services of Carteret County.* Marshallberg, N.C.: Grandma Publications, 1992.

Wilmington Morning Star. *Diana!* Indianapolis, Ind.: New Books International, 1984.

Wilson, Elizabeth Jean. *A Guide to Salt Marsh Plants Common to North Carolina*. Raleigh, N.C.: UNC Sea Grant Program, 1981.

Works Progress Administration. *The Ocean Highway: New Brunswick, New Jersey, to Jacksonville, Florida*. New York: Modern Age Books, 1938.

Wrenn, Tony. *Wilmington, North Carolina: An Architectural and Historical Portrait*. Charlottesville, Va.: University Press of Virginia, 1984.

Wright, Sarah Bird. *Ferries of America: A Guide to Adventurous Travel*. Atlanta: Peachtree Publishers, 1987.

————. *Islands of the South and Southeastern United States*. Atlanta: Peachtree Publishers, 1989.

Young, Claiborne S. *Cruising Guide to Coastal North Carolina*. Winston-Salem, N.C.: John F. Blair, Publisher, 1983.

Index

Calloway, Cab, 224
Camp Davis, 157, 160, 165-66, 167
Camp Glenn, 79
Camp Lejeune Marine Corps Base, 83, 134, 135, 153-54, 155, 156
Canada, 64, 306, 313, 334
Cape Canaveral, Florida, 160
Cape Carteret, 101, 134, 135, 143
Cape Fear, 267, 280, 283, 284, 285, 289, 290-91
Cape Fear Club, 210
Cape Fear Lighthouse, 289
Cape Fear Memorial Bridge, 194
Cape Fear Museum, 176, 177, 184-86
Cape Fear Pilots Association, 272
Cape Fear River: at Bald Head Island, 281, 282, 285, 289; at Belville, 255; at Brunswick Town, 201, 261; at Carvers, 326; at Oak Island, 293, 300; at Orton, 257; at Pleasure Island, 228, 230, 235, 238; at Rocky Point, 171; at Town Creek, 256; at Wilmington, 176, 185, 194, 200; description of, 253-54; northeast portion of, 156, 253; northwest portion of, 253
Cape Fear River Ferry, 317, 326
Cape Hatteras, 254
Cape Hatteras Lighthouse, 17, 18, 19, 289
Cape Hatteras National Seashore, 27
Cape Hatteras (research vessel), 84
Cape Henry, Virginia, 287
Capel House, 297
Cape Lookout (the cape), 16, 18, 20, 21, 22, 23, 24, 82, 89
Cape Lookout Bight, 20, 21, 23-24, 27, 44
Cape Lookout Development Company, 24
Cape Lookout (former village), 20, 31
Cape Lookout Lighthouse, 2, 3, 17-20, 22, 27, 40, 289
Cape Lookout National Seashore, 3-33, 40, 42
Cape Lookout National Seashore Visitor Center, 16, 40
Cape Point, 20, 22, 23

Capps, John, 87
Captain Bill's Restaurant, 85
Captain Charlie's Complex, 289-90
Captain Elijah Willis House, 132
Captain J. N. Maffitt, 194
Captain Thomas, 285
Capt. Winner, 231
Carolco Pictures, 179
Carolco Studios, 177-79
Carolina bays, 138, 139, 140, 166, 321-22, 323, 330
Carolina Beach, 89, 186, 214, 215, 228-32, 236, 242
Carolina Beach Boardwalk, 215, 230
Carolina Beach Fishing Pier, 232
Carolina Beach Inlet, 232
Carolina Beach State Park, 215, 228-30
Carolina Beach Yacht Basin, 232
Carolina City, 79-80
Carolina Exploration Company, 163
Carolina Power and Light Company, 267
Carolina Yacht Club, 221
Carrere and Hastings, 190
Carrot Island, 55, 56, 59, 69-71, 72; wild horses of, 55, 56, 71
Carruthers-Forbes House, 104, 121
Carteret Academy, 54, 72
Carteret County: Cape Lookout portion of, 2-33; Beaufort portion of, 57-75; Bogue Banks portion of, 89-103; Down East portion of, 34-55; Morehead City portion of, 77-89; White Oak River portion of, 142-43
Carteret County Courthouse, 54, 55
Carteret County Courthouse of 1786, 56
Carteret County Historical Society, 79
Carteret County Jail (former), 57
Carteret County Museum of History, 77, 78, 79
Carteret County Parks and Recreation Department, 39
Cart Island, 69
Carvers, 316
Casino, The, 221

Cassatt, Mary, 198
Caswell Beach, 292, 293, 299-302
Caswell, Richard, 116, 117, 173, 273, 302
Catfish Lake, 134, 135, 140-41
Cedar Grove Cemetery, 130
Cedar Island, 2, 3, 16, 34, 35, 45, 48, 51-53
Cedar Island National Wildlife Refuge, 35, 51
Cedar Island-Ocracoke Ferry, 2, 16, 35
Cedar Point Tideland Trail, 139, 143
Centenary United Methodist Church, 128
Central School, 130
Chadwick House, 54, 63
Chadwick, Mary, 63
Chadwick, Mary Frances, 18
Chadwick, Robert, 63
Challenger, 68
Chandler's Wharf, 176, 195-96
Channing, Edward, 174
Chapel Hill, 191
Charles V, 283
Charles Slover House, 104, 132
Charleston, 58, 62, 82, 109, 158, 178, 285, 286
Charles Towne, 255
Charlie, the alligator, 253
Chase, H. M., 219
Chatham County, 253
Chattawka, 107, 108
Chautauqua, New York, 108
Chermont, 105
Cherry, Gregg, 117
Chester B'nai Sholom Synagogue, 104, 128
Chiang Kai-shek, Mrs., 63
Chicago, Illinois, 179
China, 63
Christ Episcopal Church, 104, 105, 112-13, 122, 131
Church of Christian Science, 211
City Hall (Wilmington), 208
City Pier, 269
Civil War: at Bald Head Island, 279, 282; at Beaufort, 59, 68, 70, 72, 74; at Bogue Banks, 90-91, 94,

---